THE 1998 ANNOTATED

INDIAN ACT

Including regulations and related constitutional provisions

Shin Imai
B.A., LL.B., LL.M.

Assisted by
Anne Marie McCollman

STATUTES OF CANADA ANNOTATED

CARSWELL
Thomson Professional Publishing

Canadian Cataloguing in Publication Data

The National Library of Canada has catalogued this publication as follows:
Canada
       [Indian Act]
       The annotated Indian Act
(Statutes of Canada annotated)
Biennial
Description based on: 1990.
"Including related treaties, statutes, and
regulations" (varies).
Continues: Canada. Indian Act.
ISSN 1197-852X
ISBN 0-459-23871-X (1998)

1. Indians of North America – Canada – Legal
status, laws, etc.   I. Title. II. Title:
Indian Act.   III. Series.

KE7704.5.C3   342.71'0872'0263   C94-300634-1
KF8205.C3

CARSWELL
Thomson Professional Publishing

One Corporate Plaza,
2075 Kennedy Road
Scarborough, Ontario
M1T 3V4

Customer Service:
Toronto: 1-416-609-8000
Elsewhere in Canada/U.S. 1-800-387-5164
Fax 1-416-298-5094

Table of Contents

Table of Contents

Preface

Changes to legislation

Significant amendments to the Indian Act which were introduced in December 1996 died on the Order Paper when the federal election was called in the spring of 1997. Consequently, the controversial *Indian Act Optional Modification Act* (Bill C-79) and the *First Nations Land Management Act* (Bill C-75) have not become law. The new Minister of Indian Affairs, Jane Stewart, does not appear to be eager to revive these changes.

The only change to the *Indian Act Regulations* was an administrative amendment to the *Indian Bands Council Method of Election Regulations*. These regulations list the Bands that hold elections under section 74 of the *Indian Act*. With the increasing number of First Nations deciding to hold custom elections outside of the *Indian Act*, it has been difficult to keep this list up to date in the regulations. These amendments facilitate keeping the list current by publishing the Minister's *Indian Bands Council Election Order* in Part II of the *Canada Gazette* from time to time.

Supreme Court of Canada cases

The Supreme Court has released five decisions since last year's volume. A sixth case was not argued because the point in contention became moot. The most significant is the Supreme Court of Canada's decision in *Delgamuukw v. British Columbia*. A summary is provided following the Preface.

In *R. v. Adams* [1996] 4 C.N.L.R. 1 (S.C.C.), a Mohawk living on the Akwesasne reserve, was fishing in a marsh on the St. Lawrence River, outside the boundaries of the reserve. He argued that he had an Aboriginal right to fish. In finding for Adams, the court made several significant findings.

- The court held that, whether the Mohawks exercised military control over the area, or fished while passing through the area on military campaigns, there was sufficient evidence to establish an Aboriginal right to fish for sustenance.

- The court found that the land had been flooded by the government, and the land surrounding the flooded area had been surrendered by the Mohawks. While Aboriginal title may have been extinguished, there was no clear and plain intention to extinguish the fishing rights.

- Aboriginal rights can exist even where there is no Aboriginal title.

- The statutory power to licence fishing infringed the Aboriginal right. The *Quebec Fisheries Regulations*, made under the *Fisheries Act*, provided that the Minister, at his discretion, could provide a special permit to fish for subsistence to an individual Indian or Inuk. The court found that such a wide discretionary power infringed the Aboriginal right. The court stated that the Crown's fiduciary duty required that the Minister's discretion be circumscribed in two ways: first, by providing specific criteria for the exercise of the discretion and second, by providing an accommodation to the existence of Aboriginal rights.

The decision in *R. v. Coté* [1996] 3 S.C.R. 139, [1996] 4 C.N.L.R. 26 was released on the same day as *Adams*. In *Coté*, a member of the Desert River Band, took a group of young people to educate them about traditional fishing in their traditional fishing territory. The territory was now a provincially designated "zone d'exploitation controlee", or "Z.E.C." ("Controlled Harvest Zone"). The court found that Coté had an Aboriginal or treaty right to fish in the area. Among the significant findings made by the court were the following.

- The court rejected Quebec's argument that there could be no Aboriginal title or Aboriginal rights in Quebec because the French did not recognize Aboriginal title.

- Coté was able to establish that the Algonquins had an Aboriginal right to fish for food in this area. The court found that educating young people was reasonably incidental to the exercise of that Aboriginal right.

- The court assumed, without deciding, that there was a Treaty of Swegatchy.

Opetchesaht Indian Band v. Canada (1997), 211 N.R. 241, 90 B.C.A.C. 1, 147 W.A.C. 1, 147 D.L.R. (4th) 1 (S.C.C.) is a case in which the Band challenged the legal status of a hydro right of way. Hydro had been granted a permit by the Minister under section 28 of the *Indian Act* for use as long as required for an electric transmission line. There was no membership surrender vote under section 37, nor an expropriation requiring the approval of the Governor in Council under section 35. The Band argued that the permit was therefore invalid. The Supreme Court upheld the validity of the easement, saying that the right of way need not be limited to any specific length of time, so long as there was an ascertainable end point. In this case, the end point would be when the right of way is no longer necessary for hydro purposes.

The definition of 'designated land'as discussed in *St. Mary's Indian Band v. Cranbrook* (1997), 147 D.L.R. (4th) 385, [1997] 3 C.N.L.R. 282 (S.C.C.). In this case, reserve land was surrendered and sold for full market value in 1966. The land was then leased for $1 per year by the federal government to the city of Cranbrook for an airport. After the creation of the "designated lands" category in 1988 (the "Kamloops Amendment"), the Band argued that the airport was designated land, and therefore part of the reserve. As such, it could be taxed under the Band's *Indian Act* by-laws. The Supreme Court found against the Band.

- The purpose of the "designated land" category was to make it clear that lands that were leased were part of the reserve, but that lands that were sold were never intended to become part of the reserve. In the case of the St. Mary's First Nation, the court found that the Band had intended to sell the land, and therefore, the land was no longer part of the reserve.

- The court did clarify, however, that in cases of surrender, the intention of the parties was more important than the "minutiae of surrender documents".

> The reason the Court has said that common law real property concepts do not apply to native lands is to prevent native intentions from being frustrated by an application of formalistic and arguably alien common law rules. Even in a case such as this where the Indian band received full legal representation prior to the surrender transaction, we must ensure that form not trump substance. It would be fundamentally unjust to impose inflexible and technical land transfer requirements upon these "autonomous actors" and conclude that the "ceased to be used for public purposes" stipulation was a condition subsequent solely because the band made the mistake of using the word "should" instead of the word "until". [C.N.L.R. p. 289]

Goodswimmer v. Canada [1997] 1 S.C.R. 309, was a case which challenged the right of a non-Indian to be elected Chief in an *Indian Act* election. The Federal Court of Appeal found that, under section 75, a chief need not be an elector of the Band. The Supreme Court of Canada quashed the appeal because the issue became moot.

Supreme Court of Canada cases expected in the next year

The rights of Indians who live off reserve will be argued before the Supreme Court in *Corbiere v. Canada* [1997] 1 F.C. 689, 41 C.R.R. (2d) 1 (Fed. C.A.). The Federal Court of Appeal granted a constitutional exemption to allow off reserve members of Batchewana to vote in their *Indian Act* elections, but then stayed the decision pending the decision of the Supreme Court of Canada.

The application of provincial sales tax will be at issue in *New Brunswick v. Union of New Brunswick Indians and Tomah* [1997] 1 C.N.L.R. 213 (C.A.). The province will try to overturn a decision by the New Brunswick Court of Appeal which exempted Indians from provincial sales tax for goods which were purchased off reserve.

In *Chippewas of Kettle & Stony Point v. Canada (Attorney General)* (1996) 31 O.R. (3d) 97, 141 D.L.R. (4th) 1, [1997] 3 C.N.L.R. 65 the Supreme Court will hear about money being paid to Band members by a land speculator during the voting process for a surrender. The Ontario Court of Appeal held that the presence of an unfair bargain, unconscionability or economic duress do not affect the validity of the surrender.

Fiduciary duties after surrender

Guerin established that there was an enforceable fiduciary duty at the time of the surrender. The Federal Court of Appeal has extended that duty to a situation after surrender in *Semiahmoo Indian Band v. Canada* (1997), 148 D.L.R. (4th) 523. In this case, the First Nation reluctantly surrendered part of its reserve when the Crown said it needed the land for the expansion of customs facilities in 1951. The land was not used for anything, and no plans for the customs facilities were even made by the Crown until 1992, after the commencement of litigation. The court held that the Crown had breached two post-surrender duties.

- First, the Crown failed to correct a mistake it made at the time of the surrender. The original surrender should have been conditional, or at least provide for a reversionary interest once the land was no longer needed for public purposes. After the surrender, the Crown had an opportunity to correct this error, but failed to do so.

- Second, the Crown failed to return the land to the Band when it became clear by 1969, that the Crown had not used the land and had no plans to use the land. When the Band asked for return of the land, the Crown should have returned the land because it had not been used.

New heading on Métis rights

This year's volume has a new heading which brings together cases dealing with rights of Métis and with those who are not registered as Indians under the *Indian Act*. The new section is located under section 35(1) of the *Constitution Act, 1982*. It is important to remember that there is a difference between the rights of Métis and the rights of Aboriginal people who are not registered under the *Indian Act*. The issues, however, overlap, and courts do not always distinguish the two very clearly.

Notes on this volume

In the interests of keeping this a portable and affordable book, I have removed the *Indian Oil and Gas Act* and regulations from this volume. The text of this statute can be found in the *Consolidated Native Law Statutes*.

The cases listed under each section are listed in the following order:

Privy Council

Courts of Canada
    Supreme Court of Canada
    Federal Court of Appeal
    Federal Court, Trial Division
    Federal tribunals

Courts of the provinces and territories, listed alphabetically by province or territory

Courts of appeal
Superior trial division courts
Provincial courts
Provincial tribunals

Shin Imai
November, 1997

Last Minute Update: Delgamuukw v. British Columbia

The Supreme Court of Canada has released its most important decision on the rights of Aboriginal peoples since its landmark decision in *R. v. Sparrow* in 1989. Chief Justice Lamer's judgment in *Delgamuukw v. British Columbia* is an impressive synthesis of the law for the last eight years, as well as a guide for future relations between Crown and Aboriginal peoples.

The Gitksan and Wet'suwet'en had asked the court for recognition of their interest in 58,000 square kilometres in British Columbia. The court proceedings were commenced by the hereditary chiefs of 71 Houses.

The original trial ended in 1991. It required 374 days to be heard, and resulted in a mammoth 400 page judgment by McEachern, C.J. In spite of the voluminous evidence and arguments presented to the judge by the First Nations, his decision was peppered with troublesome observations about the racial inferiority of Aboriginal people. For example, rather than accepting evidence of societal laws and customs of the Gitksan and Wet'suwet'en peoples, McEachern, C.J. expressed the view that "they more likely acted as they did because of survival instincts" ([1991] 3 W.W.R. 97 at p. 372).

The views of McEachern, C.J. were repudiated by the British Columbia Court of Appeal in 1993, and now have been repudiated by the Supreme Court of Canada. In fact, it was the trial judge's refusal to take seriously the oral histories of the Gitksan and Wet'suwet'en which led the Supreme Court of Canada to order a new trial.

Chief Justice Lamer wrote the main decision for the Supreme Court of Canada, with Justices Cory, Major and McLachlin concurring. A second decision by Mr. Justice La Forest (concurred in by Madam Justice L'Heureux-Dubé) arrived at the same result, but through somewhat different reasoning.

Oral histories

The Supreme Court ordered a new trial because the trial judge had erred in refusing to admit, or in giving no independent weight to oral histories. Chief Judge Lamer affirmed the importance of considering oral histories on equal footing with other types of historical evidence.

> Notwithstanding the challenges created by the use of oral histories as proof of historical facts, the laws of evidence must be adapted in order that this type of evidence can be accommodated and placed on an equal footing with the types of historical evidence that courts are familiar with, which largely consists of historical documents. [at para.87]

Three general features of Aboriginal title

The Supreme Court stated in earlier cases that Aboriginal title is a *sui generis* interest in land. In *Delgamuukw* this concept is further elaborated by the recognition that the definition of Aboriginal title must refer to both the common law and Aboriginal law.

> ... [aboriginal title] is also *sui generis* in the sense that its characteristics cannot be completely explained by reference either to the common law rules of real property or to the rules of property found in aboriginal legal systems. As with other aboriginal rights, it must be understood by reference to both common law and aboriginal perspectives. [at para. 112]

The court outlined three general features of Aboriginal title.

1. Aboriginal land can only be alienated to the Crown in the right of Canada. [at para.113]

2. The source of Aboriginal title arises from the prior occupation of Canada. This prior occupation is relevant in two ways:

> (i) at common law, occupation is proof of possession; consequently, occupation prior to the assertion of British sovereignty is proof of possession [at para.114 and para.149]

> (ii) prior to the assertion of British sovereignty, Aboriginal law determined the legitimacy of the occupation; consequently, Aboriginal title must partly rely on "pre-existing systems of aboriginal law." [at para.114,and para.148]

3. Aboriginal title is held communally by the "aboriginal nation" and decisions are made by that community. [at para. 115]

Content of Aboriginal title

Chief Justice Lamer sets out two propositions to describe the content of Aboriginal title.

1. Aboriginal title provides exclusive use and occupation of the land for a variety of purposes.

The Supreme Court's view of Aboriginal title is different from its view of other Aboriginal activity such as hunting and fishing. Aboriginal activities must be related to the distinctive culture of Aboriginal peoples (as set out in *R. v. Van der Peet*). On the other hand, Aboriginal title can support other activities related to the use of the land.

> Aboriginal title encompasses the right to use the land held pursuant to that title for a variety of purposes, which need not be aspects of those aboriginal practices, cultures and traditions which are integral to *distinctive aboriginal cultures*. [at para. 117]

While this statement appears to be very wide, and could, as the Chief Justice seems to imply, include mining, the second proposition places an important limitation on the possible uses of the land.

2. The uses of Aboriginal title land must be consistent with the group's attachment to the land.

The court, in a very perceptive balancing move, puts limits on the use of the land using insights provided by Aboriginal peoples about their special relationship to the land.

> ... there will exist a special bond between the group and the land in question such that the land will be part of the definition of the group's distinctive culture. It seems to me that these elements of aboriginal title create an inherent limitation on the uses to which the land, over which such title exists, may be put. For example, if occupation is established with reference to the use of the land as a hunting ground, then the group that successfully claims aboriginal title to that land may not use it in such a fashion as to destroy its value for such a use (e.g., by strip mining it). Similarly, if a group claims a special bond with the land because of its ceremonial or cultural significance, it may not use the land in such a way as to destroy that relationship (e.g., by developing it in such a way that the bond is destroyed, perhaps by turning it into a parking lot.) [at para. 128]

These words will clearly be welcomed by those members of Aboriginal communities who favour continuing a special relationship to the land. It is clear that this judgment does not provide the basis for uncontrolled exploitation of Aboriginal lands unless the land is first surrendered to the federal Crown. [at para. 131]

Recognition under section 35(1) of the Constitution Act, 1982

The court finds that Aboriginal title was recognized at common law before 1982, and is now "constitutionalized in its full form." [at para. 133] Chief Judge Lamer quickly adds that Aboriginal rights which have not been recognized at common law may also receive constitutional protection: "The existence of an aboriginal right at common law is therefore sufficient, but not necessary, for the recognition and affirmation of that right by s. 35(1)". [para. 136]

Proof of Aboriginal title

Chief Justice Lamer outlines three criteria for establishing the existence of Aboriginal title.

1. The land must have been occupied prior to the assertion of British sovereignty.

The point in time for establishing the existence of an Aboriginal practice or custom was the *point of contact* with the Europeans (*R. v. Van der Peet*). In the case of Aboriginal title, the point in time is the date of the assertion of British sovereignty. However, there may be circumstances, such as in the case of dispossession after the arrival of the Europeans, where possession after the assertion of sovereignty may be relevant in establishing Aboriginal title. [at para. 145]

In order to establish occupation, courts should take into account both the physical occupation required at common law as well as relevant Aboriginal laws which "might include, but are not limited to, a land tenure system or laws governing land use." [para. 148]

2. There must be continuity in the possession between the present and the pre-sovereignty occupation.

While present occupation could be used to support a claim for pre-sovereignty occupation, the court attempts to ensure that the requirement is somewhat flexible. There need not be an "unbroken chain of continuity", and a change in the nature of the occupation would not preclude a claim. [at para. 153]

3. The occupation must be exclusive.

The requirement of "exclusive occupation" has been troublesome in the past because it has imposed notions of territoriality associated with nation states, or notions of private property associated with fee simple ownership. Chief Justice Lamer, however, appears to use the term in a more expansive way, underscoring the importance of Aboriginal laws which delineate boundaries between Aboriginal nations for various purposes. Using this approach, then, the Chief Justice is able to allow room for the possibility of joint title among Aboriginal nations using the same territory. [at para. 158]

Laws which infringe Aboriginal title must be justified

In *R. v. Sparrow*, the Supreme Court held that a law which infringed an Aboriginal right was not valid if it did not have a valid legislative objective, or if it was enacted in breach of the Crown's fiduciary duty.

In *Delgamuukw* the *Sparrow* approach is used, but the tests are varied to apply to Aboriginal title.

1. "Compelling and substantial" legislative objective.

The list of legitimate legislative objectives are very wide.

> In my opinion, the development of agriculture, forestry, mining, and hydroelectric power, the general economic development of the interior of British Columbia, protection of the environment or endangered species, the building of infrastructure and the settlement of foreign populations to support those aims, are the kinds of objectives that are consistent with this purpose and, in principle, can justify the infringement of aboriginal title. Whether a particular measure or government act can be explained by reference to one of those objectives, however, is ultimately a question of fact that will have to be examined on a case-by-case basis. [at para. 165]

The breadth of activity which is justified, is balanced by two requirements described below. First, there are clearly articulated requirements for compensation and consultation. Second, only the federal Crown can extinguish Aboriginal title — the provincial Crown is constitutionally incapable.

2. Crown's fiduciary duty

In *Sparrow*, the Crown was required, if it were infringing an Aboriginal right, to take steps which would ensure that the Crown was fulfilling its fiduciary duty to the Aboriginal people involved.

The first move made by the Chief Justice in *Delgamuukw* is to create two categories for analysing the fiduciary duty.

(i) The "form"

The first category is the "form" that the duty takes. This "form" could be consultation, ensuring that there is as little infringement as possible, providing compensation, and so on.

(ii) The "degree of scrutiny"

The second category is the "degree of scrutiny". By this, the Chief Justice suggests that there can be a range of standards in the responses to the Aboriginal interest. For example, *Sparrow* required an absolute priority for Aboriginal food fishing, but in the case of commercial fishing, *Gladstone* required only that the government "take into account" the existence and importance of Aboriginal rights.

The second move made by the Chief Justice is to apply these two categories to three aspects of Aboriginal title.

(i) The right to exclusive use and occupation of land

If the right to exclusive use is to be infringed, the degree of scrutiny should be based on the less stringent test suggested in *Gladstone*.

> this might entail, for example, that governments accommodate the participation of aboriginal peoples in the development of the resources of British Columbia, that the conferral of fee simples for agriculture, and of leases and licences for forestry and mining reflect the prior occupation of aboriginal title lands, that economic barriers to aboriginal uses of their lands (e.g., licensing fees) be somewhat reduced. This list is illustrative and not exhaustive. [at para. 167]

(ii) The right to choose uses for the land - consultation and consent

The fiduciary duty may satisfied by addressing the right to choose through the form of consultation. The degree of consultation would depend on the circumstances.

> In occasional cases, when the breach is less serious or relatively minor, it will be no more than a duty to discuss important decisions that will be taken with respect to lands held pursuant to aboriginal title. Of course, even in these rare cases when the minimum acceptable standard is consultation, this consultation must be in good faith, and with the intention of substantially addressing the concerns of the aboriginal peoples whose lands are at issue. In most cases, it will be significantly deeper than mere consultation. Some cases may even require the full consent of an aboriginal nation, particularly when provinces enact hunting and fishing regulations in relation to aboriginal lands. [at para. 168]

(iii) The economic component of the land

The Chief Justice states that fiduciary duty will have to address the economic component the form of through "fair compensation" .[at para. 169].

The right of self-government

The Supreme Court held that the errors made at trial made it impossible to consider the issue of self-government. In addition, it was observed that the parties in *Delgamuukw* had framed the issue of self-government too broadly for consideration.

In my view, the court was wise to defer the issue for another day. Self-government raises complex issues concerning the relationship of Aborginal laws to Crown laws; and complex issues internal to the Aboriginal communities, especially in relation to laws promulgated by Band Councils which are statutory bodies created by the *Indian Act*. It is likely that these issues can be only be resolved through a series of cases which address different aspects of the self-government issue. The Report of the Royal Commission on Aboriginal Peoples (which the Chief Justice mentions) will undoubtedly provide useful guidance in the coming years.

Power of the province to extinguish Aboriginal rights

Under section 91(24) of the *Constitution Act, 1867*, the federal government has authority over "Indians and Lands reserved for Indians." This brings all Aboriginal rights under exclusive federal authority and only the federal government can extinguish those rights.

> The core of Indianness encompasses the whole range of aboriginal rights that are protected by s. 35(1). Those rights include rights in relation to land; that part of the core derives from s. 91(24)'s reference to "Lands reserved for the Indians". But those rights also encompass practices, customs and traditions which are not tied to land as well; that part of the core can be traced to federal jurisdiction over "Indians". Provincial governments are prevented from legislating in relation to both types of aboriginal rights. [at para. 178]

Provincial laws of general application may apply to Indians through section 88 of the *Indian Act*. However, such provincial laws cannot extinguish Aboriginal rights because section 88 was not enacted with extinguishment in mind.

> I see nothing in the language of the provision which even suggests the intention to extinguish aboriginal rights. Indeed, the explicit reference to treaty rights in s. 88 suggests that the provision was clearly not intended to undermine aboriginal rights.[at para. 183]

The province argued that "Lands reserved for Indians" only included reserve lands. The Supreme Court rejected that argument stating that the federal government had jurisdiction over all lands held pursuant to Aboriginal title. Only the federal government could extinguish that title. [at para. 174]

Duty to negotiate

Issues relating to Aboriginal rights and Aboriginal title are complex, and courts often encourage the parties to resolve their differences through negotiation. In this case, we see the strongest statement to come out of the Supreme Court on the duty of the Crown to negotiate in good faith.

> ... the Crown is under a moral, if not a legal, duty to enter into and conduct those negotiations in good faith. Ultimately, it is through negotiated settlements, with good faith and give and take on all sides, reinforced by the judgments of this Court, that we will achieve what I stated in *Van der Peet*, ... to be a basic purpose of s. 35(1) — "the reconciliation of the pre-existence of aboriginal societies with the sovereignty of the Crown". Let us face it, we are all here to stay. [at para. 186]

Exhortations to negotiate without providing some guidance to the parties on the terms of the negotiations are not very useful. And negotiations which are conducted when there is great inequality in bargaining power do not lead to durable results. In this case, however, the Supreme Court has laid down clear guidelines, and clearly sought to ensure that the parties have greater equality of bargaining power. Hopefully, the groundwork has been laid for a renewed relationship between the Crown and Aboriginal nations.

Table of Cases

All references are to section numbers of the Indian Act, with the following execeptions: Indian Band Election Regulation *IBER*, Indian Reserve Traffic Regulations *IRTR*, Constitution Act 1867 *CA 1867*, Constitution Act 1930 *CA 1930*, Constitution Act 1982 *CA 1982*, Jay Treaty *JT*, Royal Proclamation *RP*

Table of Cases

Table of Cases

INDIAN ACT

Indian Act

An Act respecting Indians

R.S.C. 1985, c. I-5, as am. R.S.C. 1985, c. 32 (1st Supp.); c. 27 (2nd Supp.), s. 10 (Schedule); c. 17 (4th Supp.); c. 43 (4th Supp.); c. 48 (4th Supp.); S.C. 1990, c. 16; 1990, c. 17; 1992, c. 51, s. 54; 1993, c. 28, s. 78 (Schedule III, items 73, 74) (not in force at date of publication); 1996, c. 23, s. 187(e)

Short Title

1. This Act may be cited as the *Indian Act*.

Interpretation

2. (1) Definitions — In this Act

"band" means a body of Indians

> **(a) for whose use and benefit in common, lands, the legal title to which is vested in Her Majesty, have been set apart before, on or after the 4th day of September 1951,**
>
> **(b) for whose use and benefit in common, moneys are held by Her Majesty, or**
>
> **(c) declared by the Governor in Council to be a band for the purposes of this Act;**

Commentary: The Band is established under the statute. In recent years, the tendency is to recognize that it has legal capacity in a wide variety of situations. For other cases on legal capacity see under "Council of the Band".

Case Law:

Definition

Isaac v. Davey (1977), 77 D.L.R. (3d) 481, [1977] 2 S.C.R. 897, 9 C.N.L.C. 134

Governor Simcoe gave a patent to the Grand River lands to the Six Nations on January 14, 1793. Until 1924, Six Nations was governed by a traditional council of hereditary Chiefs. In 1924, the federal government declared by Order in Council, that Six Nations was to be governed according to the elected procedure set out in the *Indian Act*.

The followers of the hereditary system argued that the Order in Council was not valid because Six Nations was not a "Band" within the meaning of the *Indian Act*.

The Supreme Court found that moneys from the sale of parts of the Grand River lands were held in trust by Canada, and therefore Six Nations came under paragraph (b) of the definition. In addition, the court observed that it was arguable that the Order in Council itself was a declaration within the meaning of paragraph (c) of the definition.

Legal Capacity — Canada

Roberts v. R., [1991] 3 F.C. 420, (sub nom. *Wewayakum Indian Band v. Canada*) 42 F.T.R. 40 (T.D.)

Although no statutory enactment specifically provides for it, there is no logical reason why an Indian band should not possess the same rights to sue as corporations, and to be subject to various resulting obligations. Those claiming to sue in the name of a band must be prepared to establish their authority to do so, if and when that authority is challenged. Such authorization may not be subject to any special laws, rules, or procedures other than those prescribed by the traditions, customs, and government of the band in question.

Otineka Development Corp. v. R., [1994] 2 C.N.L.R. 83, 94 D.T.C. 1234, [1994] 2 C.T.C. 2424 (T.C.C.)

Two corporations owned by the Opaskwayak Cree Nation (the Pas Indian Band) were exempt from taxation because the band is a Canadian municipality for the purposes of s. 149(1)(d) of the *Income Tax Act*. The effect of the powers conferred on the band by Parliament and the exercise of those powers by the band, has been to create a form of self-government that is central to the functioning of a municipality; the entity exercising that form of self-government is a municipality within the ordinary meaning of the word.

Legal Capacity — British Columbia

Cache Creek Motors Ltd. v. Porter (1979), 14 B.C.L.R. 13 (Co. Ct.)

This case follows the *Mintuck* decision, and agrees that the band can be sued and is legally capable of acting on its own behalf on all matters except those in which the Minister's involvement is required by the Act.

Legal Capacity — Manitoba

Mintuck v. Valley River Band No. 63A (1977), 75 D.L.R. (3d) 589, 9 C.N.L.C. 210, [1977] 2 W.W.R. 309, 2 C.C.L.T. 1 (Man. C.A.)

A member of a Band leased reserve lands from the federal government for farming purposes. He ceased farming because of harassment from members of the Band. The Band Council then purported to "cancel" the lease and took possession of the farm. The court found that the Band could be sued in tort. Two of the three judges thought a representation order was necessary because the Band itself was not a suable entity.

R. v. Cochrane (1977), 9 C.N.L.C. 486, [1977] 3 W.W.R. 660 (Man. Co. Ct.)

The court found that "a band is neither a natural person nor a corporation", but fell within the definition of "mail contractor" for the purposes of the *Post Office Act*.

Legal Capacity — Nova Scotia

Afton Band of Indians v. Nova Scotia (Attorney General) (1978), 29 N.S.R. (2d) 226, 9 C.N.L.C. 8, 15 A.P.R. 226, 3 R.P.R. 298, 85 D.L.R. (3d) 454 (N.S. S.C.)

A representation order is necessary for the Band to bring an application under the provincial *Quieting of Titles Act*.

Legal Capacity — Ontario

Clow Darling Ltd. v. Big Trout Lake Band of Indians (1989), [1990] 4 C.N.L.R. 7, 70 O.R. (2d) 56 (Ont. Dist. Ct.)

The Band's statutory authority provides it with the legal status to sue or be sued in its own name, and a representation order is unnecessary.

— See also *King v. Gull Bay Indian Band* (1983), 38 C.P.C. 1 (Ont. Co. Ct.)*Bannon v. Pervais*, [1990] 2 C.N.L.R. 17, 68 O.R. (2d) 276 (Ont. Dist. Ct.)

Legal Capacity — Saskatchewan

R. v. Peter Ballantyne Band, [1987] 1 C.N.L.R. 67, 47 M.V.R. 299, 45 Sask. R. 33 (Sask. Q.B.)

A vehicle registered to the Band received a parking ticket. The court found that the Band was an entity which could own property, and therefore was an "owner" within the meaning of the *Vehicles Act*. A conviction was entered against the Band for breaching the municipal by-law.

Custody of child

Re C. and V.C. (1982), 40 B.C.L.R. 234, [1983] 3 C.N.L.R. 58 (Prov. Ct.)

An Indian band is not a "person" capable of having custody of a child.

C.A.S. Winnipeg v. Big Grassy Indian Band (1982), 13 Man. R. (2d) 320 (C.A.)

It was held that a band is not a suitable guardian for a child since it is not a "child caring agency".

Tom v. Winnipeg C.A.S., [1982] 2 W.W.R. 212, 132 D.L.R. (3d) 187, [1982] 1 C.N.L.R. 170 (Man. C.A.)

In this case it was also held that a band is not a suitable guardian for a child and may not be granted custody of a child band member.

Trespass

Joe v. Findlay, [1981] 3 W.W.R. 60, [1981] 3 C.N.L.R. 58, 26 B.C.L.R. 376, 122 D.L.R. (3d) 377 (B.C. C.A.)

The Squamish Band successfully brought an action for trespass against a Band member who was occupying reserve land without authority.

— See also *Mathias v. Findlay*, [1978] C.N.L.B. No.4 130, 4 W.W.R. 653 (B.C. S.C.)

Johnson v. British Columbia Hydro & Power Authority (1981), 27 B.C.L.R. 50, [1981] 3 C.N.L.R. 63, 16 C.C.L.T. 10, 123 D.L.R. (3d) 340 (B.C. S.C.)

In 1971, B.C. Hydro constructed a power line across the Suewoa reserve of the Mowachaht Band, on Vancouver Island. B.C. Hydro did not get the consent of the Band and constructed the line knowing that they had not followed proper procedures. Proceedings were commenced in 1979 when the Band received legal advice. The court granted an injunction against B.C. Hydro and awarded general and exemplary damages for trespass to the reserve.

"Band List" means a list of persons that is maintained under section 8 by a band or in the Department;

"child" includes a child born in or out of wedlock, a legally adopted child and a child adopted in accordance with Indian custom;

Commentary: For cases related to the eligibility for registration or Band membership, see sections 5–14.

Case Law: *Natural Parents v. Supt. of Child Welfare*, [1976] 2 S.C.R. 751, [1976] 1 W.W.R. 699, 21 R.F.L. 267, 60 D.L.R. (3d) 148, 6 N.R. 491

The Supreme Court of Canada held that the general definition in s. 2 is confined to the adoption of an Indian child and is limited to an Indian child of Indian parents. An adoption of such a child by non-Indians does not extinguish the child's status:

> The fact that an Indian child may be the subject of an order for permanent custody or the fact that an Indian child may be adopted by non-Indian parents does not, in my view, terminate or destroy any rights that child as an Indian may have under the *Indian Act* nor terminate or destroy the child's status as an Indian.

— See also *Nelson v. C.A.S. Eastern Manitoba*, [1975] 5 W.W.R. 45, 21 R.F.L. 222, 56 D.L.R. (3d) 567 (Man. C.A.)

Michell v. Dennis, [1984] 2 W.W.R. 449, 51 B.C.L.R. 27 (S.C.)

The change in the definition of "child" to include a child adopted in accordance with Indian custom may permit the adopting parent to bring an action under a *Family Relief Compensation Act*.

N. v. Children's Aid Society of Eastern Manitoba, [1975] 5 W.W.R. 45, 21 R.F.L. 222, 56 D.L.R. (3d) 567 (Man. C.A.)

The adoption provisions of the *Child Welfare Act* do not affect the rights of the child under the *Indian Act.* (This case was decided before *Natural Parents,* but is consistent with *Natural Parents*).

"council of the band" means

(a) in the case of a band to which section 74 applies, the council established pursuant to that section,

(b) in the case of a band to which section 74 does not apply, the council chosen according to the custom of the band, or, where there is no council, the chief of the band chosen according to the custom of the band;

Commentary: Although some cases do not clearly distinguish between the legal capacity of a "Band" and a "Band Council", the distinction is important in some contexts. For other cases on legal capacity see under "Band".

The cases on election disputes listed here deal with "custom" elections. For cases on elections conducted under the *Indian Act,* see sections 74–79.

Case Law:

Legal Capacity of a Band Council

Francis v. Canada, [1982] 4 C.N.L.R. 94, (sub nom. *St. Regis Indian Band Council v. P.S.A.C.)* [1982] 2 S.C.R. 72, 82 C.L.L.C. 14, 208, 139 D.L.R. (3d) 9, 44 N.R. 136

The court finds that a Band Council is an employer within the meaning of the *Canada Labour Code.*

> While the Act does not provide that [the Band Council] shall be incorporated, it does grant to this body substantial legislative powers which, if exercised, would require the employment of staff to secure the implementation of its by-laws. (C.N.L.R. at p. 97–98)

Chippewas of the Nawash First Nation v. Canada (Minister of Indian and Northern Affairs) (1996), [1997] 1 C.N.L.R. 1, 41 Admin. L.R. (2d) 232, 116 F.T.R. 37 (T.D.)

The federal government, pursuant to the *Access to Information Act,* proposed to release two Band Council Resolutions (B.C.R.'s) from the First Nation to an individual. The B.C.R.'s dealt with a federal Bill which would have changed the land regime under the *Indian Act.* The First Nation objected to the release of the information.

Under s. 13 of the federal *Access to Information Act,* information could not be disclosed if it was obtained in confidence from other government bodies, including provinces and "municipal or regional governments" established pursuant to provincial legislation. The court held that two B.C.R.'s sent in confidence to the Minister could be disclosed to a third party because Band Councils were not established pursuant to provincial legislation.

The court also rejected the First Nation's arguments relating to breach of fiduciary duty, and breach of s. 15 of the *Charter of Rights and Freedoms.*

Roseau River Tribal Council v. James, [1989] 4 C.N.L.R. 149 (Can. Adj. L.R.B.)

An Indian band council is run in a manner similar to a municipal council, and its public servants cannot undermine the service expected of a public body. Hence, employees of the Native Alcohol and Drug Addiction Program who were dismissed for publicly criticizing the direction of the tribal council were in breach of their duty of loyalty to their employer, and their employment validly terminated. Their right to free expression under the Charter was not infringed.

Telecom Leasing Canada (TLC) Ltd. v. Enoch Indian Band of Stony Plain Indian Reserve No. 135 (1992), 133 A.R. 355, [1993] 1 W.W.R. 373, 5 Alta. L.R. (3d) 81, [1994] 1 C.N.L.R. 206 (Q.B.)

In addition to the exercise of those powers expressly set out in the Act requiring ministerial approval, a band council is free to contract in the same way as any other party, subject to the laws of general application. Accordingly, a council has the power to guarantee, on behalf of the band, the performance of a related company under a purchase-lease agreement. When the council discussed the motion to approve the agreement, it understood that the guarantee was an integral part of the financing arrangement, and in passing the motion, it approved the guarantee. The guarantee, which the council then executed, was valid.

Chadee v. Norway House First Nation, [1997] 10 W.W.R. 335, 25 C.C.E.L. (2d) 1, 43 Admin. L.R. (2d) 92, 139 D.L.R. (4th) 589, 113 Man. R. (2d) 110, [1997] 2 C.N.L.R. 48 (C.A.)

Mr. Chadee was employed as an education director for the First Nation for six years. He was dismissed without cause and given one month's wages. The Court of Appeal upheld a trial decision to provide six months wages for unjust dismissal.

The court rejected the argument raised by the lawyer for the First Nation, that the First Nation was an agent of the Crown, and therefore, could dismiss any employees at pleasure (ie. without notice). The court held that, to determine whether the Band was acting as an agent of the Crown, it was necessary to look at the degree of control exercised by the federal government. In this case, the court held that the federal government did not exercise control.

> The evidence before us in the presence case does not indicate a level of ministerial control which would lead to the conclusion that the Norway House First Nation was acting as agent for the Crown. The evidence focused upon the relationship between the Norway House First Nation and the plaintiff himself. It would seem that his hiring was entirely the decision of the band council. There is nothing on the record which indicates that the Minister influenced, let alone controlled, the decision to establish the position of director of education or to choose the plaintiff to fill that position. From the record, there is nothing to indicate that the Minister had anything to do with the terms of the employment contract. There is no evidence that the Minister was informed or consulted when Mr. Chadee's responsibilities changed. And the Minister was not involved in Mr. Chadee's dismissal. (W.W.R. p. 344)

[The court distinguished *Whitebear Band Council v. Carpenters Provincial Council*, which found, in that case, that the Band Council was an agent of the Crown.]

Kucey v. Peter Ballantyne Band Council, [1987] 3 W.W.R. 438, 16 C.P.C. (2d) 59, [1987] 3 C.N.L.R. 68, 57 Sask. R. 29 (C.A.)

Band councils are given rights to contract and may be sued in their own name. A Chief may be ordered to attend an examination for discovery as a representative of the council.

— See also *Whitebear Band v. Carpenters Provincial Council (Saskatchewan)*, [1982] 3 W.W.R. 554, [1982] 3 C.N.L.R. 181, 135 D.L.R. (3d) 128, 15 Sask. R. 37 (C.A.)

Relationship of Chief and Council to the Band

Williams Lake Indian Band v.Abbey, [1992] 4 C.N.L.R. 21, (sub nom. *Gilbert v. Abbey*) [1992] B.C.W.L.D. 1783 (B.C. S.C.)

A former Chief received, while in office, payments from the Band for her student loan, and private school tuition for her children. The court ordered her to pay the money back, and observed,

> There can be no question that a duly-elected chief as well as the members of a band council are fiduciaries as far as all other members of the band are concerned. The chief upon being elected, undertakes to act in the interests of the members of the band. The members of the band are vulnerable to abuse by the fiduciary of his or her position, and a fiduciary undertakes not to allow his or her interest to conflict with the duty that he or she has undertaken. [C.N.L.R. at p.23]

Leonard v. Gottfriedson (1981), 21 B.C.L.R. 326, [1982] 1 C.N.L.R. 60 (B.C. S.C.)

The Kamloops Band challenged the possession of land by a son of a former chief. The court found that the son was not in lawful possession, and commented "It should be apparent that the chief and councillors of a band are in a position of trust relative to the interests of the band generally, the band's assets and the members of the band." [C.N.L.R. at p.64]

> Just as the exercise of a power by a municipality is required to be exercised in strict accord with the statute, to protect the interests of the inhabitants, so, it seems to me, and on the same principle, the council's powers under the *Indian Act* are to be exercised strictly in accord with the Act in the interests of the benefit and protection of the Indians. [C.N.L.R. at p.71]

Barry v. Garden River Band of Ojibway (1997), 33 O.R. (3d) 782, 147 D.L.R. (4th) 615 (C.A.)

As part of a land claim settlement, the First Nation set aside $1 million for a per capita distribution to members of the Band. A dispute developed over two issues: the repayment of moneys paid out to women who were enfranchised before 1985 (section 64.1 of the *Indian Act*) and the fiduciary duty of the Band Council to make payments to all members of the Band.

In this case, the women who had been involuntarily enfranchised before 1985 had been paid out less than $1,000 of the Band moneys when they lost status. Although they were not required to pay this money back upon regaining status under Bill C-31, the Band proposed to deduct the payments from the amounts to be distributed under the land claim settlement.

The court found that the Band Council was a trustee and had a duty as a trustee to distribute the land claim money equally among all the beneficiaries. In this case, the Band had decided to reduce the amounts paid out to the enfranchised women, but decided *not* to reduce the distribution of members who owed money to the Band for other reasons. The court found that this was a breach of trust.

There was a breach of trust as well when the Band Council decided not to distribute moneys to children of the enfranchised women who were entitled to become Band members, but who had not yet been put on the Band list. The court held that the Band Council had a duty to identify and locate all the members of the Band.

Federal Court Jurisdiction over Band Councils in General

Gabriel v. Canatonquin, [1980] 2 F.C. 792, [1981] 4 C.N.L.R. 61 (F.C.A.)

The Council of an Indian Band is a "federal board, commission or other tribunal" within the meaning of the *Federal Court Act*, even if the Council is elected according to custom.

— See also, *Rider v. Ear*, [1979] 6 W.W.R. 226, [1979] 4 C.N.L.R. 119, 103 D.L.R. (3d) 168 (Alta.S.C.)

Parisier v. Ocean Man First Nation (1996), 108 F.T.R. 297

The Ocean Man First Nation conducted an election for Chief and Council pursuant to the provisions in its Constitution. There was a tie for one of the Councillor positions. The Electoral Officer appointed under the Ocean Man Constitution declared one of the candidates the winner based on her past experience as a member of council. The Constitution, however, required that the Electoral Officer conduct a run-off election within fifteen days.

According to the Constitution, election disputes were to go to the Court of Queen's Bench and dealt with according to the *Controverted Elections Act* of Saskatchewan. The Federal Court, however, held that the Ocean Man First Nation Constitution could not oust jurisdiction of the Federal Court. Finding that the Electoral Officer was a "federal board, commission or other tribunal" within the meaning of the *Federal Court Act*, the court quashed her decision.

Repap Manitoba Inc. v. Mathias Colomb Indian Band (1996), [1997] 1 C.N.L.R. 176, 47 C.P.C. (3d) 118, 110 Man. R. (2d) 125 (C.A.)

Repap, a forestry company, sought an injunction against members of the First Nation who were obstructing its logging operations.

The court confirmed that a Band Council was a federal board which could only be enjoined in the Federal Court of Canada. However, a Band, and individual members of a Band, could be enjoined by a Manitoba court.

Coalition to Save Northern Flood v. Canada, [1995] 9 W.W.R. 457, 102 Man. R. (2d) 223, 93 W.A.C. 223 (C.A.)

At a Band meeting a group called "Quorum of Chief and Council" are mandated to negotiate agreement on behalf of the Band. A group of Band members calling itself the Coalition tried to stop the Quorum from negotiating. The Court finds that "Quorum" was not exercising authority under the *Indian Act*, but rather authority from Band meeting. Therefore, it was not a federal board, and the matter was not within the exclusive jurisdiction of the Federal Court. The matter could be heard in Manitoba's Queen's Bench.

Chapman v. Chicago (1991), 5 O.R. (3d) 220, 52 O.A.C. 308 (Div. Ct.)

While a Band Council is a federal board within the meaning of the *Federal Court Act*, a Band is not. In this case, the Ontario Court (General Division) had jurisdiction to appoint a receiver *for the Band*, while an election dispute was being dealt with through the federal court system.

Elections by Band custom — Canada

Gabriel v. Canatonquin, [1980] 2 F.C. 792, [1981] 4 C.N.L.R. 61 (F.C.A.)

The Council of an Indian Band is a "federal board, commission or other tribunal" within the meaning of the *Federal Court Act*, even if the Council is elected according to custom.

— See also, *Lameman v. Gladue* (1995), 90 F.T.R. 319 (Fed. T.D.)*Whitefish v. Canada (Department of Indian & Northern Development)*, [1986] 1 C.N.L.R. 180, [1985] 5 W.W.R. 664, 41 Sask. R. 257 (Sask. Q.B.)

Lameman v. Cardinal, [1997] F.C.J. No. 1518 (T.D.)

The Beaver Lake First Nation reverted to custom elections in 1984. Under the *Beaver Lake Tribal Election Law* an Appeals Officer found that there had been a corrupt practice in an election where a new Chief and Council was elected. The Appeals Officer reinstated the former Chief and Council and ordered that a new election be called.

The court reviewed the decision of the Appeals Officer and found that he had failed to provide information to the candidates about his findings. He therefore failed in a minimal duty of fairness. The Federal Court also found that the *Tribal Election Law* did not give the Appeals Officer authority to call a new election.

Lower Similkameen Indian Band v. Allison (1996), [1997] 1 F.C. 475, 122 F.T.R. 1 (T.D.)

Members of the Council of the Band began an action for a declaration that they were the duly elected office holders against former members of Council. The five individual defendants counterclaimed that the custom election was null and void. The court held that it did not have jurisdiction to decide the case because the proper procedure should have been judicial review, not an action.

Crow v. Blood Indian Band Council (1996), 107 F.T.R. 270, [1997] 3 C.N.L.R. 76 (T.D.)

The Blood Tribe had a Custom Election By-law. Crow was elected as a councillor under this by-law. He was removed as a councillor by the rest of Chief and Council for misconduct. His removal was done according to a process described in the Election By-law, and, under the Election By-law, Crow was not allowed to stand for re-election.

Crow challenged the validity of the Election By-law on two major grounds. First, Crow argued that, even in custom elections, the *Indian Act* procedures, such as section 78, should continue to apply. The court rejected this argument, and observed,

> ... those bands that are not subject to a s.74 ministerial order may select their band council in accordance with their band's custom, unimpeded by the Act. Section 2 of the *Indian Act* recognizes that the council of the band may be "chosen" according to the custom of the band. In my

view, use of the word "chosen" suggests that the manner by which the band council is selected does not necessarily require an election; for example, the Band Chief position may be hereditary. [F.T.R. at 276]

The second challenge was based on violations of the *Charter of Rights and Freedoms*. The court pointed out that, whether the *Charter* applied at all to custom elections was a difficult question. The court avoided having to make a decision on this point because it found that, even if the *Charter* applied, there was no violation of the *Charter*.

Bone v. Sioux Valley Indian Band No. 290 (1996), 107 F.T.R. 133, 3 C.N.L.R. 54 (T.D.)

The First Nation held two plebiscites to determine whether to revert to custom elections. The majority of voters were in favour on both occasions. A draft Election Code was in existence at the time of the plebiscites. The Election Code stated that Regulations would be drafted and submitted to the community for approval.

A dispute arose following the election held under the Election Code. An Election Appeals Tribunal established under the Code ordered a new election, based on a residency requirement provided in the Regulations.

The court held that the there was evidence of community support for the Code, but that there was no evidence that the Regulations had been submitted to the community for approval, as required by the Code. The court, therefore, upheld the Code, but did not uphold the Regulations.

The court also observed that custom elections arose out of the inherent power of the Band, not from a delegation under the *Indian Act*.

> Accordingly, I do not think that the power of the Band to choose its council in a customary manner is a "power conferred on the Band" as is contemplated by subsection 2(3)(a) of the *Indian Act*. Rather it is an inherent power of the Band; it is a power the Band has always had, which the *Indian Act* only interferes with in limited circumstances, as provided for under s. 74 of the Act. Thus, in my view the Band may exercise this inherent power unrestrained by subsection 2(3)(a) of the *Indian Act*. [p. 141]

Gadwa v. Kehewin Cree Nation (1996), 109 F.T.R. 12 (T.D.)

An amendment was made to the election provisions of Kehewin Indian Law Number One at a meeting of seventy band members. There are over 500 electors in the Band. Although the Law did not provide for a method for amendments, the court struck down the amendment on the basis that not sufficient time nor details were provided in the notice for the meeting.

Big "C" First Nation v. Big "C" First Nation Election Appeal Tribunal (1994), [1995] 2 C.N.L.R. 54, (sub nom. *Cheecham v. Piche*) 80 F.T.R. 49 (T.D.)

The Federal Court had jurisdiction to prohibit a hearing by an Election Appeal Tribunal established under the *First Nation's Election Regulations*.

Frank v. Bottle (1993), [1994] 2 C.N.L.R. 45, 65 F.T.R. 89 (T.D.)

The council of the Blood Tribe, elected under the tribe's customary election by-law, is a "federal board, commission or other tribunal" which is within the jurisdiction of the Federal Court in relation to relief sought under s. 18 of the *Federal Court Act*.

Sparvier v. Cowessess Indian Band No. 73, [1993] 3 F.C. 142, 13 Admin. L.R. (2d) 266, 63 F.T.R. 242, [1994] 1 C.N.L.R. 182 (T.D.)additional reasons at [1993] 3 F.C. 175, 13 Admin. L.R. (2d) 266 at 293, 66 F.T.R. 266 [1994] 1 C.N.L.R. 182 at 205 (T.D.)

Elections for chief and council were conducted according to custom. An appeal tribunal was established by custom to hear disputes about elections. The court held that the appeal tribunal was a federal board within the meaning of the *Federal Court Act*.

Bigstone v. Big Eagle (1992), [1993] 1 C.N.L.R. 25, 52 F.T.R. 109 (T.D.)

The *Indian Act* does not require that a Band constitution providing for "custom" elections be approved by a referendum. Rather, the practice must be based upon a "broad consensus." Innovative measures may have to be taken to establish contemporary "custom."

The Federal Court, Trial Division has exclusive jurisdiction to issue injunctions against Indian band councils, insofar as they purport to exercise powers under the *Indian Act*, regardless of whether the councils have been elected by custom or under the Act.

Joe v. John (1990), 34 F.T.R. 280, [1991] 3 C.N.L.R. 63 (T.D.)

John was elected Chief of the Miawpukek Band of Micmac Indians in a custom election. The Federal Court had jurisdiction to deal with a complaint by Joe that John was expending Band moneys on payments to lawyers and accountants to retain control of the Band.

Elections by Band custom — British Columbia

Napoleon v. Garbitt, [1997] B.C.J. No. 1250 (B.C. S.C.)

In 1988, the Saulteau First Nation decided to have custom elections. The Government Law which the community developed provided for a selection for Chief which differed markedly from the secret vote regime of the *Indian Act*. Under this scheme, each of the five families on the reserve elected a Headman by consensus. The five Headmen, in consultation with the Council of Elders then selected a Chief. In 1996 a general meeting of the Band recommended changes to the process, and an election was held with some of those changes in place. Under the Government Law, however, amendments to the election process could not be made at a Band meeting. A controversy developed about the validity of the election held after the changes made in 1996 at the general Band meeting.

After reviewing the history of the custom elections since 1988, the court found that the procedures in the Government Law were not followed in practice: the custom was to seek consensus by informal votes or band meetings. The court upheld the amendments made at the Band meeting.

James v. Jules, [1995] 3 C.N.L.R. 90 (B.C. Prov.Ct.)

The Kamloops Band holds elections under "custom" and has *Custom Election Regulations*. These regulations provide that the Provincial Court is to hear disputes concerning the elections. In this case, the court took jurisdiction and dismissed a challenge based on conflict of interest. The judge commented about conflict of interest:

> Standards which apply when electing public officials in large urban populations may not be workable for the Kamloops Indian band. That is a decision properly made by the members of the Kamloops Indian Band. [C.N.L.R. 100]

"Department" means the Department of Indian Affairs and Northern Development;

"designated lands" means a tract of land or any interest therein the legal title to which remains invested in Her Majesty and in which the band for whose use and benefit it was set apart as a reserve has, otherwise than absolutely, released or surrendered its rights or interests, whether before or after the coming into force of this definition;

Case Law: *St. Mary's Indian Band v. Cranbrook (City)* (1997), 147 D.L.R. (4th) 385, [1997] 3 C.N.L.R. 282 (S.C.C.)

A 1966 surrender by the Band contained the following provision:

> And that should any time the said lands cease to be used for public purposes they will revert to the St. Mary's Indian Band free of charge.

The land was surrendered and sold for full market value at that time. The land was then leased for $1 per year by the federal government to the city of Cranbrook for an airport. After the creation of the "designated lands" category in 1988 (the "Kamloops Amendment"), the Band argued that the airport was designated land, and therefore part of the reserve. As such, it could be taxed under the Band's *Indian Act* by-laws.

The Supreme Court held that the Kamloops Amendment was enacted to make it clear that lands that were *leased* were part of the reserve, but that lands that were *sold* were never intended to become part of the reserve. In the case of the St. Mary's First Nation, the court found that the Band had intended to sell the land, and therefore, the land was no longer part of the reserve.

The Chief Justice commented on the meaning of the words 'otherwise than absolutely' in the definition of designated lands (s.2(1))

> Why did Parliament use this broad "otherwise than absolutely" language? If its express intention was to keep surrenders for sale outside the reserve, why did Parliament not define "designated lands" in a more explicit manner? I offer one convincing response: Parliament must have selected the broad "otherwise than absolutely" phraseology in order to account for other contingencies — to allow, at one end, for other limited forms of surrenders, such as a right of way, to be considered designated land, and to ensure, at the other end, that other forms of permanent surrenders such as exchange or gift remain beyond our notions of reserve land. [C.N.L.R. p. 294]

"elector" means a person who

(a) is registered on a Band List,

(b) is of the full age of eighteen years, and

(c) is not disqualified from voting at band elections;

"estate" includes real and personal property and any interest in land;

"Indian" means a person who pursuant to this Act is registered as an Indian or is entitled to be registered as an Indian;

Commentary: Cases have generally found that a corporation is not an "Indian" (unless the court pierces the corporative veil). For cases on whether an individual is an "Indian" for the purpose of hunting rights, see cases under *Natural Resources Transfer Agreement* and under *Constitution Act*, 1982, s. 35.

Case Law: *Four B. Manufacturing Ltd. v. U.G.W.*, [1979] 4 C.N.L.R. 21, [1980] 1 S.C.R. 1031

Four B. made shoes on the Tyendinaga reserve. The company was owned by four members of the Band, and employed mostly Band members. The court found that there was not anything specifically Indian about "an employer who happens to be an Ontario corporation, privately owned by Indians" (C.N.L.R. p.25).

Kostyshyn (Johnson) v. West Region Tribal Council Inc. (1992), [1994] 1 C.N.L.R. 94, 55 F.T.R. 48 (T.D.)

Because a tribal council is a corporation, it cannot have the benefit of ss. 89 or 90, and its account can be subject to garnishment.

Stony Plain Indian Reserve No. 135, Re, [1982] 1 C.N.L.R. 133, [1982] 1 W.W.R. 302, 130 D.L.R. (3d) 636, 35 A.R. 412 (Alta. C.A.)

A corporation with head offices on reserve, and with shareholders who are all Indians is not an "Indian". The court states, "... the status of a corporation as a legal entity which exists independently of the character or status of its shareholders is recognized in law. It follows that the status of any or all of its shareholders, or the presence of a registered office on or off a reservation, has no bearing on the status accorded it at law." (C.N.L.R at p.154.).

Western Industrial Contractors Ltd. v. Sarcee Development Ltd., [1979] 3 W.W.R. 631, 98 D.L.R. (3d) 424, 15 A.R. 309 (Alta. C.A.)

Sarcee Development was a Band-owned corporation. The Band surrendered reserve land to the federal government for 75 years, and the corporation leased the land back from the federal government. The court held that the corporation was not an Indian. Therefore, a provincial builder's lien could apply against the corporation and the corporation's interest in the lease. However, the provincial legislation could not apply to the Band's reversionary interest in the land, because that fell within "lands reserved for Indians."

Sarcee Gravel Products Inc. v. Alberta (Worker's Compensation Board) (1994), [1995] 3 C.N.L.R. 193, [1995] 2 W.W.R. 246, 161 A.R. 305, 24 Alta. L.R. (3d) 389 (Alta. Q.B.)

The Tsuu T'ina Nation created a provincial corporation to conduct gravel extraction. The corporation was wholly owned by the Band and all profits went to the Nation. The corporation challenged the assessment of a provincial workers' compensation levy. The court held that the corporation was not an Indian, and therefore, was not exempt from the levy.

Northwest/Prince Rupert Assessor, Area No. 25 v. N & V Johnson Services Ltd. (1990), 1 M.P.L.R. (2d) 170, 49 B.C.L.R. (2d) 173, [1991] 1 W.W.R. 527, 73 D.L.R. (4th) 170, [1991] 1 C.N.L.R. 90 (C.A.)

The shareholders of a corporation that operated a service station and restaurant on a reserve were band members. The corporation had obtained a lease of the lands from the Ministry of Indian and Northern Affairs, and s. 34 of the *B.C. Assessment Act*, R.S.B.C. 1979, c. 21 provided that Crown lands occupied by parties other than the Crown were liable to assessment for taxation. The court declined to lift the corporate veil and exempt the corporation from assessment pursuant to s. 87 of the *Indian Act* because there were no grounds to justify it. There was no ambiguity in the provincial legislation or in s. 87 to be resolved in favour of the taxpayer.

Westbank Property Management Ltd. v. Kelowna Assessor, Area No. 19 (1991), [1993] 1 C.N.L.R. 176 (B.C. S.C.)

The status of individual shareholders could not, except in special circumstances, affect the status of a company. Where the company was wholly owned and operated by a status Indian, and leased Indian lands, the Court would not lift the corporate veil to exempt the corporation from taxation.

Celtic Shipyards 1988 Ltd. v. Marine Workers' and Boilermakers' Industrial Union, Local 1 (1994), [1995] 3 C.N.L.R. 41, 94 C.L.L.C. 16,068 (B.C.L.R.B.)

The Board upheld the application of provincial labour legislation to a commercial fishing company owned by the Musqueam Band. The Board found that, in this case, the owner was the corporation, not the Band. There was nothing "Indian" about the company as it was engaged in ordinary industrial activity, and the company was not exercising an Aboriginal right to fish.

Kinookimaw Beach Assn. v. R., [1979] 4 C.N.L.R. 101, [1979] 6 W.W.R. 84, 102 D.L.R. (3d) 333 (Sask.C.A.)

Seven First Nations were the sole shareholders of a not-for-profit corporation. The corporation was established to develop a surrendered reserve for recreation purposes. The court held that the corporation was not an "Indian", and therefore was not exempt from paying provincial taxes.

"Indian moneys" means all moneys collected, received or held by Her Majesty for the use and benefit of Indians or bands;

"Indian Register" means the register of persons that is maintained under section 5;

"intoxicant" includes alcohol, alcoholic, spirituous, vinous, fermented malt or other intoxicating liquor or combination of liquors and mixed liquor a part of which is spir-

ituous, vinous, fermented or otherwise intoxicating and all drinks or drinkable liquids and all preparations or mixtures capable of human consumption that are intoxicating;

Case Law: *R. v. Campbell* (1996), [1997] 1 C.N.L.R. 120, [1997] 2 W.W.R. 195, 112 C.C.C. (3d) 107, 41 C.R.R. (2d) 175, 5 C.R. (5th) 133, 142 D.L.R. (4th) 496, 113 Man. R. (2d) 288 (C.A.)

The accused lived off reserve. He was charged with violating a Moose Lake Indian Reserve by-law by being intoxicated on the reserve.

The lawyer for the accused argued that the words "intoxicant" and "intoxicated" were too vague, and therefore, the by-law was invalid. The court took the opposite view, stating

> The evidence in the present case supports the view that the safety of Moose Lake residents is at risk due to overindulgence in alcohol and other intoxicants by some. This state of affairs is not unique to the Moose Lake Reserve. The empowerment of local bands to deal with the problem, if it exists, is thus a valid social objective, as is the enactment of the law by a band faced with the problem.

> We would likely impede the band's objective if we were to construe the word "intoxicated" as being too vague. I therefore prefer to construe it as meaning any recognizable degree of intoxication. This construction of the by-law supports sobriety on the reserve and avoids any clash with the doctrine of vagueness. [C.N.L.R. p. 126-127]

"member of a band" means a person whose name appears on a Band List or who is entitled to have his name appear on a Band List;

"mentally incompetent Indian" means an Indian who, pursuant to the laws of the province in which he resides, has been found to be mentally defective or incompetent for the purposes of any laws of that province providing for the administration of estates of mentally defective or incompetent persons;

"Minister" means the Minister of Indian Affairs and Northern Development;

"registered" means registered as an Indian in the Indian Register;

"Registrar" means the officer in the Department who is in charge of the Indian Register and the Band List maintained in the Department;

"reserve"

> **(a) means a tract of land, the legal title to which is vested in Her Majesty, that has been set apart by Her Majesty for the use and benefit of a band, and**

> **(b) except in subsection 18(2), sections 20 to 25, 28, 36 to 38, 42, 44, 46, 48 to 51, 58, 60 and the regulations made under any of those provisions, includes designated lands;**

Case Law:

General

R. v. Nikal, [1996] 5 W.W.R. 305, 19 B.C.L.R. (3d) 201, 105 C.C.C. (3d) 481, 196 N.R. 1, 133 D.L.R. (4th) 658, 74 B.C.A.C. 161, [1996] 1 S.C.R. 1013

The *ad medium filum aquae* presumption did not apply in this case, so that the Bulkley River did not form part of the Moricetown reserve.

R. v. Lewis, [1996] 5 W.W.R. 348, 19 B.C.L.R. (3d) 244, 105 C.C.C. (3d) 523, 133 D.L.R. (4th) 700, 196 N.R. 165, [1996] 1 S.C.R. 921, [1996] 3 C.N.L.R. 131

The *ad medium filum aquae* presumption did not apply to the navigable rivers, such as the Squamish River. Therefore, the river was not part of the reserve.

Re Stony Plain Indian Reserve No. 135 (1982), 35 A.R. 412, [1982] 1 W.W.R. 302, 130 D.L.R. (3d) 636, [1982] 1 C.N.L.R. 133 (C.A.)

Once land is surrendered by a band and granted in fee simple to a grantee, it ceases to be a "reserve" under this Act.

Joe v. Findlay, [1981] 3 W.W.R. 60, 26 B.C.L.R. 376, 122 D.L.R. (3d) 377 (C.A.)

The court held that the use and benefit of reserve land accrues to and comes into existence as an enforceable right vested in the entire band; it is a collective right of the band members as a body and not a right of band members individually.

— See also *Mathias v. Findlay*, [1978] 4 W.W.R. 653 (B.C. S.C.)

Creation of a Reserve

Canadian Pacific Ltd. v. Paul, [1989] 1 C.N.L.R. 47, [1988] 2 S.C.R. 654, 53 D.L.R. (4th) 487, 89 N.R. 325 (S.C.C.)

In 1851 lands were conveyed from the estate of an owner to the Queen as represented by the Lieutenant-Governor of New Brunswick. The deed stated that it was being purchased "for the use of the Melicette Tribe of Indians .... during the [pleasure] of Her Majesty in Lieu of a Tract of land of which the said Indians have been wrongfully deprived as is alleged".

The court found that, although there was no formal allotment of the lands, on acquisition, the lands were *de facto* allotted to the First Nation.

Erasmus v. R., [1992] 2 F.C. 681, [1993] 1 C.N.L.R. 59, 92 D.T.C. 6301, [1992] 2 C.T.C. 21, 145 N.R. 321 (C.A.)

The setting aside of lands under the *Territorial Lands Act* is not equivalent to the creation of a "reserve".

Hay River v. R., [1980] 1 F.C. 262, 101 D.L.R. (3d) 184 (T.D.)

The Federal Court noted that, while the *Indian Act* gives a definition of "reserve", it does not deal with the creation of a reserve. The court stated:

> ... the authority to set apart Crown lands for an Indian reserve in the Northwest Territories appears to remain based entirely on the Royal Prerogative, not subject to any statutory limitation. [F.C. p. 265]

"superintendent" includes a commissioner, regional supervisor, Indian superintendent, assistant Indian superintendent and any other person declared by the Minister to be a superintendent for the purposes of this Act, and with reference to a band or a reserve, means the superintendent for that band or reserve;

"surrendered lands" means a reserve or part of a reserve or any interest therein, the legal title to which remains vested in Her Majesty, that has been released or surrendered by the band for whose use and benefit it was set apart.

(2) The expression "band" with reference to a reserve or surrendered lands means the band for whose use and benefit the reserve or the surrendered lands were set apart.

(3) Unless the context otherwise requires or this Act otherwise provides

(a) a power conferred upon a band shall be deemed not to be exercised unless it is exercised pursuant to the consent of a majority of the electors of the band, and

(b) a power conferred upon the council of a band shall be deemed not to be exercised unless it is exercised pursuant to the consent of a majority of the councillors of the band present at a meeting of the council duly convened.

R.S. 1985, c. 32 (1st Supp.), s. 1; c. 17 (4th Supp.), s. 1.

Case Law:

Powers of band and council of band

Bone v. Sioux Valley Indian Band No. 290 (1996), 107 F.T.R. 133 (T.D.)

The court observed that custom elections arose out of the inherent power of the Band, not from a delegation under the *Indian Act*.

Accordingly, I do not think that the power of the Band to choose its council in a customary manner is a "power conferred on the Band" as is contemplated by subsection 2(3)(a) of the *Indian Act*. Rather it is an inherent power of the Band; it is a power the Band has always had, which the *Indian Act* only interferes with in limited circumstances, as provided for under section 74 of the Act. Thus, in my view the Band may exercise this inherent power unrestrained by subsection 2(3)(a) of the *Indian Act*. [p. 141]

Leonard v. Gottfriedson (1982), 21 B.C.L.R. 326, [1982] 1 C.N.L.R. 60 (S.C.)

In an *obiter* comment, the court stated that the requirements of this subsection should be followed. There is no authority for a band council to exercise its power by individual consent to a resolution in writing. The use of a Department of Indian Affairs form headed "Band Council Resolution" as if it were a written resolution, simply signed by members of a council without reference to any meeting, neglects the requirements set out in this section and may invalidate the declaration made.

Basque v. Woodstock Indian Band (1996), 175 N.B.R. (2d) 241, 446 A.P.R. 241 (C.A.)

Basque was a contractor who did work for the Band and was owed over $99,000. The Band challenged the validity of the claim. The court held that there was a valid oral contract. The contract had been authorized by a resolution passed at a meeting at which there were a quorum of councillors who authorized the Chief to enter into the contract.

Heron Seismic Services Ltd. v. Peepeekisis Indian Band (1990), 87 Sask. R. 66, 74 D.L.R. (4th) 308, (sub nom. *Heron Seismic Services Ltd. v. Muscowpetung Indian Band*) [1991] 2 C.N.L.R. 52 (Q.B.) (Q.B.)affirmed (1991), 86 D.L.R. (4th) 767 (Sask. C.A.)

Contracts must be approved or authorized by a duly passed resolution of the band council before a band can be contractually bound.

Administration

3. (1) Minister to administer Act — **This Act shall be administered by the Minister of Indian Affairs and Northern Development, who shall be the superintendent general of Indian Affairs.**

(2) Authority of Deputy Minister and chief officer — **The Minister may authorize the Deputy Minister of Indian Affairs and Northern Development or the chief officer in charge of the branch of the Department relating to Indian affairs to perform and exercise any of the duties, powers and functions that may be or are required to be performed or exercised by the Minister under this Act or any other Act of the Parliament of Canada relating to Indian affairs.**

Case Law: *Isaac v. Davey*, 5 O.R. (2d) 610, 51 D.L.R. (3d) 170, 16 N.R. 29affirmed [1977] S.C.R. 897, 77 D.L.R. (3d) 481, 16 N.R. 29

> No express provision of the *Indian Act*, and no implied underlying policy of that Act make the members of an elected council agents of the Crown. [51 D.L.R. p. 183]

Badger v. Canada (1990), 38 F.T.R. 43, [1991] 2 C.N.L.R. 17affirmed (1992), 146 N.R. 79, 57 F.T.R. 311n (C.A.)

The predecessor to section 74 of the *Indian Act*, (S.C. 1951, c.29, s.73) provided that an order from the Governor in Council was necessary to bring Band elections under the *Indian Act*. Such an order was made in 1952. In 1956, the section was amended to permit the Minister to make such an order. In 1982, the Band voted to return to Band custom elections, and the Deputy Minister of Indian Affairs issued an instrument returning the Band to custom elections. In 1986, a Band member challenged the authority of the Deputy Minister to make that decision.

The court found that the Minister could now exercise the authority which the Governor in Council had previously exercised. In addition, under section 3, the Minister had the authority to delegate the decision to the Deputy Minister.

Application of Act

4. (1) Application of Act — **A reference in this Act to an Indian does not include any person of the race of aborigines commonly referred to as Inuit.**

(2) Act may be declared inapplicable — **The Governor in Council may by proclamation declare that this Act or any portion thereof, except sections 5 to 14.3 or sections 37 to 41, shall not apply to**

(a) any Indians or any group or band of Indians,

(b) any reserve or any surrendered lands or any part thereof,

and may by proclamation revoke any such declaration.

(2.1) Authority confirmed for certain cases — **For greater certainty, and without restricting the generality of subsection (2), the Governor in Council shall be deemed to have had the authority to make any declaration under subsection (2) that he has made in respect of section 11, 12 or 14, or any provision thereof, as each section or provision read immediately prior to April 17, 1985.**

(3) Certain sections inapplicable to Indians living off reserves — **Sections 114 to 122 and, unless the Minister otherwise orders, sections 42 to 52 do not apply to or in respect of any Indian who does not ordinarily reside on a reserve or on lands belonging to Her Majesty in right of Canada or a province.**

R.S. 1985, c. 32 (1st Supp.), s. 2.

Commentary: The word **"Indian"** in s. 91(24) of the *Constitution Act, 1867* includes Inuit (*Re: Eskimo*, [1939] S.C.R. 104). This section, added in 1951, states that, in spite of federal legislative authority over Inuit, this legislation does not apply to them.

Case Law:

"Ordinarily reside"

A.G. Can. v. Canard, [1976] 1 S.C.R. 170, [1975] 3 W.W.R. 1, 52 D.L.R. (3d) 548, 4 N.R. 91

"**Ordinarily reside**" is a matter of fact that must be determined in each case. Factors to be considered include the general mode of life, bodily presence and the intention of remaining, and duration of stay.

4.1 Provisions that apply to all band members — A reference to an Indian in any of the following provisions shall be deemed to include a reference to any person whose name is entered in a Band List and who is entitled to have it entered therein: the definitions "band", "Indian moneys" and "mentally incompetent Indian" in section 2, subsections 4(2) and (3) and 18(2), sections 20 and 22 to 25, subsections 31(1) and (3) and 35(4), sections 51, 52, 52.2 and 52.3, subsections 58(3) and 61(1), sections 63 and 65, subsections 66(2) and 70(1) and (4), section 71, paragraphs 73(g) and (h), subsection 74(4), section 84, paragraph 87(a), section 88, subsection 89(1) and paragraph 107(b).

R.S. 1985, c. 48 (4th Supp.), s. 1.

Indian Register

5. (1) Indian Register — There shall be maintained in the Department an Indian Register in which shall be recorded the name of every person who is entitled to be registered as an Indian under this Act.

(2) Existing Indian Register — The names in the Indian Register immediately prior to April 17, 1985 shall constitute the Indian Register on April 17, 1985.

(3) Deletions and additions — The Registrar may at any time add to or delete from the Indian Register the name of any person who, in accordance with this Act, is entitled or not entitled, as the case may be, to have his name included in the Indian Register.

(4) Date of change — The Indian Register shall indicate the date on which each name was added thereto or deleted therefrom.

(5) Application for registration — The name of a person who is entitled to be registered is not required to be recorded in the Indian Register unless an application for registration is made to the Registrar.

R.S. 1985, c. 32 (1st Supp.), s. 4.

Commentary: This section provides for registration as Indians under this Act. Most registered Indians belong to Bands. Where Bands control their own membership under section 10 of the *Indian Act*, there may be individuals who are registered, but who do not belong to the Band, and there may be Band members who are not registered as Indians.

Case Law: *Landry v. Canada (Ministre des Affaires Indiennes & du Nord)* (1996), 118 F.T.R. 184 (T.D.)

The Registrar had decided that the applicants were incorrectly registered, and proposed to take their names off the Indian Register under section 5(3). The judge held that the Federal Court could not judicially review the the action of the Registrar under section 5(3) because the adding or deleting of a name "was of no legal effect." The proper course was to file a protest under section 14.2 after the Registrar had added or deleted the name from the Register.

6. (1) Persons entitled to be registered — Subject to section 7, a person is entitled to be registered if

(a) that person was registered or entitled to be registered immediately prior to April 17, 1985;

(b) that person is a member of a body of persons that has been declared by the Governor in Council on or after April 17, 1985 to be a band for the purposes of this Act;

(c) the name of that person was omitted or deleted from the Indian Register, or from a Band List prior to September 4, 1951, under subparagraph 12(1)(a)(iv), paragraph 12(1)(b) or subsection 12(2) or under subparagraph 12(1)(a)(iii) pursuant to an order made under subsection 109(2), as each provision read immediately prior to April 17, 1985, or under any former provision of this Act relating to the same subject-matter as any of those provisions;

(d) the name of that person was omitted or deleted from the Indian Register, or from a Band List prior to September 4, 1951, under subparagraph 12(1)(a)(iii) pursuant to an order made under subsection 109(1), as each provision read immediately prior to April 17, 1985, or under any former provision of this Act relating to the same subject-matter as any of those provisions;

(e) the name of that person was omitted or deleted from the Indian Register, or from a Band List prior to September 4, 1951,

(i) under section 13, as it read immediately prior to September 4, 1951, or under any former provision of this Act relating to the same subject-matter as that section, or

(ii) under section 111, as it read immediately prior to July 1, 1920, or under any former provision of this Act relating to the same subject-matter as that section; or

(f) that person is a person both of whose parents are or, if no longer living, were at the time of death entitled to be registered under this section.

(2) Idem — Subject to section 7, a person is entitled to be registered if that person is a person one of whose parents is or, if no longer living, was at the time of death entitled to be registered under subsection (1).

(3) Deeming provision — For the purposes of paragraph (1)(f) and subsection (2),

(a) a person who was no longer living immediately prior to April 17, 1985 but who was at the time of death entitled to be registered shall be deemed to be entitled to be registered under paragraph (1)(a); and

(b) a person described in paragraph (1)(c), (d), (e), or (f) or subsection (2) who was no longer living on April 17, 1985 shall be deemed to be entitled to be registered under that provision.

R.S. 1985, c. 32 (1st Supp.), s. 4; c. 43 (4th Supp.), s. 1.

Commentary: Major changes were made in 1985 to the membership provisions. Prior *Indian Acts* had facilitated the voluntary and involuntary loss of registration (called "enfranchisement") of Indian men and women for a number of reasons. One notorious provision resulted in the loss of registration of

Indian women who married men who were not registered Indians. Indian men, on the other hand, did not lose status, and their non-Indian wives gained status. The 1985 amendments (Bill C-31) attempted to remove discriminatory provisions, and re-register most of those who had lost registered status.

Case Law: *Sawridge Band v. Canada*, [1997] F.C.J. No. 794 (F.C.A.)

Three bands in Treaties 6, 7 and 8 challenged amendments (made under Bill C-31 in 1985) which reinstated Indian women who had lost status when they had married non-Indian men. The Bands claimed that they had a "woman follows man" custom which meant that women marrying non-Band members left the Band. It was argued that the *Indian Act* amendments violated this custom by requiring that these women be reinstated to the Band list. The Band was unsuccessful at trial, and appealed, citing in part, a reasonable apprehension of bias on part of the trial judge, Muldoon, J.

The Court of Appeal cited many examples of "critical, perjorative language" on the part of the Muldoon, J. about constitutional and statutory provisions relating to Aboriginal peoples. Comments included comparing Indians to adolescents, referring to Aboriginal rights as racist, and making derogatory comments about the recognition of Métis in the Constitution. The Court of Appeal found that there was a reasonable apprehension of bias and sent the matter back for a new trial.

7. (1) Persons not entitled to be registered — The following persons are not entitled to be registered:

(a) a person who was registered under paragraph 11(1)(f), as it read immediately prior to April 17, 1985, or under any former provision of this Act relating to the same subject-matter as that paragraph, and whose name was subsequently omitted or deleted from the Indian Register under this Act; or

(b) a person who is the child of a person who was registered or entitled to be registered under paragraph 11(1)(f), as it read immediately prior to April 17, 1985, or under any former provision of this Act relating to the same subject-matter as that paragraph, and is also the child of a person who is not entitled to be registered.

(2) **Exception** — Paragraph (1)(a) does not apply in respect of a female person who was, at any time prior to being registered under paragraph 11(1)(f), entitled to be registered under any other provision of this Act.

(3) **Idem** — Paragraph (1)(b) does not apply in respect of the child of a female person who was, at any time prior to being registered under paragraph 11(1)(f), entitled to be registered under any other provision of this Act.

R.S. 1985, c. 32 (1st Supp.), s. 4.

Commentary: The old section 11(1)(f) was the provision which entitled non-Indian women to be registered if they were married to, or widows of, registered Indian men.

Band Lists

8. Band Lists — There shall be maintained in accordance with this Act for each band a Band List in which shall be entered the name of every person who is a member of that band.

R.S. 1985, c. 32 (1st Supp.), s. 4.

Case Law: *McArthur v. Canada (Registrar, Department of Indian Affairs and Northern Development) (1992),* 91 D.L.R. (4th) 666, 102 Sask. R. 300, [1992] 4 C.N.L.R. 33 (Q.B.)

In drawing up membership lists for two bands reconstituted on the lands of an extant band, the Registrar gave full hearing to protests, and did not breach the rules of natural justice. The lists were therefore properly constituted. In addition, the negotiating parties and the interim band councils were properly chosen pursuant to law and custom.

9. (1) Band Lists maintained in Department — Until such time as a band assumes control of its Band List, the Band List of that band shall be maintained in the Department by the Registrar.

(2) Existing Band Lists — The names in a Band List of a band immediately prior to April 17, 1985 shall constitute the Band List of that band on April 17, 1985.

(3) Deletions and additions — The Registrar may at any time add to or delete from a Band List maintained in the Department the name of any person who, in accordance with this Act, is entitled or not entitled, as the case may be, to have his name included in that List.

(4) Date of change — A Band List maintained in the Department shall indicate the date on which each name was added thereto or deleted therefrom.

(5) Application for entry — The name of a person who is entitled to have his name entered in a Band List maintained in the Department is not required to be entered therein unless an application for entry therein is made to the Registrar.

R.S. 1985, c. 32 (1st Supp.), s. 4.

10. (1) Band control of membership — A band may assume control of its own membership if it establishes membership rules for itself in writing in accordance with this section and if, after the band has given appropriate notice of its intention to assume control of its own membership, a majority of the electors of the band gives its consent to the band's control of its own membership.

(2) Membership rules — A band may, pursuant to the consent of a majority of the electors of the band,

(a) after it has given appropriate notice of its intention to do so establish membership rules for itself; and

(b) provide for a mechanism for reviewing decisions on membership.

(3) Exception relating to consent — Where the council of a band makes a by-law under paragraph 81(p.4) bringing this subsection into effect in respect of the band, the consents required under subsections (1) and (2) shall be given by a majority of the members of the band who are of the full age of eighteen years.

(4) Acquired rights — Membership rules established by a band under this section may not deprive any person who had the right to have his name entered in the Band List for that band, immediately prior to the time the rules were established, of the right to have his name so entered by reason only of a situation that existed or an action that was taken before the rules came into force.

(5) Idem — For greater certainty, subsection (4) applies in respect of a person who was entitled to have his name entered in the Band List under paragraph 11(1)(c) immediately before the band assumed control of the Band List if that person does not subsequently cease to be entitled to have his name entered in the Band List.

(6) Notice to the Minister — Where the conditions set out in subsection (1) have been met with respect to a band, the council of the band shall forthwith give notice to the Minister in writing that the band is assuming control of its own membership and shall provide the Minister with a copy of the membership rules for the band.

(7) Notice to band and copy of Band List — On receipt of a notice from the council of a band under subsection (6), the Minister shall, if the conditions set out in subsection (1) have been complied with, forthwith

  (a) give notice to the band that it has control of its own membership; and

  (b) direct the Registrar to provide the band with a copy of the Band List maintained in the Department.

(8) Effective date of band's membership rules — Where a band assumes control of its membership under this section, the membership rules established by the band shall have effect from the day on which notice is given to the Minister under subsection (6), and any additions to or deletions from the Band List of the band by the Registrar on or after that day are of no effect unless they are in accordance with the membership rules established by the band.

(9) Band to maintain Band List — A band shall maintain its own Band List from the date on which a copy of the Band List is received by the band under paragraph (7)(b), and, subject to section 13.2, the Department shall have no further responsibility with respect to that Band List from that date.

(10) Deletions and additions — A band may at any time add to or delete from a Band List maintained by it the name of any person who, in accordance with the membership rules of the band, is entitled or not entitled, as the case may be, to have his name included in that list.

(11) Date of change — A Band List maintained by a band shall indicate the date on which each name was added thereto or deleted therefrom.

R.S. 1985, c. 32 (1st Supp.), s. 4.

Case Law:

Section 10(1)

Gros-Louis v. Nation Huronne-Wendat, [1990] 1 C.N.L.R. 46, 24 F.T.R. 245 (T.D.)

The Minister's decision can only be made once the conditions of s. 10(1) have been complied with. An action prior to a decision to annul a vote on the membership rules is premature.

Section 10(2)

Twinn v. Can. (Min. of Indian Affairs & Nor. Dev.), [1987] 3 F.C. 368, 26 Admin. L.R. 197, 10 F.T.R. 48, 37 D.L.R. (4th) 270, (sub nom. *Twinn v. McKnight)* [1988] 1 C.N.L.R. 159

Anyone might have access to a band's membership rules under the federal *Access to Information Act.*

Section 10(10)

Ermineskin v. Ermineskin Band Council, [1995] 96 F.T.R. 181 (T.D.)

A woman who became a member of the Band through marriage had her name removed from the Band list after her spouse died. The Band has its own membership code. The court held that the Band must act fairly in making its decisions. In this case, however, the court decided not to interfere in the Band Council decision because the woman had been informed of an opportunity to appeal to the Band membership as a whole, and she had not availed herself of that opportunity.

Section 10(11)

Omeasoo v. Can. (Min. of Indian Affairs & Nor. Dev.), [1989] 1 C.N.L.R. 110, 24 F.T.R. 130

Proposed band membership rules cannot be amended by a band council resolution.

11. (1) Membership rules for Departmental Band list — Commencing on April 17, 1985, a person is entitled to have his name entered in a Band List maintained in the Department for a band if

(a) the name of that person was entered in the Band List for that band, or that person was entitled to have his name entered in the Band List for that band, immediately prior to April 17, 1985;

(b) that person is entitled to be registered under paragraph 6(1)(b) as a member of that band;

(c) that person is entitled to be registered under paragraph 6(1)(c) and ceased to be a member of that band by reason of the circumstances set out in that paragraph; or

(d) that person was born on or after April 17, 1985 and is entitled to be registered under paragraph 6(1)(f) and both parents of that person are entitled to have their names entered in the Band List or, if no longer living, were at the time of death entitled to have their names entered in the Band List.

(2) Additional membership rules for Departmental Band List — Commencing on the day that is two years after the day that an Act entitled *An Act to amend the Indian Act,* introduced in the House of Commons on February 28, 1985, is assented to, or on such earlier day as may be agreed to under section 13.1, where a band does not have control of its Band List under this Act, a person is entitled to have his name entered in a Band List maintained in the Department for the band

(a) if that person is entitled to be registered under paragraph 6(1)(d) or (e) and ceased to be a member of that band by reason of the circumstances set out in that paragraph; or

(b) if that person is entitled to be registered under paragraph 6(1)(f) or subsection 6(2) and a parent referred to in that provision is entitled to have his name entered in the Band List or, if no longer living, was at the time of death entitled to have his name entered in the Band List.

(3) **Deeming provision** — For the purposes of paragraph (1)(d) and subsection (2),

(a) a person whose name was omitted or deleted from the Indian Register or a band list in the circumstances set out in paragraph 6(1)(c), (d) or (e) who was no longer living on the first day on which the person would otherwise be entitled to have the person's name entered in the Band List of the band of which the person ceased to be a member shall be deemed to be entitled to have the person's name so entered; and

(b) a person described in paragraph (2)(b) shall be deemed to be entitled to have the person's name entered in the Band List in which the parent referred to in that paragraph is or was, or is deemed by this section to be, entitled to have the parent's name entered.

(4) **Where band amalgamates or is divided** — Where a band amalgamates with another band or is divided so as to constitute new bands, any person who would otherwise have been entitled to have his name entered in the Band List of that band under this section is entitled to have his name entered in the Band List of the amalgamated band or the new band to which he has the closest family ties, as the case may be.

R.S. 1985, c. 32 (1st Supp.), s. 4; c. 43 (4th Supp.), s. 2.

Case Law: *McArthur v. Canada (Registrar, Department of Indian Affairs and Northern Development)* (1992), 91 D.L.R. (4th) 666, 102 Sask. R. 300, [1992] 4 C.N.L.R. 53 (Sask. Q.B.)

In drawing up membership lists for two bands reconstituted on the lands of an extant band, the Registrar gave full hearing to protests, and did not breach the rules of natural justice. The lists were therefore properly constituted. In addition, the negotiating parties and the interim band councils were properly chosen pursuant to law and custom.

12. **Entitlement with consent of band** — Commencing on the day that is two years after the day that an Act entitled *An Act to amend the Indian Act*, introduced in the House of Commons on February 28, 1985, is assented to, or on such earlier day as may be agreed to under section 13.1, any person who

(a) is entitled to be registered under section 6, but is not entitled to have his name entered in the Band List maintained in the Department under section 11, or

(b) is a member of another band,

is entitled to have his name entered in the Band List maintained in the Department for a band if the council of the admitting band consents.

R.S. 1985, c. 32 (1st Supp.), s. 4.

13. **Limitation to one Band List** — Notwithstanding sections 11 and 12, no person is entitled to have his name entered at the same time in more than one Band List maintained in the Department.

R.S. 1985, c. 32 (1st Supp.), s. 4.

13.1 (1) **Decision to leave Band List control with Department** — A band may, at any time prior to the day that is two years after the day that an Act entitled *An Act to amend the Indian Act*, introduced in the House of Commons on February 28,

1985, is assented to, decide to leave the control of its Band List with the Department if a majority of the electors of the band gives its consent to that decision.

(2) **Notice to the Minister** — Where a band decides to leave the control of its Band List with the Department under subsection (1), the council of the band shall forthwith give notice to the Minister in writing to that effect.

(3) **Subsequent band control of membership** — Notwithstanding a decision under subsection (1), a band may, at any time after that decision is taken, assume control of its Band List under section 10.

R.S. 1985, c. 32 (1st Supp.), s. 4.

13.2 (1) Return of control to Department — A band may, at any time after assuming control of its Band List under section 10, decide to return control of the Band List to the Department if a majority of the electors of the band gives its consent to that decision.

(2) **Notice to the Minister and copy of membership rules** — Where a band decides to return control of its Band List to the Department under subsection (1), the council of the band shall forthwith give notice to the Minister in writing to that effect and shall provide the Minister with a copy of the Band List and a copy of all the membership rules that were established by the band under subsection 10(2) while the band maintained its own Band List.

(3) **Transfer of responsibility to Department** — Where a notice is given under subsection (2) in respect of a Band List, the maintenance of that Band List shall be the responsibility of the Department from the date on which the notice is received and from that time the Band List shall be maintained in accordance with the membership rules set out in section 11.

R.S. 1985, c. 32 (1st Supp.), s. 4.

13.3 Entitlement retained — A person is entitled to have his name entered in a Band List maintained in the Department pursuant to section 13.2 if that person was entitled to have his name entered, and his name was entered, in the Band List immediately before a copy of it was provided to the Minister under subsection 13.2(2), whether or not that person is also entitled to have his name entered in the Band List under section 11.

R.S. 1985, c. 32 (1st Supp.), s. 4.

Notice of Band Lists

14. (1) Copy of Band List provided to band council — Within one month after the day an Act entitled *An Act to amend the Indian Act*, introduced in the House of Commons on February 28, 1985, is assented to, the Registrar shall provide the council of each band with a copy of the Band List for the band as it stood immediately prior to that day.

(2) **List of additions and deletions** — Where a Band List is maintained by the Department, the Registrar shall, at least once every two months after a copy of the Band List is provided to the council of a band under subsection (1), provide the council of the band with a list of the additions to or deletions from the Band List not included in a list previously provided under this subsection.

(3) **Lists to be posted** — The council of each band shall, forthwith on receiving a copy of the Band List under subsection (1), or a list of additions to and deletions from its Band List under subsection (2), post the copy or the list, as the case may be, in a conspicuous place on the reserve of the band.

R.S. 1985, c. 32 (1st Supp.), s. 4.

Inquiries

14.1 Inquiries relating to Indian Register or Band Lists — The Registrar shall, on inquiry from any person who believes that he or any person he represents is entitled to have his name included in the Indian Register or a Band List maintained in the Department, indicate to the person making the inquiry whether or not that name is included therein.

R.S. 1985, c. 32 (1st Supp.), s. 4.

Protests

14.2 (1) Protests — A protest may be made in respect of the inclusion or addition of the name of a person in, or the omission or deletion of the name of a person from, the Indian Register, or a Band List maintained in the Department, within three years after the inclusion or addition, or omission or deletion, as the case may be, by notice in writing to the Registrar, containing a brief statement of the grounds therefor.

(2) **Protest in respect of Band List** — A protest may be made under this section in respect of the Band List of a band by the council of the band, any member of the band or the person in respect of whose name the protest is made or his representative.

(3) **Protest in respect of Indian Register** — A protest may be made under this section in respect of the Indian Register by the person in respect of whose name the protest is made or his representative.

(4) **Onus of proof** — The onus of establishing the grounds of a protest under this section lies on the person making the protest.

(5) **Registrar to cause investigation** — Where a protest is made to the Registrar under this section, he shall cause an investigation to be made into the matter and render a decision.

(6) **Evidence** — For the purposes of this section, the Registrar may receive such evidence on oath, on affidavit or in any other manner, whether or not admissible in a court of law, as in his discretion he sees fit or deems just.

(7) Decision final — Subject to section 14.3, the decision of the Registrar under subsection (5) is final and conclusive.

R.S. 1985, c. 32 (1st Supp.), s. 4.

Case Law:

Section 14.2(2)

Landry v. Canada (Ministre de Affaires Indiennes & du Nord) (1996), 118 F.T.R. 184 (T.D.)

The Registrar had decided that the applicants were incorrectly registered, and proposed to take their names off the Indian Register under section 5(3). The judge held that the Federal Court could not judicially review the action of the Registrar under section 5(3) because the adding or deleting of a name "was of no legal effect." The proper course was to file a protest under section 14.2 after the Registrar had added or deleted the name from the Register.

Section 14.2(5)

Ermineskin Band Council v. Can. (Reg. of Indian & Nor. Affairs), [1986] 3 F.C. 447, [1987] 2 C.N.L.R. 70, 5 F.T.R. 313 (T.D.)

The Registrar has a duty to render a decision on a protest.

14.3 (1) Appeal — Within six months after the Registrar renders a decision on a protest under section 14.2,

  (a) in the case of a protest in respect of the Band List of a band, the council of the band, the person by whom the protest was made, or the person in respect of whose name the protest was made or his representative, or

  (b) in the case of a protest in respect of the Indian Register, the person in respect of whose name the protest was made or his representative,

may, by notice in writing, appeal the decision to a court referred to in subsection (5).

(2) Copy of notice of appeal to the Registrar — Where an appeal is taken under this section, the person who takes the appeal shall forthwith provide the Registrar with a copy of the notice of appeal.

(3) Material to be filed with the court by Registrar — On receipt of a copy of a notice of appeal under subsection (2), the Registrar shall forthwith file with the court a copy of the decision being appealed together with all documentary evidence considered in arriving at that decision and any recording or transcript of any oral proceedings related thereto that were held before the Registrar.

(4) Decision — The court may, after hearing an appeal under this section,

  (a) affirm, vary or reverse the decision of the Registrar; or

  (b) refer the subject-matter of the appeal back to the Registrar for reconsideration or further investigation.

(5) Court — An appeal may be heard under this section

  (a) in the Province of Quebec, before the Superior Court for the district in which the band is situated or in which the person who made the protest resides, or for such other district as the Minister may designate;

  (a.1) in the Province of Ontario, before the Ontario Court (General Division);

(b) in the Province of New Brunswick, Manitoba, Saskatchewan or Alberta, before the Court of Queen's Bench;

(c) in the Province of Prince Edward Island or Newfoundland, before the Trial Division of the Supreme Court; or

(c.1) [Repealed 1992, c. 51, s. 54.]

(d) in the Provinces of Nova Scotia and British Columbia, the Yukon Territory or the Northwest Territories, before the Supreme Court.

R.S. 1985, c. 32 (1st Supp.), s. 4; c. 27 (2d Supp.), s. 10 (Schedule); 1990, c. 16, s. 14; c. 17, s. 25; 1992, c. 51, s. 54; 1993, c. 28, s. 78 (Schedule III, item 73).

> **(d) in the Provinces of Nova Scotia and British Columbia, the Yukon Territory, the Northwest Territories or Nunavut, before the Supreme Court.**
>
> [1993, c. 28, s. 78 (Schedule III, item 73). Not in force at date of publication.]

Case Law:

Section 14.3(4)

Sparrow v. Can. (Dept. of Indian & Nor. Affairs) (1988), 15 B.C.L.R. (2d) 363, [1988] 2 C.N.L.R. 172 (Co. Ct.)

A court may refer a decision back to the Registrar with recommendations.

Payments in Respect of Persons Ceasing to be Band Members

15. (1) Commutation of payments under former Act — [Repealed R.S. 1985, c. 32 (1st Supp.), s. 5.]

(2) [Repealed R.S. 1985, c. 32 (1st Supp.), s. 5.]

(3) [Repealed R.S. 1985, c. 32 (1st Supp.), s. 5.]

(4) [Repealed R.S. 1985, c. 32 (1st Supp.), s. 5.]

(5) Where, prior to the 4th day of September 1951, any woman became entitled, under section 14 of the *Indian Act*, chapter 98 of the Revised Statutes of Canada, 1927, or any prior provisions to the like effect, to share in the distribution of annuities, interest moneys or rents, the Minister may, in lieu thereof, pay to such woman out of the moneys of the band an amount equal to ten times the average annual amounts of such payment made to her during the ten years last preceding or, if they were paid for less than ten years, during the years they were paid.

R.S. 1985, c. 32 (1st Supp.)., s. 5.

16. (1) Transferred member's interest — [Repealed R.S. 1985 c. 32, (1st Supp.), s. 6.]

(2) A person who ceases to be a member of one band by reason of his becoming a member of another band is not entitled to any interest in the lands or moneys held by Her Majesty on behalf of the former band but he is entitled to the same interest in

common in lands and moneys held by Her Majesty on behalf of the latter band as other members of that band.

R.S. 1985, c. 32 (1st Supp.), s. 6.

(3) [Repealed R.S. 1985, c. 32 (1st Supp.), s. 6.]

Case Law: *Sabattis v. Oromocto Indian Band*, [1989] 2 C.N.L.R. 158 (N.B. Q.B.)

This provision provides an element of certainty, and was held to apply where a land claims settlement was reached in 1983 in respect of land taken from a band by the Crown in 1953, to band members who left the band after 1953 and before 1983.

New Bands

17. (1) Minister may constitute new bands — The Minister may, whenever he considers it desirable,

(a) amalgamate bands that, by a vote of a majority of their electors, request to be amalgamated; and

(b) constitute new bands and establish Band Lists with respect thereto from existing Band Lists, or from the Indian Register, if requested to do so by persons proposing to form the new bands.

(2) **Division of reserves and funds** — Where pursuant to subsection (1) a new band has been established from an existing band or any part thereof, such portion of the reserve lands and funds of the existing band as the Minister determines shall be held for the use and benefit of the new band.

(3) **No protest** — No protest may be made under section 14.2 in respect of the deletion from or the addition to a Band List consequent on the exercise by the Minister of any of his powers under subsection (1).

R.S. 1985, c. 32 (1st Supp.), s. 7.

Reserves

18. (1) Reserves to be held for use and benefit of Indians — Subject to this Act, reserves are held by Her Majesty for the use and benefit of the respective bands for which they were set apart; and subject to this Act and to the terms of any treaty or surrender, the Governor in Council may determine whether any purpose for which lands in a reserve are used or are to be used is for the use and benefit of the band.

(2) **Use of reserves for schools, etc.** — The Minister may authorize the use of lands in a reserve for the purpose of Indian schools, the administration of Indian affairs, Indian burial grounds, Indian health projects or, with the consent of the council of the band, for any other purpose for the general welfare of the band, and may take any lands in a reserve required for such purposes, but where an individual Indian, immediately prior to such taking, was entitled to the possession of such lands, compensation for such use shall be paid to the Indian, in such amount as may be agreed be-

tween the Indian and the Minister, or, failing agreement, as may be determined in such manner as the Minister may direct.

Commentary: *Guerin*, the leading case on this section, held that land rights of First Nations were not created by section 18, but pre-existed it; and that the Crown has a fiduciary duty arising from the fact that land can only be surrendered to the Crown. For cases on the fiduciary duty upon surrender, see cases listed under section 53.

For cases on Crown fiduciary duties in general, see under the heading "Fiduciary duty" in the annotations for section 35(1) of the *Constitution Act, 1982*.

There are no provisions in the *Indian Act* stating how reserves are created. Cases on this issue are annotated under section 2(1), "reserves".

Case Law:

Section 18(1)

Derrickson v. Derrickson, [1986] 3 W.W.R. 193, [1986] 1 S.C.R. 285, 1 B.C.L.R. (2d) 273, 50 R.F.L. (2d) 337, 65 N.R. 278, [1986] 2 C.N.L.R. 45, 26 D.L.R. (4th) 175

The court found that provincial matrimonial property legislation relating to the possession and ownership of the matrimonial home could not apply to matrimonial homes on reserves. In the course of the discussion, the court stated,

> The purpose of [subsection 18(1)] is to ensure that lands reserved for Indians are and remain used for the use and benefit of the band. [W.W.R. at p.200]

Guerin v. R., [1984] 2 S.C.R. 335, 36 R.P.R. 1, 20 E.T.R. 6, [1984] 6 W.W.R. 481, 59 B.C.L.R. 301, [1985] 1 C.N.L.R. 120, 13 D.L.R. (4th) 321, 55 N.R. 161

The court described the source of the Indian interest in land as follows:

> Their interest in their lands is a pre-existing legal right not created by Royal Proclamation, by s.18(1) of the *Indian Act*, or by any other executive order or legislative provision.

> It does not matter, in my opinion, that the present case is concerned with the interest of an Indian Band in a reserve rather than with unrecognized aboriginal title in traditional tribal lands. The Indian interest in the land is the same in both cases. [S.C.R. at p.379]

The nature of the Indian interest and the fiduciary obligation of the Crown is described as follows:

> Indians have a legal right to occupy and possess certain lands, the ultimate title to which is in the Crown. While their interest does not, strictly speaking, amount to beneficial ownership, neither is its nature completely exhausted by the concept of a personal right. It is true that the *sui generis* interest which the Indians have in the land is personal in the sense that it cannot be transferred to a grantee, but it is also true, as will presently appear, that the interest gives rise upon surrender to a distinctive fiduciary obligation on the part of the Crown to deal with the land for the benefit of the surrendering Indians. These two aspects of Indian title go together, since the Crown's original purpose in declaring the Indians' interest to be inalienable otherwise than to the Crown was to facilitate the Crown's ability to represent the Indians in dealings with third parties. The nature of the Indians' interest is therefore best characterized by its general inalienability, coupled with the fact that the Crown is under an obligation to deal with the land on the Indians' behalf when the interest is surrendered. Any description of Indian title which goes beyond these two features is both unnecessary and potentially misleading. [S.C.R. at p.382]

Callie v. R., [1991] 2 F.C. 379, 40 E.T.R. 276, (sub nom. *Callie v. Canada*) 41 F.T.R. 59 (T.D.)

Section 18(1) of the *Indian Act* is not the source of the fiduciary obligation respecting reserve lands; rather, that source is the pre-existing Aboriginal interest in the land.

Horn v. M.N.R., [1989] 3 C.N.L.R. 59 (T.C.C.)

Section 18(1) has nothing to do with the residence of the Crown as a contractual debtor.

Joe v. Findlay, [1981] 3 W.W.R. 60, 26 B.C.L.R. 376, 122 D.L.R. (3d) 377 (C.A.)

The reserves are set apart for the band as a whole and individual band members do not have a right of individual possession except by application of the Act. There is no tenancy in common by band members.

R. v. Stevenson, [1986] 5 W.W.R. 737, [1987] 1 C.N.L.R. 136, 42 Man. R. (2d) 133, leave to appeal to C.A. refused [1987] 1 W.W.R. 767, [1987] 2 C.N.L.R. 144

Lands are held by Her Majesty for the use and benefit of a band and are not owned by a band.

18.1 Children of band members — A member of a band who resides on the reserve of the band may reside there with his dependent children or any children of whom he has custody.

R.S. 1985, c. 32 (1st Supp.), s. 8.

Commentary: While children of Band members who reside on reserve have a right to reside on the reserve as well, rights of residence in general can be addressed in by-laws made under sections 81(1)(p.1) and 81(1)(p.2).

19. Surveys and subdivisions — The Minister may

(a) authorize surveys of reserves and the preparation of plans and reports with respect thereto,

(b) divide the whole or any portion of a reserve into lots or other subdivisions, and

(c) determine the location and direct the construction of roads in a reserve.

Possession of Lands in Reserves

20. (1) Possession of lands in a reserve — No Indian is lawfully in possession of land in a reserve unless, with the approval of the Minister, possession of the land has been alloted to him by the council of the band.

(2) Certificate of Possession — The Minister may issue to an Indian who is lawfully in possession of land in a reserve a certificate, to be called a Certificate of Possession, as evidence of his right to possession of the land described therein.

(3) Location Tickets issued under previous legislation — For the purposes of this Act, any person who, on the 4th day of September 1951, held a valid and subsisting Location Ticket issued under *The Indian Act*, 1880, or any statute relating to the same subject-matter, shall be deemed to be lawfully in possession of the land to which the location ticket relates and to hold a Certificate of Possession with respect thereto.

(4) Temporary possession — Where a possession of land in a reserve has been allotted to an Indian by the Council of the band, the Minister may, in his discretion, withhold his approval and may authorize the Indian to occupy the land temporarily and may prescribe the conditions as to use and settlement that are to be fulfilled by the Indian before the Minister approves of the allotment.

(5) Certificate of Occupation — Where the Minister withholds approval pursuant to subsection (4), he shall issue a Certificate of Occupation to the Indian, and the Certificate entitles the Indian, or those claiming possession by devise or descent, to occupy the land in respect of which it is issued for a period of two years from the date thereof.

(6) Extension and approval — The Minister may extend the term of a Certificate of Occupation for a further period not exceeding two years, and may, at the expiration of any period during which a Certificate of Occupation is in force

(a) approve the allotment by the council of the band and issue a Certificate of Possession if in his opinion the conditions as to use and settlement have been fulfilled, or

(b) refuse approval of the allotment by the council of the band and declare the land in respect of which the Certificate of Occupation was issued to be available for re-allotment by the council of the band.

Commentary: Sections 20–28 set out the framework by which band members may obtain and exercise possession of reserve lands. Trespass cases are listed under section 20 (where lawful possession by an Indian is in dispute), section 30 (offence) and section 31 (where Federal government can bring action against non-Indian trespasser). For cases on the authority of a Band to bring an action for trespass, see under section 2(1), "Band".

Case Law:

Section 20(1) — Canada

Derrickson v. Derrickson, [1986] 1 S.C.R. 285, [1986] 3 W.W.R. 193, 1 B.C.L.R. (2d) 273, 50 R.F.L. (2d) 337, 26 D.L.R. (4th) 175, [1986] 2 C.N.L.R. 45, 65 N.R. 278

A court cannot make an order for possession or for partition and sale of reserve land under provincial legislation. It can, however, under the *Family Relations Act*, make an order for compensation for the purpose of adjusting the division of family assets between spouses.

— See also *Sandy v. Sandy* (1979), 27 O.R. (2d) 248, 13 R.F.L. (2d) 81, 107 D.L.R. (3d) 659 (C.A.); *Laforme v. Laforme* (1984), 33 R.F.L. (2d) 69, [1984] 2 C.N.L.R. 88 (Ont. Co. Ct.)

Paul v. Paul, [1986] 1 S.C.R. 306, [1986] 3 W.W.R. 210, 1 B.C.L.R. (2d) 290, 50 R.F.L. (2d) 355, 26 D.L.R. (4th) 196, [1986] 2 C.N.L.R. 74

The provincial law (*Family Relations Act*), could not be used for an order for interim occupancy of the family residence on the reserve to one spouse. Both possession and occupation are dealt with by the *Indian Act*, and an order under provincial law would be in conflict with this.

Campbell v. Elliott, [1988] 4 C.N.L.R. 45, (sub nom. *Campbell v. Cowichan Band of Indians*) 23 F.T.R. 43 (T.D.)

Band councils are trustees of band assets and must act with fairness in making allotments.

Section 20(1) — Alberta

Bigstone Cree Nation v. Boskoyous (1996), 180 A.R. 398, [1997] 2 C.N.L.R. 13 (Master)

This was a dispute between the Band and an individual who claimed membership, but who was not a Band member. The individual repaired and occupied a house, which he claimed had been abandoned. The Band had allocated the house to another family. The court held that the Band has the authority to allot land, and an individual cannot get squatter's rights.

Section 20(1) — British Columbia

Joe v. Findlay, [1981] 3 W.W.R. 60, 26 B.C.L.R. 376, 122 D.L.R. (3d) 377 (C.A.)

Individual possession must be obtained by an allotment by the band council:

> ... there is no statutory provision enabling the individual band members alone to exercise through possession the right of use and benefit which is held in common for all band members. [D.L.R. 380]

Joe v. Findlay (1987), 12 B.C.L.R. (2d) 166, [1987] 2 C.N.L.R. 75 (S.C.)

The band council can decide on who may possess reserve land and a vote of the whole band is not required.

Leonard v. Gottfriedson (1982), 21 B.C.L.R. 326, [1982] 1 C.N.L.R. 60 (S.C.)

In a case where members of council merely signed a government form entitled "Band Council Resolution", did not have a duly convened meeting and did not pass a resolution as required by s. 2(3)(b), an alleged allotment of land to a band member was not valid, and thus there was nothing to submit for ministerial approval.

Mathias v. Findlay, [1978] 4 W.W.R. 653 (B.C. S.C.)

It was held that for this section to be enforceable, possession of land in the reserve must be in the band, not in the Crown:

> The scheme of the Act for the management of reserve lands by Indian bands would be impeded if such a fundamental legal remedy as ejectment were not available to the band suing in its own behalf before the ordinary courts of the province. [p. 657]

Section 20(1) — Manitoba

Mintuck v. Valley River Band No. 63A, [1977] 2 W.W.R. 309, 2 C.C.L.T. 1, 75 D.L.R. (3d) 589 (Man. C.A.)

An action under this section by an individual for possession, or by a band council for removal of a member not in lawful possession, should not include the Crown as a party since possession is in the band rather than the Crown. The action should be properly commenced in a court of the province, not in Federal Court.

A band council that granted a ten-year lease of a portion of reserve land to a member, then after a few years assisted in the harassment of the tenant which caused him to vacate the farm land, was liable to pay damages to the member in an action based on intimidation and unlawful interference with economic interest.

Section 20(2)

George v. George, [1997] 2 CNLR 62 (B.C.C.A.)

In *Derrickson v. Derrickson*, the Supreme Court of Canada held that, where the husband held a matrimonial home under a Certificate of Possession, the wife could not use the provisions of provincial family law to gain possession of that matrimonial home. However, the wife could obtain a compensation order based on the value of the property.

In this case, the husband was in occupation of the matrimonial home, but there was no Certificate of Possession issued. The husband argued that, as he was *not* legally in possession of the matrimonial home pursuant to section 20(1), the court could not make a compensation order with respect to the property. Both spouses were members of the Burrard Indian Band.

The court held that a Certificate of Possession under section 20(2) was not necessary in order to have lawful possession. In this case, the court inferred lawful possession from a course of conduct by the Chief and Council and by the Department of Indian Affairs. In particular, the court relied on the fact that the loan application from the Canada Mortgage and Housing Corporation (CMHC), for building a house on the subject property was signed by the Chief, and approved by Indian Affairs.

Westbank Indian Band v. Normand (1993), [1994] 3 C.N.L.R. 197 (B.C. S.C.)

Upon the issuance of a Certificate of Possession, all the incidents of ownership vests in the holder of the Certificate. Therefore a claim for damages to the land by flooding had to be made by the individual. An action by the band for those damages was not sustainable.

21. Register — **There shall be kept in the Department a register, to be known as the Reserve Land Register, in which shall be entered particulars relating to Certificates of Possession and Certificates of Occupation and other transactions respecting lands in a reserve.**

22. Improvements on lands — **Where an Indian who is in possession of lands at the time they are included in a reserve made permanent improvements thereon before that time, he shall be deemed to be in lawful possession of such lands at the time they are so included.**

23. Compensation for improvements — **An Indian who is lawfully removed from lands in a reserve upon which he has made permanent improvements may, if the Minister so directs, be paid compensation in respect thereof in an amount to be determined by the Minister, either from the person who goes into possession or from the funds of the band, at the discretion of the Minister.**

24. Transfer of possession — **An Indian who is lawfully in possession of lands in a reserve may transfer to the band or to another member of the band the right to possession of the land, but no transfer or agreement for the transfer of the right to possession of lands in a reserve is effective until it is approved by the Minister.**

Case Law: *Cooper v. Tsartlip Indian Band* (1996), [1997] 1 C.N.L.R. 45, 199 N.R. 126, 118 F.T.R. 309 (note) (Fed. C.A.)

Cooper claims to have bought a lot on reserve from the Smiths in 1942, but the transfer was not registered in the Reserve Land Register. In 1982, the Smiths sold the land in question to the Band, and the transaction was registered in the Reserve Land Register after the requisite approval by the Minister.

The court held that the first transfer was not valid because it did not conform with the requirements of the *Indian Act*. Therefore, Cooper could not claim the land, although he may have some other claim against the Smiths or the Band.

— See also *Jones Estate v. Louis* (1996), 108 F.T.R. 81, 3 C.N.L.R. 85 (T.D.)*Okanagan Indian Band v. Canada (Registrar of Indian Lands)* (1996), 106 F.T.R. 158 (T.D.)

Simpson v. Ryan (1996), 106 F.T.R. 158 (T.D.)

Simpson held property on the Duck Lake reserve under a certificate of possession. In 1989 he transferred the land to himself and one of his daughters, Ziprick, as joint tenants. In 1993, he wanted to use the land for a mobile home park. His daughter objected. He argued that the transfer to the joint tenancy was not valid because there had been no Band Council approval of the transfer.

The court held that under s. 24, there was no "implicit or explicit" requirement for Band approval, and, as a holder of a Certificate of Possession, he was therefore vested with all the incidents of ownership, with the exception of the legal title itself, which remains with the Crown. The transfer was, therefore, valid.

25. (1) Indian ceasing to reside on reserve — An Indian who ceases to be entitled to reside on a reserve may, within six months or such further period as the Minister may direct, transfer to the band or another member of the band the right to possession of any lands in the reserve of which he was lawfully in possession.

(2) Where an Indian does not dispose of his right of possession in accordance with subsection (1), the right to possession of the land reverts to the band, subject to the payment of the Indian who was lawfully in possession of the land, from the funds of the band, of such compensation for permanent improvements as the Minister may determine.

26. Correction of Certificate or Location Tickets — Whenever a Certificate of Possession or Occupation or a Location Ticket issued under *The Indian Act*, 1880, or any statute relating to the same subject-matter was, in the opinion of the Minister, issued to or in the name of the wrong person, through mistake, or contains any clerical error or misnomer, or wrong description of any material fact therein, the Minister may cancel the Certificate or Location Ticket and issue a corrected Certificate in lieu thereof.

27. Cancellation of Certificates or Location Tickets — The Minister may, with the consent of the holder thereof, cancel any Certificate of Possession or Occupation or Location Ticket referred to in section 26, and may cancel any Certificate of Possession or Occupation or Location Ticket that in his opinion was issued through fraud or in error.

28. (1) Grants, etc., of reserve lands void — Subject to subsection (2), a deed, lease, contract, instrument, document or agreement of any kind whether written or oral, by which a band or a member of a band purports to permit a person other than a member of that band to occupy or use a reserve or to reside or otherwise exercise any rights on a reserve is void.

(2) Minister may issue permits — The Minister may by permit in writing authorize any person for a period not exceeding one year, or with the consent of the council of the band for any longer period, to occupy or use a reserve or to reside or otherwise exercise rights on a reserve.

Commentary: Prior to an amendment in 1956, this section permitted the Minister to grant a one year permit only. Other methods of alienating reserve land to non-members includes s. 35 (Lands Taken for Public Purposes), ss. 37–39 (Surrenders and Designations) and s. 58 (Uncultivated and Unused Lands).

Case Law:

Section 28(1)

R. v. Devereux, [1965] S.C.R. 567, 51 D.L.R. (2d) 546

> The scheme of the *Indian Act* is to maintain intact for bands of Indians, reserves set apart for them regardless of the wishes of any individual Indian to alienate for his own benefit any portion of the reserve of which he may be a locatee. [D.L.R. p. 550]

Shubenacadie Indian Band v. Canada (Human Rights Commission), [1997] F.C.J. No. 1481 (T.D.)

The Band Council received funds from the federal government to administer welfare. The federal government permitted the Band to provide welfare to non-Indian spouses if they were permitted to reside on the reserve. In this case, the Band refused to pay welfare to a non-Indian spouse. The court held that the *Canadian Human Rights Act* had been violated because the Band was discriminating on the basis of race.

One of the arguments raised by the Band was that the Band could not authorize the residence of non-Indian spouses, even if it wanted to, because it would be a breach of section 28. The court rejected this argument. According to the court, section 28 only applied to commercial transactions, and was not referrable to non-Indians living on reserve as spouses of Band members.

Sheard v. Chippewas of Rama First Nation Band Council (1996), 42 Admin L.R. (2d) 265, 114 F.T.R. 44 (T.D.)

Sheard was a member of the First Nation. She leased a house from the Band Council and resided with her common law spouse, Weston, a non-native and their children. One day, the Band Council passed a Band Council Resolution ordering Weston off the reserve, citing safety concerns with Weston. The Band claimed that Weston did not have a right to reside on the reserve because of s. 28(1).

The court found that Sheard and Weston had not been given notice of the meeting where the BCR was discussed, had not been given disclosure of the basis for the concerns, and were not given an opportunity to respond. The court granted the judicial review and quashed the decision.

M.D. Sloan Consultants Ltd. v. Derrickson (1991), 61 B.C.L.R. (2d) 370, 85 D.L.R. (4th) 449, 9 B.C.A.C. 241, 19 W.A.C. 241 (C.A.)

Section 28(1) does not automatically operate to void a lease of premises which are in part located on reserve lands. The principal of the defendant corporation from which the premises were leased was a band official, and the evidence supported the contention that the parties had negotiated a long term lease. Given that part of the lease related to land outside of the reserve, the section did not operate so as to invalidate the entire agreement. Furthermore, the defendant could have applied to the Crown for a lease in the plaintiff's favour, and the plaintiff could have called upon him to do so. The operation of s. 28(1) was not such as to dissolve all of the defendant's contractual obligations to the plaintiff.

Sampson v. Locations West Property Management Ltd. (1993), 82 B.C.L.R. (2d) 157 (B.C. C.A.)

The Crown entered into a lease with a company which created a mobile home park on reserve lands. The residents of the park subleased from the company. The company went into default and the lease was cancelled. When the main lease was cancelled, the residents (the sublessees) ceased to have a right to remain on the reserve by virtue of section 28.

Section 28(2)

Opetchesaht Indian Band v. Canada (1997), 211 N.R. 241, 90 B.C.A.C. 1, 147 W.A.C. 1, 147 D.L.R. (4th) 1 (S.C.C.)

A right of way was granted to B.C. Hydro in 1959 across the reserve "for such a period of time as the said right-of-way is required for the purpose of an electric transmission line." The question was whether the land should have been alienated through a surrender (s. 37) or an expropriation (s. 35) as opposed to a permit under this section.

Major J., for the majority held that the "period" of time in this case was acceptable.

> The end point of a permit need not be defined in terms of a specific calendar date as long as it is ascertainable. The only requirement is that the end of the period be capable of ascertainment so that it does not constitute a grant in perpetuity. In the instant case, the end point of the permit arises when the easement is no longer required for power transmission. [D.L.R. p. 12]

He then went on to say that, while there was some overlap between section 37 and section 28(2), the two sections were aimed at two different situations.

In the case of sales, dispositions and long-term leases or alienations permanently disposing of any Indian interest in reserve land, surrender is required, involving the vote of all members of the band. On the other hand in the case of rights of use, occupation or residence for a period of longer than one year, only band council approval is required. [D.L.R. p.17]

In her dissent, McLachlin, J., points out that when the legislation was being enacted, the Minister of Indian Affairs noted that this section was to be used for things of a temporary nature. It was not to be used for "major long term alienations of Indian interests in their reserve lands." [D.L.R. p. 28]

Millbrook Indian Band v. Nor. Counties Residential Tenancies Bd. (1978), 93 D.L.R. (3d) 230, 28 N.S.R. (2d) 268, 43 A.P.R. 268 (C.A.)

A lease to a non-Indian of reserve land for residential purposes is void without permission of the Minister, and such a person is not entitled to seek the benefits of provincial residential tenancies legislation.

— See also *Springbank Dehydration Ltd. v. Charles*, [1978] 1 F.C. 188 (T.D.)

29. Exemption from seizure — Reserve lands are not subject to seizure under legal process.

Case Law: *Palm Dairies Ltd. v. R.*, [1979] 1 F.C. 53, 91 D.L.R. (3d) 665 (T.D.)

Lands of the Sarcee Nation were surrendered for seventy-five years, and leased back to Sarcee Developments. The court found that these lands continued to be reserved for the Indians, and therefore within exclusive federal jurisdiction. The provincial *Builders' Lien Act* did not apply to such lands.

West. Int. Contr. Ltd. v. Sarcee Dev. Ltd., [1979] 3 W.W.R. 631, 98 D.L.R. (3d) 424, 15 A.R. 309 (C.A.)

Sarcee Developments was a Band-owned corporation. The Band surrendered reserve land to the federal government for 75 years, and the corporation leased the land back from the federal government. The court held that the corporation was not an Indian. Therefore, a provincial builder's lien could apply against the corporation and the corporation's interest in the lease. However, the provincial legislation could not apply to the Band's reversionary interest in the land, because that fell within "lands reserved for Indians."

Trespass on Reserve

30. Penalty for trespass — A person who trespasses on a reserve is guilty of an offence and is liable on summary conviction to a fine not exceeding fifty dollars or to imprisonment for a term not exceeding one month, or to both.

Commentary: The *Indian Act* does not define **"trespass"**. Therefore, common law principles developed with respect to trespass on non-Indian land should be applied in determining whether an act amounts to trespass pursuant to this section.

Trespass cases are listed under section 20 (where lawful possession by an Indian is in dispute), section 30 (offence) and section 31 (where Federal government can bring action against non-Indian trespasser). For cases on the authority of a Band to bring an action for trespass, see under section 2(1), "Band".

Case Law: *R. v. Whiskeyjack*, [1985] 2 W.W.R. 481, 35 Alta. L.R. (2d) 269, 16 D.L.R. (4th) 231, 17 C.C.C. (3d) 245, 58 A.R. 81, [1985] 2 C.N.L.R. 167 (C.A.)

A special constable appointed under provincial legislation to enforce this section is a peace officer for limited purposes. His powers are not derived from provincial legislation but merely limited by it.

R. v. Bernard (1991), 118 N.B.R. (2d) 361, [1992] 3 C.N.L.R. 33, 296 A.P.R. 361 (Q.B.)

A sheriff who entered the Eel Ground reserve to execute an order for recovery of personal property as a result of a default payment under a conditional sales contract, is not a trespasser.

R. v. Crosby (1982), 54 C.C.C. (2d) 497, [1982] 1 C.N.L.R. 102 (Ont. C.A.)

A provincial court judge has jurisdiction to hear and dispose of a charge under s. 30. Section 31 is concerned with civil proceedings and does not affect proceedings under this section.

R. v. Yang (G.S.) (1996), 15 O.T.C. 45 (Gen.Div.)

Special Investigators acting under authority of the provincial *Tobacco Act* entered Six Nations reserve to conduct surveillance on illegal tobacco sales. They followed a van of the accused, a non-native, and charged him off reserve. The court noted in passing that investigators of Special Investigations were trespassing on the reserve.

White c. Leduc (1991), 42 Q.A.C. 105, [1992] R.L. 384

The granting by the Crown of a retroactive lease to certain reserve lands had the effect of eliminating the *mens rea* of the offence of trespassing by giving the accused a "colour of right" to enter the lands in question. The accused had rented a chalet on Indian lands for several years, and was ordered to leave the reserve because the owner of the chalet did not have a lease issued by the Department of Indian Affairs. The owner subsequently applied for the lease, which was granted before the accused was convicted of trespassing, and which was retroactive to the period covered by the indictments.

R. v. Pinay, [1990] 4 C.N.L.R. 71, 83 Sask. R. 287 (Q.B.)

A provincial official entering upon a reserve to serve a statement of claim is not a trespasser within the meaning of s. 30.

31. (1) Information by Attorney General — Without prejudice to section 30, where an Indian or a band alleges that persons other than Indians are or have been

    (a) unlawfully in occupation or possession of,

    (b) claiming adversely the right to occupation or possession of, or

    (c) trespassing upon

a reserve or part of a reserve, the Attorney General of Canada may exhibit an information in the Federal Court of Canada claiming, on behalf of the Indian or the band, the relief or remedy sought.

(2) Information deemed action by Crown — An information exhibited under subsection (1) shall, for all purposes of the *Federal Court Act*, be deemed to be a proceeding by the Crown within the meaning of that Act.

(3) Existing remedies preserved — Nothing in this section shall be construed to impair, abridge or otherwise affect any right or remedy that, but for this section, would be available to Her Majesty or to an Indian or a band.

Commentary: Trespass cases are listed under section 20 (where lawful possession by an Indian is in dispute), section 30 (offence) and section 31 (where Federal government can bring action against non-Indian trespasser). For cases on the authority of a Band to bring an action for trespass, see under section 2(1), "Band".

Case Law:

Section 31(1)

Smith v. R., [1983] S.C.R. 554, 147 D.L.R. (3d) 237, 47 N.R. 132

A unanimous decision of the Supreme Court of Canada held that an absolute surrender of lands by Indians leaves no retained or other interest in the federal Crown under s. 91(24) of the *Constitution Act, 1867.* The federal Crown had no legislative authority in surrendered lands and did not have the status to commence an action for their recovery.

R. v. Devereux, [1965] S.C.R. 567, 51 D.L.R. (2d) 546, [1965] 6 C.N.L.C. 236

Under this section, either the Band or an individual can ask the Crown to bring an action. In this case, the court gave judgment for Her Majesty on behalf of the Six Nations Band in an action against a non-Indian who was occupying a farm on reserve without authority under the *Indian Act.*

R. v. Weremy (1943), 9 C.N.L.C. 534, [1943] Ex. C.R. 44, [1943] 1 D.L.R. 9 (Ex.Ct.)

The court upheld the authority of the federal Crown to recover Brokenhead Band reserve lands, which had been the subject of a survey error.

Section 31(3)

Custer v. Hudson's Bay Co. Developments Ltd., [1983] 1 C.N.L.R. 1, [1983] 1 W.W.R. 566, 20 Sask. R. 89, 141 D.L.R. (3d) 722 (Sask. C.A.)

The existence of section 31 does not remove the ability of the band or its members to maintain an action for trespass.

> But the fact the Crown has been empowered to bring an action does not, in our opinion, preclude a band, or a member thereof, in possession of reserve lands, from commencing or maintaining an action in trespass in relation to such lands, independent of action by the Crown. We think that is made quite clear by subsection (3), which expressly preserves the rights and remedies of Indians and Indian Bands, with respect to claims against non-Indians for wrongful occupation or possession of reserve lands. [C.N.L.R. at p.3]

Sale or Barter of Produce

32. (1) Sale or barter of produce — A transaction of any kind whereby a band or a member thereof purports to sell, barter, exchange, give or otherwise dispose of cattle or other animals, grain or hay, whether wild or cultivated, or root crops or plants or their products from a reserve in Manitoba, Saskatchewan or Alberta, to a person other than a member of that band, is void unless the superintendent approves the transaction in writing.

(2) Exemption — The Minister may at any time by order exempt a band and the members thereof or any member thereof from the operation of this section, and may revoke any such order.

33. Offence — Every person who enters into a transaction that is void under subsection 32(1) is guilty of an offence.

Roads and Bridges

34. (1) Roads, bridges, etc. — A band shall ensure that the roads, bridges, ditches and fences within the reserve occupied by that band are maintained in accordance with instructions issued from time to time by the superintendent.

(2) Idem — Where, in the opinion of the Minister, a band has not carried out the instructions of the superintendent given under subsection (1), the Minister may cause the instructions to be carried out at the expense of the band or any member thereof and may recover the cost thereof from any amounts that are held by Her Majesty and are payable to the band or such member.

Case Law: *Brick Cartage Ltd. v. R.*, [1965] 1 Ex. C.R. 102

The owner of a truck sued the federal government for damages to the truck resulting from the collapse of a bridge on an Indian reserve. The court held that the band, its council or servants were not agents of the Crown. In addition it held that there was no evidence to show that the Crown had any authority, responsibility, or control in relation to the maintenance of the bridge. The action was dismissed. It would appear from this case that this section does not impose a duty on the Crown to issue instructions, but only on the band to carry out any instructions issued.

Lands Taken for Public Purposes

35. (1) Taking of lands by local authorities — Where by an Act of the Parliament of Canada or a provincial legislature, Her Majesty in right of a province, a municipal or local authority or a corporation is empowered to take or to use lands or any interest therein without the consent of the owner, the power may, with the consent of the Governor in Council and subject to any terms that may be prescribed by the Governor in Council, be exercised in relation to lands in a reserve or any interest therein.

(2) Procedure — Unless the Governor in Council otherwise directs, all matters relating to compulsory taking or using of lands in a reserve under subsection (1) are governed by the statute by which the powers are conferred.

(3) Grant in lieu of compulsory taking — Whenever the Governor in Council has consented to the exercise by a province, authority or corporation of the powers referred to in subsection (1), the Governor in Council may, in lieu of the province, authority or corporation taking or using the lands without the consent of the owner, authorize a transfer or grant of such lands to the province, authority or corporation, subject to any terms that may be prescribed by the Governor in Council.

(4) Payment — Any amount that is agreed upon or awarded in respect to the compulsory taking or using of land under this section or that is paid for a transfer or grant of land pursuant to this section shall be paid to the Receiver General for the use and benefit of the band or for the use and benefit of any Indian who is entitled to compensation or payment as a result of the exercise of the powers referred to in subsection (1).

Commentary: This section, and its predecessors, are often cited in Orders in Councils relating to highways, railways and hydro-electric projects on reserve lands. Other methods of alienating reserve land to non-members includes s. 28 (Minister May Issue Permits for Reserve Lands), ss. 37–39 (Surrenders and Designations) and s. 58 (Uncultivated and Unused Lands).

Case Law:

Canada

Kruger v. R., [1986] 1 F.C. 3, 32 L.C.R. 65, 17 D.L.R. (4th) 591, [1985] 3 C.N.L.R. 15, 58 N.R. 231leave to appeal to S.C.C. refused, 33 L.C.R. 192n, 62 N.R. 102n

Expropriation of reserve land (in 1938 and 1942) by the Crown to develop an airport was valid.

Canadian Pacific Ltd. v. Matsqui Indian Band, [1996] 3 F.C. 373, 134 D.L.R. (4th) 555, 111 F.T.R. 161 (T.D.)

The Matsqui First Nation passed a by-law imposing tax on railways which passed through their reserve. The court held that the lands, which had been surrendered or taken under the *Indian Act* for railway rights-of-way, were no longer part of the reserve. The court held that the lands were granted to the railway companies until the lands were no longer necessary for railway purposes. The rights of way were determinable fee simple lands, not easements or conditional interests in land. Consequently, the First Nation did not have the jurisdiction to impose the tax.

British Columbia

Moses v. R. in Right of Can., [1979] 5 W.W.R. 100, 12 B.C.L.R. 308 (C.A.)

The province has the right to resume up to one twentieth of the land in reserves in British Columbia for making roads or other works of public utility.

Osoyoos Indian Band v. Oliver (Town) (1997), 145 D.L.R. (4th) 552 (B.C. S.C.)

In 1957, land was expropriated from the Band for irrigation canal purposes under section 35 of the *Indian Act*, R.S.C. 1952, c. 149. The province was given management and control of the lands. In 1996, the Band attempted to impose a tax on this land.

The court held that the expropriated lands were either absolutely transferred to the province, or were transferred only until they were no longer needed for irrigation canal purposes. In either case, the lands were no longer reserve lands, and therefore were not "land, or interest in land, in the reserve" within s. 83. The fact that the mines and minerals may have been reserved for the Band did not affect the status of the surface rights.

A.G. Can. v. C.P., [1986] 1 C.N.L.R. 1, [1986] B.C.W.L.D. 3036 (S.C.)

Pursuant to the wording of the *Indian Act* and the *Railways Act*, the court ordered the return of railway lands originally expropriated from the Penticton Band, once C.P. no longer needed the land for railway purposes.

Eli v. Royal Bank (1985), 68 B.C.L.R. 353, 24 D.L.R. (4th) 127 (S.C.)

Under subsection 35(4), compensation money is to go to the federal government. In this case, a lawyer transferred the money directly to the Band, and was criticized by the court.

Manitoba

R. v. Stevenson, [1986] 5 W.W.R. 737, [1987] 1 C.N.L.R. 136 (Man. Q.B.)leave to appeal to Man.C.A. refused, [1987] 2 C.N.L.R. 144 (Man. C.A.)

The court upheld the validity of the transfer of a bridge located on a reserve to the province under section 35.

Ontario

Chippewas of Kettle & Stony Point v. M.M. Dillon Ltd., [1996] 1 C.N.L.R. 99 (Ont. Gen. Div.)

Land set aside as a reserve under Treaty No. 29 of 1827 could be appropriated by the *War Measures Act*. In this case, no provision of the *Indian Act* was relied upon.

Quebec

Lazare v. St. Lawrence Seaway Authority, [1957] Que. S.C. 5, 5 C.N.L.C. 238

The court rejected Khanawake's claim that their reserves could not be expropriated for the St.Lawrence Seaway.

Saskatchewan

Mathias Colomb Band of Indians v. Saskatchewan Power Corp., [1994] 2 W.W.R. 457, 13 C.E.L.R. (N.S.) 245, 92 Man. R. (2d) 105, 111 D.L.R. (4th) 83, [1994] 4 C.N.L.R. 50 (C.A.)leave to appeal to S.C.C. refused [1994] 5 W.W.R. lvin, 111 D.L.R. (4th) viin, 174 N.R. 235n (S.C.C.)

Saskatchewan Power proposes to construct a dam in Saskatchewan. The First Nation is located in Manitoba, but argues that the dam will affect its lands. The court held that the First Nation should have standing to argue that Saskatchewan Power needs to obtain authority under Manitoba statutes, particularly because s. 35 requires approval of the Governor in Council for any provincial taking from Indian reserves.

Special Reserves

36. Reserves not vested in the Crown — Where lands have been set apart for the use and benefit of a band and legal title thereto is not vested in Her Majesty, this Act applies as though the lands were a reserve within the meaning of this Act.

Case Law: *Isaac v. Davey* (1977), 77 D.L.R. (3d) 481, [1977] 2 S.C.R. 897, 9 C.N.L.C. 134, 16 N.R. 29

It was argued that the patent of the Grand River lands to the Six Nations which had been granted by Governor Simcoe on January 14, 1793, was effective to pass title to the Six Nations in fee simple.

The court held that even if that were the case, section 36 would operate to make the *Indian Act* apply to those lands as if they were reserves.

Re Stony Plain Indian Reserve No. 135 (1982), 35 A.R. 412, [1982] 1 W.W.R. 302, 130 D.L.R. (3d) 636, [1982] 1 C.N.L.R. 133 (C.A.)

In a reference which asked if surrendered lands cease to be "lands reserved for the Indians" if the lands in fee simple are held in trust, in perpetuity, by someone for the benefit of the band and its members, the court held (in this instance at (D.L.R.) p. 658):

> ... the band has not ceded an iota of these benefits and usufructs appurtenant to a reserve; it has been at specific pains to state its retention of them [in the trust]. The change in title of the land from Her Majesty to the grantee cannot effect the scope and operation of the trust ... the land falls within s. 36 and remains a reserve for the purposes of the Act. In our view, if such a grant were made, it would come within s. 36 and the *Indian Act* would apply.

Jules v. Harper Ranch Ltd., [1989] 3 C.N.L.R. 67 (B.C. S.C.), leave to appeal to C.A. refused [1991] 1 C.N.L.R. vin (B.C. C.A.), application for judicial review denied, (sub. nom. *Kamloops Indian Band v. Harper Ranch Ltd.* (1991), 81 D.L.R. (4th) 323 (B.C. C.A.)

The defendant was the owner of the land pursuant to a certificate of title under British Columbia's *Land Titles Act*. The plaintiff band claimed that the lands constituted a special reserve under s. 36 of the *Indian Act*, or were subject to an express or constructive trust in the band's favour. The plaintiff's claim was based upon Aboriginal title and the allotment of a reserve by the provincial governor in 1862. The governor had authority in 1862 to set aside Indian reserves and to bind the imperial Crown, and there was a fair question to be tried as to whether the *Land Titles Act* extinguished the plaintiff's rights. An interlocutory injunction was granted in favour of the plaintiff Indian band restraining the defendant developer from entering onto or interfering with certain lands while the plaintiff's claim to the land was adjudicated.

Petro-Canada Inc. v. Capot-Blanc (1992), 72 B.C.L.R. (2d) 28, 95 D.L.R. (4th) 69, [1993] 1 C.N.L.R. 72 (S.C.)

Fuel purchased by an Indian band for use on the reserve, and on adjacent land held in trust for the band, was exempt from sales tax, notwithstanding the fact that the fuel was delivered to the band at a location off the reserve. The paramount location of the vehicles in which the fuel was used was on the reserve, and the adjacent trust lands constituted part of the reserve by the application of s.36.

Surrenders and Designations

37. (1) Sales — Lands in a reserve shall not be sold nor title to them conveyed until they have been absolutely surrendered to Her Majesty pursuant to subsection 38(1) by the band for whose use and benefit in common the reserve was set apart.

(2) Other transactions — Except where this Act otherwise provides, lands in a reserve shall not be leased nor an interest in them granted until they have been surrendered to Her Majesty pursuant to subsection 38(2) by the band for whose use and benefit in common the reserve was set apart.

R.S. 1985, c. 17 (4th Supp.), s. 2.

Commentary: Before this section was amended in 1988, there was no category for "designation". Instead, lands were either surrendered absolutely, or conditionally. There was some doubt about whether lands conditionally surrendered (with a reversionary interest in the Band, such as a lease), ceased to be reserve lands. The 1988 amendment clarified the situation by recognizing that bands could "designate" lands so that the lands could remain reserve lands after a surrender. Cases decided prior to the amendment should be read with care to ensure their continued relevance.

For cases on the fiduciary duty upon surrender, see cases listed under section 53.

See the definitions of "designated lands", "reserve" and "surrendered lands" in section 2. Other methods of alienating reserve land to non-members include sections 28 (Minister may issue permits for reserve lands), section 35 (Lands taken for public purposes) and section 58 (Uncultivated and unused lands).

Case Law:

General

Opetchesaht Indian Band v. Canada (1997), 211 N.R. 241, 90 B.C.A.C. 1, 147 W.A.C. 1, 147 D.L.R. (4th) 1 (S.C.C.)

A right of way was granted to B.C. Hydro in 1959 across the reserve "for such a period of time as the said right-of-way is required for the purpose of an electric transmission line." The question was whether the land should have been alienated through a surrender (s. 37) or an expropriation (s. 35), as opposed to a permit under s. 28.

Major, J., said that, while there was some overlap between s. 37 and s. 28(2), the two sections were aimed at two different situations.

> In the case of sales, dispositions and long-term leases or alienations permanently disposing of any Indian interest in reserve land, surrender is required, involving the vote of all members of the band. On the other hand in the case of rights of use, occupation or residence for a period of longer than one year, only band council approval is required. [D.L.R. p. 17]

Guerin v. R., [1984] 2 S.C.R. 335, [1984] 6 W.W.R. 481, 59 B.C.L.R. 301, 36 R.P.R. 1, 20 E.T.R. 6, 13 D.L.R. (4th) 321, [1985] 1 C.N.L.R. 120, 55 N.R. 161

The Supreme Court of Canada found that the Crown had an enforceable fiduciary duty to Indians. In this case, the Crown's agents promised to lease reserve land to a third party on certain specified terms. After surrender, the Crown entered into a lease on different, less favourable terms with an exclusive golf club. According to the court,

> The purpose of this surrender requirement is clearly to interpose the Crown between the Indians and prospective purchasers or lessees of their land, so as to prevent the Indians from being exploited. [S.C.R. p.383]

The court went on to indicate that the courts should take into account oral terms as understood by the Band.

> .. the Crown, in my view, was not empowered by the surrender document to ignore the oral terms which the Band understood would be embodied in the lease. The oral representations form the backdrop against which the Crown's conduct in discharging its fiduciary obligation must be measured. They inform and confine the field of discretion within which the Crown was free to act. [S.C.R. p. 388]

The Band was awarded damages of $10,000,000.

Easterbrook v. R., [1931] S.C.R. 210, 4 C.N.L.C. 304

In 1821, the "British Indian Chiefs of St. Regis" purported to enter into a 999 year agreement for the lease of 160 acres for a farm on Cornwall Island. In 1875, the Department of Indian Affairs registered the lease and began collecting the yearly rental. The validity of the lease was challenged in this court case.

Relying on the Royal Proclamation of 1763, the court found that the Band could not convey a lease directly to a third party. In addition, there had been no surrender vote. The court found that the lease was void *ab initio*, and there was no other authority for the lessee to remain in possession of the lands.

> It is true that, during the latter part of the term of ninety-nine years, the annual rent of $10 was received at the Department of Indian Affairs, and presumably distributed as belonging to the income of the band or the Indians of the reserve; but that circumstance could not serve to validate a lease which was void at law, nor even to create a tenancy from year to year under conditions which the law prohibited. [C.N.L.C. at p. 315]

— See also *R. v. McMaster*, [1926] Ex.C.R. 68, 4 C.N.L.C. 359

Chippewas of Kettle & Stony Point v. Canada (A.G.) (1996), 31 O.R. (3d) 97, 95 O.A.C. 365, 141 D.L.R. (4th) 1, 6 R.P.R. (3d) 185 (C.A.)Leave to appeal to the Supreme Court of Canada granted, May 29, 1997

The First Nation challenged the validity of a surrender of reserve lands in 1927 under the *Indian Act* of that day (R.S.C. 1906, c. 81, ss. 48–50). In this case, the private purchaser was present at the Band meeting where the surrender vote was discussed, and presented each voter with a $5.00 payment. A few months after the vote in favour of the surrender, he provided each of the voters with an additional $10.00. The purchaser paid $85 per acre for the reserve, but less than three months after obtaining the land, he flipped half the land and sold it to third parties for $300 per acre.

The Court of Appeal decided that the presence of an unfair bargain, unconscionability or economic duress do not affect the validity of the surrender of land. The court did not set aside the surrender, but left open the possibility of an action against the federal Crown for breach of fiduciary duty.

Skerryvore Ratepayers' Assn. v. Shawanaga Indian Band (1993), 16 O.R. (3d) 390, 36 R.P.R. (2d) 23, 50 M.V.R. (2d) 9, 109 D.L.R. (4th) 449, [1994] 2 C.N.L.R. 61, 68 O.A.C. 69 (C.A.)leave to appeal to S.C.C. refused (1994) 17 O.R. (3d) xvii 38 R.P.R. (2d) 245n 2 M.V.R. (3d) 311n [1994] 3 C.N.L.R. vin (S.C.C.)

A branch road built by the band across the reserve from the highway did not become a public highway when federal officials asked the province to improve the road or by virtue of the *Municipal Act*, R.S.O. 1980, c. 302 which declares that all roads passing through Indian lands are public highways. An intention to dedicate the road as a public highway could not be derived from the band's actions. In any event, the common law doctrine of dedication is inconsistent with the nature of Indian title, which is inalienable and can only be surrendered to the Crown in right of Canada.

Effect of surrender

A.G. Canada v. Giroux (1916), 53 S.C.R. 172, 30 D.L.R. 125

Reserve land surrendered to the Crown to be sold may be purchased by an individual Indian. However, the land does not thereby become a reserve.

Canadian Pacific Ltd. v. Matsqui Indian Band, [1996] 3 F.C. 373, 134 D.L.R. (4th) 555, 111 F.T.R. 161 (T.D.)

The Matsqui First Nation passed a by-law imposing tax on railways which passed through their reserve. The court held that the lands, which had been surrendered or taken under the *Indian Act* for railway rights-of-way were no longer part of the reserve. The court held that the land was granted to the railway companies until the land was no longer necessary for railway purposes. The rights of way were determinable fee simple lands, not easements or conditional interests in land. Consequently, the First Nation did not have the jurisdiction to impose the tax.

Western Industrial Contractors Ltd. v. Sarcee Developments Ltd., [1979] 2 C.N.L.R. 107, [1979] 3 W.W.R. 631, 98 D.L.R. (3d) 424, 15 A.R. 309 (Alta. C.A.)

A surrender of reserve lands with a condition that it return to reserve status after 75 years was not an absolute surrender. It was clear that the Band retained a beneficial interest.

— See also *Palm Dairies Ltd. v. R.*, [1979] 2 C.N.L.R. 43, 91 D.L.R. (3d) 665, [1979] 1 F.C. 531 (Fed. Ct. T.D.)

Re Stony Plain Indian Reserve No. 135 (1982), 35 A.R. 412, [1982] 1 W.W.R. 302, 130 D.L.R. (3d) 636, [1982] 1 C.N.L.R. 133 (C.A.)

The Alberta Court of Appeal held at (D.L.R.) p. 653:

> ... an absolute surrender followed by a disposition of the reserved lands frees the land from the Indian burden ... if the band retains the reversion the burden remains at least in so far as the reversionary interest is concerned.

The band may thus choose to give up their rights to the land and the legislative authority of the federal Parliament forever, or retain such in their reversionary interests. Further, this section must be construed and applied in light of the duties of the Minister under section 53(1).

St. Mary's Indian Band v. Cranbrook (City) (1997), 147 D.L.R. (4th) 385, [1997] 3 C.N.L.R. 282 (S.C.C.)

A 1966 surrender by the Band contained the following provision:

> And that should any time the said lands cease to be used for public purposes they will revert to the St. Mary's Indian Band free of charge.

The land was surrendered and sold for full market value at that time. The land was then leased for $1 per year by the federal government to the city of Cranbrook for an airport. After the creation of the "designated lands" category in 1988 (the "Kamloops Amendment"), the Band argued that the airport was designated land, and therefore part of the reserve. As such, it could be taxed under the Band's *Indian Act* by-laws.

The Supreme Court held that the Kamloops Amendment was enacted to make it clear that lands that were *leased* were part of the reserve, but that lands that were *sold* were never intended to become part of the reserve. In the case of the St. Mary's First Nation, the court found that the Band had intended to sell the land, and therefore, the land was no longer part of the reserve.

In coming to this decision, the court reiterated that it would not interpret the intention of the parties by relying on the "minutiae of surrender documents." The Chief Justice goes on to say,

> The reason the Court has said that common law real property concepts do not apply to native lands is to prevent native intentions from being frustrated by an application of formalistic and arguably alien common law rules. Even in a case such as this where the Indian band received full legal representation prior to the surrender transaction, we must ensure that form not trump substance. It would be fundamentally unjust to impose inflexible and technical land transfer requirements upon these "autonomous actors" and conclude that the "ceased to be used for public purposes" stipulation was a condition subsequent solely because the band made the mistake of using the word "should" instead of the word "until". [C.N.L.R. p. 289]

Surrey v. Peace Arch Ent. Ltd. (1970), 74 W.W.R. 380 (B.C. C.A.)

A surrender under the Act is not a surrender in the conveyancing sense. Indians are forbidden from leasing or conveying reserve lands, and this function must be performed by a government official. A surrender for the purpose of leasing land is a conditional surrender. Such land is still within the category of lands described in s. 91(24) of the *Constitution Act*, 1867 as "lands reserved for Indians". Where land was reserved for Indians in 1887, and they still maintain a reversionary interest in it, the exclusive legislative jurisdiciton remains with the federal Parliament and provincial or municipal laws, including municipal zoning, building, water service and sewage disposal by-laws, cannot be enforced against the non-Indian lessee.

Gitanmaax Indian Band v. British Columbia Hydro & Power Authority (1991), 84 D.L.R. (4th) 562 (B.C. S.C.)

A reference in the authorizing Order in Council that the sale of certain lands by an Indian band was "for power purposes" was descriptive only, and not an underlying condition of the sale. The land therefore did not revert back to the band by operation of law when the power station was dismantled, and the land no longer used for those purposes.

38. (1) Surrender to Her Majesty — A band may absolutely surrender to Her Majesty, conditionally or unconditionally, all of the rights and interests of the band and its members in all or part of a reserve.

(2) Designation — A band may, conditionally or unconditionally, designate by way of a surrender to Her Majesty that is not absolute, any right or interest of the band and its members in all or part of a reserve, for the purpose of its being leased or a right or interest therein being granted.

R.S. 1985, c. 17 (4th Supp.), s. 2.

Commentary: See commentary under section 37. See the *Constitution Act, 1867*, for cases which hold that, upon surrender, the land becomes provincial Crown land.

39. (1) How lands surrendered or designated — An absolute surrender or designation is void unless

> **(a) it is made to Her Majesty;**
>
> **(b) it is assented to by a majority of the electors of the band**
>
> > **(i) at a general meeting of the band called by the council of the band,**
> >
> > **(ii) at a special meeting of the band called by the Minister for the purpose of considering a proposed absolute surrender or designation, or**

(iii) **by a referendum as provided in the regulations; and**

(c) **it is accepted by the Governor in Council.**

(2) **Minister may call meeting or referendum** — Where a majority of the electors of a band did not vote at a meeting or referendum called pursuant to subsection (1), the Minister may, if the proposed absolute surrender or designation was assented to by a majority of the electors who did vote, call another meeting by giving thirty days notice thereof or another referendum as provided in the regulations.

(3) **Assent of band** — Where a meeting is called pursuant to subsection (2) and the proposed absolute surrender or designation is assented to at the meeting or referendum by a majority of the electors voting, the surrender or designation shall be deemed, for the purposes of this section, to have been assented to by a majority of the electors of the band.

(4) The Minister may, at the request of the council of the band or whenever he considers it advisable, order that a vote at any meeting under this section shall be by secret ballot.

(5) Every meeting under this section shall be held in the presence of the superintendent or some other officer of the Department designated by the Minister.

R.S. 1985, c. 17 (4th Supp.), s. 3.

Commentary: The public meeting provision is carried forward from the Royal Proclamation of 1763, which required that lands of the Indians could only be sold to the Crown "at some public Meeting or Assembly of the said Indians."

Case Law: *Cardinal v. R.*, [1982] 1 S.C.R. 508, [1982] 3 W.W.R. 673, 133 D.L.R. (3d) 513 at 522, 41 N.R. 300

Prior legislation (*Indian Act*, R.S.C. 1906, c. 81, s. 49(1)), which required that no surrender "shall be valid ... unless the ... surrender shall be assented to by a majority of the male members of the band ... at a meeting ... thereof summoned for that purpose", was interpreted as requiring that a majority of the eligible male members of the band be present at a meeting called for the purpose of voting on the surrender of lands, and that a majority of those present vote in favour of surrendering the lands. The present Act is clearer as to the requirements of the vote.

St. Ann's Island Shooting & Fishing Club v. R., [1950] 2 D.L.R. 225, [1950] S.C.R. 211, 5 C.N.L.C. 608

In reviewing the effect of a predecessor to this section (*Indian Act*, R.S.C. 1906, c.81, s.51) the court held that an Order in Council is necessary for a valid surrender.

Luke v. R. (1991), 42 F.T.R. 241, (sub nom. *Lower Kootenay Indian Band v. Canada)* [1992] 2 C.N.L.R. 54 (F.C.T.D.)

Following *St. Ann's Island Shooting & Hunting Club* and *Easterbrook* in the interpretation of s.51 of the *Indian Act*, R.S.C. 1927, c.98, the court found that a 1934 lease was void *ab initio* for lack of the Order in Council.

> Clearly, that section is more than a technicality. It is the ultimate protection to ensure that Indians are not taken advantage of by unscrupulous or negligent administrators. [C.N.L.R. at p.107]

Port Franks Properties Ltd. v. R. (1979), 99 D.L.R. (3d) 28, [1981] 3 C.N.L.R. 86 (F.C.T.D.)

The Department of National Defence traced its claim to land at Ipperwash from a surrender. In this case, there was a surrender vote on October 18, 1928, and the land was conveyed on June 27, 1929. The surrender was not accepted by the Privy Council until August 7, 1929. The court held that all of the statutory procedures must be followed, but that all steps need not all be completed prior to the date of the conveyance for there to be a valid conveyance.

[Note: although this case purports to follow St. Ann's Island Shooting Club, *it appears to be a misreading of the facts of that case]*

Chippewas of Kettle & Stony Point v. Canada (A.G.) (1996), 31 O.R. (3d) 97, 95 O.A.C. 365, 141 D.L.R. (4th) 1, 6 R.P.R. (3d) 185 (C.A.)Leave to appeal to the Supreme Court of Canada granted, May 29, 1997

The First Nation challenged the validity of a surrender of reserve lands in 1927 under the *Indian Act* of that day (R.S.C. 1906, c. 81, ss. 48–50). In this case, the private purchaser was present at the Band meeting where the surrender vote was discussed, and presented each voter with a $5.00 payment. A few months after the vote in favour of the surrender, he provided each of the voters with an additional $10.00. The purchaser paid $85 per acre for the reserve land, but less than three months after obtaining the land, he flipped half the land and sold it to third parties for $300 per acre.

The court found that there was nothing wrong with the presence of the private purchaser at the Band meeting. As well, the court found that the payment of money did not change the "true intent" of the majority of the Band, which was to sell the land. While upholding the validity of the surrender, the court left open the possibility of a case of breach of fiduciary duty against the federal Crown for the alleged "bribes" and exploitation.

Logan v. Styres (1959), 20 D.L.R. (2d) 416, [1959] O.W.N. 361, 5 C.N.L.C. 261 (Ont. H.C.)

The hereditary chiefs of the Six Nations brought an action against the elected Chief and Council to stop the surrender of a portion of the reserve. The judge found that "a great majority" of the members of Six Nations did not subscribe to the system of elections imposed under the *Indian Act*, and that these individuals did not vote on surrenders. Consequently, the two surrender votes saw 54 people voting (37 in favour) and 53 people voting (30 in favour). There were about 3,600 eligible voters.

While observing that "it is difficult to see what advantage would accrue to the Six Nations Indians by surrendering the land in question", the judge nevertheless upheld the validity of the surrender and the subsequent Order in Council.

Related Provisions: See the *Indian Referendum Regulations* for rules on referendums.

40. Certification — **A proposed absolute surrender or designation that is assented to by the band in accordance with section 39 shall be certified on oath by the superintendent or other officer who attended the meeting and by the chief or a member of the council of the band and then submitted to the Governor in Council for acceptance or refusal.**

R.S. 1985, c. 17 (4th Supp.), s. 4.

Case Law: *Chippewas of Kettle & Stony Point v. Canada (Attorney General)* (1995), 24 O.R. (3d) 654, [1996] C.N.L.R. 54 (Gen. Div.)affirmed on other grounds (1996), 31 O.R. (3d) 97, 141 D.L.R. (4th) 1, 6 R.P.R.(3d) 185, 95 O.A.C. 365 (C.A.)

The court may go behind the Order in Council to determine whether the proper procedure was followed to obtain the surrender.

41. Effect of surrenders and designations — **An** absolute surrender or designation shall be deemed to confer all rights that are necessary to enable Her Majesty to carry out the terms of the surrender or designation.

R.S. 1985, c. 17 (4th Supp.), s. 4.

Descent of Property

42. (1) Powers of Minister with respect to property of deceased Indians — Unless otherwise provided in this Act, all jurisdiction and authority in relation to matters and causes testamentary, with respect to deceased Indians, is vested exclusively in the Minister, and shall be exercised subject to and in accordance with regulations of the Governor in Council.

(2) Regulations — The Governor in Council may make regulations for providing that a deceased Indian who at the time of his death was in possession of land in a reserve shall, in such circumstances and for such purposes as the regulations prescribe, be deemed to have been at the time of his death lawfully in possession of that land.

(3) Application of regulations — Regulations made under this section may be made applicable to estates of Indians who died before, on or after the 4th day of September 1951.

Case Law: *Sampson v. Gosnell Estate* (1989), 35 B.C.L.R. (2d) 125, 32 E.T.R. 164, 57 D.L.R. (4th) 299 (C.A.)

A claim for a declaration of entitlement to an intestate's estate by virtue of an agreement during life is not a "cause testamentary" within the meaning of this section, and therefore the Federal Court does not have exclusive jurisdiction over the matter.

Related Provisions: Under section 4(3), sections 42-52 may not apply if an individual is not ordinarily resident on reserve.

The *Indian Estates Regulations* [C.R.C. 1978, c. 954] may be relevant.

43. Particular powers — Without restricting the generality of section 42, the Minister may

    (a) appoint executors of wills and administrators of estates of deceased Indians, remove them and appoint others in their stead;

    (b) authorize executors to carry out the terms of the wills of deceased Indians;

    (c) authorize administrators to administer the property of Indians who die intestate;

    (d) carry out the terms of wills of deceased Indians and administer the property of Indians who die intestate; and

    (e) make or give any order, direction or finding that in his opinion it is necessary or desirable to make or give with respect to any matter referred to in section 42.

Case Law: *A.G. Can. v. Canard*, [1976] 1 S.C.R. 170, [1975] 3 W.W.R. 1, 52 D.L.R. (3d) 548, 4 N.R. 91

Sections 42 and 43 do not create an inequality before the law by reason of race under the Bill of Rights.

Related Provisions: Under section 4(3), sections 42-52 may not apply if an individual is not ordinarily resident on reserve.

The *Indian Estates Regulations* may be relevant.

44. (1) Courts may exercise jurisdiction with consent of Minister — The court that would have jurisdiction if the deceased were not an Indian may, with the consent of the Minister, exercise, in accordance with this Act, the jurisdiction and authority conferred upon the Minister by this Act in relation to testamentary matters and causes and any other powers, jurisdiction and authority ordinarily vested in that court.

(2) Minister may refer a matter to the court — The Minister may direct in any particular case that an application for the grant of probate of the will or letters of administration shall be made to the court that would have jurisdiction if the deceased were not an Indian, and the Minister may refer to such court any question arising out of any will or the administration of any estate.

(3) Orders relating to lands — A court that is exercising any jurisdiction or authority under this section shall not without the consent in writing of the Minister enforce any order relating to real property on a reserve.

Commentary: Note that the court exercises the jurisdiction under the *Indian Act*. The court does not administer provincial legislation.

Case Law: *Johnson v. Pelkey*, [1997] B.C.J. No. 1290 (B.C. S.C.)

Albert Pelkey was a member of the Tsawout Band. He died leaving substantial amounts of cash and property. The Minister of Indian Affairs consented to the transfer of his authority and jurisdiction of the Supreme Court of British Columbia.

The court noted that it not only had the Minister's powers under the *Indian Act*, it also had "any other powers, jurisdiction and authority ordinarily vested in that court." This meant that the court could refer to common law and to precedents related to testamentary dispositions by non-Indians.

Related Provisions: Under section 4(3), sections 42-52 may not apply if an individual is not ordinarily resident on reserve.

The *Indian Estates Regulations* may be relevant.

Wills

45. (1) Indians may make wills — Nothing in this Act shall be construed to prevent or prohibit an Indian from devising or bequeathing his property by will.

(2) Form of will — The Minister may accept as a will any written instrument signed by an Indian in which he indicates his wishes or intention with respect to the disposition of his property upon his death.

(3) Probate — No will executed by an Indian is of any legal force or effect as a disposition of property until the Minister has approved the will or a court has granted probate thereof pursuant to this Act.

Related Provisions: Under section 4(3), sections 42-52 may not apply if an individual is not ordinarily resident on reserve.

The *Indian Estates Regulations* may be relevant.

46. (1) Minister may declare will void — The Minister may declare the will of an Indian to be void in whole or in part if he is satisfied that

(a) the will was executed under duress or undue influence;

(b) the testator at the time of execution of the will lacked testamentary capacity;

(c) the terms of the will would impose hardship on persons for whom the testator had a responsibility to provide;

(d) the will purports to dispose of land in a reserve in a manner contrary to the interest of the band or contrary to this Act;

(e) the terms of the will are so vague, uncertain or capricious that proper administration and equitable distribution of the estate of the deceased would be difficult or impossible to carry out in accordance with this act; or

(f) the terms of the will are against the public interest.

(2) Where will declared void — Where a will of an Indian is declared by the Minister or by a court to be wholly void, the person executing the will shall be deemed to have died intestate, and where the will is so declared to be void in part only, any bequest or devise affected thereby, unless a contrary intention appears in the will, shall be deemed to have lapsed.

Case Law:

Section 46(1)(a)

Johnson v. Pelkey, [1997] B.C.J. No. 1290 (B.C.S.C.)

Albert Pelkey was a member of the Tsawout Band. He died leaving substantial amounts of cash and property. The Minister of Indian Affairs consented to the transfer of his authority and jurisdiction to the Supreme Court of British Columbia.

The court declared the will void because of incapacity and undue influence.

Section 46(1)(d)

Pronovost v. Can. (Min. of Indian Affairs & Nor. Dev.), [1985] 1 F.C. 517, [1986] 1 C.N.L.R. 51 (C.A.)

A testator's bequeathing of reserve land to his daughters subject to a life estate to his wife, thus creating a legacy with a substitution, is not contrary to the intention of the Act.

Section 46(2)

Pronovost v. Can. (Min. of Indian Affairs & Nor. Dev.), supra

The Minister's discretion is subject to review.

Related Provisions: Under section 4(3), sections 42-52 may not apply if an individual is not ordinarily resident on reserve.

The *Indian Estates Regulations* may be relevant.

Appeals

47. Appeal to Federal Court — A decision of the Minister made in the exercise of the jurisdiction or authority conferred upon him by section 42, 43 or 46 may, within two months from the date thereof, be appealed by any person affected thereby to the

Federal Court of Canada, if the amount in controversy in the appeal exceeds five hundred dollars or if the Minister consents to an appeal.

R.S. 1985, c. 10 (2d Supp.), ss. 64, 65.

Related Provisions: Under section 4(3), sections 42-52 may not apply if an individual is not ordinarily resident on reserve.

The *Indian Estates Regulations* may be relevant.

Distribution of Property on Intestacy

48. (1) Surviving spouse's share — Where the net value of the estate of an intestate does not, in the opinion of the Minister, exceed seventy-five thousand dollars or such other amount as may be fixed by order of the Governor in Council, the estate shall go to the widow.

(2) Idem — Where the net value of the estate of an intestate, in the opinion of the Minister, exceeds seventy-five thousand dollars, or such other amount as may be fixed by order of the Governor in Council, seventy-five thousand dollars, or other such amount as may be fixed by order of the Governor in Council, shall go to the widow, and

   (a) if the intestate left no issue, the remainder shall go to the widow;

   (b) if the intestate left one child, one-half of the remainder shall go to the widow; and

   (c) if the intestate left more than one child, one-third of the remainder shall go to the widow,

and where a child has died leaving issue and such issue is alive at the date of the intestate's death, the widow shall take the same share of the estate as if the child had been living at that date.

(3) Where children not provided for — Notwithstanding subsections (1) and (2),

   (a) where in any particular case the Minister is satisfied that any children of the deceased will not be adequately provided for, he may direct that all or any part of the estate that would otherwise go to the widow shall go to the children, and

   (b) the Minister may direct that the widow shall have the right, during her widowhood, to occupy any lands on a reserve that were occupied by her deceased husband at the time of his death.

(4) Distribution to issue — Where an intestate dies leaving issue his estate shall be distributed, subject to the rights of the widow, if any, *per stirpes* among such issue.

(5) Distribution to father and mother — Where an intestate dies leaving no widow or issue his estate shall go to his father and mother in equal shares if both are living, but if either of them is dead the estate shall go to the survivor.

(6) Distribution to brothers, sisters and their issue — Where an intestate dies leaving no widow or issue or father or mother his estate shall go to his brothers and sisters in equal shares, and if any brother or sister is dead the children of the deceased brother or sister shall take the share their parents would have taken if living, but where the only persons entitled are children of deceased brothers and sisters, they shall take per capita.

(7) **Next-of-kin** — Where an intestate dies leaving no widow, issue, father, mother, brother or sister, and no children of any deceased brother or sister, his estate shall go to his next-of-kin.

(8) **Distribution among next-of-kin** — Where the estate goes to the next-of-kin it shall be distributed equally among the next-of-kin of equal degree of consanguinity to the intestate and those who legally represent them, but in no case shall representation be admitted after brothers' and sisters' children, and any interest in land in a reserve shall vest in Her Majesty for the benefit of the band if the nearest of kin of the intestate is more remote than a brother or sister.

(9) **Degrees of kindred** — For the purposes of this section, degrees of kindred shall be computed by counting upward from the intestate to the nearest common ancestor and then downward to the relative, and the kindred of the half-blood shall inherit equally with those of the whole-blood in the same degree.

(10) **Descendants and relatives born after intestate's death** — Descendants and relatives of the intestate begotten before his death but born thereafter shall inherit as if they had been born in the lifetime of the intestate and had survived him.

(11) **Estate not disposed of by will** — All such estate as is not disposed of by will shall be distributed as if the testator had died intestate and had left no other estate.

(12) **No dower or estate by curtesy** — No widow is entitled to dower in the land of her deceased husband dying intestate, and no husband is entitled to an estate by curtesy in the land of his deceased wife so dying, and there is no community of real or personal property situated on a reserve.

(13) [Repealed R.S. 1985, c. 32 (1st Supp.), s. 9.]

(14) [Repealed R.S. 1985, c. 32 (1st Supp.), s. 9.]

(15) **Definition of "widow"** — This section applies in respect of an intestate woman as it applies in respect of an intestate male, and for the purposes of this section the word "widow" includes "widower".

R.S. 1985, c. 32 (1st Supp.), s. 9; c. 48 (4th Supp.), s. 2.

(16) [Repealed R.S. 1985, c. 48, (4th Supp.), s. 2(3).]

Related Provisions: Under section 4(3), sections 42-52 may not apply if an individual is not ordinarily resident on reserve.

The *Indian Estates Regulations* may be relevant.

49. Devisee's entitlement — A person who claims to be entitled to possession or occupation of lands in a reserve by devise or descent shall be deemed not to be in lawful possession or occupation of that land until the possession is approved by the Minister.

Related Provisions: Under section 4(3), sections 42-52 may not apply if an individual is not ordinarily resident on reserve.

The *Indian Estates Regulations* may be relevant.

50. (1) Non-resident of reserve — A person who is not entitled to reside on a reserve does not by devise or descent acquire a right to possession or occupation of land in that reserve.

(2) Sale by superintendent — Where a right to possession or occupation of land in a reserve passes by devise or descent to a person who is not entitled to reside on a reserve, that right shall be offered for sale by the superintendent to the highest bidder among persons who are entitled to reside on a reserve and the proceeds of the sale shall be paid to the devisee or descendant, as the case may be.

(3) Unsold lands revert to bands — Where no tender is received within six months or such further period as the Minister may direct after the date when the right to possession or occupation is offered for sale under subsection (2), the right shall revert to the band free from any claim on the part of the devisee or descendant, subject to the payment, at the discretion of the Minister, to the devisee or descendant, from the funds of the band, of such compensation for permanent improvements as the Minister may determine.

(4) Approval required — The purchaser of a right to possession or occupation of land under subsection (2) shall be deemed not to be in lawful possession or occupation of the land until the possession is approved by the Minister.

Case Law:

Section 50(2)

R. v. Devereux, [1965] S.C.R. 567, 51 D.L.R. (2d) 546

Attempted arrangements to enable a person to acquire occupancy of land are irrelevant and do not assist in a claim for possession.

Related Provisions: Under section 4(3), sections 42-52 may not apply if an individual is not ordinarily resident on reserve.

The *Indian Estates Regulations* may be relevant.

Mentally Incompetent Indians

51. (1) Powers of Minister generally — Subject to this section, all jurisdiction and authority in relation to the property of mentally incompetent Indians is vested exclusively in the Minister.

(2) Particular powers — Without restricting the generality of subsection (1), the Minister may

(a) appoint persons to administer the estates of mentally incompetent Indians;

(b) order that any property of a mentally incompetent Indian shall be sold, leased, alienated, mortgaged, disposed of or otherwise dealt with for the purpose of

(i) paying his debt or engagements,

(ii) discharging encumbrances on his property,

(iii) paying debts or expenses incurred for his maintenance or otherwise for his benefit, or

(iv) paying or providing for the expenses of future maintenance; and

(c) make such orders and give such directions as he considers necessary to secure the satisfactory management of the estates of mentally incompetent Indians.

(3) **Property off reserve** — The Minister may order that any property situated off a reserve and belonging to a mentally incompetent Indian shall be dealt with under the laws of the province in which the property is situated.

Related Provisions: Under section 4(3), sections 42-52 may not apply if an individual is not ordinarily resident on reserve.

The *Indian Estates Regulations* may be relevant.

Guardianship

52. Property of infant children — The Minister may administer or provide for the administration of any property to which infant children of Indians are entitled, and may appoint guardians for such purposes.

Case Law: *Dir. of Recovery & Maintenance v. W.S.* (1983), 24 Alta. L.R. (2d) 133, [1983] 3 C.N.L.R. 65 (Prov. Ct.)

This section allows the Minister to administer oil and gas royalties paid as per capita distribution to infant band members.

Related Provisions: Under section 4(3), sections 42-52 may not apply if an individual is not ordinarily resident on reserve.

The *Indian Estates Regulations* may be relevant.

Money of Infant Children

52.1 (1) Distribution of capital — The council of a band may determine that the payment of not more than three thousand dollars, or such other amount as may be fixed by order of the Governor in Council, in a year of the share of a distribution under paragraph 64(1)(a) that belongs to an infant child who is a member of the band is necessary or proper for the maintenance, advancement or other benefit of the child.

(2) Procedure — Before making a determination under subsection (1), the council of the band must

(a) post in a conspicuous place on the reserve fourteen days before the determination is made a notice that it proposes to make such a determination; and

(b) give the members of the band a reasonable opportunity to be heard at a general meeting of the band held before the determination is made.

(3) **Minister's duty** — Where the council of the band makes a determination under subsection (1) and notifies the Minister, at the time it gives its consent to the distribution pursuant to paragraph 64(1)(a), that is has made that determination and that, before making it, it complied with subsection (2), the Minister shall make a payment described in subsection (1) for the maintenance, advancement or other benefit of the child to a parent or person who is responsible for the care and custody of the child or, if so requested by the council on giving its consent to that distribution, to the council.

R.S. 1985, c. 48 (4th Supp.), s. 3.

52.2 Money of infant children of Indians — The Minister may, regardless of whether a payment is made under section 52.1, pay all or part of any money administered by the Minister under section 52 that belongs to an infant child of an Indian to a parent or person who is responsible for the care and custody of the child or otherwise apply all or part of that money if

(a) the Minister is requested in writing to do so by the parent or the person responsible; and

(b) in the opinion of the Minister, the payment or application is necessary or proper for the maintenance, advancement or other benefit of the child.

R.S. 1985, c. 48 (4th Supp.), s. 3.

52.3 (1) Attaining majority — Where a child of an Indian attains the age of majority, the Minister shall pay any money administered by the Minister under section 52 to which the child is entitled to that child in one lump sum.

(2) **Exception** — Notwithstanding subsection (1), where requested in writing to do so before a child of an Indian attains the age of majority by a parent or a person who is responsible for the care and custody of the child or by the council of the band of which the child is a member, the Minister may, instead of paying the money in one lump sum, pay it in instalments during a period beginning on the day the child attains the age of majority and ending not later than the day that is three years after that day.

R.S. 1985, c. 48 (4th Supp.), s. 3.

52.4 Relief — Where, in a proceeding in respect of the share of a distribution under paragraph 64(1)(a) or of money belonging to an infant child that was paid pursuant to section 52.1, 52.2 or 52.3, it appears to the court that the Minister, the band, its council or a member of that council acted honestly and reasonably and ought fairly to be relieved from liability in respect of the payment, the court may relieve the Minister, band, council or member, either in whole or in part, from liability in respect of the payment.

R.S. 1985, c. 48 (4th Supp.), s. 3.

52.5 (1) Effect of payment — The receipt in writing from a parent or person who is responsible for the care and custody of an infant child for a payment made pursuant to section 52.1 or 52.2

(a) discharges the duty of the Minister, the band, its council and each member of that council to make the payment to the extent of the amount paid; and

(b) discharges the Minister, the band, its council and each member of that council from seeing to its application or being answerable for its loss or misapplication.

(2) Idem — The receipt in writing from the council of the band of which an infant child is a member for a payment made pursuant to section 52.1

(a) discharges the duty of the Minister to make the payment to the extent of the amount paid; and

(b) discharges the Minister from seeing to its application or being answerable for its loss or misapplication.

R.S. 1985, c. 48, (4th Supp.), s. 3.

Management of Reserves and Surrendered and Designated Lands

53. (1) Transactions re surrendered and designated lands — The Minister or a person appointed by the Minister for the purpose may, in accordance with this Act and the terms of the absolute surrender or designation, as the case may be,

(a) manage or sell absolutely surrendered lands; or

(b) manage, lease or carry out any other transaction affecting designated lands.

(2) Grant where original purchaser dead — Where the original purchaser of surrendered lands is dead and the heir, assignee or devisee of the original purchaser applies for a grant of the lands, the Minister may, upon receipt of proof in such manner as he directs and requires in support of any claim for the grant and upon being satisfied that the claim has been equitably and justly established, allow the claim and authorize a grant to issue accordingly.

(3) Departmental employees — No person who is appointed pursuant to subsection (1) or who is an officer or servant of Her Majesty employed in the Department may, except with the approval of the Governor in Council, acquire directly or indirectly any interest in absolutely surrendered or designated lands.

R.S. 1985, c. 17 (4th Supp.), s. 5.

Commentary: Courts have placed a high standard on the conduct of the Crown with respect to surrenders. In *Guerin*, the Supreme Court of Canada held that the Crown had an enforceable fiduciary duty.

Case Law:

General

St. Ann's Island Shooting & Fishing Club Ltd. v. R., [1950] S.C.R. 211, [1950] 2 D.L.R. 225, 5 C.N.L.C. 608

In 1882, there was a surrender by the Chippewas and Pottawatomie Indians of Walpole Island for leasing part of their reserve to the club. The lease, drawn up in 1881, was for five years, renewable for another five year term. The Superintendent entered into further leases which extended beyond the term.

Taschereau, J.finds that the 1882 surrender was valid, but that the surrender did not authorize the Superintendent, "at the expiration of the lease, to enter into fresh agreements with the appellant nearly 50 years later, and in which can be found different conditions." [C.N.L.C. at p.613].

Rand J. comments that the statutory requirement for an Order in Council authorizing the leases could not be delegated to the Superintendent General.

> The language of the statute embodies the accepted view that these aborigines are, in effect, wards of the state, whose care and welfare are a political trust of the highest obligation. For that reason, every such dealing with their privileges must bear the imprint of Governmental approval, and it would be beyond the power of the Governor in Council to transfer that responsibility to the Superintendent General. [C.N.L.C. at p.616]

Fiduciary duty

Blueberry River Indian Band v. Canada (Department of Indian Affairs & Northern Development) (1995), 130 D.L.R. (4th) 193, [1995] 4 S.C.R. 344, 190 N.R. 89, 102 F.T.R. 60 (note)

The Band surrendered their mineral rights for lease in 1940. In 1945, there was a further surrender of the reserve for lease or for sale. In 1948, the Department of Indian Affairs sold the land, including the minerals, to the Department of Veterans Affairs.

The court found that, after the surrender, there was a duty on the Crown to act in the best interests of the Indians. The department did not discuss the sale of the mineral rights with the band before selling those rights. The court found that it was a breach of fiduciary duty to sell, rather than lease, the mineral rights in 1948.

Guerin v. R., [1984] 2 S.C.R. 335, [1984] 6 W.W.R. 481, 59 B.C.L.R. 301, 36 R.P.R. 1, 20 E.T.R. 6, 13 D.L.R. (4th) 321, [1985] 1 C.N.L.R. 120, 55 N.R. 161

In this case, the Crown's agents promised to lease reserve land on certain specified terms. After the surrender, the Crown entered into a lease on different, less favourable terms with an exclusive golf club. The Supreme Court of Canada found that the Crown had an enforceable fiduciary duty to Indians.

> An Indian Band is prohibited from directly transferring its interest to a third party. Any sale or lease of land can only be carried out after a surrender has taken place, with the Crown then acting on the Band's behalf. The Crown first took this responsibility upon itself in the Royal Proclamation of 1763. It is still recognized in the surrender provisions of the *Indian Act*. The surrender requirement, and the responsibility it entails, are the source of a distinct fiduciary obligation owed by the Crown to the Indians. [S.C.R. at p.376]

Semiahmoo Indian Band v. Canada (1997), 148 D.L.R. (4th) 523, 215 N.R. 241 (C.A.)

The reserve of the Semiahmoo First Nation is located near the border between British Columbia and the United States. In 1951 the federal government requested that the Band surrender 22.4 acres of its 382 acre reserve, citing a need to expand its custom facility. The Band reluctantly voted for an absolute surrender knowing that the government could expropriate the land (as it had done previously with a different parcel of the reserve). The land was never developed, and no plans were made for an expansion of the customs facility until 1992, after the Band began the court action.

The court held that there had been a breach of a pre-surrender fiduciary duty by the Crown in 1951, because of the failure to ensure that the land was going to be used for a public purpose. Although a claim for this breach of fiduciary duty was barred by a British Columbia limitation period, there were two breaches of fiduciary duties which occurred after the surrender.

First, the Crown failed to correct a mistake it made at the time of the surrender. The original surrender should have been conditional, or at least provide for a reversionary interest once the land was no longer needed for public purposes. After the surrender, the Crown had an opportunity to correct this error, but failed to do so.

Second, the Crown failed to return the land to the Band when it became clear by 1969, that the Crown had not used the land and had no plans to use the land. When the Band asked for return of the land, the Crown should have returned the land because it had not been used.

The Crown was ordered that the land be restored to the reserve, and that compensation be paid to the Band.

Luke v. R. (1991), 42 F.T.R. 241, (sub nom. *Lower Kootenay Indian Band v. Canada)* [1992] 2 C.N.L.R. 54 (Fed. T.D.)

There was a purported surrender in 1934 for fifty years. The lease did not contain an escalator clause, and the Band was unhappy with the lease. In 1948, the Department of Indian Affairs discovered that there was no Order in Council accepting the surrender, but did not tell the Band until 25 years later.

The court finds that the Crown was both negligent and in breach of fiduciary duty to continue with the lease that was void *ab initio*. In addition, the Crown was in breach of its fiduciary duty by failing to terminate the lease when it had an opportunity to do so because of breaches by the lessee.

54. Assignments — Where absolutely surrendered lands are agreed to be sold and letters patent relating thereto have not issued, or where designated lands are leased or an interest in them granted, the purchaser, lessee or other person who has an interest in the absolutely surrendered or designated lands may, with the approval of the Minister, assign all or part of that interest to any other person.

R.S. 1985, c. 17 (4th Supp.), s. 6.

55. (1) Surrendered and Designated Lands Register — There shall be kept in the Department a register, to be known as the Surrendered and Designated Lands Register, in which shall be entered particulars in connection with any transaction affecting absolutely surrendered or designated lands.

(2) Conditional assignment — A conditional assignment shall not be registered.

(3) Proof of execution — Registration of an assignment may be refused until proof of its execution has been furnished.

(4) Effect of registration — An assignment registered under this section is valid against an unregistered assignment or an assignment subsequently registered.

R.S. 1985, c. 17 (4th Supp.), s. 7(1).

Case Law: *Palm Dairies Ltd. v. R.*, [1979] 2 C.N.L.R. 43, 91 D.L.R. (3d) 665, [1979] 1 F.C. 53 (Fed. T.D.)

In rejecting a motion for the registration of a builders' lien in the surrendered lands register, the court states:

> The Crown's argument is that s. 55 of the *Indian Act* does not encompass any builders' lien and this is a compelling argument. A builders' lien is a document which may be filed in the Land Titles Office pursuant to the provisions of the *Builders' Lien Act* but can the Registrar under the *Indian Act* somehow be directed to register a lien in the federal registry when there is no specific authority for any such registration. The answer must be in the negative. [C.N.L.R. at p. 51]

56. Certificate of registration — Where an assignment is registered there shall be endorsed on the original copy thereof a certificate of registration signed by the Minister or by an officer of the Department authorized by him to sign such certificates.

57. Regulations — The Governor in Council may make regulations

(a) authorizing the Minister to grant licences to cut timber on surrendered lands, or, with the consent of the council of the band, on reserve lands;

(b) imposing terms, conditions and restrictions with respect to the exercise of rights conferred by licences granted under paragraph (a);

(c) providing for the disposition of surrendered mines and minerals underlying lands in a reserve;

(d) prescribing the penalty not exceeding one hundred dollars or imprisonment for a term of three months, or both, that may be imposed on summary conviction for contravention of any regulation made under this section; and

(e) providing for the seizure and forfeiture of any timber or minerals taken in contravention of any regulation made under this section.

58. (1) Uncultivated or unused lands — Where land in a reserve is uncultivated or unused, the Minister may, with the consent of the council of the band,

(a) improve or cultivate such land and employ persons therefor, and authorize and direct the expenditure of so much of the capital funds of the band as he considers necessary for such improvement or cultivation including the purchase of such stock, machinery or material or for the employment of such labour as the Minister considers necessary;

(b) where the land is in the lawful possession of any individual, grant a lease of such land for agricultural or grazing purposes or for any purpose that is for the benefit of the person in possession; and

(c) where the land is not in the lawful possession of any individual, grant for the benefit of the band a lease of such land for agricultural or grazing purposes.

(2) **Distribution of proceeds** — Out of the proceeds derived from the improvement or cultivation of lands pursuant to paragraph (1)(b), a reasonable rent shall be paid to the individual in lawful possession of the lands or any part thereof, and the remainder of the proceeds shall be placed to the credit of the band, but if improvements are made on the lands occupied by an individual, the Minister may deduct the value of such improvements from the rent payable to such individual under this subsection.

(3) **Lease at request of occupant** — The Minister may lease for the benefit of any Indian, on application of that Indian for that purpose, the land of which the Indian is lawfully in possession without the land being designated.

(4) Disposition of grass, timber, non-metallic substances, etc. — Notwithstanding anything in this Act, the Minister may, without an absolute surrender or designation

(a) dispose of wild grass or dead or fallen timber, and

(b) with the consent of the council of the band, dispose of sand, gravel, clay and other non-metallic substances upon or under lands in a reserve, or, where such consent cannot be obtained without undue difficulty or delay, may issue temporary permits for the taking of sand, gravel, clay and other non-metallic substances upon or under lands in a reserve, renewable only with the consent of the council of the band, and the proceeds of such transactions shall be credited to band funds or shall be divided between the band and the individual Indians in lawful possession of the lands in such shares as the Minister may determine.

R.S. 1985, c. 17 (4th Supp.), s. 8.

(5) Proceeds — The proceeds of the transactions referred to in subsection (4) shall be credited to band funds or shall be divided between the band and the individual Indians in lawful possession of the lands in such shares as the Minister may determine.

R.S., c. I-6, s. 58.

Commentary: Other methods of alienating reserve land to non-members include s. 28 (Minister May Issue Permits for Reserve Lands), s. 35 (Lands Taken for Public Purposes) and ss. 37–39 (Surrenders and Designations).

Case Law:

Section 58(3)

R. v. Devereux, [1965] S.C.R. 567, 51 D.L.R. (2d) 546

There are only two ways under the Act for a non-Indian to be in possession of reserve land: by a lease made by the Minister for the benefit of any Indian under s. 58(3), or under a permit by s. 28(2).

Northwest/Prince Rupert Assessor Area No. 25 v. N & V Johnson Services Ltd., [1988] 5 W.W.R. 438, 25 B.C.L.R. 322, [1988] 4 C.N.L.R. 83 (S.C.)affirmed (1990), [1991] 1 W.W.R. 527, 49 B.C.L.R. (2d) 173, 1 M.P.L.R. (2d) 170 (C.A.)

A corporation is not an Indian even if wholly owned by Indians and land held under this section by a corporation may be taxed under provincial law.

Boyer v. Canada, [1986] 2 F.C. 393, 26 D.L.R. (4th) 284, [1986] 4 C.N.L.R. 53, 65 N.R. 305 (C.A.)leave to appeal to S.C.C. refused (1986), 72 N.R. 365n (S.C.C.)

A former chief of the Batchewana First Nation had a certificate of occupation approved by the Band Council and the Minister. He then decided to lease the land for development to a corporation of which he and his wife were sole shareholders. The chief and council had initially approved in principle the leasing of the land to the corporation. However, the council objected to the final lease provisions and argued that the Minister did not have authority to approve the lease without the consent of council. The Federal Court of Appeal held that the lease was legal and that s. 58(3) of the *Indian Act* did not require the Minister to obtain the First Nation's consent before agreeing to the lease.

59. Adjustment of contracts — The Minister may, with the consent of the council of a band,

(a) reduce or adjust the amount payable to Her Majesty in respect of a transaction affecting absolutely surrendered lands, designated lands or other lands in a reserve or the rate of interest payable thereon; and

(b) reduce or adjust the amount payable to the band by an Indian in respect of a loan made to the Indian from band funds.

R.S. 1985, c. 17 (4th Supp.), s. 9.

60. (1) Control over lands — The Governor in Council may at the request of a band grant to the band the right to exercise such control and management over lands in the reserve occupied by the band as the Governor in Council considers desirable.

(2) Withdrawal — The Governor in Council may at any time withdraw from a band a right conferred upon the band under subsection (1).

Management of Indian Moneys

61. (1) Indian moneys to be held for use and benefit — Indian moneys shall be expended only for the benefit of the Indians or bands for whose use and benefit in common the moneys are received or held, and subject to this Act and to the terms of any treaty or surrender, the Governor in Council may determine whether any purpose for which Indian moneys are used or are to be used is for the use and benefit of the band.

(2) Interest — Interest upon Indian moneys held in the Consolidated Revenue Fund shall be allowed at a rate to be fixed from time to time by the Governor in Council.

Case Law:

Section 61(1)

Desjarlais v. Can. (Min. of Indian Affairs & Nor. Dev.), [1988] 2 C.N.L.R. 62, (sub nom. *Sandy Bay Indian Band v. Can. (Min. of Indian Affairs & Nor. Dev.))* 18 F.T.R. 316 (T.D.)

This section reinforces the obligation of the Crown to look after Indian money.

Chisholm v. R., [1948] Ex. C.R. 370, [1948] 3 D.L.R. 797

The Crown is not liable to pay a just account due from a band to a creditor from money held by the Crown for the band.

Dir. of Recovery & Maintenance v. W.S. (1983), 24 Alta. L.R. (2d) 133, [1983] 3 C.N.L.R. 65 (Prov. Ct.)

Oil and gas royalties paid by companies from the production on native reserve lands and governed by the *Indian Oil and Gas Act* are Indian moneys under this section.

62. Capital and revenue — All Indian moneys derived from the sale of surrendered lands or the sale of capital assets of a band shall be deemed to be capital moneys of the band and all Indian moneys other than capital moneys shall be deemed to be revenue moneys of the band.

63. Payments to Indians — Notwithstanding the *Financial Administration Act,* where moneys to which an Indian is entitled are paid to a superintendent under any lease or agreement made under this Act, the superintendent may pay the moneys to the Indian.

64. (1) Expenditure of capital moneys with consent — With the consent of the council of a band, the Minister may authorize and direct the expenditure of capital moneys of the band

(a) to distribute per capita to the members of the band an amount not exceeding fifty per cent of the capital moneys of the band derived from the sale of surrendered lands;

(b) to construct and maintain roads, bridges, ditches and water courses on the reserves or on surrendered lands;

(c) to construct and maintain outer boundary fences on reserves;

(d) to purchase land for use by the band as a reserve or as an addition to a reserve;

(e) to purchase for the band the interest of a member of the band in lands on a reserve;

(f) to purchase livestock and farm implements, farm equipment, or machinery for the band;

(g) to construct and maintain on or in connection with a reserve such permanent improvements or works as in the opinion of the Minister will be of permanent value to the band or will constitute a capital investment;

(h) to make to members of the band, for the purpose of promoting the welfare of the band, loans not exceeding one-half of the total value of

(i) the chattels owned by the borrower, and

(ii) the land with respect to which he holds or is eligible to receive a Certificate of Possession,

and may charge interest and take security therefor;

(i) to meet expenses necessarily incidental to the management of lands on a reserve, surrendered lands and any band property;

(j) to construct houses for members of the band, to make loans to members of the band for building purposes with or without security and to provide for the guarantee of loans made to members of the band for building purposes; and

(k) for any other purpose that in the opinion of the Minister is for the benefit of the band.

(2) Expenditure of capital moneys in accordance with by-laws — The Minister may make expenditures out of the capital moneys of a band in accordance with by-laws made pursuant to paragraph 81(p.3) for the purpose of making payments to any person whose name was deleted from the Band List of the band in an amount not exceeding one per capita share of the capital moneys.

R.S. 1985, c. 32 (1st Supp.), s. 10.

Case Law:

Section 64(1)(a)

Fox v. Peterson Livestock Ltd., [1982] 2 W.W.R. 204, 17 Alta. L.R. (2d) 311, 131 D.L.R. (3d) 716, 35 A.R. 471 (C.A.)

Moneys that have not been declared payable under this section are only an expectation of a gratuitous distribution by the Minister. Not being due or accruing due, such moneys are not subject to an equitable execution.

Dir. of Recovery & Maintenance v. W.S. (1983), 24 Alta. L.R. (2d) 133, [1983] 3 C.N.L.R. 65 (Prov. Ct.)

Oil and gas royalties earned by a band may be paid as per capita distribution to band members. The withholding of a portion or all of such money to infant band members is a policy only, not contained in statute or regulations, and does not have the force of law.

Section 64(1)(k)

Can. (Min. of Indian Affairs & Nor. Dev.) v. Oromocto Indian Band, [1987] 4 C.N.L.R. 38, 77 N.B.R. (2d) 150, 195 A.P.R. 150 (Q.B.)

The Minister must approve expenditures of capital money, and a band may not pay the chief and councillors large fees for negotiating a land claims settlement without specific approval for the same.

64.1 (1) Limitation in respect of paragraphs 6(1)(c), (d) and (e) — A person who has received an amount that exceeds one thousand dollars under paragraph 15(1)(a), as it read immediately prior to April 17, 1985, or under any former provision of this Act relating to the same subject-matter as that paragraph, by reason of ceasing to be a member of a band in the circumstances set out in paragraph 6(1)(c), (d) or (e) is not entitled to receive an amount under paragraph 64(1)(a) until such time as the aggregate of all amounts that he would, but for this subsection, have received under paragraph 64(1)(a) is equal to the amount by which the amount that he received under paragraph 15(1)(a), as it read immediately prior to April 17, 1985, or under any former provision of this Act relating to the same subject-matter as that paragraph, exceeds one thousand dollars, together with any interest thereon.

(2) Additional limitation — Where the council of a band makes a by-law under paragraph 81(p.4) bringing this subsection into effect, a person who has received an amount that exceeds one thousand dollars under paragraph 15(1)(a), as it read immediately prior to April 17, 1985, or under any former provision of this Act relating to the same subject-matter as that paragraph, by reason of ceasing to be a member of the band in the circumstances set out in paragraph 6(1)(c), (d) or (e) is not entitled to receive any benefit afforded to members of the band as individuals as a result of the expenditure of Indian moneys under paragraphs 64(1)(b) to (k), subsection 66(1) or subsection 69(1) until the amount by which the amount so received exceeds one thousand dollars, together with any interest thereon, has been repaid to the band.

(3) Regulations — The Governor in Council may make regulations prescribing the manner of determining interest for the purpose of subsections (1) and (2).

R.S. 1985, c. 32 (1st Supp.), s. 11.

Case Law: *Barry v. Garden River Band of Ojibways* (1997), 33 O.R. (3d) 782, 147 D.L.R. (4th) 615 (C.A.)

As part of a land claim settlement, the First Nation set aside $1 million for a per capita distribution to members of the Band. A dispute developed over two issues: the repayment of moneys paid out to women who were enfranchised before 1985 (section 64.1 of the Indian Act) and the fiduciary duty of the Band Council to make payments to all members of the Band.

In this case, the women who had been involuntarily enfranchised before 1985 had been paid out less than $1,000 of the Band moneys when they lost status. Although they were not required to pay this money back upon regaining status under Bill C-31, the Band proposed to deduct the payments from the amounts to be distributed under the land claim settlement. The court held that the Band had no authority to recoup the moneys paid out upon enfranchisement because the amount was less than $1,000.00.

65. Expenditure of capital — The Minister may pay from capital moneys

(a) compensation to an Indian in an amount that is determined in accordance with this Act to be payable to him in respect of land compulsorily taken from him for band purposes, and

(b) expenses incurred to prevent or suppress grass or forest fires or to protect the property of Indians in cases of emergency.

66. (1) Expenditure of revenue moneys with consent of band — With the consent of the council of a band, the Minister may authorize and direct the expenditure of revenue moneys for any purpose that in his opinion will promote the general progress and welfare of the band or any member of the band.

(2) Minister may direct expenditure — The Minister may make expenditures out of the revenue moneys of the band to assist sick, disabled, aged or destitute Indians of the band and to provide for the burial of deceased indigent members of the band and to provide for the payment of contributions under the *Employment Insurance Act* on behalf of employed persons who are paid in respect of their employment out of moneys of the band.

(2.1) Idem — The Minister may make expenditures out of the revenue moneys of a band in accordance with by-laws made pursuant to paragraph 81(l)(p.3) for the purpose of making payments to any person whose name was deleted from the Band List of the band in an amount not exceeding one per capita share of the revenue moneys.

(3) Expenditure of revenue moneys with authority of Minister — The Minister may authorize the expenditure of revenue moneys of the band for all or any of the following purposes, namely:

(a) for the destruction of noxious weeds and the prevention of the spreading or prevalence of insects, pests or diseases that may destroy or injure vegetation on Indian reserves;

(b) to prevent, mitigate and control the spread of diseases on reserves, whether or not the diseases are infectious or communicable;

(c) to provide for the inspection of premises on reserves and the destruction, alteration or renovation thereof;

(d) to prevent overcrowding of premises on reserves used as dwellings;

(e) to provide for sanitary conditions in private premises on reserves as well as in public places on reserves; and

(f) for the construction and maintenance of boundary fences.

R.S. 1985, c. 32 (1st Supp.), s. 12.

67. Recovery of certain expenses — Where money is expended by Her Majesty for the purpose of raising or collecting Indian moneys, the Minister may authorize the recovery of the amount so expended from the moneys of the band.

68. Maintenance of dependants — Where the Minister is satisfied that an Indian

(a) has deserted his spouse or family without sufficient cause,

(b) has conducted himself in such a manner as to justify the refusal of his spouse or family to live with him, or

(c) has been separated by imprisonment from his spouse and family,

the Minister may order that payments of any annuity or interest money to which that Indian is entitled shall be applied to the support of the spouse or family or both the spouse and family of that Indian.

R.S. 1985 (1st Supp.), c. 32, s. 13.

Commentary: The case law appears to be clear that provincial legislation on support payments is not inconsistent with this section, and applies to Indians on reserves. For cases which find that a provincial Director of Enforcement Maintenance may garnishee wages of a spouse residing on reserve, see section 89.

Case Law: *Re Baptiste; Dir. of Maintenance and Recovery v. Potts* (1979), 20 A.R. 196, [1979] 6 W.W.R. 560, 12 R.F.L. (2d) 144, 102 D.L.R. (3d) 553 (Q.B.).

Section 68 gives the Minister a discretionary power to divert only "annuity or interest money" and does not give a power to attach other sources of income. A provincial statute such as the *Alberta Maintenance and Recovery Act*, provides means whereby a mother may obtain support from the putative father's other resources. A mother may use such provincial legislation, which is not in conflict with this limited section, and such law is of general application in the province and applies under s. 88.

69. (1) Management of revenue moneys by band — The Governor in Council may by order permit a band to control, manage and expend in whole or in part its revenue moneys and may amend or revoke any such order.

(2) Regulations — The Governor in Council may make regulations to give effect to subsection (1) and may declare therein the extent to which this Act and the *Financial Administration Act* shall not apply to a band to which an order made under subsection (1) applies.

Related Provisions: Bands that may control, manage and expend in whole or in part their revenue moneys are set out in the *Indian Bands Revenue Moneys Regulations*, C.R.C. 1978, c. 953, as amended.

Loans to Indians

70. (1) **Loans to Indians** — The Minister of Finance may from time to time authorize advances to the Minister out of the Consolidated Revenue Fund of such sums of money as the Minister may require to enable him

(a) to make loans to bands, groups of Indians or individual Indians for the purchase of farm implements, machinery, livestock, motor vehicles, fishing equipment, seed grain, fencing materials, materials to be used in native handicrafts, any other equipment, and gasoline and other petroleum products, or for the making of repairs or the payment of wages, or for the clearing and breaking of land within reserves,

(b) to expend or to lend money for the carrying out of cooperative projects on behalf of Indians, or

(c) to provide for any other matter prescribed by the Governor in Council.

(2) **Regulations** — The Governor in Council may make regulations to give effect to subsection (1).

(3) **Accounting** — Expenditures that are made under subsection (1) shall be accounted for in the same manner as public moneys.

(4) **Repayment** — The Minister shall pay to the Receiver General all moneys that he receives from bands, groups of Indians or individual Indians by way of repayments of loans made under subsection (1).

(5) **Limitation** — The total amount of outstanding advances to the Minister under this section shall not at any one time exceed six million and fifty thousand dollars.

(6) **Report to Parliament** — The Minister shall within fifteen days after the termination of each fiscal year or, if Parliament is not then in session, within fifteen days after the commencement of the next ensuing session, lay before Parliament a report setting out the total number and amount of loans made under subsection (1) during that year.

Farms

71. (1) **Minister may operate farms** — The Minister may operate farms on reserves and may employ such persons as he considers necessary to instruct Indians in farming and may purchase and distribute without charge, pure seed to Indian farmers.

(2) **Application of profits** — The Minister may apply any profits that result from the operation of farms pursuant to subsection (1) on reserves to extend farming operations on the reserves or to make loans to Indians to enable them to engage in farming or other agricultural operations or he may apply such profits in any way that he considers to be desirable to promote the progress and development of the Indians.

Treaty Money

72. Treaty money payable out of C.R.F. — Moneys that are payable to Indians or to Indian bands under a treaty between Her Majesty and the band and for the payment of which the Government of Canada is responsible, may be paid out of the Consolidated Revenue Fund.

Regulations

73. (1) **Regulations** — The Governor in Council may make regulations

(a) for the protection and preservation of fur-bearing animals, fish and other game on reserves;

(b) for the destruction of noxious weeds and prevention of the spreading or prevalence of insects, pests or diseases that may destroy or injure vegetation on Indian reserves;

(c) for the control of the speed, operation and parking of vehicles on roads within reserves;

(d) for the taxation, control and destruction of dogs and for the protection of sheep on reserves;

(e) for the operation, supervision and control of pool rooms, dance halls and other places of amusement on reserves;

(f) to prevent, mitigate and control the spread of diseases on reserves, whether or not the diseases are infectious or communicable;

(g) to provide medical treatment and health services for Indians;

(h) to provide compulsory hospitalization and treatment for infectious disease among Indians;

(i) to provide for the inspection of premises on reserves and the destruction, alteration or renovation thereof;

(j) to prevent overcrowding of premises on reserves used as dwellings;

(k) to provide for sanitary conditions in private premises on reserves as well as in public places on reserves;

(l) for the construction and maintenance of boundary fences; and

(m) for empowering and authorizing the council of a band to borrow money for band projects or housing purposes and providing for the making of loans out of moneys so borrowed to members of the band for housing purposes.

(2) The Governor in Council may prescribe the penalty, not exceeding a fine of one thousand dollars or imprisonment for a term not exceeding three months, or both, that may be imposed on summary conviction for contravention of a regulation made under subsection (1).

(3) The Governor in Council may make orders and regulations to carry out the purposes and provisions of this Act.

Related Provisions: See: *Indian Reserve Traffic Regulations*, C.R.C. 1978, c. 959, *infra*; *Indian Reserve Waste Disposal Regulations*, C.R.C. 1978, c. 960, *infra*.

Elections of Chiefs and Band Councils

74. (1) Elected councils — Whenever he deems it advisable for the good government of a band, the Minister may declare by order that after a day to be named therein the council of the band, consisting of a chief and councillors, shall be selected by elections to be held in accordance with this Act.

(2) Composition of council — Unless otherwise ordered by the Minister, the council of a band in respect of which an order has been made under subsection (1) shall consist of one chief, and one councillor for every one hundred members of the band, but the number of councillors shall not be less than two nor more than twelve and no band shall have more than one chief.

(3) Regulations — The Governor in Council may, for the purposes of giving effect to subsection (1), make orders or regulations to provide

(a) that the chief of a band shall be elected by

(i) a majority of the votes of the electors of the band, or

(ii) a majority of the votes of the elected councillors of the band from among themselves, but the chief so elected shall remain a councillor, and

(b) that the councillors of a band shall be elected by

(i) a majority of the votes of the electors of the band, or

(ii) a majority of the votes of the electors of the band in the electoral section in which the candidate resides and that he proposes to represent on the council of the band.

(4) Electoral sections — A reserve shall for voting purposes consist of one electoral section, except that where the majority of the electors of a band who were present and voted at a referendum or a special meeting held and called for the purpose in accordance with the regulations have decided that the reserve should for voting purposes be divided into electoral sections and the Minister so recommends, the Governor in Council may make orders or regulations to provide that the reserve shall for voting purposes be divided into not more than six electoral sections containing as nearly as may be an equal number of Indians eligible to vote and to provide for the manner in which electoral sections so established shall be distinguished or identified.

Commentary: Sections 74–80 only apply to councils that are the subject of a declaration under subsection 74(1). These Bands are listed in the *Indian Bands Council Order*, SOR/97-138.

Cases related to councils that are elected by custom are listed under section 2(1) under "Council of the Band".

Case Law: *Isaac v. Davey* (1977), 77 D.L.R. (3d) 481, [1977] 2 S.C.R. 897, 9 C.N.L.C. 134

On January 14, 1793, Governor Simcoe provided a patent of the Grand River lands to the Six Nations. Until 1924, the Six Nations were governed by a hereditary council. In 1924, the federal government declared that the Band should have *Indian Act* elections pursuant to Orders in Council in 1924 and 1951.

The traditional people, who wanted to return to the hereditary system, blocked the council elected under the *Indian Act* from entering the Council House. The court found that the Orders in Council were valid, and observed that the declaration itself may bring the Six Nations under the definition of "Band" found in section 2 of the *Indian Act*.

Badger v. Canada (1990), [1991] 1 F.C. 191, [1991] 2 C.N.L.R. 17, 38 F.T.R. 43, affirmed (1992), 57 F.T.R. 311n (C.A.)

The predecessor to section 74 of the *Indian Act*, (S.C. 1951,c.29,s.73) provided that an order from the Governor in Council was necessary to bring Band elections under the *Indian Act*. Such an order was made in 1952. In 1956, the section was amended to permit the Minister to make such an order. In 1982, the Band voted to return to Band custom elections, and the Deputy Minister of Indian Affairs issued an instrument returning the Band to custom elections. In 1986, a Band member challenged the authority of the Deputy Minister to make that decision.

The court found that the Minister could now exercise the authority which the Governor in Council had previously exercised. In addition, under section 3, the Minister had the authority to delegate the decision to the Deputy Minister. The court held:

> The power of the Minister to issue or repeal a declaration under present s.74(1) with respect to bringing a band's election under the *Indian Act* is in no way conditioned on the holding of a referendum or the adoption of a band council resolution. While it is no doubt highly important that the Minister have regard to the views of the Band, to the extent that those can be ascertained, the Act in no way requires some formal expression of those views such as by referendum or band council resolution. [F.T.R. at p. 47]

Six Nations Traditional Hereditary Chiefs v. Canada (Minister of Indian & Northern Affairs) (1991), 43 F.T.R. 132, [1992] 3 C.N.L.R. 156 (T.D.)

A referendum scheduled by the Minister to determine a dispute over the manner of conducting elections was within the Minister's discretion. The Minister was not illegally delegating authority to the voters, since the ultimate purpose was to provide the Minister with information.

Related Provisions: Also see: *Indian Band Election Regulations*, C.R.C. 1978, c. 952; *Indian Band Council Procedure Regulations*, C.R.C. 1978, c. 950; *Indian Band Council Borrowing Regulations*, C.R.C. 1978, c. 949; *Indian Referendum Regulations*, C.R.C. 1978, c. 957; *Indian Band Council Election Order* SOR/97-138.

75. (1) Eligibility — No person other than an elector who resides in a section may be nominated for the office of councillor to represent that section on the council of the band.

(2) Nomination — No person may be a candidate for election as chief or councillor unless his nomination is moved and seconded by persons who are themselves eligible to be nominated.

Case Law: *Goodswimmer v. Canada (Minister of Indian Affairs & Northern Development)*, [1995] 3 C.N.L.R. 72, 93 F.T.R. 79, 180 N.R. 184 (C.A.)appeal to S.C.C. quashed because the issue was moot, 208 N.R. 302, [1997] 1 S.C.R. 309

The members of the Sturgeon Lake Indian Band elected a chief who was not registered under the *Indian Act*, but who was married to a member of the Band. The court found that the chief need not be an "elector" in order to be a chief, although it was clear that councillors must be "electors".

76. (1) Regulations governing elections — The Governor in Council may make orders and regulations with respect to band elections and, without restricting the generality of the foregoing, may make regulations with respect to

(a) meetings to nominate candidates;

(b) the appointment and duties of electoral officers;

(c) the manner in which voting shall be carried out;

(d) election appeals; and

(e) the definition of residence for the purpose of determining the eligibility of voters.

(2) Secrecy of voting — The regulations made under paragraph (1)(c) shall make provision for secrecy of voting.

Case Law: *Walkem v. Draney*, [1981] 2 F.C. 287, [1982] 3 C.N.L.R. 178 (T.D.)

It was held that neither the regulations nor the *Indian Act* requires that an electoral officer be a person qualified to vote in accordance with s. 77 [re-en. R.S.C. 1985 (1st Supp.), c. 32, s. 14], even when the electoral officer has the duty to cast a vote to break a tie.

Perley v. Higgins (1986), 56 N.B.R. (2d) 6, 146 A.P.R. 6, [1986] 1 C.N.L.R. 45 (N.B. Q.B.)

The District Manager has the authority to call a special meeting of council in accordance with the requirements of the regulations. A majority of the council constitutes a quorum and matters are to be decided by a majority vote.

Related Provisions: Indian Band Election Regulations, C.R.C. 1978, c. 952.

77. (1) Eligibility of voters for chief — A member of a band who has attained the age of eighteen years and is ordinarily resident on the reserve is qualified to vote for a person nominated to be chief of the band and, where the reserve for voting purposes consists of one section, to vote for persons nominated as councillors.

(2) Councillor — A member of a band who is of the full age of eighteen years and is ordinarily resident in a section that has been established for voting purposes is qualified to vote for a person nominated to be councillor to represent that section.

R.S. 1985, c. 32 (1st Supp.), s. 14.

Case Law: *Corbiere v. Canada (Minister of Indian & Northern Affairs)* (1996), [1997] 1 F.C. 689, 41 C.R.R. (2d) 1, 122 F.T.R. 319 (note), 206 N.R. 85, 142 D.L.R. (4th) 122 (C.A.)leave to appeal to S.C.C. granted (April 24, 1997), Doc. 25708 (S.C.C.)

(Note that this decision has been stayed pending an appeal to the Supreme Court of Canada, 206 N.R. 122, [1996] F.C. No.1620)

Like many Bands, the membership of Batchewana grew when the *Indian Act* was changed by Bill C-31 in 1985. By 1991, only 468 members lived on reserve, while 958 lived off reserve. The off reserve members were not allowed to vote. The court found that this provision discriminated against them, and breached section 15 of the *Constitution Act, 1982*. The court granted a constitutional exemption for the Batchewana Band only: this section was not struck down generally.

78. (1) Tenure of office — Subject to this section, chiefs and councillors hold office for two years.

(2) Vacancy — The office of chief or councillor becomes vacant when

    (a) the person who holds that office

        (i) is convicted of an indictable offence,

        (ii) dies or resigns his office, or

        (iii) is or becomes ineligible to hold office by virtue of this Act; or

    (b) the Minister declares that in his opinion the person who holds that office

        (i) is unfit to continue in office by reason of his having been convicted of an offence,

        (ii) has been absent from meetings of the council for three consecutive meetings without being authorized to do so, or

        (iii) was guilty, in connection with an election, of corrupt practice, accepting a bribe, dishonesty or malfeasance.

(3) Disqualification — The Minister may declare a person who ceases to hold office by virtue of subparagraph (2)(b)(iii) to be ineligible to be a candidate for chief or councillor for a period not exceeding six years.

(4) Special election — Where the office of chief or councillor becomes vacant more than three months before the date when another election would ordinarily be held, a special election may be held in accordance with this Act to fill the vacancy.

Case Law: *Crow v. Blood Band Indian Council* (1996), 107 F.T.R. 270, [1997] 3 C.N.L.R. 76 (T.D.)

A member of Council was removed pursuant to the Blood Custom Election Bylaw, and was barred from running in the next election. The court upheld the Custom Election Bylaw and held that section 78 of the *Indian Act* did not apply to custom elections.

Jock v. R. (1991), 41 F.T.R. 189, (sub nom. *Jock v. Canada (Minister of Indian & Northern Affairs)*) [1991] 2 F.C. 355, (sub nom. *Jock v. Canada*) [1992] 1 C.N.L.R. 103

An Indian band council is a federal board within the meaning of ss. 2 and 18 of the *Federal Court Act* and hence the Trial Division of the Federal Court has jurisdiction to grant a writ of *quo warranto* against individual members of the council. However, it declined to exercise that power when band traditionalists sought to challenge the election held for Grand Chief and band council. By seeking the relief two years after the election, the applicants were guilty of undue delay, and were not entitled to *quo warranto*. In addition, if the applicants were disqualified from pursuing internal election appeal procedures, it was their own fault.

Sault v. Mississaugas of the New Credit Indian Band Council, [1989] 2 F.C. 701, [1990] 1 C.N.L.R. 140, 25 F.T.R. 241 (T.D.)

A band councillor can only be suspended in accordance with this section of the *Indian Act*.

Smith v. R., [1972] F.C. 561, 28 D.L.R. (3d) 93 (T.D.)

Parliament intended to provide a system of periodic general elections to elect an entire council, with special elections under s. 78(4) to elect persons to fill vacancies. The position of chief or councillor may become vacant under ss. 78(2), 79 or by other provisions. The term of a person elected to fill a vacant position does not carry on beyond the next council general election.

79. Governor in Council may set aside election — The Governor in Council may set aside the election of a chief or a councillor on the report of the Minister that he is satisfied that

(a) there was corrupt practice in connection with the election;

(b) there was a violation of this Act that might have affected the result of the election; or

(c) a person nominated to be a candidate in the election was ineligible to be a candidate.

Case Law: *Bear v. Can. (Min. of Indian & Nor. Affairs)* (1989), 33 Admin. L.R. 147, [1989] 1 C.N.L.R. 45 (Fed. C.A.)

Under s. 79(*b*) it is the Governor in Council's decision which is legally binding. The Minister's report has no legally binding operative effect of its own and, therefore, the court does not have jurisdiction to set aside the Minister's decision and report.

Baptiste v. Goodstoney Indian Band (1989), 31 F.T.R. 282, (sub nom. *Stoney Indian Tribe v. Goodstoney Indian Band)* [1991] 1 C.N.L.R. 34

The applicants sought a declaration setting aside the election of band chiefs and councillors, on the grounds that the elections were not in accordance with tribal customs. However, an interim injunction preventing the chiefs and councillors from performing any functions relating to their elected duties was refused because there were no allegations that the officials were misconducting themselves in their official capacities.

80. Regulations respecting band and council meetings — The Governor in Council may make regulations with respect to band meetings and council meetings and, without restricting the generality of the foregoing, may make regulations with respect to

(a) presiding officers at such meetings;

(b) notice of such meetings;

(c) the duties of any representative of the Minister at such meetings; and

(d) the number of persons required at the meeting to constitute a quorum.

Commentary: The Chief and members of council have a duty as fiduciaries to the Band as a whole (see annotations under section 2(1) "Council"). Therefore, they must avoid conflicts of interests.

Case Law: *Williams Lake Indian Band v. Abbey* (1992), , (sub nom. *Gilbert v. Abbey)* [1992] 4 C.N.L.R. 21 (B.C. S.C.)

The court ordered the repayment of student loans and private school tuition fees which the defendant had received from the Band during her term as Chief.

> Chief Abbey upon the band council considering the payment of any account in which she had an interest was obliged to make full disclosure of that interest to the band council. She was obliged to not participate in the band council's discussions with respect to any of the transactions in which she had an interest, and by participate I refer to her participating in the discussions preceding the voting and to her voting on any motion dealing with any transaction in which she had an interest. [C.N.L.R. at p.24]

— See also *Leonard v. Gottfriedson* (1981), 21 B.C.L.R. 326, [1982] 1 C.N.L.R. 60 (B.C. S.C.)

Related Provisions: *Indian Band Council Procedure Regulations*, C.R.C. 1978, c. 950.

Powers of the Council

81. (1) By-laws — The council of a band may make by-laws not inconsistent with this Act or with any regulation made by the Governor in Council or the Minister, for any or all of the following purposes, namely:

(a) to provide for the health of residents on the reserve and to prevent the spreading of contagious and infectious diseases;

(b) the regulation of traffic;

(c) the observance of law and order;

(d) the prevention of disorderly conduct and nuisances;

(e) the protection against and prevention of trespass by cattle and other domestic animals, the establishment of pounds, the appointment of pound-keepers, the regulation of their duties and the provision for fees and charges for their services;

(f) the construction and maintenance of water courses, roads, bridges, ditches, fences and other local works;

(g) the dividing of the reserve or a portion thereof into zones and the prohibition of the construction or maintenance of any class of buildings or the carrying on of any class of business, trade or calling in any such zone;

(h) the regulation of the construction, repair and use of buildings, whether owned by the band or by individual members of the band;

(i) the survey and allotment of reserve lands among the members of the band and the establishment of a register of Certificates of Possession and Certificates of Occupation relating to allotments and the setting apart of reserve lands for common use, if authority therefor has been granted under section 60;

(j) the destruction and control of noxious weeds;

(k) the regulation of bee-keeping and poultry raising;

(l) the construction and regulation of the use of public wells, cisterns, reservoirs and other water supplies;

(m) the control and prohibition of public games, sports, races, athletic contests and other amusements;

(n) the regulation of the conduct and activities of hawkers, peddlers or others who enter the reserve to buy, sell or otherwise deal in wares or merchandise;

(o) the preservation, protection and management of fur-bearing animals, fish and other game on the reserve;

(p) the removal and punishment of persons trespassing upon the reserve or frequenting the reserve for prohibited purposes;

(p.1) the residence of band members and other persons on the reserve;

(p.2) to provide for the rights of spouses and children who reside with members of the band on the reserve with respect to any matter in relation to which the council may make by-laws in respect of members of the band;

(p.3) to authorize the Minister to make payments out of capital or revenue moneys to persons whose names were deleted from the Band List of the band;

(p.4) to bring subsection 10(3) or 64.1(2) into effect in respect of the band;

(q) with respect to any matter arising out of or ancillary to the exercise of powers under this section; and

(r) the imposition on summary conviction of a fine not exceeding one thousand dollars or imprisonment for a term not exceeding thirty days, or both, for violation of a by-law made under this section.

(2) **Power to restrain by order where conviction entered** — Where any by-law of a band is contravened and a conviction entered, in addition to any other remedy and to any penalty imposed by the by-law, the court in which the conviction has been entered, and any court of competent jurisdiction thereafter, may make an order prohibiting the continuation or repetition of the offence by the person convicted.

(3) **Power to restrain by court action** — Where any by-law of a band passed is contravened, in addition to any other remedy and to any penalty imposed by the by-law, such contravention may be restrained by court action at the instance of the band council.

R.S. 1985, c. 32 (1st Supp.), s. 15.

Commentary: By-laws made under this section may supersede conflicting federal legislation, such as the *Fisheries Act*, as well as provincial legislation incorporated through section 88.

For cases on the legal status of Band Councils, see under section 2(1), "Band".

Case Law:

Section 81(1)

R. v. Sam, [1986] 1 C.N.L.R. 129 (B.C. Prov. Ct.)

A band by-law has no effect outside the reserve.

R. v. Bear (1982), 35 N.B.R. (2d) 181, 88 A.P.R. 181, [1982] 3 C.N.L.R. 78 (Q.B.)

By-laws enacted under this section and coming within s. 82 are statutory instruments within the meaning of the *Statutory Instruments Act*, 1970–71–72 (Can.), c. 38 [now R.S.C. 1985, c. S-22], but are exempt from publication in the Canada Gazette (*Statutory Instruments Regulations*, C.R.C. 1978, c. 1509). They are not instruments of which judicial notice is required to be taken.

Section 81(1)(c)

Eastmain Band v. Gilpin, [1988] 3 C.N.L.R. 15, [1988] R.J.Q. 1987 (Prov. Ct.)

A curfew by-law may provide for a curfew for those under 16 years.

Section 81(1)(m)

St. Mary's Indian Band v. Canada (Minister of Indian Affairs & Northern Development), [1995] 3 F.C. 461, 127 D.L.R. (4th) 686, 100 F.T.R. 148 (T.D.)affirmed (1996), 198 N.R. 394, 136 D.L.R. (4th) 767, 118 F.T.R. 318 (note), [1997] 1 C.N.L.R. 206 (C.A.), leave to S.C.C. refused (February 20, 1997) Doc. 25537 (S.C.C.)

The court supported the Minister's disallowance of a by-law to regulate gambling on reserve. First, the court held that Parliament had not intended this provision to cover gambling. Second, the Criminal Code provisions on gaming were more specific than the *Indian Act* by-law provisions, so that, as a matter of statutory interpretation, the Criminal Code provisions took precedence.

R. v. Gladue (1987), 30 C.C.C. (3d) 308, [1987] 4 C.N.L.R. 92 (Alta. Prov. Ct.)

This subsection does not give a band power to control lotteries or gambling.

Section 81(1)(o)

R. v. Lewis, [1996] 5 W.W.R. 348, 19 B.C.L.R. (3d) 244, 105 C.C.C. (3d) 52, 3133 D.L.R. (4th) 700 (S.C.C.)

A by-law on fishing passed under this section will offer a defence to a charge under the federal *Fisheries Act.* The court states,

> I believe it is clear that Parliament's intention in enacting s. 81(1) as a whole and in particular paragraph (o) was to provide a mechanism by which Band Councils could assume management over certain activities within the territorial limits of their constituencies. [W.W.R. p. 376]

In this case, however, the fishing occurred on the Squamish River. The court held that the river was not part of the reserve; and that the by-law did not extend to waters adjacent to the reserve. Three members of the Squamish Nation were convicted under the *Fisheries Act.*

R. v. Nikal, [1996] 5 W.W.R. 305, 19 B.C.L.R. (3d) 201, 105 C.C.C. (3d) 481, 196 N.R. 1, 133 D.L.R. (4th) 658 (S.C.C.)

The Bulkley River flowed through the Moricetown First Nation reserve. The court held that the *ad medium filum aquae* doctrine did not operate to make the river part of the reserve, and that the First Nation did not have an exclusive fishery. Therefore, the Moricetown fishing by-law did not apply to fishing on the river.

R. v. Vidulich (1988), 22 B.C.L.R. (2d) 238, [1988] 2 C.N.L.R. 145 (Co. Ct.), reversed on other grounds 37 B.C.L.R. (2d) 391, [1989] 3 C.N.L.R. 167 (C.A.)

A band by-law might be able to allow the sale of fish to non-Indians.

R. v. Jimmy, [1987] 5 W.W.R. 755, 15 B.C.L.R. (2d) 145, [1987] 3 C.N.L.R. 77 (C.A.)

A by-law approved by the Minister may regulate fishing on a reserve and offer a defence to an Indian charged under the *Fisheries Act.*

R. v. Billy, [1982] 1 C.N.L.R. 99 (B.C. C.A.)

This paragraph alone, without evidence of a by-law of a band council, is not inconsistent with the *Fisheries Regulations.*

R. v. Alfred, [1994] 3 C.N.L.R. 88 (B.C. S.C.)

A by-law made under s. 81(o) purported to permit the sale of fish. The accused sold fish caught on reserve to a person off reserve. The court held that the by-law could not operate off reserve.

R. v. Baker, [1983] 4 C.N.L.R. 73 (B.C. Co. Ct.)

A by-law becomes a statutory instrument and has the force of law and is effective within the boundaries of the reserve. When a properly drafted and enacted by-law is inconsistent with a federal law, such as the *Fisheries Regulations,* the application of the federal law ceases at the boundaries of the reserve.

R. v. Ward, [1989] 2 C.N.L.R. 142, 45 C.C.C. (3d) 280, 93 N.B.R. (2d) 370, 238 A.P.R. 370 (N.B.C.A.)leave to appeal to S.C.C. refused (1989), 101 N.R. 235n, 92 N.B.R. (2d) 360n, 236 A.P.R. 360n (S.C.C.)

The validity of a section of a by-law is to be determined by examining the by-law as a whole to determine its purpose. A section that allowed unlimited fishing by any means and which could not be categorized as being for the preservation, protection and management of fish on the reserve, was saved by reference to other sections in the by-law which did have those objects.

Section 81(1)(p)

Gingrich v. R. (1958), 31 C.R. 306, 29 W.W.R. 471, 122 C.C.C. 279 (Alta. C.A.)

The Act does not define "trespassing", so the common law must be looked at for a definition. The powers of council are not to decide what constitutes trespassing, but are limited to removing and punishing trespassers:

> In other words the council cannot by establishing a system of permits to be given to individual persons to go on the Reserve, create the offence of trespass by those who enter the Reserve without such a permit. There must first be a trespass before the power of the council to remove and punish can be exercised. [C.C.C. p. 280]

Section 81(p.1)

Six Nations of the Grand River Band Council v. Henderson (1996), [1997] 1 C.N.L.R. 202 (Ont. Gen. Div.)

The Band Council passed a by-law which prohibited non-Indian spouses from residing on reserve. The court found that this by-law contravened section 15(1) of the *Charter of Rights and Freedoms*. However, the judge was persuaded that the socio-economic circumstances of the Band and the overcrowding were sufficient to justify the by-law under section 1 of the *Charter*.

Section 81(3)

Re Stacey and Montour (1981), 63 C.C.C. (2d) 61 (Que. C.A.)

> The powers conferred by s. 81 are first of all, powers to regulate, and to regulate only 'administrative statutes'. In other words, a band council has, in this area, the same sort of legislative powers as those possessed by the council of a municipal corporation. The power to give effect to regulations cannot extend beyond these administrative statutes; they are accessory and nothing more. [p. 68]

82. (1) Copies of by-laws to be sent to Minister — A copy of every by-law made under the authority of section 81 shall be forwarded by mail by the chief or a member of the council of the band to the Minister within four days after it is made.

(2) Effective date of by-law — A by-law made under section 81 comes into force forty days after a copy thereof is forwarded to the Minister pursuant to subsection (1), unless it is disallowed by the Minister within that period, but the Minister may declare the by-law to be in force at any time before the expiration of that period.

Case Law: *Twinn v. Can. (Min. of Indian Affairs & Nor. Dev.),* [1987] 3 F.C. 368, 26 Admin. L.R. 197, 10 F.T.R. 48, 37 D.L.R. (4th) 270, (sub nom. *Twinn v. McKnight)* [1988] 1 C.N.L.R. 159

There is no requirement that a notice of disallowance be sent to the band. The Minister is not required to give reasons for disallowance and such disallowance may be made by a delegate of the Minister.

83. (1) Money by-laws — Without prejudice to the powers conferred by section 81, the council of a band may, subject to the approval of the Minister, make by-laws for any or all of the following purposes, namely,

> **(a) subject to subsections (2) and (3), taxation for local purposes of land, or interests in land, in the reserve, including rights to occupy, possess or use land in the reserve;**

(a.1) the licensing of businesses, callings, trades and occupations;

(b) the appropriation and expenditure of moneys of the band to defray band expenses;

(c) the appointment of officials to conduct the business of the council, prescribing their duties and providing for their remuneration out of any moneys raised pursuant to paragraph (a);

(d) the payment of remuneration, in such amount as may be approved by the Minister, to chiefs and councillors, out of any moneys raised pursuant to paragraph (a);

(e) the enforcement of payment of amounts that are payable pursuant to this section, including arrears and interest;

(e.1) the imposition and recovery of interest on amounts that are payable pursuant to this section, where those amounts are not paid before they are due, and the calculation of that interest;

(f) the raising of money from band members to support band projects; and

(g) with respect to any matter arising out of or ancillary to the exercise of powers under this section.

(2) **Restrictions on expenditures** — An expenditure made out of moneys raised pursuant to subsection (1) must be so made under the authority of a by-law of the council of the band.

(3) **Appeals** — A by-law made under paragraph (1)(a) must provide an appeal procedure in respect of assessments made for the purposes of taxation under that paragraph.

(4) **Minister's approval** — The Minister may approve the whole or a part only of a by-law made under subsection (1).

(5) **Regulations re by-laws** — The Governor in Council may make regulations not inconsistent with this section respecting the exercise of the by-law making powers of bands under this section.

(6) **By-laws must be consistent with regulations** — A by-law made under this section remains in force only to the extent that it is consistent with the regulations made under subsection (5).

R.S. 1985, c. 17 (4th Supp.), s. 10.

Case Law: *Matsqui Indian Band v. Canadian Pacific Ltd.*, [1995] 1 S.C.R. 3, 26 Admin. L.R. 1, 122 D.L.R. (4th) 129, [1995] 2 C.N.L.R. 92, 85 F.T.R. 79n, 177 N.R. 325

The First Nation, pursuant to its by-laws assessed a tax on Canadian Pacific. The by-law provided that an appeal of the assessment could be made to a tribunal established under the by-law. The Supreme Court granted Canadian Pacific's request to by-pass the tribunal to bring their challenge to the by-law directly to the Federal Court. (See *Canadian Pacific Ltd. v. Matsqui Indian Band* below for result of hearing in Federal Court.)

In coming to their decision, six of the judges agreed that promoting the development of Aboriginal self-government was a policy objective which could be considered by the trial judge. They also agreed that the fact that band members might serve on the tribunal did not give rise to a reasonable apprehension of bias. However, two of the judges felt that the by-law did not do enough to ensure the independence of the tribunal.

Canadian Pacific Ltd. v. Matsqui Indian Band (1996), 134 D.L.R. (4th) 555, 111 F.T.R. 161, [1996] 3 F.C. 373 (Fed. T.D.)

The Matsqui First Nation passed a by-law imposing tax on railways which passed through their reserve. The court held that title to the lands vested in the railways through surrenders and authorized takings, so that the First Nation did not have the jurisdiction to impose the tax.

The court observed, however, that the by-laws were meant to enhance self-government, so that the by-laws could discriminate among various types of property, even though such power is not specifically mentioned in the *Indian Act*.

Osoyoos Indian Band v. Oliver (Town) (1997), 145 D.L.R. (4th) 552 (B.C. S.C.)

In 1957, land was expropriated from the Band for irrigation canal purposes under s. 35 of the *Indian Act*, R.S.C. 1952, c.149. The province was given management and control of the lands. In 1996, the Band attempted to impose a tax on this land.

The court held that the expropriated lands were either absolutely transferred to the province, or were transferred only until they were no longer needed for irrigation canal purposes. In either case, the lands were no longer reserve lands, and therefore were not "land, or interest in land, in the reserve" within s. 83. The fact that the mines and minerals may have been reserved for the Band did not affect the status of the surface rights.

Westbank First Nation v. British Columbia Hydro and Power Authority, [1997] 2 C.N.L.R. 229 (B.C. S.C.)

The First Nation passed a taxing by-law and taxed B.C. Hydro for the use of the right-of-way which crossed the Tsinstikeptum Reserve. The court held that B.C. Hydro was exempt from taxation because B.C. hydro was an agent of the provincial Crown, and, by virtue of section 125 of the *Constitution Act, 1867*, the province is immune from taxation.

Although B.C. Hydro does not pay taxes to the province or municipalities either, it does give annual grants roughly equivalent to the taxes to those bodies. The court noted that it was unfair that B.C Hydro did not pay anything to Bands, but felt that the matter could only be remedied by Parliament or the provincial Legislature.

84. Recovery of taxes — Where a tax that is imposed upon an Indian by or under the authority of a by-law under section 83 is not paid in accordance with the by-law, the Minister may pay the amount owing together with an amount equal to one-half of one per cent thereof out of moneys payable out of the funds of the band to the Indian.

85. [Repealed R.S. 1985, c. 17 (4th Supp.), s. 11.]

85.1 (1) By-laws relating to intoxicants — Subject to subsection (2), the council of a band may make by-laws

(a) **prohibiting the sale, barter, supply or manufacture of intoxicants on the reserve of the band;**

(b) **prohibiting any person from being intoxicated on the reserve;**

(c) **prohibiting any person from having intoxicants in his possession on the reserve; and**

(d) **providing for exceptions established pursuant to paragraph (b) or (c).**

(2) Consent of electors — A by-law may not be made under this section unless it is first assented to by a majority of the electors of the band who voted at a special meeting of the band called by the council of the band for the purpose of considering the by-law.

(3) Copies of by-laws to be sent to Minister — A copy of every by-law made under this section shall be sent by mail to the Minister by the chief or a member of the council of the band within four days after it is made.

(4) Offence — Every person who contravenes a by-law made under this section is guilty of an offence and is liable on summary conviction

    (a) in the case of a by-law made under paragraph (1)(a), to a fine of not more than one thousand dollars or to imprisonment for a term not exceeding six months or to both; and

    (b) in the case of a by-law made under paragraph (1)(b) or (c), to a fine of not more than one hundred dollars or to imprisonment for a term not exceeding three months or to both.

R.S. 1985, c. 32 (1st Supp.), s. 16.

Case Law: *Laforme v. Mississaugas of the New Credit First Nation Indian Band* (1996), 115 F.T.R. 303 (T.D.)

Marvin Laforme was a member of the First Nation, and operated a restaurant on the reserve. He challenged the wording of the by-law made by the Band pursuant to this section, arguing that certain provisions in the by-law were not authorized by the *Indian Act*. The by-law was upheld.

R. v. Campbell (1996), [1997] 1 C.N.L.R. 120, 5 C.R. (5th) 133, [1997] 2 W.W.R. 195, 112 C.C.C. (3d) 107, 41 C.R.R. (2d) 175, 142 D.L.R. (4th) 496, 113 Man. R. (2d) 288, 131 W.A.C. 288 (C.A.)

The accused lived off reserve. He was charged with violating a Moose Lake Indian Reserve by-law by being intoxicated on the reserve. The lawyer for the accused argued that the by-law was invalid because it was discriminatory. The court took the opposite view for three reasons.

    1. The law was validly made pursuant to s. 91(24) of the *Constitution Act, 1867*

    2. The law was freely adopted by the residents of Moose Lake: it was not imposed on them through Parliament

    3. It does not authorize a band to make different laws for different people, but only to make an enforceable policy choice for the governance of all people on the reserve. [C.N.L.R. p.125]

R. v. LaForme, [1996] 1 C.N.L.R. 193 (Ont. Prov. Div.)

Accused were selling intoxicants contrary to a by-law passed under section 85.1 of the *Indian Act*. The court found that the by-law did not contravene section 15 of the Charter.

The by-law contained a clause which was not authorized under the *Indian Act*, but that clause could be severed.

86. Proof — A copy of a by-law made by the council of a band under this Act, if it is certified to be a true copy by the superintendent, is evidence that the by-law was duly made by the council and approved by the Minister, without proof of the signature or official character of the superintendent, and no such by-law is invalid by reason of any defect in form.

Case Law: *R. v. Bear* (1983), 35 N.B.R. (2d) 181, 88 A.P.R. 181, [1983] 3 C.N.L.R. 78 (Q.B.)

A court cannot take judicial notice of an Indian band by-law. It is incumbent on the party relying on a by-law to adduce proof of it in admissible form. Section 86 requires that it be certified by the superintendent. Registration and certification as a true copy by the Privy Council are not sufficient as proof.

Taxation

87. (1) Property exempt from taxation — Notwithstanding any other Act of the Parliament of Canada or any Act of the legislature of a province, but subject to section 83, the following property is exempt from taxation, namely:

(a) the interest of an Indian or a band in reserve or surrendered lands; and

(b) the personal property of an Indian or band situated on a reserve.

(2) Idem — No Indian or band is subject to taxation in respect of the ownership, occupation, possession or use of any property mentioned in paragraph (*a*) or (*b*) or is otherwise subject to taxation in respect of any such property.

(3) Idem — No succession duty, inheritance tax or estate duty is payable on the death of any Indian in respect of any such property mentioned in paragraphs (1)(*a*) or (*b*) or the succession thereto if the property passes to an Indian, nor shall any such property be taken into account in determining the duty payable under the *Dominion Succession Duty Act*, chapter 89 of the Revised Statutes of Canada, 1952, or the tax payable under the *Estate Tax Act*, chapter E-9 of the Revised Statutes of Canada, 1970, on or in respect of other property passing to an Indian.

R.S., c. I-6, s. 87; 1980-81-82-83, c. 47, s. 25.

Commentary: Cases under this section overlap with cases under ss. 89 and 90, especially on the issue of personal property situated on a reserve.

Corporations are generally not considered as "Indians" and therefore cannot take advantage of these tax provisions (See cases under section 2(1) — "Indians")

Case Law:

General

Williams v. Canada, [1992] 1 S.C.R. 877, 41 C.C.E.L. 1, 90 D.L.R. (4th) 129, [1992] 3 C.N.L.R. 181, 92 D.T.C. 6320, [1992] 1 C.T.C. 225, 136 N.R. 161, 53 F.T.R. 104n

This case set out an important new "connecting factors" test in determining whether the property was "situated on a reserve." Mr. Justice Gonthier suggested that the proper approach was one which (at C.N.L.R. p. 190)

> analyzes the matter in terms of categories of property and types of taxation. For instance, connecting factors may have different relevance with regard to unemployment insurance benefits than in respect of employment income, or pension benefits. The first step is to identify the various connecting factors which are potentially relevant. These factors should then be analyzed to determine what weight they should be given in identifying the location of the property, in light of three considerations: (1) the purpose of the exemption under the *Indian Act*; (2) the type of property in question; and (3) the nature of the taxation of that property.

Canadian Pacific Ltd. v. Matsqui Indian Band, [1996] 3 F.C. 373, 134 D.L.R. (4th) 555, 111 F.T.R. 161 (T.D.)

The Matsqui First Nation passed a by-law imposing tax on railways which passed through their reserve. The court held that title to the lands vested in the railways through surrenders and authorized takings, so that the land was no longer reserve lands. Consequently, the First Nation did not have the jurisdiction to impose the tax.

The court, in passing, rejected the argument that s. 87 of the *Indian Act* exempted Band members from taxation by the Band under s. 83. The exemption under s. 87 applied only to taxation by outside governments.

Leighton v. B.C. (1989), 35 B.C.L.R. (2d) 216, [1989] 4 W.W.R. 654, 57 D.L.R. (4th) 657 (C.A.)

The word "situated" in s. 87(b) does not refer only to the permanent location of property. For the purposes of determining whether property is "situated on a reserve", the pattern of use and safe keeping of property must be examined to establish its paramount location. Neither tangible personal property nor its Indian owner can be taxed with respect to the use of the property off the reserve if the paramount location of the property remains on the reserve.

Metlakatla Ferry Service Ltd. v. R. (1987), 12 B.C.L.R. (2d) 308, 37 D.L.R. (4th) 322, [1987] 2 C.N.L.R. 95 (C.A.)

Section 87 should be liberally interpreted in favour of Indians and the term **"property"** should not be confined to tangible, physical property. The lease of a ferry was held to be not subject to tax. The court did not address the issue of whether a band-owned corporation was an Indian.

Brown v. R. in Right of B.C., [1980] 3 W.W.R. 360, 20 B.C.L.R. 64, 107 D.L.R. (3d) 705 (C.A.)

Section 87 is *intra vires* the federal Parliament's power to legislate under s. 91(24) of the *Constitution Act, 1867*, and does not encroach the provincial jurisdiction over property and civil rights.

Customs and Excise Tax

Francis v. R., [1956] S.C.R. 618, 3 D.L.R. (2d) 641, 56 D.T.C. 1077

The section does not give Indians immunity from general legislation such as the *Customs Act*, R.S.C. 1985 (2d Supp.), c. 1.

Saugeen Indian Band v. Canada, [1990] 2 C.N.L.R. 166, 1 F.C. 403, 1 T.S.T. 2233 (Fed. C.A.)

The Band bought certain goods which were used on the reserve. The price of the goods included the federal sales tax, which had already been paid by the manufacturer, wholesaler, or vendor. The Band argued that it was exempt from taxation, and therefore not responsible for paying the amount equivalent to the federal tax. The court found that these were not taxes on property but rather, taxes on business transactions. The court also found that, even though the cost of the taxes was passed on to the Band, the taxes were not paid by the Band, but by the vendor. Therefore, the federal government was not taxing the property of the Band.

Mohawk Council of Akwesasne v. Canada (Minister of National Revenue), [1997] F.C.J. No. 882 (F.C.T.D.)

Akwesasne is a Mohawk reserve which straddles the Canada-U.S.A. border as well as the Ontario-Quebec border. In 1988, Chief Mike Mitchell crossed the border with one washing machine, 10 blankets, 20 Bibles, various articles of used clothing, one case of lubricating motor oil, 10 loaves of bread, two pounds of butter, four gallons of whole milk, six bags of cookies and 12 cans of soup. He told customs officials that these were gifts for a ceremonial dinner at the neighbouring Mohawk reserve of Tyendinaga to commemorate the renewal of trade ties with that community. Chief Mitchell refused to pay the duty of $361.64 claiming an Aboriginal right, and rights under the Jay Treaty. He did not rely on s. 87 for the exemption.

Although the court found that an existing Aboriginal right exempted Mitchell from paying duty on those items, it did not find that the Jay Treaty was applicable.

R. v. McBride (1989), [1990] 2 C.N.L.R. 158 (Ont. Dist. Ct.)

Indians are not exempt from paying duty on goods brought across the Canada-U.S. border where such importation is in contravention of the *Customs Act*, R.S.C. 1985 (2d Supp.), c. 1. Any rights in this regard which may have existed by way of convention or custom are extinguished by the valid statutory enactment.

R. v. Poitras, [1994] 7 W.W.R. 686, [1994] 3 C.N.L.R. 157 (Sask. Q.B.)

The accused were charged with customs and excise tax offences related to the sale of tobacco. The court held that custom duties were imposed upon the importation of goods. They were not taxes on personal property situate on a reserve.

Health Care Tax

R. v. Johnston (1966), 5 W.W.R. 565, 49 C.R. 203, 56 D.L.R. (2d) 749 (Sask. C.A.)(followed in *R. v. Swimmer*, [1971] 1 W.W.R. 756, 3 C.C.C. (2d) 92, 17 D.L.R. (3d) 476 (Sask. C.A.))

Indians not living on a reserve are liable for paying a hospitalization tax imposed by a provincial government in the absence of any agreement by the federal government that it will pay the tax.

Income Tax

Nowegijick v. R., [1983] 1 S.C.R. 29, 144 D.L.R. (3d) 193, [1983] C.T.C. 20, 83 D.T.C. 5041, 46 N.R. 41, [1943] 2 C.N.L.R. 89

An Indian is not required to pay tax on income earned from a corporation with its head office on a reserve, and while he is living on the reserve. Income and taxable income are personal property. Dickson, J. stated:

> ... I do not agree ... that the effect of s. 87 of the *Indian Act* is only to exempt what can properly be classified as direct taxation on property. Section 87 provides that "the personal property of an Indian ... on a reserve" is exempt from taxation; but it also provides that "no Indian ... is ... subject to taxation in respect of any such property". The earlier words certainly exempt certain property from taxation; but the latter words also exempt certain persons from taxation in respect of such property. As I read it, s. 87 creates an exemption for both persons and property. It does not matter then that the taxation of employment income may be characterized as a tax on persons, as opposed to a tax on property. [S.C.R. p. 41]

Folster v. Canada, [1997] F.C.J. No. 664 (F.C.A.)

The Norway House Indian Hospital was once located on the reserve. Although it was moved off reserve, it served primarily Indian patients. Marianne Folster was a member of the First Nation and resided on the reserve. She argued that her employment income from her work as an administrator at the hospital should be exempt from income tax. The court of appeal agreed.

The court applied the "connecting factors" test from *Williams*. The court reviewed the residence of the employer (in this case the Crown) and the uncertainty of determining where the Crown resided. The court commented on the guidelines issued by the Department of National Revenue, but decided to depart from them.

> As is evident, the guidelines understandably are based largely on the residence of the employer and the location where the duties of the employee are performed. While these factors may be useful for the determination of whether employment income falls within section 87, a central premise of Williams is that, in the final analysis, the relative weighting of connecting factors must proceed on a case by case basis. Consequently, although guidelines may assist in routine cases, it is not possible to establish, in advance, the precise formula by which employment income is to be assessed in all cases.

> On the facts of this case, the residence of the taxpayer, the nature of the service performed, the history of the institution in question, and the circumstances surrounding the employment all received great weight in the purposive interpretation of section 87. On the contrary, the residence of the employer, even if that could be determined, and the metes and bounds location

where the duties were performed, although certainly relevant, were granted less weight than in other cases. [paras. 31–32]

Snow v. M.N.R., [1979] C.T.C. 227, 79 D.T.C. 5177, 102 D.L.R. (3d) 191 (Fed. C.A.)

Income earned off a reserve by an Indian is subject to income tax as stated by Le Dain, J. at (C.T.C.) p. 227:

> In our opinion, section [87] contemplates taxation in respect of specific personal property *qua* property and not taxation in respect of taxable income as defined by the *Income Tax Act*, which, while it may reflect items that are personal property, is not itself personal property ...

Poker v. Canada (Minister of National Revenue), [1995] 1 F.C. 561, [1995] 1 C.N.L.R. 85, 94 D.T.C. 6658, [1995] 1 C.T.C. 84, 84 F.T.R. 295 (T.D.)

Two residents of Norway House Indian Band claimed exemption from taxation on employment income. The court applied the connecting factors test set out in *Williams v. Canada, supra*. P. was employed at a school off reserve, but her employer and her employment income was on reserve. Her work was connected to the reserve, and most of her students were Indians. Her income was exempt.

The court found that the income of the second person was not exempt. She appealed and succeeded in *Folster v. Canada*, above.

Laforme v. Minister of National Revenue (1991), , (sub nom. *Laforme v. R.)* 91 D.T.C. 5372, (sub nom. *Laforme v. Canada)* [1991] 2 C.T.C. 28 (Fed. T.D.)

Section 87 of the *Indian Act* does not expressly render any provisions of the *Income Tax Act*, S.C. 1970–71–72, c. 63 inapplicable. Therefore, a native appellant seeking to take advantage of the right of appeal to the Tax Court must do so only in accordance with the terms of the *Income Tax Act*.

R. v. Nat. Indian Brotherhood, [1979] 1 F.C. 103, 92 D.L.R. (3d) 333, [1978] C.T.C. 680, 78 D.T.C. 6488 (T.D.)

Salaries paid by an Indian non-profit corporation located in Ottawa to Indian employees were, until paid, simply contract debts owed by a corporation not on a reserve. The s. 87 exemption does not extend beyond the ordinary meaning of the words and expressions used in it. Neither can the payment of salaries be considered to be personal property as defined by s. 90 which would deem them to be situate on a reserve. Thus salaries received by Indians from a corporation with its head office and major work location outside a reserve are subject to income tax.

Greyeyes v. R., [1978] 2 F.C. 385, 84 D.L.R. (3d) 196, [1978] C.T.C. 91, 78 D.T.C. 6043 (T.D.)

A scholarship paid to an Indian by the Department of Indian Affairs in accordance with a treaty obligation to provide education and to attend a university not on a reserve was the personal property of an Indian situated on a reserve and thus not taxable. Section 87 prevails over any contrary intention expressed by the *Income Tax Act*.

Recalma v. Canada (1996), 96 D.T.C. 1520, [1996] 3 C.T.C. 2272 (headnote only) (T.C.C.)

Recalma lived on the Qualicam Beach reserve in southern British Columbia. He made investments at a bank branch located on the Squamish reserve. He attempted to claim an exemption from tax for the income from the investments. The court held that the income was from mainstream economic activity located and structured off reserve. Because the income was not situated on reserve, it was taxable.

Dixon v. Minister of National Revenue, [1995] 3 C.N.L.R. 60, [1995] 2 C.T.C. 2095 (T.C.C.)

Two Quebec Crees claimed exemption from income tax on income earned in 1976. The two had worked for the Grand Council of the Crees on land which became reserve by Order in Council in 1978. The Tax Court held that the income was *not* tax exempt because the land was not reserve at the time that the income was earned.

Brant v. Canada (Minister of National Revenue) (1992), 92 D.T.C. 2274, [1992] 2 C.T.C. 2633 (T.C.C.)

Brant worked as an auditor for Revenue Canada and resided on a reserve. The court found that the income he earned from the government was in the "commercial mainstream". Therefore, his income was not tax exempt.

McNab v. Canada, [1992] 4 C.N.L.R. 52, [1992] 2 C.T.C. 2545 (T.C.C.)

The salary of an employee of the Saskatchewan Treaty Indian Women's Council was exempt from income tax, even though most of her work was performed outside of the reserve. The court cited a number of factors: the Council's registered office was on the reserve, and its purpose was to assist Indian women on the reserves; the employee's legal residence was on the reserve; she was paid at the reserve 75 per cent of the time; and her work was with and for the benefit of Indians on reserves.

Henry v. M.N.R., 87 D.T.C. 338, [1987] 2 C.T.C. 2013 (T.C.C.)

It was held that certain amounts the taxpayer received by way of severance payment were reasonably attributable to the taxpayer's duties of employment on a reserve and that they were therefore exempt from taxation pursuant to the Remission Order.

Wavey v. Minister of National Revenue, 91 D.T.C. 905, (sub nom. *Kirkness v. Minister of National Revenue*) [1991] 2 C.T.C. 2028 (T.C.C.)

Status Indians employed by the federal government a few hundred yards outside the legal boundary of a reserve are not exempt from income taxation under s. 87 of the *Indian Act*.

Horn v. M.N.R., [1989] 3 C.N.L.R. 59 (T.C.C.)

A federal government employee who works in the National Capital area but takes vacations and sick leave on the reserve is not exempt from income tax in respect of that part of her employment income relating to time spent on the reserve. In this case all tests indicate that the situs of the wages is off the reserve.

Boadway v. M.N.R., [1980] C.T.C. 2382, 80 D.T.C. 1321 (T.R.B.)

An Indian woman who marries a non-Indian under the former s. 12(1)(b) is liable to pay tax from the date of her marriage, which is the date she ceases to be entitled to be registered. The fact that her name may remain on the list of registered Indians is immaterial since it is only for administrative purposes.

Sioui v. Quebec (Deputy Minister of Revenue) (1996), 142 D.L.R. (4th) 742 (Que.C.A.)

A member of the Lorette Huron Band had a commercial business on the Lorette reserve. He refused to collect provincial taxes, and the Quebec government applied for an injunction to close his business. One of his defences was that the Murray Treaty of 1760 guaranteed the Hurons autonomy in their territory, so that he was not under an obligation to collect taxes for the Quebec government. He relied on the statement in the treaty which allowed the Hurons free exercise of their "customs" (see *R. v. Sioui*, for text of the treaty).

The court of appeal upheld the conviction at trial, saying that "customs" only referred to a way of life, cultural habits, traditional hunting or fishing, etc.

Vachon c. Commission d'appel en matiere de lesions professionelles, [1997] 1 C.N.L.R. 234 (Que. S.C.)

A member of the Betsiamites Reserve was injured at work. While he was employed, he did not have to pay income tax. However, his workers' compensation payments were calculated on an amount that assumed payment of income tax. The court held that the amount of tax was only a factor used to calculate the workers'compensation payments. Since there was no actual tax remitted, there was no conflict with the *Indian Act*.

Kinookimaw Beach Assn. v. R. in Right of Sask., [1979] 6 W.W.R. 84, 102 D.L.R. (3d) 333 (Sask. C.A.)

The courts will not lift the corporate veil of a corporation wholly owned and controlled by Indian bands, operating on a reserve, to allow the operation of the tax exemption of s. 87. Culliton, C.J.S., of the Saskatchewan Court of Appeal:

> To grant to the association the exemption from taxation provided for in s. 87 of the *Indian Act* would be to destroy the legal obligations of the association as an independent corporate entity and to determine its obligations by the character of its shareholders. [W.W.R. p. 89]

The corporation was liable to pay taxes assessed under provincial education and health tax legislation.

— See also: *Northwest/Prince Rupert Assessor, Area No. 25 v. N & V Johnson Services Ltd.*, [1988] 5 W.W.R. 438, 25 B.C.L.R. 322, [1988] 4 C.N.L.R. 83 (S.C.)affirmed (1990) [1991] 1 W.W.R. 527, 49 B.C.L.R. (2d) 173, 1 M.P.L.R. (2d) 170, 73 D.L.R. (4th) 170, [1991] 1 C.N.L.R. 90 (C.A.)

Land Taxes

Kamsack v. Can. Nor. Town Properties Co., [1924] S.C.R. 80

Reserve land was surrendered to the Crown who agreed with the defendant that they could sell it to purchasers, who would receive a title from the Crown; the defendant would share the profit with the Crown for the band. The court held that the defendant did not have title, occupation or an interest in the land that would make them liable for a municipal tax assessment.

Sammartino v. A.G.B.C., [1972] 1 W.W.R. 24, 22 D.L.R. (3d) 194 (B.C. C.A.)

Where a taxing statute imposes a tax on an occupier of land, a non-Indian who occupies reserve land is liable to be taxed even if his lease is void for non-compliance with the requirements of the *Indian Act*. Such a statute is not *ultra vires* a provincial legislature since it taxes the occupant and does not legislate in any way with respect to "lands reserved for the Indians".

Mission (District) v. Dewdney/Alouette Assessor, Area No. 13 (1992), [1993] 1 C.N.L.R. 66 (B.C. S.C.)

Section 87 overrides any other taxing statute applying to Indian interest in reserve or surrendered lands. Hence, a status Indian's leasehold interest in lands held in trust by the Crown for another band was exempt from assessment under both the provincial *Assessment Act* and the *Municipal Act*.

Prov. Mun. Assessor v. Harrison, [1971] 3 W.W.R. 735, 20 D.L.R. (3d) 208 (Man. Q.B.), following *Vancouver v. Chow Chee*, [1942] 1 W.W.R. 72, 57 B.C.R. 104 (C.A.)

Although Indian reserve land is not subject to taxation, the leasehold interest of a non-Indian is taxable and is not protected by the *Indian Act*.

Re Kane, [1940] 1 D.L.R. 390 at 396 (N.S. Co. Ct.)

The 1927 Act, R.S.C. 1927, c. 98, ss. 102–104, was considered to be "exhaustive on the subject of Indian taxation so as to exclude provincial legislation". Thus, a city by-law assessing a poll tax on all male residents had no application to unenfranchised Indians living off a reserve.

Sales Tax — British Columbia

Danes v. R. in Right of B.C.; Watts v. R. in Right of B.C. (1985), 61 B.C.L.R. 257, 18 D.L.R. (4th) 253, [1985] 2 C.N.L.R. 19 (C.A.)

An Indian who purchases an item on a reserve is not liable for sales tax on the purchase. "Situated" means "located" and even if the item, such as a motor vehicle, will be used off the reserve it comes within the definition since it does not depend on a degree of permanence. Sales tax is payable at the time of the sale only, not later when the vehicle is registered.

Sales Tax — New Brunswick

Union of New Brunswick Indians v. New Brunswick (Minister of Finance) (1996), 135 D.L.R. (4th) 193, 178 N.B.R. (2d) 1, 454 A.P.R. 1, [1997] 1 C.N.L.R. 213 (C.A.)

In 1993, the province ordered retailers to either collect provincial sales tax from registered Indians or to deliver the goods to the reserve. The majority of the court ruled that the provincial orders were not valid.

> The benefit of s. 87 is essentially referable to the use and consumption of personal property on a reserve; the pattern of use and safekeeping of the property is therefore an appropriate way of determining what chattels shall be exempt from the provincial sales tax, just as it is an appropriate way of determining whether those chattels shall be exempt from seizure under s. 89. A literal interpretation of s. 87 would lead to an erosion of the entitlement of Indians qua Indians under s. 87 and an unjustifiable difference in the interpretation of the terms "situated on a reserve" in companion sections 87 and 89 of the *Indian Act*. [para 31]

Sales Tax — Newfoundland

Miawpukek Indian Band v. Newfoundland (Minister of Finance) (1995), [1996] 1 C.N.L.R. 115, 130 Nfld. & P.E.I.R. 164, 405 A.P.R. 164 (T.D.)

The Band bought two bookshelves and used them on reserve. The Band argued that the "connecting factors" test, developed in *Williams v. Canada*, should be used to determine whether the Band was required to pay provincial sales tax. The court held that the tax exemption would only apply where the transaction occurred on the reserve. The "connecting factors" test did not apply to tangible property where the situs of the transaction was clear.

Sales Tax — Quebec

Jean Vassiliou Inc. c. Québec (Ministre du Revenu), [1990] R.D.F.Q. 255, (sub nom. *Jean Vassiliou Inc. c. Québec (Department of Revenue)*) 3 T.C.T. 5357 (C.Q.)

A vendor is entitled to benefit from an exemption for sales to native people where the sales are made off the reserve but are delivered to the reserve. Certificates attesting to that state of affairs are not mandatory.

Sales Tax — Prince Edward Island

Dumville Restaurants Ltd. v. Prince Edward Island (Minister of Finance & Tourism) (1989), 77 Nfld. & P.E.I.R. 291, 240 A.P.R. 291, 3 T.C.T. 5017, 1 T.S.T. 3177 (P.E.I. T.D.)

Section 10(2) of the provincial *Revenue Tax Act*, R.S.P.E.I. 1974, c. R-14 [now R.S.P.E.I. 1974, c. R-14], which exempts Indians from liability to pay certain sales taxes, does not violate s. 15 of the Charter of Rights and Freedoms.

Tobacco and Gasoline Taxes — British Columbia

Tseshaht Indian Band v. British Columbia (1992), 69 B.C.L.R. (2d) 1, 94 D.L.R. (4th) 97, [1992] 4 C.N.L.R. 171, 15 B.C.A.C. 1, 27 W.A.C. 1 (C.A.)leave to appeal to S.C.C. granted (1993), 75 B.C.L.R. (2d) xxxii (note), 151 N.R. 240 (note) (S.C.C.). The appeal has been discontinued.

Notwithstanding s. 87, an Indian band can be required to remit an amount equal to the sales tax when purchasing gasoline and tobacco products for re-sale to both Indian and non-Indian purchasers. Payment of an amount equal to tax is not in itself the payment of a tax. A quota system — whereby a band is authorized to purchase a percentage of its gasoline without paying an amount equal to tax, to reflect the volume of sales to Indian as opposed to non-Indians purchasers — was *intra vires* the province. Such a quota system simply relieved retailers of the requirements to remit amounts equal to tax when it was predictable that the ultimate consumers would not pay tax.

Chehalis Indian Band v. B.C., [1987] 3 C.N.L.R. 44, (sub nom. *Chehalis Indian Band v. B.C. (Dir. Motor Fuel Tax Act)*) [1989] 1 C.N.L.R. 62 (C.A.)affirmed 31 B.C.L.R. (2d) 333, 53 D.L.R. (4th) 761

A band sought repayment of tax paid on gasoline sold on the reserve to Indians. Since the band did not purchase the gasoline, it was not entitled to a rebate. A provincial licence must be obtained and provincial sales tax must be collected by an Indian merchant on a reserve selling to non-Indian customers. In an *obiter* comment, the court stated that no licence is required or tax imposed if all customers are Indians.

Petro-Canada Inc. v. Fort Nelson Indian Band (1992), 72 B.C.L.R. (2d) 28, [1993] 1 C.N.L.R. 72, 95 D.L.R. (4th) 69 (S.C.)

When a manufacturer or producer contracts with an Indian band, s. 87 does not relieve the non-Indian party of its sales tax and excise tax obligations. These costs may be incorporated into the purchase price, but this is a matter of agreement. A band is exempt from provincial gasoline tax if (1) the fuel at the time the tax is to be levied is the personal property of the band and (2) the paramount location of the vehicles using the fuel is on the reserve.

Tobacco and Gasoline Taxes — Nova Scotia

R. v. Murdock (1996), 154 N.S.R. (2d) 1, 452 A.P.R. 1, 38 C.R.R. (2d) 15 (C.A.)

[For a related case, which followed this case, see R. v. Johnson (1996), 156 N.S.R. (2d) 71, 461 A.P.R. 71 (C.A.)]

Johnson, a Mik'maq from the Millbrook Reserve bought tobacco from Murdock, a Mohawk from Six Nations, Johnson sold the tobacco to both members of the Band and to non-natives. The court found that there were no Aboriginal rights in this case, and upheld the quota system for allocating tobacco to Indian communities. Convictions with jail sentences were upheld.

> The appellants, if anything, may have established an existing aboriginal right to use tobacco for personal comsumption and for ceremonial purposes although the trial judge did not make such a finding.

> Even if one were to conclude that this use of tobacco constitutes an aboriginal right of some sort, in the absence of evidence, the appellants have failed to prove that the scope of the obriginal right to use tobacco extends to include Mi'kmaq Indians dealing, or trading in to-bacco between different Indians or Indian Bands in different parts of Canada. And it clearly would not involve selling tobacco to non-natives. [N.S.R. p. 56]

R. v. Johnson (1993), 120 N.S.R. (2d) 414, 332 A.P.R. 414, [1994] 1 C.N.L.R. 129 (C.A.)leave to appeal to S.C.C. granted (1993), 164 N.R. 79n (S.C.C.), granting of leave quashed (October 4, 1994), Doc. No. 23593 (S.C.C.)

Section 87 does not exempt Indians from prepaying tax to wholesalers on purchases made off reserve where provincial legislation of general application requires it.

Johnson v. Nova Scotia (A.G.) (1990), 96 N.S.R. (2d) 140, 253 A.P.R. 140, 3 T.C.T. 5148, [1990] 2 C.N.L.R. 62 (C.A.)leave to appeal to S.C.C. refused (1990), [1991] 1 C.N.L.R. vin, 100 N.S.R. (2d) 180n, 272 A.P.R. 180n, 124 N.R. 319n (S.C.C.)

A regulatory scheme requiring native persons to remit tax on tobacco products to wholesale vendors, and to apply for a later rebate of the amount, was held to be beyond the scope of the authorizing legisla-tion. It was a patent attempt to extend the application of the provincial *Health Services Tax Act* without legislative authority.

R. v. Stevens, [1991] 3 C.N.L.R. 149 (N.S. Prov. Ct.)

A registered Indian is entitled to purchase diesel oil on a reserve without paying provincial diesel oil tax and is further entitled to use and consume the tax-free diesel oil off reserve lands without being subject to prosecution or penalty.

Tobacco and Gasoline Taxes — Ontario

Bomberry v. Ontario (Minister of Revenue) (1989), 70 O.R. (2d) 662, [1989] 3 C.N.L.R. 27, 34 O.A.C. 17, 2 T.C.T. 4234, 63 D.L.R. (4th) 526 (Div. Ct.)appeal to Ont. C.A. dismissed as abandoned October 21, 1993 [1994] 2 C.N.L.R. vi

A provincial quota system, aimed at limiting the amount of tax-exempt cigarettes that retail dealers on reserves could purchase from wholesalers, was not authorized by the *Tobacco Tax Act*, R.S.O. 1980, c. 502 [now R.S.O. 1990, c. T.10]. As well, the quota directly infringed the right of status Indians under s. 87 to be exempt from tax on personal property located on the reserve. It overstepped provincial jurisdiction and intruded into federal authority over Indians.

Hill v. Ont. (Min. of Revenue) (1985), 50 O.R. (2d) 765, 18 D.L.R. (4th) 537, [1986] 1 C.N.L.R. 22 (H.C.)*Bernard v. N.B. (Min. of Fin.)* (1987), 31 D.L.R. (4th) 303, [1987] 2 C.N.L.R. 57, 75 N.B.R. (2d) 215, 188 A.P.R. 215 (Q.B.)

The *Tobacco Tax Act* is one of general application in a province and Indians on a reserve are not exempt by s. 87. The seller of cigarettes is not taxed; the individual purchasers are taxed. The seller is an agent for the purpose of collecting the tax.

Tobacco and Gasoline Taxes — Saskatchewan

R. v. Merasty, [1997] 3 C.N.L.R. 241 (Sask. Prov. Ct.)

The accused was a member of the Flying Dust Band of Saskatchewan. He purchased 15,000 litres of tax exempt fuel on the Ermineskin reserve in Alberta and was charged after transporting the fuel to Saskatchewan. The court found that the Saskatchewan *Fuel Tax Act*, which required retailers to prepay tax on the fuel, was valid, and not in contravention of section 87.

Unemployment Insurance

Williams v. Canada, [1992] 1 S.C.R. 877, 41 C.C.E.L. 1, 90 D.L.R. (4th) 129, [1992] 3 C.N.L.R. 181, 92 D.T.C. 6320, [1992] 1 C.T.C. 225, 136 N.R. 161, 53 F.T.R. 104n (S.C.C.)

Two factors are important in deciding whether unemployment insurance benefits are taxable: first, the location of the income earned giving rise to the benefit, and second, the residence of the person receiving the benefit. In this case, a registered Indian residing on reserve qualified for unemployment insurance benefits as the result of employment on the reserve. The court held that benefits in this case were exempt from taxation, and clearly left open the question of whether the result would have been different if the individual had not resided on reserve.

M.N.R. v. Iroquois of Caughnawaga, [1997] C.T.C. 49, 77 D.T.C. 5127, 73 D.L.R. (3d) 414, 15 N.R. 377 (C.A.)

Unemployment insurance premiums are not a tax on property and thus not exempt by s. 87, which only exempts what can properly be classified as direct taxation on property.

Utility Tax

Brown v. R. in Right of B.C., [1980] 3 W.W.R. 360, 20 B.C.L.R. 64, 107 D.L.R. (3d) 705 (C.A.)

A provincial tax on the purchase price of electricity is a tax "in respect of" personal property and thus an Indian resident on a reserve is not subject to such taxation.

Delisle v. Shawinigan Water & Power Co. (1941), 79 Que. S.C. 353, [1941] 4 D.L.R. 556

An amount imposed by a supplier of electricity on its customers to equal the sales tax payable by it to the federal *Special War Revenue Act* was not a tax on the plaintiff Indian. The tax was payable by the supplier and was indirectly collected, in accordance with law, from the consumer. The court found there was no tax on the Indian who received electricity at his home on the reserve, since a tax is an enforced contribution, not a voluntary payment, and the consumer voluntarily chose electricity as the means to illuminate his home. Payment by an increase in the cost of goods by reason of a tax on the supplier or manufacturer is not a tax imposed on real or personal property.

Miscellaneous

Sarcee Gravel Products Inc. v. Alberta (Worker's Compensation Board) (1994), [1995] 3 C.N.L.R. 193, [1995] 2 W.W.R. 246, 161 A.R. 303, 24 Alta. L.R. (3d) 389 (Q.B.)

The Tsuu T'ina Nation created a provincial corporation to conduct gravel extraction. The corporation was wholly owned by the Band and all profits go the Nation. The corporation challenged the assessment of a provincial workers' compensation levy. The provincial law exempted "any Industry carried on by an Indian or Band on a Reserve". The court held that the corporation was not an Indian for the purposes of the provincial exemption, and therefore, was not exempt from the levy. (*See Auger where provincial exemption was found to apply*)

Auger v. Alberta (Workers' Compensation Board) (1989), 61 D.L.R. (4th) 660 (Alta. Q.B.)affirmed (1990), 111 A.R. 2, 76 Alta. L.R. (2d) 195, 33 C.C.E.L. 75, 73 D.L.R. (4th) 357 (C.A.), leave to appeal to S.C.C. refused (1992), 125 A.R. 160n, 83 Alta. L.R. (2d) lxvin, 86 D.L.R. (4th) viiin, 7 C.R.R. (2d) 384n (S.C.C.)

In this case, all parties made submissions to the effect that employer contributions to the provincial accident fund were not taxes but a levy solely for the establishment and maintenance of a compensation fund. (The court did not have to deal with this issue because Alberta legislation exempted bands from the workers compensation scheme.)

A.G. Que. v. Williams (1944), 82 C.C.C. 166, [1944] 4 D.L.R. 488 (Que. S.C.)

A business licence fee of general application and scope that is imposed for administrative costs of providing a registration certificate and not as a means of collecting revenue for the state must be paid by Indian merchants operating a business on a reserve.

— See also *R. v. Groslouis* (1944), 81 C.C.C. 167, [1944] R.L. 12 (Que. S.C.)

R. v. Bob (1991), 3 C.R. (4th) 348, [1991] 2 C.N.L.R. 104, 88 Sask. R. 302, 6 C.R.R. (2d) 144 (C.A.)

Members of an Indian band were charged with conducting a bingo on reserve for charitable purposes without a provincial licence. The court found that, in other respects, the bingo would have complied with the conditions of a licence, had one been issued.

The province cancelled the licence when the band refused to pay a fee of 2 per cent of the prizes awarded. The court found that the "2 per cent fee" was, in fact, a tax, and therefore exempt under s.87 of the *Indian Act*.

Legal Rights

88. General provincial laws applicable to Indians — Subject to the terms of any treaty and any other Act of the Parliament of Canada, all laws of general application from time to time in force in any province are applicable to and in respect of Indians in the province, except to the extent that such laws are inconsistent with this Act or any order, rule, regulation or by-law made thereunder, and except to the extent that such laws make provision for any matter for which provision is made by or under the Act.

Commentary:

Provincial authority

Provincial laws apply to Indians in two ways, according to the Supreme Court of Canada in *Dick v. R.*. First, provincial laws apply directly to Indians of their own force (*ex propio vigore*) as long as the laws do not invade exclusive federal authority over Indians and lands reserved for Indians, or are inconsistent with a federal law. (See commentary under s.91(24), *Constitution Act, 1867*). Second, s. 88 operates to incorporate into federal law, those provincial laws of general application which *do* invade exclusive federal authority. That is, a provincial law which affects "Indianness" or derogates from the "status and capacities" of Indians can become a valid federal law through s. 88. The operation of the incorporated statute is subject, of course to treaties and other exceptions mentioned in s. 88. In *Delgamuukw v. British*

Columbia the Supreme Court of Canada held that provincial laws, either on their own, or through section 88, could not legislate in relation to Aboriginal rights.

Application of provincial laws through s. 88

The "laws of general application" referred to in s. 88 are provincial laws. This section (unlike section 35(1) of the *Constitution Act, 1982*) does not provide for the primacy of treaties over *federal* laws (See *R. v. George*). This section makes provincial laws of general application which are brought in through s. 88 (ie. laws which affect "Indianness", etc.) subject to treaties.

Lands

Note that this section does not permit application of provincial laws to lands reserved for Indians.

Relevant constitutional provisions

There is considerable overlap with cases on division of powers under s. 91(24) of the *Constitution Act, 1867* as well as cases on treaties under s. 35(1) of the *Constitutional Act, 1982*.

Case Law:

General — Canada

Sioui v. Quebec (Attorney General), [1990] 1 S.C.R. 1025, 70 D.L.R. (4th) 427, [1990] 3 C.N.L.R. 127, 56 C.C.C. (3d) 225, 109 N.R. 22

> Section 88 of the *Indian Act* is designed specifically to protect the Indians from provincial legislation that might attempt to deprive them of rights protected by a treaty. A legislated change in the use of the territory thus does not extinguish rights otherwise protected by treaty. [C.N.L.R. p. 153]

Dick v. R., [1985] 2 S.C.R. 309, [1986] 1 W.W.R. 1, 69 B.C.L.R. 184, 23 D.L.R. (4th) 33, 22 C.C.C. (3d) 129, [1985] 4 C.N.L.R. 55, 62 N.R. 1

> I believe that a distinction should be drawn between two categories of provincial laws. There are, on the one hand, provincial laws which can be applied to Indians without touching their Indianness, like traffic legislation; there are on the other hand, provincial laws which cannot apply to Indians without regulating them qua Indians. [C.N.L.R. p.71]

The laws of the second type which touch "Indianness" are incorporated through s. 88 while laws of the first type apply *ex propio vigore*.

Kruger v. R., [1978] 1 S.C.R. 104, [1977] 4 W.W.R. 300, 34 C.C.C. (2d) 377, 75 D.L.R. (3d) 434, 14 N.R. 945

Under s. 88 Indians are brought within provincial regulatory legislation in the absence of treaty or federal statutory protection. The provincial law, however, must be of general application and not be in relation to Indians. Dickson, J., giving the judgment of the court, said:

> There are two indicia by which to discern whether or not a provincial enactment is a law of general application. It is necessary to look first to the territorial reach of the Act. If the Act does not extend uniformly throughout the territory, the inquiry is at an end and the question is answered in the negative. If the law does extend uniformly throughout the jurisdiction, the intention and effects of the enactment need to be considered. The law must not be "in relation to" one class of citizens in object and purpose. But the fact that a law may have graver consequence to one person than to another does not, on that account alone, make the law other than one of general application. There are few laws which have a uniform impact. The line is crossed, however, when an enactment, though in relation to another matter, by its effect impairs the status or capacity of a particular group. [W.W.R. p. 304]

Natural Parents v. Supt. of Child Welfare, [1976] 2 S.C.R. 751, [1976] 1 W.W.R. 699, 21 R.F.L. 267, 60 D.L.R. (3d) 148, 6 N.R. 491

At issue was the applicability of provincial adoption legislation to an Indian child. The court found that provincial legislation applied, only through incorporation by the *Indian Act*. Laskin, J. said at (D.L.R.) p. 154:

> ... adoption legislation which would, if applicable as provincial legislation *simpliciter*, consti-tute a serious intrusion into the Indian family relationship. It is difficult to conceive what would be left of exclusive federal power in relation to Indians if such provincial legislation was held to apply to Indians.

R. v.George, [1966] S.C.R. 267, 47 C.R. 382, 55 D.L.R. (2d) 386, [1966] 3 C.C.C. 137

Treaties are supreme in relation to provincial law but do not take precedence over federal legislation. This was held by a 6 to 1 decision of the Supreme Court of Canada, when Martland, J. said:

> [Section] 88 was not intended to be a declaration of the paramountcy of treaties over federal legislation. The reference to treaties was incorporated in a section the purpose of which was to make provincial laws applicable to Indians, so as to preclude any interference with rights under treaties resulting from the impact of provincial legislation. [C.C.C. p. 151]

General — Alberta

Re Stony Plain Indian Reserve No. 135 (1982), 35 A.R. 412, [1982] 1 W.W.R. 302, 130 D.L.R. (3d) 636, [1982] 1 C.N.L.R. 133 (C.A.)

Section 88 does not relate to surrenders since it is concerned only with provincial laws that apply to Indians themselves, and not to land reserved for Indians.

General — British Columbia

Delgamuukw v. British Columbia, [1993] 5 W.W.R. 97, 104 D.L.R. (4th) 470 (C.A.)leave to appeal to S.C.C. granted [1994] 3 W.W.R. lxvin, 109 D.L.R. (4th) viin (S.C.C.), appeal revised to include leave to cross-appeal [1994] 2 C.N.L.R. vin (S.C.C.)

Macfarlane, J.A. said at (5 W.W.R.) p. 172:

> Aboriginal rights fall within the ambit of the core values of Indians described above, and to which s. 88 has been held to apply. Thus s. 88, while not authorizing extinguishment of aborig-inal rights, may authorize provincial interference with aboriginal rights; provincial laws may affect, regulate, diminish, impair or suspend the exercise of an aboriginal right. Of course, the operation of such incorporated laws is subject to s. 35 of the *Constitution Act, 1982*.

R. v. Dick, [1993] 5 W.W.R. 446, 80 B.C.L.R. (2d) 62, [1993] 4 C.N.L.R. 63 (C.A.)

The fact that s. 88 incorporates provincial laws which affect "Indianness" does not mean that s. 88 is inconsistent with s. 35(1) of the *Constitution Act*, 1982, although the particular law incorporated may be inconsistent with s. 35(1).

R. v. Alphonse, [1993] 5 W.W.R. 401, 80 B.C.L.R. (2d) 17, [1993] 4 C.N.L.R. 19, 83 C.C.C. (3d) 417 (C.A.)

1. A provincial law which affects Aboriginal rights can be incorporated into federal law by s. 88.

2. A provincial law so incorporated would have to be justified under the *Sparrow* tests.

3. Section 88 only applies to "status" Indians. Therefore, Metis, Inuit and "non-status" Indians are im-mune from provincial laws which affect their "Indianness".

Re Williams Estate and Trustee Act; Re Indian Act (1960), 32 W.W.R. 686 (B.C. S.C.)

The plain wording of this section must be looked at, and it is very clear that the test is inconsistent, which means something at variance or incompatible or contrary.

Child Welfare Legislation — Canada

Natural Parents v. Superintendent of Child Welfare, [1976] 2 S.C.R. 751, [1976] 1 W.W.R. 699, 21 R.F.L. 267, 60 D.L.R. (3d) 148, 6 N.R. 491

See note, *supra.* Followed in *Sahanatien v. Smith*, [1982] 2 F.C. 807, 134 D.L.R. (3d) 172, [1983] 1 C.N.L.R. 151 (Fed. T.D.)

Child Welfare Legislation — Alberta

Re Baptiste; Dir. of Maintenance and Recovery v. Potts (1979), 20 A.R. 196, [1979] 6 W.W.R. 560, 12 R.F.L. (2d) 144, 102 D.L.R. (3d) 553 (Q.B.)

A parent or guardian is obligated to contribute to the support and maintenance of a child in ward care when so ordered by the court. This applies to Indians on reserves as to all residents of a province.

Child Welfare Legislation — British Columbia

Alexander v. Maxime (1995), 4 B.C.L.R. (3d) 294, [1995] B.C.W.L.D. 943, [1995] W.D.F.L. 657, 56 B.C.A.C. 97, 92 W.A.C. 97, [1996] 1 C.N.L.R. 1 (C.A.)

The Spallumcheen First Nation, pursuant to its child welfare by-law, changed custody of a child from his grandmother, to his mother. The grandmother, who lived in Vancouver, refused to give up custody of the child. She challenged the validity of the First Nation by-law. The Court of Appeal did not decide on whether the by-law was authorized under the *Indian Act.* However, the court upheld the exercise of *parens patriae* jurisdiction by the court below to stay the Spallumcheen custody in order to determine the best interests of the child.

Re Family & Child Services Act (British Columbia), [1990] 4 C.N.L.R. 14 (B.C. Prov. Ct.)

The provincial *Family and Child Service Act*, 1980, S.B.C. 1980, c. 11 has application to Aboriginal children in the care of residents on a reserve. The right to determine whether children are in need of protection, and the power to implement remedies, are not Aboriginal rights protected by s. 35 of the *Constitution Act*, 1982.

Re C. and V.C. (1982), 40 B.C.L.R. 234, [1983] 3 C.N.L.R. 58 (Prov. Ct.)

Provincial child welfare legislation applies to Indians on reserves.

Child Welfare Legislation — Manitoba

Nelson v. C.A.S. Eastern Manitoba, [1975] 5 W.W.R. 45, 21 R.F.L. 222, 56 D.L.R. (3d) 567 (Man. C.A.)

Provincial laws apply to the adoption of an Indian child by non-Indians.

Northwest Child & Family Services Agency v. T. (S.J.) (1990), 70 D.L.R. (4th) 418, 65 Man. R. (2d) 38, [1991] 1 C.N.L.R. 82 (Q.B.)

This case was a determination of the effect of a regulation under the *Manitoba Child and Family Services Act*, S.M. 1985–86, c. 8. The Indian child services agency only had jurisdiction within the reserve, not over band members residing outside the reserve.

Dir. of Child Welfare for Manitoba v. B., [1979] 6 W.W.R. 229, [1981] 4 C.N.L.R. 62 (Man. Prov. Ct.)

Provincial child welfare legislation applies to Indians on reserves.

Child Welfare Legislation — Ontario

Weechi-it-te-win Child & Family Services v. M. (D.), [1992] 3 C.N.L.R. 165 (Ont. Prov. Div.)

The *Ontario Child and Family Services Act* applies without exemption to Indian children.

Family Law — Canada

Derrickson v. Derrickson, [1986] 1 S.C.R. 285, [1986] 3 W.W.R. 193, 1 B.C.L.R. (2d) 273, 50 R.F.L. (2d) 337, 26 D.L.R. (4th) 175, [1986] 2 C.N.L.R. 45, 65 N.R. 278

A wife in a divorce proceeding asked for half of the husband's property located on the Westbank reserve, under the provincial *Family Relations Act*. The property was held by the husband through a certificate of possession in his name.

The court held that the division of property provisions could not apply of its own force to Indian lands because possession of lands was the "very essence" of the exclusive federal authority under 91(24). The court also held that the provincial provisions could not be referentially incorporated through section 88 because the provincial provisions were in actual conflict with provisions in the *Indian Act* relating to possession of land.

However, as the *Indian Act* did not provide for compensation in lieu of division of property, the court could order compensation for the purpose of adjusting the division of family assets.

Paul v. Paul, [1986] 1 S.C.R. 306, [1986] 3 W.W.R. 210, 1 B.C.L.R. (2d) 290, 50 R.F.L. (2d) 355, 26 D.L.R. (4th) 196, [1986] 2 C.N.L.R. 74

Provincial provisions on interim exclusive occupation of the matrimonial home could not apply on reserve for the same reasons as in *Derrickson*.

Family Law — Alberta

Potts v. Potts (1991), 31 R.F.L. (3d) 66, [1991] 3 W.W.R. 11, 77 D.L.R. (4th) 369, 113 A.R. 276, 78 Alta. L.R. (2d) 240, [1992] 1 C.N.L.R. 182 (C.A.)

The *Maintenance Enforcement Act* is an act of general application which applies on reserve through section 88. Because there was no conflict with provisions in the *Indian Act*, the provincial statute was valid.

Family Law — British Columbia

Simpson v. Ziprick (1995), 126 D.L.R. (4th) 754, 10 B.C.L.R. (3d) 41 (S.C.)

Members of the Okanagan Indian Band held a certificate of possession as joint tenants. One of the joint tenants applied for partition under the provincial *Partition of Property Act*. The court followed the Supreme Court of Canada in *Derrickson v. Derrickson* and found that the provincial statute was not made applicable by section 88. The court also found that any common law right or English statute law right to partition were subject to the provisions of the *Indian Act*.

George v. George (1992), 95 D.L.R. (4th) 333, [1993] 2 C.N.L.R. 112 (B.C. S.C.)

While the *Indian Act* prevented the real property from being sold or divided, a spouse was entitled under the *B.C. Family Relations Act* to be compensated for her interest in the matrimonial home. That interest was calculated as one-half of its rental value over her lifetime.

Family Law — Ontario

Sandy v. Sandy (1979), 27 O.R. (2d) 248, 13 R.F.L. (2d) 81, 107 D.L.R. (3d) 659 (C.A.)

Reserve lands are not within the definition of "matrimonial home" in the provincial legislation. There could be no order for partition and sale. (Followed in *Laforme v. Laforme* (1984), 33 R.F.L. (2d) 69, [1984] 2 C.N.L.R. 88 (Ont. Co. Ct.))

Dir. of Support & Custody Enforcement v. Nowegejick, [1989] 2 C.N.L.R. 27 (Ont. Fam. Ct.)

Registered Indians are exempt from garnishment by non-Indians, but not when the dispute is between two Indians. In that case, the provincial support and custody legislation applies.

Family Law — Saskatchewan

Standing v. Standing (1991), 37 R.F.L. (3d) 90, 96 Sask. R. 13 (Q.B.)

The court may take the value of property situated on a reserve into account in calculating the net worth of the parties in proceedings under the *Matrimonial Property Act*, even though it does not have jurisdiction to divide the property.

Bellegarde v. Walker (1987), 6 R.F.L. (3d) 317, 36 D.L.R. (4th) 700, [1987] 4 C.N.L.R. 28, 57 Sask. R. 197 (Q.B.)

It has been held that the *Saskatchewan Enforcement of Maintenance Orders Act*, S.S. 1984–85–86, c. E-9.2, applies as a law of general application to Indians on a reserve.

Hunting and Fishing — Canada

R. v. Jack, [1985] 2 S.C.R. 332, [1986] 1 W.W.R. 21, 69 B.C.L.R. 201, 21 D.L.R. (4th) 641, 21 C.C.C. (3d) 482, [1985] 4 C.N.L.R. 88, 62 N.R. 14

A provincial wildlife act applies to all persons and is a statute of general application and thus applicable to all Indians. It does not prevent Indians from exercising their historic religious practices, since there are other ways to exercise those practices (such as storing wild meat for ceremonials). (Note that this case was decided before section 35(1) of the *Constitution Act*, 1982 was enacted.)

Dick v. R., [1985] 2 S.C.R. 309, [1986] 1 W.W.R. 1, 69 B.C.L.R. 184, 23 D.L.R. (4th) 33, 22 C.C.C. (3d) 129, [1985] 4 C.N.L.R. 55, 62 N.R. 1

The court assumed, without deciding, that the provincial *Wildlife Act* was a law which touched upon "Indianness". Therefore, the provincial law could not apply of its own force, and had to be incorporated through section 88.

R. v. George, [1966] S.C.R. 267, 47 C.R. 382, 55 D.L.R. (2d) 386, [1966] 33 C.C.C. 137

Section 88 is intended to make Indians subject to provincial laws of general application. It does not make any legislation of the Parliament of Canada subject to the terms of any treaty. Thus the *Migratory Birds Convention Act*, a federal statute, was not restricted by this section, and applied to Indians. (Note that this case was decided before section 35(1) of the *Constitution Act*, 1982 was enacted.)

R. v. Sikyea, [1964] S.C.R. 642, 49 W.W.R. 306, 44 C.R. 266, 50 D.L.R. (2d) 80

The courts held that Indians are subject to the *Migratory Birds Convention Act*. (Note that this case was decided before section 35(1) of the *Constitution Act, 1982* was enacted.)

Hunting and Fishing — Alberta

R. v. Napolean, [1985] 6 W.W.R. 302, 21 C.C.C. (3d) 515, [1986] 1 C.N.L.R. 86 (B.C. C.A.)leave to appeal to S.C.C. refused (1985), 21 C.C.C. (3d) 515n, 63 N.R. 319n

Provincial legislation which sets safety standards for the use of firearms is of general application.

Hunting and Fishing — British Columbia

R. v. Alphonse, [1993] 5 W.W.R. 401, 80 B.C.L.R. (2d) 17, [1993] 4 C.N.L.R. 19, 83 C.C.C. (3d) 417 (C.A.)*R. v. Dick*, [1993] 5 W.W.R. 446, 80 B.C.L.R. (2d) 62, [1993] 4 C.N.L.R. 63 (C.A.)

The *Wildlife Act* is a law of general application and is referentially incorporated as a federal law. Like a federal law, it is of no force and effect where it would unjustifiably infringe aboriginal rights.

Hunting and Fishing — New Brunswick

R. v. Paul (1993), 110 D.L.R. (4th) 382, 142 N.B.R. (2d) 55, 364 A.P.R. 55, [1994] 2 C.N.L.R. 167 (C.A.)*R. v. McCoy* (1993), 141 N.B.R. (2d) 185, 361 A.P.R. 185, 109 D.L.R. (4th) 433, [1994] 2 C.N.L.R. 129 (C.A.)

Treaty rights do not include hunting in an unsafe manner. Provincial laws on night hunting apply to Indians with treaty hunting rights.

Hunting and Fishing — Nova Scotia

R. v. Julian (1978), 26 N.S.R. (2d) 156, 40 A.P.R. 156 (C.A.)

An Indian who wounded a deer on a reserve and tracked it off the reserve where it died, was convicted under the provincial game law of possession of deer meat out of season. (Note that this case was decided before section 35(1) of the *Constitution Act, 1982* was enacted.)

R. v. Paul (1977), 24 N.S.R. (2d) 313, 35 A.P.R. 313 (C.A.)

It has been held that the provincial requirement for a hunter to possess a hunting licence applies to Indians off a reserve in Nova Scotia, that the offence of not having a licence is one of strict liability, and that *mens rea* is not an element of the offence. (Note that this case was decided before section 35(1) of the *Constitution Act, 1982* was enacted.)

R. v. Isaac (1975), 13 N.S.R. (2d) 460 (C.A.)

Hunting is use of land, so provincial hunting laws do not apply on reserve.

Hunting and Fishing — Ontario

R. v. Hare, [1985] 3 C.N.L.R. 139, 20 C.C.C. (3d) 1, 9 O.A.C. 161 (C.A.)

The words "subject to the terms of any treaty" apply only to provincial legislation; federal legislation may restrict treaty hunting rights. (Note that this case arose before section 35(1) of the *Constitution Act, 1982* was enacted.)

R. v. Moses, [1970] 3 O.R. 314, 13 D.L.R. (3d) 50, [1970] 5 C.C.C. 356 (Dist. Ct.)

Provincial laws did not apply to Indians hunting on unoccupied Crown land.

Hunting and Fishing — Saskatchewan

R. v. Fiddler, [1980] 6 W.W.R. 5, [1982] 1 C.N.L.R. 110 (Sask. Prov. Ct.)

A section in a wildlife act that is designed for the safety of all persons does not place undue hardship on Indians.

Liquor Offences — Alberta

R. v. Shade (1952), 4 W.W.R. (N.S.) 430, 14 C.R. 56, 102 C.C.C. 316 (Alta. Dist. Ct.)

Sections of the *Indian Act* (now repealed) which dealt with intoxication on reserve excluded the application of provincial laws on public drunkenness.

Liquor Offences — Nova Scotia

R. v. Gloade (1987), 72 N.S.R. (2d) 247, 173 A.P.R. 247, [1987] 1 C.N.L.R. 87 (C.A.)leave to appeal to S.C.C. refused 75 N.S.R. (2d) 270n, 186 A.P.R. 270n, 72 N.R. 160n

Provincial liquor control acts apply to Indians on a reserve without touching their "Indianness" and the provincial legislation therefore does not come within s. 88.

Liquor Offences — Ontario

R. v. Pawis, [1972] 2 O.R. 516, 6 C.C.C. (2d) 322 (Dist. Ct.)

The *Indian Act* provision in respect to possession of liquor on a reserve made provincial laws inapplicable to Indians on reserves. Provincial laws would apply to those reserves which have a proclamation under s. 4(2) declaring that ss. 95 to 102 do not apply to the reserve, or when a proclamation is issued pursuant to s. 98(1).

Liquor Offences — Saskatchewan

R. v. Bear (1968), 63 W.W.R. 754 (Sask. Dist. Ct.)

The *Liquor Act*, R.S.S. 1965, c. 382, applied on a reserve in Saskatchewan where an Indian was charged with having liquor in a place other than a dwelling house.

Liquor Offences — Yukon

R. v. Peters (1967), 57 W.W.R. 727, 50 C.R. 68, [1967] 2 C.C.C. 19 (Y.T. C.A.)

A broad and liberal interpretation should be made when considering whether a provincial act is inconsistent with the *Indian Act*. It held that the *Indian Act* made provisions for use and possession of intoxicants by Indians and thus the *Yukon Liquor Ordinance*, S.Y. 1958, c. 67, did not apply to Indians.

R. v. Carlick (1966), 47 C.R. 302, [1966] 3 C.C.C. 323 (Y.T. Police Mag. Ct.)

The *Yukon Territory Ordinance* does not apply to Indians when the *Indian Act* makes provision for the specific subject matter of the ordinance, such as being intoxicated in a public place.

Bruce v. Yukon Territory, [1994] 3 C.N.L.R. 25 (Y.T. Terr. Ct.)

Prohibition of liquor does not touch on "Indianness."

Seizure Legislation — Canada

Mitchell v. Sandy Bay Indian Band, [1990] S.C.R. 85, [1990] 5 W.W.R. 97, 71 D.L.R. (4th) 193, 67 Man. R. (2d) 81, [1990] 3 C.N.L.R. 46, 3 T.C.T. 5219, 110 N.R. 241

The *Garnishment Act*, R.S.M. 1987, c. G20 is a law of general application and is applicable to Indians except to the extent that it is inconsistent with the *Indian Act*.

Seizure Legislation — Manitoba

Mintuck v. Valley River Band No. 63A (No. 2), [1978] 2 W.W.R. 159, 83 D.L.R. (3d) 324 (Man. Q.B.)

Provincial garnishment legislation applies to Indians.

Fires on Reserves — Manitoba

R. v. Sinclair, [1978] 6 W.W.R. 37 (Man. Prov. Ct.)

Provincial law concerning the setting of fires does not apply to land reserved for Indians.

Fires on Reserves — Saskatchewan

R. v. Fiddler, [1993] 3 W.W.R. 594, 108 Sask. R. 5, [1994] 1 C.N.L.R. 121 (Sask. Q.B.)

As a general rule, provincial laws apply to Indians and Indian lands, with the exception of laws that seek to regulate Indians *qua* Indians, or regulate their use of reserve lands. Section 15(a) of the *Saskatchewan Prairie and Forest Fires Act*, which prohibited the starting of a fire without taking adequate precautions to control it, is a safety law of general application, and not an attempt to regulate the use of land. Even if s. 15(a) had touched the "Indianness" of the accused, s. 88 of the *Indian Act* would operate so as to make s. 15(a) applicable against him.

89. (1) Restriction on mortgage, seizure, etc., on property on reserve —

Subject to this Act, the real and personal property of an Indian or a band situated on a reserve is not subject to charge, pledge, mortgage, attachment, levy, seizure, distress or execution in favour or at the instance of any person other than an Indian or a band.

(1.1) Exception — Notwithstanding subsection (1), a leasehold interest in designated lands is subject to charge, pledge, mortgage, attachment, levy, seizure, distress and execution.

(2) Conditional sales — A person who sells to a band or a member of a band a chattel under an agreement whereby the right of property or right of possession thereto remains wholly or in part in the seller, may exercise his rights under the agreement notwithstanding that the chattel is situated on a reserve.

R.S. 1985, c. 17 (4th Supp.), s. 12.

Commentary: Cases under this section overlap with cases under ss. 87 and 90, especially on the issue of personal property situated on a reserve.

Case Law:

General

Alberta (Workers' Compensation Board) v. Enoch Indian Band (1993), 141 A.R. 204, [1993] 8 W.W.R. 77, 11 Alta. L.R. (3d) 305, 20 C.P.C. (3d) 192, 106 D.L.R. (4th) 279, [1994] 2 C.N.L.R. 3 (C.A.)

Assignment of a debt to a collection agency run by an Indian does not render the execution "in favour of an Indian" since the agency was accountable to the non-Indian creditor for 85 per cent of monies garnished. An agreement between band and trust company, which deemed the band's account to be held at the trust company's on-reserve head office even though the account was serviced at an off-reserve branch, does not bind a creditor or collection agency.

Potts v. Potts (1991), 3 R.F.L. (3d) 174, [1991] 5 W.W.R. 639, 80 Alta. L.R. (2d) 395, 81 D.L.R. (4th) 329 (Q.B.)

Clear, independent and unequivocal knowledge on the part of an attached Indian band that the attachment is for the benefit of an Indian removes the need for the attaching party to provide further notice to that effect.

Mintuck v. Valley River Band No. 63A (No. 2), [1978] 2 W.W.R. 159, 83 D.L.R. (3d) 324 (Man. Q.B.)

An Indian may garnishee Indian property.

Kingsclear Indian Band v. J.E. Brooks & Associates Ltd. (1991), 2 P.P.S.A.C. (2d) 151 (N.B. C.A.)

The fact that a band has waived its s. 89 rights as against the Crown in consideration for a loan and chattel mortgage does not preclude the band from exercising those rights against a third party judgment creditor who has seized the mortgaged personal property.

R. v. Bernard (1991), 118 N.B.R. (2d) 361, 296 A.P.R. 361, [1992] 3 C.N.L.R. 33 (Q.B.)

Section 89 does not apply to chattels owned by a corporation.

Campbell v. Sandy, [1956] O.W.N. 441, 4 D.L.R. (2d) 754 (Co. Ct.)

Under s. [89] of the *Indian Act* an Indian judgment debtor is still exempt from execution if he has no property or interests outside the reserve. The judgment creditor, however, is entitled to examine him on judgment summons to ascertain whether he has or not and he stands in no better position so far as the examination is concerned than any other person. If on the examination it appears that he has property or interests outside the reserve and therefore subject to execution, an order can be made against him. [D.L.R. p. 756]

Syrette v. Sewell, [1997] 1 C.N.L.R. 207 (Ont. Small Claims Ct.)

The defendants were police officers. Following a court order in favour of the non-Native wife of the plaintiff Syrette, the officers seized the vehicle of the plaintiff from the Rankin reserve. The plaintiff was a member of the Band. The court found that the seizure was prohibited under s.89. The police officers were ordered to pay damages to the plaintiff.

Bellegarde v. Qu'Appelle Indian Residential School Council Inc. (1991), 92 Sask. R. 285, (sub nom. *Bellegarde v. Araquod)* 83 D.L.R. (4th) 327 (C.A.)

Garnishment proceedings, directed against a school located on a reserve that employed the debtor, were dismissed where the creditor failed to establish that he was a status Indian. The school enjoyed the protection of s. 89(1) of the Act.

Situated on Reserve — Canada

Westbank Indian Band v. Robertson, [1990] 4 C.N.L.R. 112, 36 F.T.R. 286

A garnishing order obtained by a non-Indian creditor requiring a bank to pay the band's debt from its bank account was set aside, as the money was deemed to be situate on the reserve, and was therefore not subject to garnishment by a non-Indian.

Situated on Reserve — British Columbia

Armstrong Growers' Assn. v. Harris (1924), 33 B.C.R. 285, [1924] 1 W.W.R. 729, [1924] 1 D.L.R. 1043 (C.A.)(decided under the former *Indian Act*, R.S.C. 1906, c. 81)

A debt owing to an Indian by a non-Indian who purchased grain grown on the reserve, is due and payable on the reserve and thus is exempt from garnishee.

Canadian Imperial Bank of Commerce v. E. & S. Liquidators, Ltd., [1994] 1 C.N.L.R. 23 (B.C. S.C.)

Funds of a registered Indian in a bank located on designated lands were protected from garnishment because they were personal property situated on a reserve.

Fricke v. Michell, [1986] 1 W.W.R. 544, 67 B.C.L.R. 227, (sub nom. *Fricke v. Moricetown Indian Band)* [1986] 1 C.N.L.R. 11 (S.C.)

Money that was appropriated by Parliament for the use and benefit of a band, paid to the band under an agreement for the provision of education, social assistance, housing, health and welfare, and unemployment works programs, and deposited in an account at a bank that was not situated on a reserve was held to be the personal property of a band situated on a reserve and thus not liable to attachment.

Geoffries v. Williams (1958), 26 W.W.R. 323, 16 D.L.R. (2d) 157 (B.C. Co. Ct.)(decided under the *Indian Act*, R.S.C. 1952, c. 149)

A debt is situate where the debtor resides. Money owed to an Indian by a debtor who does not reside on the reserve is not the personal property of an Indian situated on a reserve and is, therefore, subject to a garnishing order issued by a creditor of the Indian.

Situated on Reserve — New Brunswick

Kingsclear Indian Band v. J.E. Brooks & Associates Ltd. (1991), 2 P.P.S.A.C. (2d) 151 (N.B. C.A.)

Parking a school bus on the reserve when it was not in use gave it sufficient connection to the reserve to bring it under the protection of s. 89(1), even when it was seized by creditors while off the reserve.

Ex parte Tenasse (1931), 2 M.P.R. 523, [1931] 1 D.L.R. 806 (N.B. C.A.)

Generally, Indian property outside of a reserve is similar to property of non-Indians and is subject to attachment in the absence of legislative protection.

Situated on Reserve — Quebec

Vincent v. Quebec (Deputy-Minister of Revenue), [1995] 3 C.N.L.R. 204 (Que. C.A.)

Moneys belonging to a member of Kahnawake were seized by the R.C.M.P. after a provincial official issued an assessment notice claiming unpaid taxes for cigarettes. The province then attempted to have the R.C.M.P. turn the money over to the province, arguing that section 89 did not apply because the R.C.M.P. had taken the money physically off the reserve. The judge found that the money had been illegally removed from the reserve, and therefore, the money continued to be protected by section 89.

Situated on Reserve — Saskatchewan

Houston v. Standingready (1990), [1991] 1 W.W.R. 744, [1991] 2 C.N.L.R. 65, 88 Sask. R. 316 (C.A.)

The bank accounts of Indians living on a reserve, which were located in financial institutions outside of the reserve, were held to be subject to garnishment by a non-Indian creditor. After obtaining judgment against a company and its Indian directors, the creditor applied for a garnishment order against the directors' personal bank accounts located off the reserve. The application was denied on the basis that the attached debts were the personal property of Indians "situated on a reserve" within the meaning of the section. On appeal, it was held that the accounts were situated at the location of the branch, which was off the reserve. There was no connection between the deposits and the occupancy of reserve lands, and hence s. 89(1) did not apply.

Support Orders

Potts v. Potts (1991), 31 R.F.L. (3d) 66, [1991] 3 W.W.R. 11, 77 D.L.R. (4th) 369, 113 A.R. 276, 78 Alta. L.R. (2d) 240, [1992] 1 C.N.L.R. 182 (C.A.)

The Peigan Band Council objected to an order to pay part of an employee's wages to the provincial Director of Maintenance Enforcement. The court found that the Director is a trustee, and the creditor a beneficiary. The Director paid the money to the creditor. The court found that section 89 did not prevent enforcement.

Agapi v. Youngpine (1994), 164 A.R. 145, [1995] A.W.L.D. 107, [1995] W.D.F.L. 148 (Q.B.)

This case followed *Potts v. Potts*, and found that section 89 was not violated if the Director of Maintenance Enforcement paid the money collected to the provincial government to repay social allowances paid to the creditor.

Dir. of Support & Custody Enforcement v. Nowegejick, [1989] 2 C.N.L.R. 27 (Ont. Fam. Ct.)

Provincial laws dealing with the enforcement of family law support orders are applicable to Indians, and garnishment laws can be used to collect debts owed to Indians within the limits of s. 89.

Bellegarde v. Walker (1987), 6 R.F.L. (3d) 317, 36 D.L.R. (4th) 700, [1987] 4 C.N.L.R. 28, 57 Sask. R. 197 (Q.B.)

This section does not prevent a garnishee under provincial enforcement of maintenance orders legislation when the wife seeking maintenance is an Indian.

Government Payments

Mitchell v. Peguis Indian Band, [1990] 2 S.C.R. 85, [1990] 5 W.W.R. 97, 71 D.L.R. (4th) 193, 67 Man. R. (2d) 81, [1990] 3 C.N.L.R. 46, 3 T.C.T. 5219, 110 N.R. 241

A refund of sales tax paid by the band to Manitoba Hydro, which the government agreed to pay, is not subject to attachment. The term **"personal property"** should be given a liberal construction, and the meaning should be the same in ss. 87 and 89.

Fox v. Peterson Livestock Ltd., [1982] 2 W.W.R. 204, 17 Alta. L.R. (2d) 311, 131 D.L.R. (3d) 716, 35 A.R. 471 (C.A.)

Money that may be received at some future time from a per capita distribution under s. 64(*a*) cannot be attached because the money is not due or accruing due. Money that may be paid to an Indian, and which is only an expectation of a gratuitous distribution by the Minister, cannot be the subject of an equitable execution such as the appointment of a receiver.

Royal Bank v. White Bear Indian Band (1991), 88 Sask. R. 289, [1992] 1 C.N.L.R. 174 (Q.B.)

Payments made to an Indian band by various federal departments, and deposited in a credit union, were not subject to attachment by virtue of the operation of s. 89(1).

Fayerman Bros. Ltd. v. Peter Ballantyne Indian Band (1986), 36 Sask. R. 76, [1986] 1 C.N.L.R. 6 (Q.B.)

Money paid by the Department of Indian Affairs and Northern Development to a bank in favour of a band is personal property of the band and not subject to attachment.

90. (1) Property deemed situated on reserve — **For the purposes of sections 87 and 89, personal property that was**

(a) purchased by Her Majesty with Indian moneys or moneys appropriated by Parliament for the use and benefit of Indians or bands, or

(b) given to Indians or to a band under a treaty or agreement between a band and Her Majesty,

shall be deemed always to be situated on a reserve.

(2) Restriction on transfer — **Every transaction purporting to pass title to any property that is by this section deemed to be situated on a reserve, or any interest in such property, is void unless the transaction is entered into with the consent of the Minister or is entered into between members of a band or between the band and a member thereof.**

(3) Destruction of property — Every person who enters into any transaction that is void by virtue of subsection (2) is guilty of an offence, and every person who, without the written consent of the Minister, destroys personal property that is by this section deemed to be situated on a reserve, is guilty of an offence.

Commentary: Cases under this section overlap with cases under ss. 87 and 89, especially on the issue of personal property situated on a reserve.

Case Law:

Section 90(1) — Canada

Mitchell v. Peguis Indian Band, [1990] 2 S.C.R. 85, [1990] 5 W.W.R. 97, 71 D.L.R. (4th) 193, [1990] 3 C.N.L.R. 46, 3 T.C.T. 5219, 110 N.R. 241, 67 Man. R. (2d) 81

Consultants for the Band sued the Band when they were not paid. The Band relied on s. 90. While the court found against the Band, LaForest, J. made the following observation about the purpose of these sections.

> In summary, the historical record makes it clear that ss. 87 and 89 of the *Indian Act*, the sections to which the deeming provision of s. 90 applies, constitute part of a legislative 'package' which bears the impress of an obligation to native peoples which the Crown has recognized at least since the signing of the Royal Proclamation of 1763. From that time on, the Crown has always acknowledged that it is honour-bound to shield Indians from any efforts by non-Natives to dispossess Indians of the property which they hold qua Indians, i.e., their land base and the chattels on that land base.
>
> It is also important to underscore the corollary to the conclusion I have just drawn. The fact that the modern-day legislation, like its historical counterparts, is so careful to underline that exemptions from taxation and distraint apply only in respect of personal property situated on reserves demonstrates that the purpose of the legislation is not to remedy the economically disadvantaged position of Indians by ensuring that Indians may acquire, hold, and deal with property in the commercial mainstream on different terms than their fellow citizens. An examination of the decisions bearing on these sections confirms that Indians who acquire and deal in property outside lands reserved for their use, deal with it on the same basis as all other Canadians. [S.C.R. p.131]

— See also *Fricke v. Michell*, [1986] 1 W.W.R. 544, 67 B.C.L.R. 227, (sub nom. *Fricke v. Moricetown Indian Band*) [1986] 1 C.N.L.R. 11 (S.C.)*Fayerman Bros. Ltd. v. Peter Ballantyne Indian Band* (1986), 36 Sask. R. 76, [1986] 1 C.N.L.R. 6 (Q.B.)

Kostyshyn (Johnson) v. West Region Tribal Council Inc. (1992), [1994] 1 C.N.L.R. 94, 55 F.T.R. 48 (T.D.)

The native tribal council being neither an Indian nor an Indian band, but rather a corporation, was not exempt from garnishment pursuant to ss. 89 and 90.

R. v. National Indian Brotherhood, [1979] 1 F.C. 103, [1978] C.T.C. 680, 92 D.L.R. (3d) 333, 78 D.T.C. 6488 (T.D.)leave to appeal to S.C.C. refused (1986), 66 N.R. 78 (note) (S.C.C.)

The National Indian Brotherhood (N.I.B.) was an organization representing registered Indian Bands. Its head office was located in Ottawa. Employees of the organization argued that they should not have to pay income tax. One of the arguments was that they were paid from moneys appropriated by Parliament for the use and benefit of Indians, and therefore their pay should be deemed to be personal property situated on a reserve.

The court held that the operative words in paragraph 90(1)(a) were "personal property *purchased* by Her Majesty". The money itself was not deemed to be situated on the reserve: only the property which was purchased was deemed to be on reserve. This property could be purchased by the Crown with two sources of funds, Indian moneys and moneys appropriated by Parliament. Consequently, the salaries themselves could not be deemed to be situated on reserve.

Matthew v. Canada, [1997] T.C.J. No. 550 (T.C.C.)

Martha Matthew was a member of the North Thompson Indian Band. She worked at the off reserve office of the Department of Indian Affairs. She did not have to pay tax for the 58 days she worked on reserve, but she was assessed income tax for the remainder of her pay. She challenged the decision, arguing that her pay was from moneys appropriated by Parliament for the use and benefit of Indians, and therefore deemed to be personal property situated on a reserve.

The court followed *R. v. The National Indian Brotherhood* (see above), and held that her income was taxable.

> Parliament refers to only two categories of personal property in subsection 90(1): First, personal property that is purchased. This property is described in paragraph (a) and that is purchased with either Indian moneys or moneys appropriated by Parliament. The second category of personal property is found in paragraph (b) and, is property that is given to Indians or to bands. [at para.24]

Horn v. M.N.R., [1989] 3 C.N.L.R. 59 (T.C.C.)

The skills, training and background of an employee of the federal government are not, and cannot be, "personal property purchased by Her Majesty" under this section, nor are that employee's wages such property. Hence, those wages are not exempt from taxation.

Section 90(1) — British Columbia

Nathanson, Schachter & Thompson v. Sarcee Band of Indians, [1994] 6 W.W.R. 203, 90 B.C.L.R. (2d) 13, 24 C.P.C. (3d) 336, [1994] 4 C.N.L.R. 58 (B.C. C.A.)Leave to appeal to the Supreme Court of Canada denied.

At issue were funds from an out-of-court settlement of a law suit which relied on breach of duties owed by the Crown. The court found that these funds did not fall within s.90(1)(b), and stated:

> I do not see how it could be said that the bargain struck in these circumstances was in discharge of the Crown's treaty obligations, or was in some way ancillary to treaty obligations. It was, in every respect, a commercial bargain such as might be concluded between any litigants intent on resolving their dispute out of court. [C.N.L.R. p. 65-66]

Section 90(1) — Manitoba

Webtech Controls Inc. v. Cross Lake Band of Indians, [1991] 3 C.N.L.R. 182 (Man. Q.B.)

Moneys in a bank account located outside a reserve which were paid to a native person pursuant to an agreement to which the Crown is a party are exempt from seizure under s. 90.

Section 90(1) — New Brunswick

Kingsclear Indian Band v. J.E. Brooks & Associates Ltd. (1991), 2 P.P.S.A.C. (2d) 151 (N.B. C.A.)

It is not necessary for the Crown to purchase personal property directly in order for the deeming provisions of s. 90(1) to take effect. A purchase made by a band by means of a loan from the Crown is sufficient to trigger the section.

Section 90(1)(b)

Sturgeon Lake Indian Band v. Tomporowski Architectural Group Ltd. (1991), 95 Sask. R. 302 (Q.B.)

Treaty monies deposited at a bank located off the reserve, which were used to pay band salaries and establish a building fund, were deemed to be situated on the reserve pursuant to s. 90(1)(b), and not subject to attachment.

Trading with Indians

91. (1) Certain property on a reserve may not be acquired — No person may, without the written consent of the Minister, acquire title to any of the following property situated on a reserve, namely:

(a) an Indian grave house;

(b) a carved grave pole;

(c) a totem pole;

(d) a carved house post; or

(e) a rock embellished with paintings or carvings.

(2) Saving — Subsection (1) does not apply to chattels referred to therein that are manufactured for sale by Indians.

(3) Removal, destruction, etc. — No person shall remove, take away, mutilate, disfigure, deface or destroy any chattel referred to in subsection (1) without the written consent of the Minister.

(4) Punishment — A person who violates this section is guilty of an offence and is liable on summary conviction to a fine not exceeding two hundred dollars or to imprisonment for a term not exceeding three months.

92. (1) Departmental employees, etc., prohibited from trading without a licence — No person who is

(a) an officer or employee in the Department,

(b) a missionary engaged in mission work among Indians, or

(c) a school teacher on a reserve,

shall, without a licence from the Minister or his duly authorized representative, trade for profit with an Indian or sell to him directly or indirectly goods or chattels, but no such licence shall be issued to a full-time officer or employee in the Department.

(2) Cancellation of licence — The Minister or his duly authorized representative may at any time cancel a licence given under this section.

(3) Punishment — A person who violates subsection (1) is guilty of an offence and is liable on summary conviction to a fine not exceeding five hundred dollars.

(4) Dismissal — Without prejudice to subsection (3), an officer or employee in the Department who contravenes subsection (1) may be dismissed from office.

Removal of Materials from Reserves

93. Removal of material from reserves — A person who, without the written permission of the Minister or his duly authorized representative,

   (a) removes or permits anyone to remove from a reserve

      (i) minerals, stone, sand, gravel, clay or soil, or

      (ii) trees, saplings, shrubs, underbrush, timber, cordwood or hay, or

   (b) has in his possession anything removed from a reserve contrary to this section,

is guilty of an offence and is liable on summary conviction to a fine not exceeding five hundred dollars or to imprisonment for a term not exceeding three months, or to both.

Case Law: *Pac. Simpson Lbr. Ltd. v. Kaisha*, [1982] 3 W.W.R. 194, 129 D.L.R. (3d) 236 (B.C. C.A.)

Related Provisions: Regulation of minerals is governed by the *Indian Oil and Gas Act*, R.S.C. 1985, c. I-7; *Indian Oil and Gas Regulations*, 1995, SOR/94-753; *Indian Mining Regulations*, C.R.C. 1978, c. 956; *Indian Timber Regulations*, C.R.C. 1978, c. 961.

94.–100 [Repealed R.S. 1985, c. 32 (1st Supp.), s. 17.]

Commentary: The courts had found these sections inoperative since they offended s. 1(b) of the Canadian Bill of Rights. See: *R. v. Hayden* (1983), [1983] 6 W.W.R. 655, 36 C.R. (3d) 187, 8 C.C.C. (3d) 33, 3 D.L.R. (4th) 361, 5 C.H.R.R. D/2121, 23 Man. R. (2d) 315leave to appeal to S.C.C. refused 8 C.C.C. (3d) 33n, 3 D.L.R. (4th) 361n, 26 Man. R. (2d) 318n*R. v. Drybones* (1970), [1970] S.C.R. 282, 71 W.W.R. 161, 10 C.R.N.S. 334, [1970] 3 C.C.C. 355, 9 D.L.R. 473

Offences, Punishment and Enforcement

101. Certificate of analysis is evidence — In every prosecution under this Act a certificate of analysis furnished by an analyst employed by the Government of Canada or by a province shall be accepted as evidence of the facts stated therein and of the authority of the person giving or issuing the certificate, without proof of the signature of the person appearing to have signed the certificate or his official character, and without further proof thereof.

102. Penalty where no other provided — Every person who is guilty of an offence against any provision of this Act or any regulation made by the Governor in Council or the Minister for which a penalty is not provided elsewhere in this Act or the regulations, is liable on summary conviction to a fine not exceeding two hundred dollars or to imprisonment for a term not exceeding three months, or to both.

103. (1) Seizure of goods — Whenever a peace officer, a superintendent or a person authorized by the Minister believes on reasonable grounds that an offence against section 33, 85.1, 90 or 93 has been committed, he may seize all goods and chattels by means of or in relation to which he believes on reasonable grounds the offence was committed.

(2) Detection — All goods and chattels seized pursuant to subsection (1) may be detained for a period of three months following the day of seizure unless during that period proceedings under this Act in respect of such offence are undertaken, in which case the goods and chattels may be further detained until such proceedings are finally concluded.

(3) Forfeiture — Where a person is convicted of an offence against the sections mentioned in subsection (1), the convicting court or judge may order that the goods and chattels by means of or in relation to which the offence was committed, in addition to any penalty imposed, are forfeited to Her Majesty and may be disposed of as the Minister directs.

(4) Search — A justice who is satisfied by information upon oath that there is reasonable ground to believe that there are upon a reserve or in any building, receptacle or place any goods or chattels by means of or in relation to which an offence against any of the sections mentioned in subsection (1) has been, is being or is about to be committed, may at any time issue a warrant under his hand authorizing a person named therein or a peace officer at any time to search the reserve, building, receptacle or place for any such goods or chattels.

R.S. 1985, c. 32 (1st Supp.), s. 19.

Case Law: *R. v. Hatchard* (1991), [1993] 1 C.N.L.R. 96 (Ont. Gen. Div.)

It was stated, *obiter*, that while band constables may not be peace officers under the Criminal Code, neither are they private citizens, and the Charter may be applicable to their activities. The *Indian Act* introduces a semblance of government-like organizations, and the power of band constables fall somewhere in between those of a peace officer and those of a private citizen.

104. Disposition of fines — Every fine, penalty or forfeiture imposed under this Act belongs to Her Majesty for the benefit of the band with respect to which or to one or more members of which the offence was committed or to which the offender, if an Indian, belongs, but the Governor in Council may from time to time direct that the fine, penalty or forfeiture shall be paid to a provincial, municipal or local authority that bears in whole or in part the expense of administering the law under which the fine, penalty or forfeiture shall be applied in the manner that he considers will best promote the purpose of the law under which the fine, penalty or forfeiture is imposed, or the administration of that law.

105. Description of Indians in writs, etc. — In any order, writ, warrant, summons or proceeding issued under this Act it is sufficient if the name of the Indian or other person referred to therein is the name given to, or the name by which the Indian or other person is known by, the person who issues the order, writ, warrant, summons or proceeding, and if no part of the name of the person is given to or known by the person issuing the order, writ, warrant, summons or proceeding, it is sufficient if the Indian or other person is described in any manner by which he may be identified.

106. Jurisdiction of magistrates — A police magistrate or a stipendiary magistrate has and may exercise, with respect to matters arising under this Act, jurisdiction over the whole county, union of counties or judicial district in which the city, town or other place for which he is appointed or in which he has jurisdiction under provincial laws is situated.

Case Law: *R. v. Crosby* (1982), 54 C.C.C. (2d) 497, [1982] 1 C.N.L.R. 102 (Ont. C.A.)

Section 106 is not the basis of jurisdiction for the trial of offences created by the *Indian Act*. Such offences are triable by the ordinary courts. Section 106 merely increases the limited territorial jurisdiction of police magistrates and stipendiary magistrates.

107. Appointment of justices — The Governor in Council may appoint persons to be, for the purposes of this Act, justices of the peace and those persons have and may exercise the powers and authority of two justices of the peace with regard to

(a) offences under this Act, and

(b) any offence against the provisions of the Criminal Code relating to cruelty to animals, common assault, breaking and entering and vagrancy, where the offence is committed by an Indian or relates to the person or property of an Indian.

Case Law: *Connolly v. Conseil des Montagnais* (1990), 128 N.R. 72 (Fed. C.A.)

Section 107 gives a justice of the peace jurisdiction only over *Indian Act* or Criminal Code offences. A band council cannot enact an administrative by-law granting the justice of the peace jurisdiction not given by the *Indian Act*.

R. v. Crosby (1982), 54 C.C.C. (2d) 497, [1982] 1 C.N.L.R. 102 (Ont. C.A.)

Although section 107 empowers the Governor in Council to appoint persons to be, for the purpose of the Act, Justices of the Peace, that section does not detract from the general assumption that offences under the Act are to be tried in the ordinary Courts of the Province in which the reserve is situate. [C.C.C. p. 502]

108. Commissioners for taking oaths — For the purposes of this Act or any matter relating to Indian affairs

(a) persons appointed by the Minister for the purpose,

(b) superintendents, and

(c) the Minister, Deputy Minister and the chief officer in charge of the branch of the Department relating to Indian affairs,

are *ex officio* commissioners for the taking of oaths.

109.–113. [Repealed R.S. 1985, c. 32 (1st Supp.), s. 20.]

Schools

114. (1) Agreements with provinces, etc. — The Governor in Council may authorize the Minister, in accordance with this Act, to enter into agreements on behalf of Her Majesty for the education in accordance with this Act of Indian children with

(a) the government of a province,

(b) the Commissioner of the Northwest Territories,

(c) the Commissioner of the Yukon Territory,

(c.1) the Commissioner of Nunavut;
              [1993, c. 28, s. 78 (Schedule III, item 74). Not in force at date of publication]

(d) a public or separate school board, and

(e) a religious or charitable organization.

(2) **Schools** — The Minister may, in accordance with this Act, establish, operate and maintain schools for Indian children.

1993, c. 28, s. 78 (Schedule III, item 74).

Case Law: *Chadee v. Norway House First Nation*, [1997] 2 C.N.L.R. 48 (Man.C.A.)

The court case arose out of an employment dispute involving the First Nation and an education director for the First Nation. The First Nation's lawyer argued that the Band was acting as an agent of the Crown pursuant to ss. 114 and 115. On this point, the court commented:

> Those provisions [ss.114–115] permit the Governor in Council or the Minister to make provision for the education of Indian children. But the sections are not mandatory. The local community is free to make its own arrangement for facilities and staff to provide a suitable educational program for its children. In doing so, the band council is not under the direction or supervision of the Minister. [W.W.R. p. 345]

Kinistino Sch. Div. 55 v. James Smith Indian Band, [1988] 5 W.W.R. 404, 66 Sask. R. 224, [1988] 4 C.N.L.R. 60 (Q.B.)affirmed (1988), [1989] 2 W.W.R. 94, [1989] 2 C.N.L.R. 67, 73 Sask. R. 236 (C.A.)

This section does not preclude a board of education from dealing directly with a band council to provide educational services.

Related Provisions: Sections 114 to 122 only apply to Indians who are ordinarily resident on reserve or resident on Crown Lands (See section 4(3)).

115. Regulations — The Minister may

(a) provide for and make regulations with respect to standards for buildings, equipment, teaching, education, inspection and discipline in connection with schools;

(b) provide for the transportation of children to and from school;

(c) enter into agreements with religious organizations for the support and maintenance of children who are being educated in schools operated by those organizations; and

(d) apply to the whole or any part of moneys that would otherwise be payable to or on behalf of a child who is attending a residential school to the maintenance of that child at that school.

Case Law: *Canada (Human Rights Commission) v. Canada (Department of Indian Affairs & Northern Development)*, [1995] 3 C.N.L.R. 28, 25 C.R.R. (2d) 230 (Fed. T.D.)

The Minister changed a funding policy which allowed students to choose schools based on their religious preference. In this case, a student attending a Catholic school 125 miles away ceased to receive funding to attend that school. The Federal Court upheld the dismissal of the complaint under the *Canadian Human Rights Act*, relying on section 67 of that statute. Section 67 immunized the *Indian Act* from the provisions of the *Canadian Human Rights Act*.

Related Provisions: Sections 114 to 122 only apply to Indians who are ordinarily resident on reserve or resident on Crown Lands (See section 4(3)).

116. (1) Attendance — Subject to section 117, every Indian child who has attained the age of seven years shall attend school.

(2) Idem — The Minister may

(a) require an Indian who has attained the age of six years to attend school;

(b) require an Indian who becomes sixteen years of age during the school term to continue to attend school until the end of that term; and

(c) require an Indian who becomes sixteen years of age to attend school for such further period as the Minister considers advisable, but no Indian shall be required to attend school after he becomes eighteen years of age.

Related Provisions: Sections 114 to 122 only apply to Indians who are ordinarily resident on reserve or resident on Crown Lands (See section 4(3)).

117. When attendance not required — An Indian child is not required to attend school if the child

(a) is, by reason of sickness or other unavoidable cause that is reported promptly to the principal, unable to attend school;

(b) is, with the permission in writing of the superintendent, absent from school for a period not exceeding six weeks in each term for the purpose of assisting in husbandry or urgent and necessary household duties;

(c) is under efficient instruction at home or elsewhere, within one year after the written approval by the Minister of such instruction; or

(d) is unable to attend school because there is insufficient accommodation in the school that the child is entitled or directed to attend.

Related Provisions: Sections 114 to 122 only apply to Indians who are ordinarily resident on reserve or resident on Crown Lands (See section 4(3)).

118. School to be attended — Every Indian child who is required to attend school shall attend such school as the Minister may designate, but no child whose parent is a Protestant shall be assigned to a school conducted under Roman Catholic auspices and no child whose parent is a Roman Catholic shall be assigned to a school conducted under Protestant auspices, except by written direction of the parent.

Case Law: *Canada (Human Rights Commission) v. Canada (Department of Indian Affairs & Northern Development)*, [1995] 3 C.N.L.R. 28, 25 C.R.R. (2d) 230 (Fed. T.D.)

The Minister changed a funding policy which allowed students to choose schools based on their religious preference. In this case, a student attending a Catholic school 125 miles away ceased to receive funding to attend that school. The Federal Court upheld the dismissal of the complaint under the *Canadian Human Rights Act*, relying on section 67 of that statute. Section 67 immunized the *Indian Act* from the provisions of the *Canadian Human Rights Act*.

Related Provisions: Sections 114 to 122 only apply to Indians who are ordinarily resident on reserve or resident on Crown Lands (See section 4(3)).

119. (1) **Truant officers** — The Minister may appoint persons, to be called truant officers, to enforce the attendance of Indian children at school, and for that purpose a truant officer has the powers of a peace officer.

(2) **Powers** — Without restricting the generality of subsection (1), a truant officer may, subject to subsection (2.1),

(a) enter any place where he believes, on reasonable grounds, that there are Indian children who are between the ages of seven and sixteen years, or who are required by the Minister to attend school;

(b) investigate any case of truancy; and

(c) serve written notice upon the parent, guardian or other person having the care or legal custody of a child to cause the child to attend school regularly thereafter.

(2.1) **Warrant required to enter dwelling-house** — Where any place referred to in paragraph (2)(a) is a dwelling-house, a truant officer may not enter that dwelling-house without the consent of the occupant except under the authority of a warrant issued under subsection (2.2).

(2.2) **Authority to issue warrant** — Where on *ex parte* application a justice of the peace is satisfied by information on oath

(a) that the conditions for entry described in paragraph (2)(a) exist in relation to a dwelling-house,

(b) that entry to the dwelling-house is necessary for any purpose relating to the administration or enforcement of this Act, and

(c) that entry to the dwelling-house has been refused or that there are reasonable grounds for believing that entry thereto will be refused,

he may issue a warrant under his hand authorizing the truant officer named therein to enter that dwelling-house subject to such conditions as may be specified in the warrant.

(2.3) **Use of force** — In executing a warrant issued under subsection (2.2), the truant officer named therein shall not use force unless he is accompanied by a peace officer and the use of force has been specifically authorized in the warrant.

(3) **Notice to attend school** — Where a notice has been served in accordance with paragraph (2)(c) with respect to a child who is required by this Act to attend school, and the child does not within three days after the service of notice attend school and continue to attend school regularly thereafter, the person upon whom the notice was served is guilty of an offence and is liable on summary conviction to a fine of not more than five dollars or to imprisonment for a term not exceeding ten days, or to both.

(4) **Further notices** — Where a person has been served with a notice in accordance with paragraph (2)(c), it is not necessary within a period of twelve months thereafter to serve that person with any other notice in respect of further non-compliance with the provisions of this Act, and whenever such person within the period of twelve months fails to cause the child with respect to whom the notice was served or any other child of whom he has charge or control to attend school and continue in regular attendance as

required by this Act, such person is guilty of an offence and liable to the penalties imposed by subsection (3) as if he had been served with the notice.

(5) **Tardiness** — A child who is habitually late for school shall be deemed to be absent from school.

(6) **Take into custody** — A truant officer may take into custody a child whom he believes on reasonable grounds to be absent from school contrary to this Act and may convey the child to school, using as much force as the circumstances require.

Related Provisions: Sections 114 to 122 only apply to Indians who are ordinarily resident on reserve or resident on Crown Lands (See section 4(3)).

120. (1) **Denomination of teacher** — Where the majority of the members of a band belongs to one religious denomination, the school established on the reserve that has been set apart for the use and benefit of that band shall be taught by a teacher of that denomination.

(2) **Idem** — Where the majority of the members of a band are not members of the same religious denomination and the band by a majority vote of those electors of the band who were present at a meeting called for the purpose requests that day schools on the reserve should be taught by a teacher belonging to a particular religious denomination, the school on that reserve shall be taught by a teacher of that denomination.

Related Provisions: Sections 114 to 122 only apply to Indians who are ordinarily resident on reserve or resident on Crown Lands (See section 4(3)).

121. **Minority religious denominations** — A Protestant or Roman Catholic minority of any band may, with the approval of and under regulations to be made by the Minister, have a separate day school or day school classroom established on the reserve unless, in the opinion of the Governor in Council, the number of children of school age does not so warrant.

Related Provisions: Sections 114 to 122 only apply to Indians who are ordinarily resident on reserve or resident on Crown Lands (See section 4(3)).

Definitions: Section 114 to 122 only apply to Indians who are ordinarily resident on reserve or resident on Crown Lands (See section 4(3).

122. **Definitions** — In sections 114 to 122

"child" means an Indian who has attained the age of six years but has not attained the age of sixteen years, and a person who is required by the Minister to attend school;

"school" includes a day school, technical school, high school and a residential school;

"truant officer" includes

    (a) a member of the Royal Canadian Mounted Police,

    (b) a special constable appointed for police duty on a reserve; and

    (c) a school teacher and a chief of the band, when authorized by the superintendent.

INDIAN ACT
REGULATIONS

Calculation of Interest Regulations

Regulations prescribing the manner of determining interest for the purpose of subsections 64.1(1) and (2) of the Indian Act

SOR/87-631

Short Title

1. These Regulations may be cited as the *Calculation of Interest Regulations*.

Interpretation

2. In these Regulations,

"Act" means the *Indian Act*;

"principal amount outstanding" means the amount received by a person under paragraph 15(1)(a) of the Act, as it read immediately prior to April 17, 1985, or under any former provision of the Act relating to the same subject-matter as that paragraph, less the sum of one thousand dollars and less the amounts withheld under subsection 64.1(1) of the Act and the amounts repaid under subsection 64.1(2) of the Act in respect of that person;

"reinstatement " means the entering of the name of a person referred to in subsection 64.1(1) or (2) of the Act in a Band List.

Application

3. These Regulations apply to persons referred to in subsections 64.1(1) and (2) of the Act who make an application for reinstatement.

Calculation of Interest

4. For the purpose of subsections 64.1(1) and (2) of the Act, interest shall be calculated

   (a) on the principal amount outstanding only;

   (b) quarterly on the average month-end balance of the principal amount outstanding;

   (c) at a rate equal to the quarterly average of the interest rates applied by the Bank of Canada to Government of Canada Treasury bills of terms of six months; and

   (d) from the date referred to in section 5.

Accrual of Interest

5. (1) Where reinstatement of a person referred to in paragraph 11(1)(c) or 11(2)(a) of the Act is made, interest accrues from the later of

(a) November 1, 1987; and

(b) subject to subsection (2), the date of signature on the application for reinstatement.

(2) Where there is a difference of more than 30 days between the date of signature on an application for reinstatement and the date on which the application is received by the Registrar, interest shall accrue from the date on which the application is received by the Registrar.

(3) Where reinstatement of a person is made pursuant to membership rules made pursuant to section 10 of the Act, interest accrues from the later of

(a) November 1, 1987; and

(b) the date of reinstatement of the person.

Method of Applying Moneys Withheld or Repaid

6. Where an amount is withheld under subsection 64.1(1) of the Act or is repaid under subsection 64.1(2) of the Act, the amount shall be applied first against the principal amount outstanding, and second against accrued interest.

7. For the purposes of section 6, the effective date on which an amount is applied shall be

(a) where the amount is withheld pursuant to subsection 64.1(1) of the Act, the date that the person would have been entitled to receive the amount but for that subsection; and

(b) where the amount is repaid pursuant to subsection 64.1(2) of the Act, the date that the amount is received by the band.

Disposal of Forfeited Goods and Chattels Regulations

Regulations respecting the disposal of goods and chattels ordered forfeited pursuant to subsection 103(3) of the Indian Act

C.R.C. 1978, c. 948

Short Title

1. These Regulations may be cited as the *Disposal of Forfeited Goods and Chattels Regulations.*

Interpretation

2. In these Regulations, "Act" means the *Indian Act.*

General

3. Goods and chattels forfeited to Her Majesty pursuant to the provisions of subsection 103(3) of the Act shall be sold at public auction following advertisement published in such local papers as the Minister may designate.

4. Where any goods and chattels have been forfeited pursuant to subsection 103(3) of the Act, anyone (other than the person accused of an offence resulting in such forfeiture, or the person in possession of such goods and chattels when the offence was committed) who claims an interest in such goods and chattels as owner, mortgagee, lien-holder or holder of any like interest, may, within 30 days after such forfeiture, apply to the Minister for a determination of his interest.

5. Where, following such application, it appears to the satisfaction of the Minister,

(a) that the claimant is innocent of any complicity in the offence resulting in such forfeiture, or of any collusion with the offender in relation thereto, and

(b) that he exercised all reasonable care in respect of the person permitted to obtain the possession of such goods and chattels to satisfy himself that they were not likely to be used contrary to the provisions of the Act, or, if a mortgagee or lien-holder, that before becoming such mortgagee or lien-holder exercised such care with respect to the mortgagor or lien-giver,

the Minister may order that the interest of the claimant be not affected by such forfeiture.

6. Where the circumstances make it appear to the Minister that the goods and chattels forfeited pursuant to subsection 103(3) of the Act should in the public interest be disposed of otherwise than by public auction, the Minister may direct that they be otherwise disposed of, in which case the direction shall prescribe such conditions and restrictions as the Minister may deem necessary or advisable.

Indian Band Council Borrowing Regulations

**Regulations respecting the borrowing of money by councils of bands
and the dispositions of such moneys**

C.R.C. 1978, c. 949

Short Title

1. These Regulations may be cited as the *Indian Band Council Borrowing Regulations.*

General

2. The council of a band may borrow money for band projects or housing purposes and may make loans out of moneys so borrowed to members of the band for housing purposes, on such terms and conditions as may be determined by the council.

Indian Bands Council Method of Election Regulations

SOR/90-46, as am. SOR/92-366; SOR/97-134

Whereas the Minister of Indian Affairs and Northern Development, pursuant to subsection 74(1) of the Indian Act, declared by the Indian Bands Council Election Order made on December 14, 1989, that the council of each of the bands set out in the schedules to the Regulations in Part II of the schedule hereto shall after December 14, 1989, be selected by elections to be held in accordance with the Act;

And Whereas the Governor in Council considers it appropriate to revoke all previous orders and regulations made pursuant to subsection 74(3) or (4) of the Indian Act and to make a single regulation in substitution therefor;

And Whereas, pursuant to subsection 74(4) of the Indian Act, a majority of the electors of each of the bands set out in Schedule III to the Regulations in Part II of the schedule hereto, who were present and voted at a referendum or a special meeting held and called for the purpose, have decided that the reserve of each of those bands should for voting purposes be divided into electoral sections and the Minister of Indian Affairs and Northern Development so recommends;

Therefore, Her Excellency the Governor General in Council, on the recommendation of the Minister of Indian Affairs and Northern Development, pursuant to subsections 74(3) and (4) of the Indian Act, is pleased hereby to

(a) revoke all orders and regulations made pursuant to subsection 74(3) or (4) of the Indian Act including the orders listed in Part I of the schedule hereto; and

(b) make, in substitution therefor, the regulations providing for the method of electing the chief and councillors of certain Indian Bands and the division of certain reserves into electoral sections in Part II of the schedule hereto.

Part I — Orders Revoked

[The list of 52 Orders is not reproduced here.]

Part II — Regulations providing for the method of electing the chief and councillors of certain Indian bands and the division of certain reserves into electoral sections

Short Title

1. These Regulations may be cited as the *Indian Bands Council Method of Election Regulations*.

Method of Election

2. The chief and the councilors of each band set out in Schedule I to the *Indian Bands Council Elections Order* shall be elected by a majority of the votes of the electors of the band.

SOR/97-134.

3. The councillors of each band set out in Schedule II to the *Indian Bands Council Elections Order* shall be elected by a majority of the votes of the electors of the band and the chief of each of those bands shall be elected by a majority of the votes of the elected councillors of the band from among themselves.

SOR/97-134.

4. The reserve of each band set out in column I of an item of Schedule III shall for voting purposes be divided into the number of electoral sections set out in column II of that item and those sections shall be distinguished and identified in accordance with the number and description in column III of that item.

5. The chief of each band set out in Schedule III to the *Indian Bands Council Elections Order* shall be elected by a majority of the votes of the electors of the band, and the councillors of each of those bands shall be elected by a majority of the votes of the electors of the band in the electoral section in which the candidate resides and that the candidate proposes to represent on the council of the band.

SOR/97-134.

Schedule I
(Section 2)

Revoked SOR/97-134.

Schedule II

Revoked SOR/97-134.

Schedule III — Bands Whose Chief is Elected by the Electors and Whose Councillors are Elected by the Electors in Electoral Sections

(Section 4)

Part I — British Columbia

Item	Column I Band	Column II Number of Electoral Sections	Column III Electoral Section Number and Description
1.	Canoe Creek	2	1. The whole of Dog Creek Reserves Nos. 1, 2, 3 and 4, Copper Johnny Meadow Reserve No. 8, Fish Lake Reserve No. 5, Timmusket Reserve No. 5A and Toby Lake Reserve No. 6. 2. The whole of Canoe Creek Reserves Nos. 1, 2 and 3 and Spilmouse Reserve No. 4.

Part II

Repealed SOR/97-134.

Part III — Ontario

Item	Column I Band	Column II Number of Electoral Sections	Column III Electoral Section Number and Description
1.	Lac Seul	4	1. Settlement of Frenchmans Head 2. Settlement of Kejick Bay 3. Settlement of Whitefish Bay 4. Settlement of Canoe River

SOR/97-134

Part IV — Nova Scotia

Item	Column I Band	Column II Number of Electoral Sections	Column III Electoral Section Number and Description
1.	Eskasoni	5	1. to 5. As set out as wards 1 to 5 on the map of the reserves entitled "Electoral Sections — Eskasoni Indian Reserves No. 3 & 3A", dated June 17, 1991 and filed with the Band Governance and Indian Estates Directorate of the Department of Indian Affairs and Northern Development on July 5, 1991.

SOR/92-366

Indian Bands Council Elections Order
SOR/97-138

1. Council Elections — The council of a band set out in Schedule I, II or III shall be selected, after the date of the coming into force of this Order, by elections to be held in accordance with the *Indian Act*.

2. Repeal — The *Indian Band Council Election Order*, made on December 14, 1989[1], is repealed.

3. Coming into Force — *This Order comes into force on March 4, 1997.*

Schedule I — Bands Whose Chief and Councillors are Elected by the Electors
(Section 1)

Part I — British Columbia

Item	Band
1.	Adams Lake
2.	Alexandria
3.	Alexis Creek
4.	Alkali Lake
5.	Anaham
6.	Anderson Lake
7.	Ashcroft
8.	Beecher Bay
9.	Bella Coola
10.	Blueberry River
11.	Bonaparte
12.	Boothroyd
13.	Boston Bar
14.	Bridge River
15.	Burns Lake
16.	Burrard
17.	Campbell River
18.	Cape Mudge
19.	Chawathil
20.	Cheam

---

[1]Not published in the *Canada Gazette* Part II

121

Item	Band
21.	Chehalis
22.	Chemainus
23.	Clayoquot
24.	Comox
25.	Cowichan
26.	Doig River
27.	Fort George
28.	Fraser Lake
29.	Gitanmaax
30.	Gitlakdamix
31.	Gitsegukla
32.	Gitwangak
33.	Glen Vowell
34.	Hagwilget
35.	Halalt
36.	Halfway River
37.	Kincolith
38.	Kispiox
39.	Kitamaat
40.	Kitselas
41.	Kitsumkalum
42.	Kitwancool
43.	Klahoose
44.	Kwicksutaineuk-Ah-Kwaw-Ah-Mish
45.	Lakalzap
46.	Lax Kw'alaams
47.	Lytton
48.	Malahat
49.	Matsqui
50.	Metlakatla
51.	Moricetown
52.	Mount Currie
53.	Musqueam
54.	Nanaimo
55.	Nanoose
56.	Nazko
57.	Neskainlith
58.	Nicomen
59.	Nooaitch
60.	North Thompson
61.	Okanagan
62.	Opetchesaht
63.	Osoyoos
64.	Oweekeno
65.	Pacheenaht

Item	Band
66.	Pauquachin
67.	Penelakut
68.	Peters
69.	Qualicum
70.	Quatsino
71.	Red Bluff
72.	Scowlitz
73.	Seabird Island
74.	Semiahmoo
75.	Shackan
76.	Skidegate
77.	Skwah
78.	Sliammon
79.	Soda Creek
80.	Songhees
81.	Sooke
82.	Soowahlie
83.	Spallumcheen
84.	Squiala
85.	Stone
86.	Stony Creek
87.	Sumas
88.	Tahltan
89.	Toosey
90.	Tsartlip
91.	Tsawout
92.	Tsawwassen
93.	Tseycum
94.	Ucluelet
95.	Upper Similkameen
96.	Westbank
97.	Whispering Pines
98.	Williams Lake

Part II — Alberta

Item	Band
1.	Driftpile
2.	Duncan's
3.	Enoch
4.	Frog Lake
5.	O'Chiese
6.	Paul
7.	Sarcee
8.	Sawridge

Item	Band
9.	Siksika Nation
10.	Sucker Creek
11.	Sunchild Cree

Part III — Saskatchewan

Item	Band
1.	Ahtahkakoop
2.	Beardy's and Okemasis
3.	Canoe Lake
4.	Carry the Kettle
5.	Day Star
6.	English River
7.	Fishing Lake
8.	Flying Dust
9.	Gordon
10.	Island Lake
11.	John Smith
12.	Kahkewistahaw
13.	Key
14.	Kinistin
15.	Makwa Sahgaiehcan
16.	Mistawasis
17.	Moosomin
18.	Mosquito-Grizzly Bear's Head
19.	Muscowpetung
20.	Muskeg Lake
21.	Muskowekwan
22.	Nut Lake
23.	Ochapowace
24.	Onion Lake
25.	Pasqua
26.	Pelican Lake
27.	Piapot
28.	Poorman
29.	Red Pheasant
30.	Sakimay
31.	Waterhen Lake
32.	White Bear
33.	Witchekan Lake

Part IV — Manitoba

Item	Band

Item	Band
1.	Berens River
2.	Birdtail Sioux
3.	Bloodvein
4.	Brokenhead
5.	Chemawawin First Nation
6.	Crane River
7.	Cross Lake
8.	Ebb and Flow
9.	Fairford
10.	Fisher River
11.	Fort Alexander
12.	God's Lake
13.	Hollow Water
14.	Indian Birch
15.	Jackhead
16.	Keeseekoowenin
17.	Lake Manitoba
18.	Lake St. Martin
19.	Little Black River
20.	Little Grand Rapids
21.	Little Saskatchewan
22.	Mathias Colomb
23.	Moose Lake
24.	Nelson House
25.	Northlands
26.	Norway House
27.	Oak Lake
28.	Oxford House
29.	Peguis
30.	Pine Creek
31.	Poplar River First Nation
32.	Rolling River
33.	Shoal River
34.	Split Lake
35.	Swan Lake
36.	The Pas
37.	Valley River
38.	Waterhen
39.	Waywayseecappo

Part V — Ontario

Item	Band
1.	Alderville
2.	Batchewana

Item	Band
3.	Beausoleil
4.	Big Grassy
5.	Brunswick House
6.	Chippewas of Georgina Island
7.	Chippewas of Kettle and Stony Point
8.	Chippewas of Nawash
9.	Chippewas of Rama
10.	Chippewas of Sarnia
11.	Chippewas of the Thames First Nation
12.	Constance Lake
13.	Couchiching
14.	Curve Lake
15.	Dokis
16.	Eagle Lake
17.	Fort Hope
18.	Fort William
19.	Garden River
20.	Ginoogaming First Nation
21.	Golden Lake
22.	Grassy Narrows
23.	Gull Bay
24.	Henvey Inlet
25.	Hiawatha First Nation
26.	Islington
27.	Lac La Croix
28.	Long Lake No. 58
29.	Magnetawan
30.	Martin Falls
31.	Matachewan
32.	Mattagami
33.	Michipicoten
34.	Mississauga
35.	Mississaugas of the Credit
36.	Mohawks of the Bay of Quinte
37.	Moose Deer Point
38.	Naicatchewenin
39.	Nicickousemenecaning
40.	Northwest Angle No. 33
41.	Northwest Angle No. 37
42.	Ojibways of Onegaming
43.	Oneidas of the Thames
44.	Osnaburgh
45.	Parry Island First Nation
46.	Pic Heron Bay
47.	Pic Mobert

Item	Band
48.	Rainy River
49.	Saugeen
50.	Scugog
51.	Seine River
52.	Serpent River
53.	Sheguiandah
54.	Sheshegwaning
55.	Shoal Lake No. 39
56.	Shoal Lake No. 40
57.	Spanish River
58.	Thessalon
59.	Wabigoon Lake Ojibway Nation
60.	Wadpole Island
61.	Washagamis Bay
62.	West Bay
63.	Whitefish Bay
64.	Whitefish Lake
65.	Whitefish River
66.	Wikwemikong

Part VI — Quebec

Item	Band
1.	Abénakis de Wôlinak
2.	Kipawa
3.	Manowan
4.	Micmacs of Gesgapegiag
5.	Nation huronne Wendat
6.	Odanak
7.	Restigouche
8.	River Desert

Part VII — New Brunswick

Item	Band
1.	Big Cove
2.	Burnt Church
3.	Edmundston
4.	Eel Ground
5.	Eel River
6.	Fort Folly
7.	Indian Island
8.	Kingsclear
9.	Oromocto
10.	Pabineau

Item	Band
11.	Red Bank
12.	Saint Mary's
13.	Tobique
14.	Woodstock

Part VIII — Nova Scotia

Item	Band
1.	Afton
2.	Annapolis Valley
3.	Bear River
4.	Chapel Island
5.	Membertou
6.	Millbrook
7.	Pictou Landing
8.	Shubenacadie
9.	Wagmatcook
10.	Whycocomagh

Schedule II — Bands Whose Councillors are Elected by the Electors and Whose Chief is Elected by the Councillors

(Section 1)

Part I — British Columbia

Item	Band
1.	Ahousaht
2.	Fort Nelson
3.	Heiltsuk
4.	Kitasoo
5.	Shuswap

Part II — Alberta

Item	Band
1.	Boyer River

Schedule III — Bands Whose Chief is Elected by the Electors and Whose Councillors are Elected by the Electors in Electoral Sections

(Section 1)

Part I — British Columbia

Item	Band
1.	Canoe Creek

Part II — Ontario

Item	Band
1.	Lac Seul

Part III — Nova Scotia

Item	Band
1.	Eskasoni

Indian Band Council Procedure Regulations

Regulations respecting procedure at Indian band council meetings

C.R.C. 1978, c. 950

Short Title

1. These Regulations may be cited as the *Indian Band Council Procedure Regulations.*

Interpretation

2. In these Regulations,

"Assistant Deputy Minister" means the Assistant Deputy Minister, Indian and Eskimo Affairs of the Department;

"council" means the council of a Band elected pursuant to section 74 of the *Indian Act*;

"Department" means the Department of Indian Affairs and Northern Development;

"Minister" means the Minister of Indian Affairs and Northern Development;

"secretary" means the person appointed by the council of a band to record the minutes of the council meetings;

"superintendent " means the Superintendent or Senior Field Officer of the Indian Affairs Branch in charge of the Agency, and includes the Indian Commissioner for British Columbia, all Regional Supervisors, all Assistants Indian Agency, and any other officer acting under the instructions of the Minister or the Assistant Deputy Minister.

Meetings of the Council

3. (1) The first meeting of the council shall be held not later than one month after its election, on a day, hour and place to be stated in a notice given to each member of the council, and meetings shall thereafter be held on such days and at such times as may be necessary for the business of the council or the affairs of the band.

(2) No member of a council may be absent from meetings of the council for three consecutive meetings without being authorized to do so by the chief of the band or superintendent, with the consent of the majority of the councillors of the band.

4. The chief of the band or superintendent may, at any time, summon a special meeting of the council, and shall summon a special meeting when requested to do so by a majority of the members of the council.

5. The superintendent shall notify each member of the council of the day, hour and place of the meeting.

Order and Proceedings

6. A majority of the whole council shall constitute a quorum, but where a council consists of nine or more members, five members shall constitute a quorum.

7. If no quorum is present within 1 hour after the time appointed for the meeting, the secretary shall call the roll and take the names of the members then present and the council shall stand adjourned until the next meeting.

8. The chief of the band or, with the consent of the majority of the councillors present at the meeting, the superintendent shall be the presiding officer.

9. (1) Upon a quorum being present, the presiding officer shall take the chair and call the meeting to order.

(2) A chairman shall be chosen

    (a) in the absence of the chief, or

    (b) where the superintendent is not chosen the presiding officer pursuant to section 8,

from among the members present who shall preside during the meeting or until the arrival of the chief or until the superintendent is chosen as the presiding officer.

10. The presiding officer shall maintain order and decide all questions of procedure.

11. The order of business at each regular meeting shall be as follows:

    (a) reading (correction, if any) and adoption of the minutes of the previous meeting;

    (b) unfinished business;

    (c) presentation and reading of correspondence and petitions;

    (d) presentation and consideration of reports of committees;

    (e) new business;

    (f) hearing deputations;

    (g) adjournment.

12. Each resolution shall be presented or read by the mover, and when duly moved and seconded and placed before the meeting by the presiding officer, shall be open for consideration.

13. After a resolution has been placed before the meeting by the presiding officer it shall be deemed to be in the possession of the council, but it may be withdrawn by consent of the majority of the council members present.

14. When any member desires to speak, he shall address his remarks to the presiding officer and confine himself to the question then before the meeting.

15. In the event of more than one member desiring to speak at one time, the presiding officer shall determine who is entitled to speak.

16. (1) The presiding officer or any member may call a member to order while speaking and the debate shall then be suspended and the member shall not speak until the point of order is determined.

(2) The member may speak only once on a point of order.

17. Any member may appeal the decision of the presiding officer to the council and all appeals shall be decided by a majority vote and without debate.

18. (1) All questions before the council shall be decided by a majority vote of the councillors present.

(2) The presiding officer shall not be entitled to vote but whenever the votes are equal the presiding officer, other than the superintendent, shall cast the deciding vote.

19. Every member present when a question is put shall vote thereon unless the council excuses him or unless he is personally interested in the question, in which case he shall not be obliged to vote.

20. A member who refuses to vote shall be deemed to vote in the affirmative.

21. Whenever a division of the council is taken for any purpose, each member present and voting shall announce his vote upon the question openly and individually to the council and, when so requested by any member, the secretary shall record the same.

22. Any member may require the question or resolution under discussion to be read for his information at any period of the debate, but not so as to interrupt a member who is speaking.

23. (1) The regular meetings shall be open to members of the band, and no member shall be excluded therefrom except for improper conduct.

(2) The presiding officer may expel or exclude from any meeting any person who causes a disturbance at the meeting.

24. The council may at the first meeting thereof appoint in lieu of the committee of the whole council the following standing committees:

(a) Finance;

(b) Roads and Bridges; and

(c) Welfare.

25. The council may appoint special committees on any matters as the interests of the band may require.

26. A majority of the members of a committee shall be a quorum.

27. The chief of the band shall *ex officio* be a member of all committees and be entitled to vote at all meetings thereof, and other members of the council may attend meetings of a committee and may with the consent of the committee take part in the discussion but shall not be entitled to vote.

28. The general duties of standing and special committees are,

(a) to report to the council from time to time as often as the interests of the band may require, all matters connected with the duties imposed on them respectively and to recommend such action by the council in relation thereto as they may deem necessary and expedient; and

(b) to consider and report upon all matters referred to them by the council or by the chief of the band.

29. Special meetings of committees shall be called at the request of the chairman or a majority of the committee or, in the absence of the chairman on request of the chief of the band or the superintendent.

30. Any representative of the Minister present at a council meeting may

(a) address the council, and explain to and advise the members thereof upon their powers and duties;

(b) explain to and advise the members thereof upon any question of procedure; and

(c) give such information as may be requested by any member of the council relating to the administration of the affairs of the band.

31. The council may make such rules of procedure as are not inconsistent with these Regulations in respect of all matters not specifically provided for thereby, as it may deem necessary.

Indian Band Election Regulations

Regulations governing Indian band elections

C.R.C. 1978, c. 952, as am. SOR/85-409

Short Title

1. These Regulations may be cited as the *Indian Band Election Regulations*.

Interpretation

2. In these Regulations

"Act" means the *Indian Act*;

"Assistant Deputy Minister" means the Assistant Deputy Minister, Indian and Eskimo Affairs of the Department of Indian Affairs and Northern Development;

"deputy electoral officer" means any person appointed by the electoral officer for the purposes of an election;

"election" means a band election held pursuant to the provisions of the Act;

"elector" means a person who

(a) is registered on a Band List,

(b) is of the full age of 21 years, and

(c) is not disqualified from voting at band elections;

"electoral officer" means the superintendent or the person appointed by the council of the band with the approval of the Minister;

"Minister" means the Minister of Indian Affairs and Northern Development;

"Superintendent " means the Superintendent or senior field officer of the Indian Affairs Branch in charge of the agency [and includes the Indian Affairs Branch in charge of the agency] [sic] and includes the Indian Commissioner for British Columbia, all Regional Supervisors and any other officer acting under the instructions of the Minister or Assistant Deputy Minister.

Related Provisions: See *Indian Act*, R.S.C. 1985, c. I-5, s. 77.

Definition of Residence for the Purpose of Determining the Eligibility of Voters

3. The following rules apply to the interpretation of the words "ordinary resident" in respect of all matters pertaining to the right of an elector to vote in an election:

(a) subject to the other provisions of this section, the question as to where a person is or was ordinarily resident at any material time or during any material period shall be determined by reference to all the facts of the case;

(b) the place of ordinary residence of a person is, generally, that place which has always been, or which he has adopted as, the place of his habitation or home, whereto, when away therefrom, he intends to return and, specifically, where a person usually sleeps in one place and has his meals or is employed in another place, the place of his ordinary residence is where that person sleeps;

(c) a person can have one place of ordinary residence only, and he shall retain such place of ordinary residence until another is acquired;

(d) temporary absence from a place of ordinary residence does not cause a loss or change of place of ordinary residence.

Nomination Meeting

4. (1) When an election is to be held, the electoral officer shall post a notice, in the form prescribed, of a meeting of the electors for the purpose of nominating candidates for election; such notice shall be posted in one or more conspicuous places in each electoral section at least 6 clear days prior to the date of the proposed nomination meeting and at least 12 clear days prior to the date set for the election.

(2) Where it is not practicable to hold a meeting for the nomination of candidates in accordance with the provisions of subsection (1), the Assistant Deputy Minister may order that the meeting be held on a date not less than 6 clear days before the day on which the election is to be held.

(3) At the time and place specified in the notice, the electoral officer shall declare the meeting open for the purpose of receiving nominations, and any person who is an elector may propose or second the nomination of any duly qualified person to serve as a chief or councillor, and the meeting shall remain open for not less than 2 hours after commencement when, if the number of persons nominated to serve on the band council does not exceed the requisite number, the electoral officer shall declare the persons so nominated to be duly elected.

(4) The electoral officer shall not close the nomination meeting until such business as he considers may properly be brought before it has been disposed of.

(5) In the event of more than the required number of persons being nominated for chief and councillors, the electoral officer shall declare that a poll will be held and shall name the time and the place where such poll shall be taken.

(6) Whenever a poll is to be taken, the electoral officer shall, without any unreasonable delay after the nomination, cause to be posted in one or more conspicuous places within the electoral section a notice to that effect in the form prescribed.

SOR/85-409, s. 1.

Manner in Which Voting Shall be Carried Out

5. (1) The electoral officer shall prepare a voters' list containing the names, in alphabetical order, of all electors.

(2) The electoral officer shall post one or more copies of the voters' list in a conspicuous place in the electoral section, and where a reserve is divided into more than one section, he shall post one or more copies of the voters' list in a conspicuous place in each section.

(3) Any elector may apply to have the voters' list revised on the ground that the name of an elector is incorrectly set out therein or the name of a person not qualified to vote is included therein.

(4) If the electoral officer is satisfied that a list should be corrected, he shall make the necessary correction therein.

(5) Ballot papers shall be prepared in the prescribed form containing the names of candidates for chief and for councillors, which names shall be listed on the ballot papers in alphabetical order.

(6) Any candidate who has been nominated may withdraw at any time after his nomination, but not later than 48 hours before the time of the opening of the poll, by filing with the electoral officer a written withdrawal of his nomination, signed by himself in the presence of the electoral officer, a justice of the peace, a notary public, or a commissioner for oaths, and any votes cast for any such candidates shall be null and void.

(7) The electoral officer shall procure or cause to be procured as many ballot boxes as there are polling places, and shall cause to be prepared a sufficient number of ballot papers for the purpose of the election.

(8) The electoral officer shall, before the poll is open, cause to be delivered to his deputy the ballot papers, materials for marking the ballot papers, and a sufficient number of directions-for-voting as may be prescribed.

(9) The electoral officer or his deputy shall provide a compartment at each polling place where the electors can mark their ballot papers free from observation, and he may appoint a constable to maintain order at such polling place.

(10) The poll shall be kept open from 9 o'clock (standard time) in the forenoon until 6 o'clock (standard time) in the afternoon of the same day, but where it appears to the electoral officer that it would be inconvenient to the electors to have the poll closed at 6

o'clock, he may order that it be kept open until not later than 8 o'clock (standard time) of the afternoon of the same day.

(11) A candidate shall be entitled to not more than two agents in a polling place at any one time.

(12) Voting at all elections shall be by ballot in the manner set forth in section 6.

(13) The electoral officer or his deputy shall, immediately before the commencement of the poll, open the ballot box and call such persons as may be present to witness that it is empty; he shall then lock and properly seal the box to prevent it being opened without breaking the seal and shall place it in view for the reception of the ballots, and the seal shall not be broken nor the box unlocked during the time appointed for taking the poll.

(14) At the request of any candidate or his agent or any elector, an oath or affirmation in the form prescribed as to his rights to vote shall be administered to any person tendering his vote at any election.

The Poll

6. (1) Where a person presents himself for the purpose of voting, the electoral officer or his deputy shall, if satisfied that the name of such person is entered on the voters' list at the polling place, provide him with a ballot paper on which to register his vote.

(2) The electoral officer or his deputy shall cause to be placed in the proper column of the voters' list a mark opposite the name of every voter receiving a ballot paper.

(3) No person who has refused to take the oath or affirmation referred to in subsection 5(14) when requested so to do shall receive a ballot paper or be permitted to vote.

(4) The electoral officer or his deputy may and when requested to do so shall explain the mode of voting to a voter.

(5) Each person receiving a ballot paper shall forthwith proceed to the compartment provided for marking ballots and shall mark his ballot paper by placing a cross opposite the name of the candidate or candidates for whom he desires to vote; he shall then fold the ballot paper so as to conceal the names of the candidates and the marks on the face of the paper but so as to expose the initials of the electoral officer or his deputy, and on leaving the compartment shall forthwith deliver the ballot paper to the electoral officer or his deputy, who shall, without unfolding the ballot paper, verify his initials and at once deposit it in the ballot box in the presence of the voter and all other persons entitled to be present in the polling place.

(6) While any voter is in the compartment for the purpose of marking his ballot paper, no other person shall, except as provided in subsection (7), be allowed in the same compartment or be in any position from which he can see the manner in which such voter marks his ballot paper.

(7) The electoral officer or his deputy, on the application of any voter who is unable to read or is incapacitated by blindness or other physical cause from voting in the manner

prescribed by subsection (5), shall assist such voter by marking his ballot paper in the manner directed by the voter in the presence of the agents of the candidates in the polling place and of no other person, and place such ballot in the ballot box.

(8) The electoral officer or his deputy shall state in the voters' list in the column for remarks opposite the name of such elector the fact that the ballot paper was marked by him at the request of the voter and the reasons therefor.

(9) A voter who has inadvertently dealt with his ballot paper in such manner that it cannot be conveniently used shall, upon returning it to the electoral officer or his deputy, be entitled to obtain another ballot paper, and the electoral officer or his deputy shall thereupon write the word "cancelled" upon the spoiled ballot paper and preserve it.

(10) Any person who has received a ballot paper and who leaves the polling place without delivering the ballot paper to the electoral officer or his deputy, in the manner provided, or if, after receiving the ballot paper, refuses to vote, shall forfeit his right to vote at the election, and the electoral officer or his deputy shall make an entry in the voters' list in the column for remarks opposite the name of such person to show that such person received the ballot paper and declined to vote, and the electoral officer or his deputy shall mark upon the face of the ballot paper the word "declined", and all ballot papers so marked shall be preserved.

(11) An elector whose name does not appear on the voters' list may vote at an election if the electoral officer or his deputy is satisfied that such person is qualified to vote.

(12) Every elector who is inside the polling place at the time fixed for closing the poll shall be entitled to vote before the poll is closed.

7. Immediately after the close of the poll the electoral officer or his deputy shall, in the presence of such of the candidates or their agents as may be present, open the ballot box and

   (a) examine the ballot papers and reject all ballot papers

      (i) that have not been supplied by him,

      (ii) by which votes have been given for more candidates than are to be elected, or

      (iii) upon which anything appears by which the voter can be identified, but no word, letter, or marks written or made or omitted to be written or made by the electoral officer or his deputy on a ballot paper shall avoid it or warrant its rejection;

   (b) declare a ballot paper containing the names of candidates for more than one office, on which votes are given for more candidates for any office than are to be elected, to be void as regards all the candidates for such office; but such ballot paper shall be good as regard the votes for any other offices in respect of which the voter has not voted for more candidates than are to be elected;

(c) subject to review on account or on an election appeal, take a note of any objection made by any candidate or his agent to any ballot paper found in the ballot box and decide any questions arising out of the objection;

(d) number such objection and place a corresponding number on the back of the ballot paper with the word "allowed" or "disallowed", as the case may be, with his initials;

(e) count the votes given for each candidate from the ballot papers not rejected and make a written statement of the number of votes given to each candidate and the number of ballot papers rejected and counted by him, which statement shall be then signed by him and such other persons authorized to be present as may desire to sign the statement.

8. Immediately after the completion of the counting of the votes the electoral officer shall publicly declare to be elected the candidate or candidates having the highest number of votes, and he shall also post in some conspicuous place a statement signed by him showing the number of votes cast for each candidate.

9. Where it appears that two or more candidates have an equal number of votes, the electoral officer shall give a casting vote for one or more of such candidates, but the electoral officer shall not otherwise be entitled to vote.

10. (1) The electoral officer shall prepare a statement in triplicate showing the total number of votes cast for each candidate, the number of rejected ballots and the names of the candidates duly declared elected.

(2) One copy of such statement shall be forwarded to the Assistant Deputy Minister, one to the regional supervisor or the Indian commissioner for the Province of British Columbia, and one copy filed in the agency office.

(3) The statement shall be signed by the electoral officer and such of the candidates or their agents as are present and desire to sign it.

Disposition of Ballot Papers

11. The electoral officer shall deposit all ballot papers in sealed envelopes with the superintendent, who shall retain them in his possession for eight weeks, and unless otherwise directed by the Minister or by a person authorized by him shall then destroy the ballot papers in the presence of two witnesses who shall make a declaration that they witnessed the destruction of those papers.

Election Appeals

12. (1) Within 30 days after an election, any candidate at the election or any elector who gave or tendered his vote at the election who has reasonable grounds for believing that

(a) there was corrupt practice in connection with the election,

(b) there was a violation of the Act or these Regulations that might have affected the result of the election, or

(c) a person nominated to be a candidate in the election was ineligible to be a candidate,

may lodge an appeal by forwarding by registered mail to the Assistant Deputy Minister particulars thereof duly verified by affidavit.

(2) Where an appeal is lodged pursuant to subsection (1), the Assistant Deputy Minister shall, within 7 days of the receipt of the appeal, forward a copy of the appeal together with all supporting documents by registered mail to the electoral officer and to each candidate in the electoral section.

(3) Any candidate may, within 14 days of the receipt of the copy of the appeal, forward to the Assistant Deputy Minister by registered mail a written answer to the particulars set out in the appeal together with any supporting documents relating thereto duly verified by affidavit.

(4) All particulars and documents filed in accordance with the provisions of this section shall constitute and form the record.

SOR/85-409, s. 4.

13. (1) The Minister may, if the material that has been filed is not adequate for deciding the validity of the election complained of, conduct such further investigation into the matter as he deems necessary, in such manner as he deems expedient.

(2) Such investigation may be held by the Minister or by any person designated by the Minister for the purpose.

(3) Where the Minister designates a person to hold such an investigation, that person shall submit a detailed report of the investigation to the Minister for his consideration.

14. Where it appears that

(a) there was corrupt practice in connection with an election,

(b) there was a violation of the Act or these Regulations that might have affected the result of an election, or

(c) a person nominated to be a candidate in an election was ineligible to be a candidate,

the Minister shall report to the Governor in Council accordingly.

Secrecy of Voting

15. (1) Every person in attendance at a polling place or at the counting of the votes shall maintain and aid in maintaining the secrecy of the voting.

(2) No person shall interfere or attempt to interfere with a voter when marking his ballot paper or obtain or attempt to obtain at the polling place information as to how a voter is about to vote or has voted.

16. The Minister may make such orders and issue such instructions as he may deem necessary from time to time for the effective administration of these Regulations.

17. Such forms as are required for the purposes of these Regulations shall be prescribed by the Minister.

18. Any person who violates any of the provisions of these Regulations is subject to the penalties provided by section 102 of the Act.

Case Law: *Derrickson v. Canada (Department of Indian Affairs & Northern Development)* (1993), 63 F.T.R. 292, [1994] 2 C.N.L.R. 36 (T.D.)

The court upheld procedures for contesting electors.

Indian Estates Regulations

Regulations respecting Indian estates elections

C.R.C. 1978, c. 954

Short Title

1. These Regulations may be cited as the *Indian Estates Regulations*.

Interpretation

2. In these Regulations

"Act" means the *Indian Act*;

"administrator " means a person appointed by the Minister to administer the property of deceased Indians and includes a person who, by reason of his office, is instructed to initiate or conclude the administration of an estate;

"Minister" means the Minister of Indian Affairs and Northern Development;

"prescribed" means prescribed by the Minister.

Notice of Death

3. (1) As soon as feasible after the death of an Indian, the superintendent shall forward a notice of the death, in the form prescribed, to the Minister.

(2) Except when otherwise ordered by the Minister for the purposes of these Regulations, the presumption of death shall arise and be determined in the manner it arises and is determined where persons other than Indians are concerned.

Inventory

4. (1) When he receives notice of the death of an Indian, or as soon thereafter as possible, the superintendent shall forward an itemized statement of inventory in the form prescribed, to the Minister, showing all the real and personal property of the deceased, the value of each item estimated as closely as possible, as well as all debts of or claims against the estate known at such time, and he shall also state therein whether the deceased left a will and give the names of all persons entitled to share in the estate and all such other information as may be required by the Minister.

(2) For the purposes of this section, the superintendent shall act in the capacity of an administrator and shall take all necessary steps for the proper safekeeping or safeguarding of the assets of the deceased and for the collection of moneys due or owing to

142

the deceased and shall dispose of the moneys so collected or held as the Minister may direct.

(3) Where the deceased had been in receipt of any pension, gratuity or allowance, any cheque or money order received by or on behalf of the deceased that had not been cashed shall be returned by the superintendent to the sender for re-issue to the order of the Receiver General for credit to the estate concerned.

Probate of Will

5. (1) Where the deceased leaves a will, the superintendent shall cause application for probate in the form prescribed to be completed and signed by the executor, if any is named in the will, unless the superintendent considers him to be incapable by reason of age or other cause to perform the duties of an executor.

(2) Where the executor named in the will refuses to act, the superintendent shall have him record his refusal in writing on the application.

(3) Where the person named in a will is unwilling to act or is considered by the superintendent to be incapable of acting, the superintendent shall complete the application.

Application for Administration

6. The superintendent shall, together with the application under section 5, or with the statement of inventory if there is no will, forward to the Minister an application for administration in the form prescribed.

Affidavits

7. All applications required under these Regulations shall be made under oath except where, by reason of remoteness or otherwise, the Minister provides that the certificate of the applicant in the form prescribed may be accepted in lieu thereof.

Advertising for Creditors, Heirs and Other Claimants

8. (1) When the application for adminstration has been forwarded to the Minister, the superintendent shall give notice to creditors, heirs and other claimants in the form prescribed that all claims against the deceased or the estate or to any interest therein are required to be filed with him in person or by mail within eight weeks from the date the notice is first posted or given.

(2) The notice referred to in subsection (1) shall be posted in the post office, in the agency office and in all such other meeting places or public places where notices are usually posted or given to the band to which the deceased belonged, and when so ordered by the Minister, may be published in such other manner or place as is deemed expedient.

(3) Any claim that has not been filed within the period prescribed in subsection (1) shall not be received unless the Minister so orders.

(4) Every claim by a creditor shall be accompanied by evidence of the debt in a form satisfactory to the Minister and, unless such evidence accompanies the notice of claim, it may be filed within 15 days of the filing of the notice.

Executors

9. Where an executor or executors have been named in a will and the will has been approved in whole by the Minister, or where an executor has been appointed by the Minister, the executor shall thereupon be considered the personal representative of the deceased and, where so ordered by the Minister, he shall act under the instructions of the administrator.

Sureties

10. The Minister may, in his discretion, order than an executor or an administrator give sureties as he deems necessary to ensure that the executor or the administrator will carry out his duties in accordance with these Regulations and his instructions.

Powers and Duties of Administrators

11. (1) The Minister may appoint an officer of the Indian and Eskimo Affairs Branch to be the administrator of estates and to supervise the administration of estates and of all the assets of deceased Indians, and may provide that for the purposes of closing an estate the administration thereof be transferred to the superintendent of the reserve to which the deceased belonged.

(2) The administrator appointed pursuant to this section or the person acting as administrator in accordance with section 4 shall be responsible to the Minister for the proper preparation of the inventory, the giving of all notices and the carrying out of all inquiries and duties that may be necessary or be ordered with respect to any matter referred to in these Regulations.

(3) Where a claim is made against an estate, the administrator may provide for payment thereof out of the assets of the estate when it appears that it is will founded; where in the opinion of the administrator the claim is doubtful or is not of the nature of a cause or matter testamentary, he shall refer it to the Minister for decision.

(4) An administrator may pay all debts owing by the estate and shall obtain receipts therefor or releases, as the case may be, and where the debt is in the nature of a loan, he may pay the balance owing or, with the consent of the heirs, transfer ownership of the security given for the loan or, with the consent of the band or of the Minister, as the case may be, sell the property upon which a lien exists to guarantee payment of the loan; he may also sell any asset real or personal for the purpose of paying debts owing by the estate, under such conditions as may be prescribed.

(5) No proceedings to establish or enforce a claim against an estate shall be valid unless the administrator is made a party thereto.

(6) The administrator may cause partial distribution to be made from the net assets of the estate to ensure the expedient administration thereof.

(7) Where a partial distribution cannot be made, or where the heirs cannot agree as to distribution, the administrator may, with the approval of the Minister, convert the net assets into cash and pay those assets to the Receiver General to be credited to the estate pending final distribution to the persons entitled thereto.

(8) Where the deceased had a deposit with a bank or other financial institution, or where such institution holds bonds or certificates on behalf of the deceased, the administrator may require the financial institution to transfer the moneys to the Receiver General for credit to the estate and to turn over to him the bonds or certificates so that he may sell them and deposit the proceeds to the credit of the estate or dispose of them in such other manner as may be prescribed.

(9) When moneys are payable to the estate of an Indian under a life insurance policy, the administrator may direct that the amount payable under the policy be paid to the Receiver General for credit to the estate.

(10) The administrator shall obtain or cause to be obtained all certificates or releases that may be required under federal or provincial statutes with respect to an estate or a succession.

(11) An administrator is empowered to do all that an executor is empowered to do where the executor refuses to act or is incapable of acting by reason of absence or sickness or for any other reason.

(12) Any bank or other financial institution or any person who makes a payment or delivers a bond or certificate under these Regulations is indemnified against any liability that may arise by reason thereof.

(13) An administrator may, if he thinks fit, and shall, if required by the Minister, lease or renew any lease of land held by the deceased and may cause to be fulfilled any contract entered into by the deceased.

(14) An administrator shall have all such powers as are required for the carrying out of the duties herein specified, and shall carry out any order or direction and abide by any finding made or given by the Minister with respect to any matter and cause testamentary.

(15) An administrator shall be accountable to the Minister for his administration.

(16) Compliance with these Regulations with respect to administration of estates shall discharge the administrator or other person complying therewith from all liability by reason of any of the assets in his hands having been paid, transmitted, remitted or otherwise dealt with in accordance therewith.

Transfer of Possession

12. (1) Where the deceased Indian had been in peaceable, public and useful possession of land on a reserve for a continuous and uninterrupted period of 30 years, transfer of possession may, at the discretion of the Minister, be presumed to have taken place and in such event the onus of proving that prescription did not run or of disproving the transfer shall be upon any person claiming adverse possession.

(2) For the purposes of this section, in calculating the 30-year period, the period of possession of the deceased, his predecessors in title and that of his heirs, may be cumulated.

Absent or Missing Heirs

13. Where heirs are found upon due inquiry to be absent or missing and notices or advertisements have been given or published in accordance with these Regulations, the moneys or assets in an estate to which they might be entitled shall be held in a special account, without interest, and unless evidence of death satisfactory to the Minister is filed or obtained, shall be held for a period of seven years after which the absent or missing heirs who have not reported by such time shall be presumed to be dead and the moneys or assets distributed accordingly to the remaining heirs or persons entitled thereto.

Woman Deemed to be a Widow

14. The Minister may direct that a woman shall be deemed to be the widow of a deceased Indian and, if there are children issue of the said woman and of the deceased Indian, that they shall be deemed to be their children, for the purposes of these Regulations,

(a) where it is established to the satisfaction of the Minister that the woman had for a period of not less than seven years immediately prior to the death of the deceased Indian with whom she had been residing and whom by law she was prevented from marrying by reason of a previous marriage either of the deceased or of herself to another person, or to whom she was married in a form not recognized by law, but maintained and publicly represented by the deceased Indian as his wife; or

(b) where there had been no prior marriage of the deceased Indian or of herself to another person, the woman establishes that she had, for a number of years immediately prior to the death of the deceased Indian with whom she had been residing, been maintained and publicly represented by the deceased Indian as his wife, whether or not there had been children of the relationship.

Will

15. Any written instrument signed by an Indian may be accepted as a will by the Minister whether or not it conforms with the requirements of the laws of general application in force in any province at the time of the death of the Indian.

Other Forms

16. The Minister may prescribe further and other notices and forms as he deems necessary for the purposes of section 42 of the Act and these Regulations.

Indian Mining Regulations

Regulations providing for the disposition of surrendered minerals underlying lands in Indian reserves

C.R.C. 1978, c. 956, as am. SOR/90-468

Short Title

1. These Regulations may be cited as the *Indian Mining Regulations*.

Interpretation

2. (1) In these Regulations,

"**Act**" means the *Indian Act*; (*Loi*)

"**assessment work**" means work performed that in the opinion of the Supervisor was performed for the purpose of discovering and developing minerals in a permit area or lease area and includes

(a) geological, geophysical, geochemical and similar surveys,

(b) core drilling, churn drilling and any other drilling method when used to provide geological information,

(c) removing overburden,

(d) drifting, crosscutting, shaft sinking, raising and similar underground work,

(e) road building, and

(f) any other type of work approved by the Supervisor; (*travaux statutaires*)

"**Department**" means the Department of Indian Affairs and Northern Development; (*ministère*)

"**Division Chief**" means the Chief, Oil and Mineral Division of the Development Branch of the Department or any person authorized by him; (*chef de la Division*)

"**lease**" means a lease issued pursuant to section 5, 6 or 19 granting the right to explore for, develop and produce minerals within the lease area; (*bail*)

"**lease area**" means the tract of land or location described in a lease; (*étendue visée par un bail*)

"**lessee**" means a person who holds a lease; (*preneur*)

"**minerals**" means naturally occurring metallic and non-metallic minerals and rock containing such minerals, but does not include petroleum, natural gas and other petroliferous minerals or any unconsolidated minerals such as placer deposits, gravel, sand, clay, earth, ash, marl and peat; (*minéraux*)

"Minister" means the Minister of Indian Affairs and Northern Development; (*Ministre*)

"permit" means a permit issued under section 5 or 6 granting the right to explore for and develop minerals within the permit area; (*permis*)

"permit area" means the tract of land or location described in a permit; (*étendue visée par un permis*)

"permittee" means a person who holds a permit; (*détenteur de permis*)

"person" means a person who has attained the age of 21 years or a corporation registered or licensed in Canada or in any province thereof; (*personne*)

"Supervisor" means the Supervisor of Indian Minerals for the Oil and Mineral Division of the Development Branch of the Department, or any person authorized by him; (*Surveillant*)

"treatment" means concentrating, smelting, refining or any similar process but does not include washing, screening, conveying, loading or other handling methods when they are not combined with treatment. (*traitement*)

(2) For the purposes of these Regulations, "section" and "legal subdivision" have the same meanings as in Part II of the *Canada Lands Surveys Act*.

Application

3. These Regulations apply with respect to surrendered mines and minerals underlying lands in a reserve, but do not apply with respect to surrendered mines and minerals underlying lands in a reserve that is situated in the Province of British Columbia

Compliance with Provincial Laws

4. Every permittee and every lessee shall comply with the laws of the province in which his permit area or lease area is situated where such laws relate to exploration for, or development, production, treatment and marketing of minerals and do not conflict with these Regulations.

Disposition of Mineral Rights

5. (1) The Division Chief may, by public advertisement or in such other manner as he considers advisable, invite tenders for mineral rights on such terms and conditions as he deems proper.

(2) Where tenders have been submitted in compliance with the terms and conditions set forth by the Division Chief, the Division Chief may issue a permit or lease to the person submitting the highest tender or may reject all tenders.

6. (1) Notwithstanding section 5, the Division Chief may, with the consent of the council of the band for whose use and benefit lands have been set apart and subject to such

terms and conditions as the council of the band may approve, issue a permit or lease with respect to minerals underlying such lands to any person upon application therefor.

(2) Every application for a permit or lease shall be accompanied by the fee therefor set out in the schedule payable to the Receiver General.

Permits

Term of Permit

7. (1) Subject to subsection (2), every permit expires one year from the date upon which it was issued.

(2) Where before the expiration of his permit a permittee makes an application in a form satisfactory to the Supervisor for extension thereof, the Supervisor, upon being satisfied that the permittee has complied with these Regulations, and with the terms and conditions of his permit, shall extend that permit for a period of one year or for such shorter period of time as the permittee may request.

(3) Every application for extension of a permit shall contain

(a) a summary of the work that has been done under the permit and the most recent extension thereof; and

(b) a summary of the work that the permittee proposes to do if the permit is extended.

8. A permittee shall not be entitled to more than three extensions of his permit unless

(a) the invitation to tender under section 5 or the permit issued under section 6 states that more than three extensions may be granted; or

(b) in the opinion of the Supervisor, the extension of the permit is required to complete exploration work in the permit area and assessment work has been performed satisfactorily.

9. Where, within 30 days after the date upon which a permit expires, the holder of the expired permit makes an application to the Supervisor for reinstatement and extension of that permit, the Division Chief may at the request of the Supervisor reinstate and extend that permit for a period not exceeding one year from the date upon which it expired.

Rental

10. (1) A permittee shall pay, unless otherwise provided in the invitation to tender under section 5 or in the permit issued under section 6, the rent for the initial term of

his permit or an extension thereof, as the case may be, in advance to the Receiver General and such rent shall be payable at the rate of

(a) $0.25 for each acre in the permit area in respect of the initial term of his permit;

(b) $0.04 per month for each acre in the permit area in respect of each of the first, second and third extensions of his permit; and

(c) $0.08 per month for each acre in the permit area in respect of any further extension.

(2) Where a permittee is issued a lease pursuant to section 19, the Division Chief shall direct the return to the permittee of any rent paid pursuant to subsection (1) that applies to the unexpired term of the permit or extension thereof, as the case may be, that was issued for the area taken under the lease.

Security Deposit

11. (1) No permit shall be issued to any person unless that person has deposited with the Division Chief a security deposit in such amount or at such rate, if any, as may be specified in the invitation to tender under section 5 or in the permit to be issued under section 6.

(2) A security deposit shall be in the form of money, bonds or promissory notes payable to the Receiver General on demand at a chartered bank or in such other form as the Division Chief deems proper.

12. Where a permit expires or is surrendered, the Division Chief, upon being satisfied that the permittee has complied with these Regulations and with the terms and conditions of his permit, shall direct that any security deposit deposited pursuant to subsection 11(1) be returned to the permittee.

Assessment Work

13. (1) During the initial term of his permit or during any extension thereof, as the case may be, every permittee shall perform assessment work acceptable to the Supervisor, of the value of

(a) $0.50 for each acre in the permit area during the initial term of his permit, and

(b) $1 for each acre in the permit area during the term of each extension of his permit,

or of such other value as may be specified in the invitation to tender under section 5 or in the permit issued under section 6.

(2) Where, in his opinion, assessment work performed near a permit area serves to evaluate the mineral potential of the permit area, the Supervisor may deem the whole or any part of the value of that work to be assessment work performed in the permit area.

14. (1) Where assessment work of the value required under subsection 13(1) is not performed, the permittee shall make a cash payment to the Receiver General in an amount equal to the difference between the value of assessment work performed and the value of assessment work required to be performed.

(2) Where the value of assessment work performed during the term of a permit or an extension thereof exceeds the value of assessment work required to be performed pursuant to subsection 13(1), the Supervisor may credit the excess value of the assessment work performed to the value of the assessment work required to be performed

(a) pursuant to subsection 13(1) during any extension or further extension of the permit; or

(b) pursuant to any lease or leases that the permittee may acquire with respect to all or any part of his permit area.

15. (1) Every permittee shall, within 90 days following the expiry of his permit and following any extension thereof, forward to the Supervisor a certified statement in duplicate itemizing the assessment work performed and the cost of performing such work during the term of his permit and any extension thereof together with any cash payment that may be required pursuant to subsection 14(1).

(2) Every permittee shall, within six months following the expiry of his permit and following any extension thereof, forward to the Supervisor copies in duplicate of all maps and technical information that serve to record the assessment work performed for the term of his permit and any extension thereof together with a report of the results obtained from the performance of that assessment work.

(3) Where the Supervisor is not satisfied with the statements, maps or technical information submitted under subsection (1) or (2), he may require the permittee to submit additional information.

Test Shipments

16. (1) Subject to subsection (2), no permittee shall produce minerals from his permit area.

(2) A permittee may, with the written consent of the Supervisor and subject to such terms and conditions as the Supervisor may prescribe in writing, produce and ship reasonable amounts of minerals for testing purposes only.

Leases

Selection

17. Where a permittee, during the term of his permit or any extension thereof, desires to obtain a lease in respect of his permit area or any part thereof, he shall make an application in duplicate therefor to the Supervisor.

18. (1) An application for a lease referred to in section 17

(a) shall be in a form satisfactory to the Division Chief;

(b) shall contain a legal description in accordance with subsection (2) or (3) of the lands in respect of which a lease is desired; and

(c) shall be accompanied by

(i) the fee therefor set out in the schedule payable to the Receiver General, and

(ii) the rental for the first year of the lease in accordance with section 24.

(2) Subject to subsection (3), lands referred to in subsection (1) shall be described by

(a) section, legal subdivision, lot or aliquot part of a lot if such lands lie within a subdivision area; or

(b) projected section, legal subdivision, lot or aliquot part of a lot if such lands do not lie within a subdivided area.

(3) Where the boundaries of a permit area or part thereof in respect of which a lease is desired do not correspond with a township survey or other legal survey or any projection thereof, the Division Chief may allow the land therein to be described by means of irregular boundaries.

19. Where a permittee has made an application for a lease in accordance with sections 17 and 18 and has complied with these Regulations and with the terms and conditions of his permit, the Division Chief shall issue a lease to him.

Entitlement

20. Every lessee who has complied with the provisions of these Regulations is entitled to all minerals found within his lease area, subject to any condition of his permit or lease acquired under section 5 or 6.

Surveys

21. Where, in the opinion of the Division Chief, it is necessary that lands in respect of which a lease is desired be surveyed for the purpose of issuing a lease pursuant to section 19, the Division Chief may require the applicant for the lease to have the boundaries of such lands surveyed by a commissioned land surveyor acting under instructions from the Surveyor General of Canada.

22. (1) Where a lease area is not surveyed before the issuance of a lease, but is subsequently surveyed by a land surveyor acting under the instructions of the Surveyor General of Canada, the Division Chief may amend the description in the lease to conform to the description supplied by the Surveyor General of Canada.

(2) Where the description in a lease is amended under subsection (1), the Division Chief shall forward to the lessee, by registered mail, a copy of the amended description.

(3) The description of lands in a lease referred to in subsection (1) shall be deemed to have been amended on the 30th day after a copy of the amended description was forwarded to the lessee by registered mail.

Term of Lease

23. (1) Subject to subsection (2), every lease expires 10 years from the date upon which it was issued unless otherwise provided in the invitation to tender under section 5 or in the lease issued under section 6 or pursuant to section 19.

(2) Where, before the expiration of a lease or a renewal thereof, a lessee applies to the Division Chief for a renewal or further renewal of the lease, and where the lessee has complied with these Regulations and with the terms and conditions of the lease or renewal thereof, the Division Chief shall issue the renewal or further renewal of the lease

    (a) for such renewal term as may be specified in the lease or, if no renewal term is specified in the lease, for a term of 10 years; or

    (b) for such shorter term than that specified in paragraph

    (c) as the lessee may request.

(3) For the purposes of subsection (2), the Division Chief may allow a lessee to group two or more of his leases within any one reserve.

(4) [Revoked SOR/90-468, s. 1(2).]

(5) Every application for renewal of a lease shall be accompanied by the fee therefor set out in the schedule payable to the Receiver General.

SOR/90-468, s. 1.

Rental

24. A lessee shall pay annual rental in advance to the Receiver General at the rate of $2 for each acre in the lease area or at such other rate as may be specified in the invitation to tender under section 5 or in the lease issued under section 6 or pursuant to section 19.

Security Deposit

25. (1) No lease shall be issued to any person unless that person has deposited with the Division Chief a security deposit in such amount or at such rate, if any, as may be specified in the invitation to tender under section 5 or in the lease to be issued under section 6 or pursuant to section 19.

(2) A security deposit shall be in the form of money, bonds or promissory notes payable to the Receiver General on demand at a chartered bank or in such other form as the Division Chief deems proper.

26. Where the Division Chief is satisfied that a lessee has complied with these Regulations and with the terms and conditions of his lease or any renewal thereof, he may, during the term of the lease, and shall, on the expiry or surrender thereof, direct that the security deposit or a portion thereof deposited pursuant to subsection 25(1) be returned to the lessee.

Assessment Work

27. (1) During each year of the term of his lease and any renewal thereof, every lessee shall perform assessment work acceptable to the Supervisor of the value of $2 for each acre in the lease area, or of such other value as may be specified in the invitation to tender under section 5 or in the lease issued under section 6 or pursuant to section 19.

(2) Where in his opinion assessment work performed near a lease area serves to evaluate the mineral potential of the lease area, the Supervisor may deem the whole or any part of the value of that work to be assessment work performed in the lease area.

28. (1) Where, during any year of a lease, assessment work of the value required under subsection 27(1) is not performed, the lessee shall make a cash payment to the Receiver General in an amount equal to the difference between the value of assessment work performed during that year and the value of the assessment work required to be performed.

(2) Where the value of assessment work performed during any year of a lease exceeds the value of assessment work required to be performed under subsection 27(1), the Supervisor may credit the excess value of the assessment work performed to the value of the assessment work required to be performed pursuant to subsection 27(1) in any succeeding year or years up to 10 years from the year in which the assessment work was performed.

29. (1) Every lessee shall, within 90 days following the completion of each year of the term of his lease or any renewal thereof, forward to the Supervisor a certified statement in duplicate itemizing the assessment work performed and the cost of performing such work during the year most recently completed, together with any cash payment that may be required pursuant to subsection 28(1).

(2) Every lessee shall, within six months following the completion of each year of the term of his lease or any renewal thereof, forward to the Supervisor copies in duplicate of all maps and technical information that serve to record the assessment work performed for the year most recently completed, together with a report of the results obtained from the performance of that assessment work.

30. [Revoked SOR/90-468, s. 2.]

Royalties

31. Unless otherwise specified in the invitation to tender under section 5 or in the lease issued pursuant to section 6 or 19, every lessee shall pay royalties on all minerals to which he is entitled that have been obtained from his lease area at the rate of five per cent of

(a) the gross revenue from the mineral output at the pithead, where the minerals are sold at the lease area before treatment; or

(b) the market value of the mineral output at the pithead, where the minerals are not sold at the lease area before treatment.

32. Notwithstanding section 31, the rate of royalty may be altered by agreement between the Division Chief and the lessee from a rate based on a percentage of the gross revenue or of the market value to the equivalent rate per ton or per cubic yard of the mineral output at the pithead.

33. Any royalty rate based upon a weight or measure of mineral output shall be adjusted annually to conform to changes in a price index or other index that is published by Statistics Canada and is chosen by the Division Chief.

34. (1) During the term of his lease and any renewal thereof, a lessee shall forward to the Supervisor within 30 days after the expiry of each period of production a royalty payment in favour of the Receiver General in respect of that period together with a statement in duplicate showing the production and sales figures upon which the payment has been calculated.

(2) Where the Supervisor is not satisfied with the amount of a royalty payment or with a statement forwarded by a lessee pursuant to subsection (1), he may require the lessee to submit further particulars in relation to the statement and, if then required by the Supervisor, the lessee shall adjust the amount of the royalty payment.

(3) A period of production consists of the three calendar months ending on the last day of March, June, September and December or of such other period of time as the Supervisor may determine.

Notice of Production

35. Every lessee, within 10 days from the commencement of production of any mineral from his lease area, shall

(a) notify the Supervisor of the commencement of production; and

(b) submit to the Supervisor such information with respect to his mining operations and production as the Supervisor may require.

Penalty and Cancellation

36. (1) Where a lessee fails to pay rental as required by section 24 or to surrender his lease within 30 days from the date on which the rental becomes payable, he is liable to a penalty of five per cent of the amount of his rental.

(2) Notwithstanding subsection (1), where in the opinion of the Division Chief a lessee has failed in respect of his lease to comply with any provision of these Regulations, the Division Chief may forward to the lessee written notice by registered mail advising him that unless he commences to remedy the failure within 30 days from the date of the mailing of the notice and continues diligently to remedy the failure his lease may be cancelled by the Minister.

(3) Where a lessee has received a notice pursuant to subsection (2), he may, within 30 days from the date of the mailing of the notice, make written application to the Minister for a hearing to consider reasons why his lease should not be cancelled.

(4) Upon receipt of an application made pursuant to subsection (3), the Minister shall appoint a time and place for a hearing and shall notify the lessee by registered mail of the time and place of the hearing not less than 10 days before the date thereof.

(5) Where, in the opinion of the Minister, a lessee has failed to comply with the requirements of a notice mailed to him pursuant to subsection (2), or at a hearing held pursuant to this section does not show adequate reason why his lease should not be cancelled, the Minister shall cancel his lease.

General

Grouping

37. The Division Chief may authorize the grouping of

(a) a permit area or a lease area within a reserve with other permit areas or lease areas within the same reserve for the purpose of

(i) providing a security deposit required under section 11 or 25, and

(ii) assessment work required to be performed under sections 13 and 27; and

(b) a lease area within a reserve with other lease areas within the same reserve for the purpose of qualifying for a renewal under subsection 23(2) or (3).

38. The Minister may authorize the grouping of a permit area or a lease area in a reserve with a permit area or lease area in another reserve or with a tract of land outside a reserve for the purpose of development or production of minerals under these Regulations, where councils of the bands for whose use and benefit the lands have been set apart in which the permit areas or lease areas are located, have approved a formula for determining the participation of the bands in revenues and other benefits derived from such development or production of minerals.

Assignment

39. (1) A permittee or lessee may assign his permit or lease or any interest therein with the approval of the Minister.

(2) Where an assignment of a permit or lease

(a) has been approved by the Minister,

(b) is unconditional, and

(c) is accompanied by the registration fee set out in the schedule payable to the Receiver General,

the assignment shall be registered in the register kept pursuant to section 55 of the Act.

Surrender

40. (1) Where a permittee or lessee has complied with these Regulations and with the terms and conditions of his permit or lease, he may at any time surrender all or part of his permit area or lease area.

(2) Subject to subsection 10(2), where a permit or lease is surrendered under subsection (1), no rental paid in relation to that permit or lease shall be returned to the permittee or lessee.

Use of Land Surface

41. Where a person requires entry to a reserve in respect of which minerals have been surrendered or where a permittee or lessee requires use of land surface in a reserve for the purpose of development or production of minerals, he shall obtain a right of entry or right to use the land in accordance with any provisions that may be made by the Minister under the Act.

Inspection

42. (1) The Supervisor may

(a) enter upon and inspect any permit area, lease area or buildings and equipment thereon;

(b) require a permittee or lessee to produce any technical, financial and other records relating to the exploration for or production of minerals from his permit area or lease area; and

(c) take samples of minerals being produced and carry out any examination that, in his opinion, is necessary.

(2) Every permittee or lessee shall render such assistance as the Supervisor may require in the performance of his duties.

Plans

43. (1) Upon the termination of his permit or extension thereof or of his lease or renewal thereof and at such other times as the Supervisor may request, a permittee or lessee, as the case may be, shall submit to the Supervisor plans and sections that show

(a) the location of all mine workings;

(b) the average valuable mineral content of all mine headings, backs and faces not currently being worked; and

(c) the surface and underground plant, roads, railways, buildings and other structures or works situated in the permit area or lease area.

(2) All plans and sections submitted pursuant to subsection (1) shall be submitted in duplicate and shall be drawn on a scale of one inch to 100 feet or on such other scale as the Supervisor may determine.

(3) Where plans and sections submitted pursuant to subsection (1) are not satisfactory to the Supervisor, the Supervisor may require the permittee or lessee to submit further plans and sections.

Information Confidential

44. Any technical information submitted by a permittee or lessee pursuant to these Regulations shall not, without the written consent of the permittee or lessee, be disclosed unless that information

(a) relates only to a permit area or a portion thereof in respect of which the permit has expired or has been surrendered; or

(b) relates only to a lease area or a portion thereof in respect of which the lease has expired or has been surrendered or cancelled.

Payment of Tax

45. Every permittee and every lessee shall pay all rates, assessments and taxes in respect of his permit area or lease area, and in respect of his operations under his permit or lease.

Appeals

46. (1) Every permittee and every lessee may appeal to the Minister from any decision of the Division Chief or Supervisor, other than a decision made under section 5, 6 or 19.

(2) Where an appeal is made under subsection (1), the Minister may make such order or declaration as he deems proper.

Schedule — Fees

(ss. 18, 23 and 39)

Column I	Column II
1. Application for permit or lease	$20
2. Registration of assignment of permit or lease	20
3. Application for renewal of lease	20

Indian Referendum Regulations

Regulations governing the holding of referendums on Indian reserves

C.R.C. 1978, c. 957; am SOR/94-369, sched. II

Short Title

1. These Regulations may be cited as the *Indian Referendum Regulations*.

Interpretation

2. In these Regulations,

"Act" means the *Indian Act*;

"Assistant Deputy Minister" means the Assistant Deputy Minister, Lands and Trust Services, Department of Indian Affairs and Northern Development;

"deputy electoral officer" means a person appointed by an electoral officer for the purposes of a referendum;

"electoral officer" means the person in charge of the local office of the Department of Indian Affairs and Northern Development or any officer of the Department of Indian Affairs and Northern Development acting under the direction of the Minister or Assistant Deputy Minister for the purposes of a referendum;

"Minister" means the Minister of Indian Affairs and Northern Development;

"prescribed" means prescribed by the Minister;

SOR/94-369, sched. II, s. 1(2).

Holding of Referendum

3. (1) The Minister may, at the request of the council of a band or whenever the Minister considers it advisable, order that a referendum be held to determine if the majority of the electors of a band are in favour of a proposed absolute surrender or designation.

(2) Subject to subsection (3), voting on a referendum held pursuant to these Regulations shall be by secret ballot.

(3) The Minister may, at the request of the council of a band or whenever the Minister considers it advisable, order that the voting on a referendum be by a show of hands or in such other manner as the council of the bank may approve.

SOR/94-369, sched. II, s. 2.

Voting by Secret Ballot

4. (1) Where a voting on a referendum is to be by secret ballot, the electoral officer shall post a notice in the form prescribed at least 30 days prior to the date of the voting, in such places as he deems necessary.

(2) The notice referred to in subsection (1) shall state

    (a) the date on which the voting shall take place;

    (b) the question to be submitted to the electors;

    (c) the hours of the day the electors may vote; and

    (d) the location of the polling booths.

5. (1) The electoral officer shall

    (a) prepare a list containing in alphabetical order the names of the electors entitled to vote on the referendum and designating the location of the polling booth where each elector shall be entitled to vote;

    (b) post a copy of the list of electors in such places as he deems necessary at least 15 days prior to the date of the voting;

    (c) prepare sufficient ballot papers in the prescribed form which shall state the questions to be submitted to the electors;

    (d) procure a sufficient number of ballot boxes; and

    (e) before the poll is open cause to be delivered to the deputy electoral officer the ballot papers and a sufficient number of lead pencils for marking the ballot papers.

(2) Any elector may apply to the electoral officer within 10 days of the posting of the list of electors to have the list revised on the grounds that

    (a) the name of an elector has been omitted therefrom;

    (b) the name of an elector is incorrectly set out therein; or

    (c) the name of a person not qualified to vote is included therein.

(3) Where the electoral officer is satisfied that a revision is necessary in the list of electors, he shall make the revision and such revision shall be final.

6. The electoral officer or the deputy electoral officer shall provide a compartment at each polling place where the elector can mark his ballot paper free from observation.

7. The electoral officer or the deputy electoral officer shall, immediately before the opening of the poll, open the ballot box and call upon such persons who may be present to witness that it is empty and shall then lock and properly seal the box and place it in view for the reception of the ballots.

8. (1) Subject to subsection (2), the polls shall be kept open from 9 o'clock in the forenoon until 6 o'clock in the afternoon of the day set for the voting on the referendum.

(2) Where it appears to the electoral officer that it would be inconvenient to the electors to have the poll closed at 6 o'clock, he may order that it be kept open for an additional period of time not exceeding 2 hours.

9. (1) The electoral officer or the deputy electoral officer after satisfying himself that a person presenting himself for the purpose of voting is entitled to vote at the polling place, shall provide such person with a ballot paper on the back of which the officer has affixed his initials, so placed, that when the ballot paper is folded the initials can be seen without unfolding the ballot paper.

(2) The electoral officer or the deputy electoral officer shall place on the list of electors a mark opposite the name of every elector receiving a ballot paper.

10. (1) The electoral officer or the deputy electoral officer shall explain the mode of voting to an elector when requested to do so by such elector.

(2) On the application of an elector who is

    (a) not able to read, or

    (b) incapacitated by blindness or other physical cause,

the electoral officer or the deputy electoral officer shall assist that elector by marking his ballot paper in the manner directed by the elector and shall place such ballot paper in the ballot box.

(3) The electoral officer or the deputy electoral officer shall make an entry in the list of electors opposite the name of the elector that the ballot was marked by him at the request of the elector and the reason therefor.

11. Except as provided in subsection 10(2), every elector receiving a ballot paper shall

    (a) proceed immediately to the compartment provided for marking the ballot paper;

    (b) mark his ballot by placing a cross ("X") under the word "YES" or "NO" opposite the question stated on the ballot paper;

    (c) fold the ballot paper so as to conceal the mark on the face of the paper but so as to expose the initials on the back of it; and

    (d) forthwith deliver it to the electoral officer or the deputy electoral officer for deposit in the ballot box.

12. (1) An elector who receives a soiled or improperly printed ballot paper, or inadvertently spoils his ballot paper in marking it shall, upon returning the ballot paper to the electoral officer or the deputy electoral officer, be entitled to another ballot paper.

(2) An elector who has received a ballot paper and

    (a) leaves the compartment for marking ballot papers without delivering the same to the electoral officer or the deputy electoral officer in the manner provided, or

    (b) refuses to vote,

shall forfeit his right to vote on the referendum and the electoral officer or the deputy electoral officer shall make an entry on the list of electors opposite the name of the elector that the elector did not return the ballot paper or refused to vote as the case may be.

13. The electoral officer or the deputy electoral officer shall allow only one elector in the compartment for marking ballot papers at any one time.

14. An elector who is inside the polling place at the time fixed for closing the poll shall be entitled to vote before the poll is closed.

15. No person shall interfere or attempt to interfere with an elector when marking his ballot paper or obtain or attempt to obtain at the polling place information as to how an elector is about to vote or has voted.

16. The electoral officer or the deputy electoral officer shall maintain peace and good order during the voting and for this purpose he may enlist the assistance of the constables, peace officers or other persons present.

17. Whenever the electoral officer or the deputy electoral officer does not understand the language spoken by the elector, he shall appoint and swear an interpreter who shall be the means of communication between him and the elector with reference to all matters required to enable such elector to vote.

18. (1) Immediately after the close of the poll the electoral officer in the presence of the deputy electoral officer and any members of the council of the band that may be present shall

(a) examine the ballot papers;

(b) reject all ballot papers

(i) that have not been supplied by him or by the deputy electoral officer,

(ii) that have been marked incorrectly, or

(iii) upon which anything appears by which an elector can be identified;

(c) count the votes given in favour of and against the question submitted in the referendum; and

(d) prepare a statement in writing of the number of votes so given and of the number of ballot papers rejected.

(2) The statement referred to in paragraph (1)(d) shall be

(a) signed by the electoral officer and by the chief or a member of the council of the band; and

(b) filed in the local office of the Department of Indian Affairs and Northern Development.

SOR/94-369, sched. II, s. 4.

19. When the results of the voting at all the polls are known to the electoral officer, he shall

    (a) immediately prepare a statement in triplicate signed by himself and by the chief or a member of the council of the band indicating

        (i) the number of electors who were entitled to vote,

        (ii) the number of electors who voted,

        (iii) the number of votes cast in favour of and against the question submitted in the referendum, and

        (iv) the number of rejected ballots; and

    (b) deliver a copy of the statement to

        (i) the Assistant Deputy Minister,

        (ii) the person in charge of the regional office of the Department of Indian Affairs and Northern Development, and

        (iii) the chief of the band.

SOR/94-369, sched. II, s. 5.

20. The electoral officer shall deposit the ballot papers used in the voting in a sealed envelope and retain it for 60 days after which time he may, unless directed otherwise by the Assistant Deputy Minister, destroy them in the presence of two witnesses.

Voting Other Than by Secret Ballot

21. (1) Where voting on a referendum is to be by a show of hands or in some other manner as ordered by the Minister and approved by the council of the band, the electoral officer shall post a notice in the form prescribed at least 30 days prior to the date of the voting, in such places as he deems necessary.

(2) The notice referred to in subsection (1) shall state

    (a) the date, time and place of the meeting where voting on the referendum shall take place; and

    (b) the question to be submitted to the electors.

22. The electoral officer shall

    (a) prepare a list of electors containing in alphabetical order the names of the electors entitled to vote on the referendum and designating the meeting place where each elector shall be entitled to attend for the purposes of voting; and

    (b) post a copy of the list of electors in such places as he deems necessary at least 15 days prior to the date of the voting.

23. (1) An elector may apply to the electoral officer within 10 days from the posting of the list of electors to have such list revised on the grounds that

    (a) the name of an elector has been omitted therefrom;

(b) the name of an elector is incorrectly set out therein; or

(c) the name of a person not qualified to vote is included therein.

(2) Where the electoral officer is satisfied that a revision is necessary in the list of electors, he shall make the revision and such revision shall be final.

24. The electoral officer or the deputy electoral officer shall maintain peace and good order during the voting and for this purpose he may enlist the assistance of constables, peace officers or other persons present.

25. Whenever the electoral officer or the deputy electoral officer does not understand the language spoken by an elector, he shall appoint and swear an interpreter who shall be the means of communication between him and the elector with reference to all matters required to enable such elector to vote.

26. The electoral officer or the deputy electoral officer shall call the meeting to order and, after explaining to the electors the purpose of the meeting and the terms of the proposed absolute surrender or designation, shall call for a vote of the electors by a show of hands or in the manner ordered by the Minister and approved by the council of the band.

SOR/94-369, sched. II, s. 6.

27. No person shall cause or attempt to cause any disturbance at a meeting or interfere or attempt to interfere with the counting of the votes.

28. (1) The electoral officer or the deputy electoral officer shall

(a) count the votes at the meeting given in favour of and against the proposed absolute surrender or designation; and

(b) prepare a statement in writing of the number of votes so given.

SOR/94-369, sched. II, s. 6

(2) The statement referred to in subsection (1) shall be

(a) signed by the electoral officer or the deputy electoral officer and by the chief or a member of the council of the band; and

(b) filed in the local office of the Department of Indian Affairs and Northern Development.

SOR/94-369, sched. II, s. 4.

29. When the results of the voting at all the meetings are known to the electoral officer, he shall

(a) immediately prepare a statement in triplicate signed by himself and by the chief or a member of the council of the band indicating

(i) the number of electors who were entitled to vote,

(ii) the number of electors who voted, and

(iii) the number of votes cast in favour of and against the proposed absolute surrender or designation; and SOR/94-369, sched. II, s. 6.

(b) deliver a copy of the statement to

(i) the Assistant Deputy Minister,

(ii) the person in charge of the regional office of the Department of Indian Affairs and Northern Development, and

(iii) the chief of the band.

SOR/94-369, sched. II, s. 5.

Subsequent Referendums

30. (1) Where the majority of the electors of a band did not vote on a referendum held to determine if the band is in favour of a proposed absolute surrender or designation, the Minister may, if the surrender was assented to by the majority of the electors who did vote, call another referendum to be held in accordance with these Regulations.

SOR/94-369, sched. II, s. 6.

(2) [Repealed SOR/94-369, sched. II, s. 3.]

Appeals

31. (1) Where a referendum is held pursuant to these Regulations, any elector who voted on the referendum and has reasonable grounds for believing that

(a) there was a violation of these Regulations that may affect the results of the referendum, or

(b) there was corrupt practice in connection with the referendum,

may, within 7 days from the date of the referendum, file an appeal by forwarding by registered mail to the Assistant Deputy Minister

(c) notice of an appeal; and

(d) a statutory declaration containing the grounds of appeal and particulars thereof.

(2) Where an appeal is filed pursuant to subsection (1), the Assistant Deputy Minister shall within 21 days from the receipt thereof forward a copy of the appeal by registered mail to the electoral officer.

(3) The electoral officer shall, within 10 days from the receipt of the appeal, forward to the Assistant Deputy Minister by registered mail a statutory declaration containing an answer to the particulars stated in the appeal.

(4) The Assistant Deputy Minister shall forward the material filed pursuant to this section to the Minister.

32. (1) The Minister may, if the material filed pursuant to section 31 is not sufficient to decide the validity of the grounds of the appeal, conduct such further investigations as he deems necessary.

(2) Subject to subsection (3) the Minister may dispose of an appeal by allowing it and calling another referendum.

(3) Where the Minister is of the opinion that the grounds of the appeal

    (a) are not established, or

    (b) do not affect the results of the referendum,

he shall dismiss the appeal.

Forms

33. The Minister may prescribe such forms as are required for the purposes of these Regulations.

Indian Reserve Traffic Regulations

Regulations governing the operation of vehicles within Indian reserves

C.R.C. 1978, c. 959

Short Title

1. These Regulations may be cited as the *Indian Reserve Traffic Regulations.*

Interpretation

2. In these Regulations,

"road" includes any roadway, driveway, street, lane or other place open to the public for the passage of vehicles;

"vehicle" means any wagon, cart, motor car, motor truck, trailer, motorcycle, traction engine, tractor, road-making machinery or other conveyance that is driven, propelled or drawn by any kind of power.

Application

3. These Regulations apply on all roads within Indian reserves.

General

4. (1) The driver of any vehicle shall bring such vehicle to a full stop when ordered to do so by any person authorized by the Minister of Indian Affairs and Northern Development to enforce these Regulations, and shall obey all directions issued by such authorized person in respect of the routing or control of traffic, including the parking of vehicles.

(2) The driver of any vehicle shall comply with the direction of any mechanical or other device or sign installed for the control or routing of traffic.

(3) The driver of any vehicle shall not drive such vehicle over any road the use of which for public traffic is prohibited by any sign or other device.

5. The person in charge of any vehicle shall not drive or ride such vehicle at any rate of speed that is excessive or dangerous, having regard to the conditions then prevailing, and the person shall keep the vehicle in such control when approaching a road intersection, or crossing for pedestrians or other purposes, as will enable him to prevent a collision with, or damage to, all other persons and vehicles.

6. The driver of any vehicle shall comply with all laws and regulations relating to motor vehicles, which are in force from time to time in the province in which the Indian reserve is situated, except such laws or regulations as are inconsistent with these Regulations.

7. No person shall park or station any vehicle upon any road unless permission to do so is designated by signs erected over or marked on the roadway.

8. No vehicle in a dangerous or unsafe condition shall be operated on any road.

9. Any person who violates any of the provisions of these Regulations shall be guilty of an offence and shall be liable, upon summary conviction, to a penalty of not less than $1 and not more than $50, or to imprisonment for a term not exceeding two months.

Case Law:

Canada

R. v. Francis (1988), [1988] 1 S.C.R. 1025, 5 M.V.R. (2d) 268, 41 C.C.C. (3d) 217, 51 D.L.R. (4th) 418, [1988] 4 C.N.L.R. 98, 217 A.P.R. 243, 85 N.B.R. (2d) 243, 85 N.R. 3

There is no conflict between the federal traffic regulations and the provincial traffic regulations. Provincial traffic regulations can be enforced on reserve.

Alberta

R. v. Twoyoungmen (1979), 16 A.R. 413, [1979] 5 W.W.R. 712, 3 M.V.R. 186, 101 D.L.R. (3d) 598, [1979] 3 C.N.L.R. 85, 48 C.C.C. (2d) 550 (C.A.)

The word **"operate"** should be limited to the narrow meaning of manner of driving. Section 72(1)(c) does not give the power to regulate vehicle insurance.

R. v. Spear Chief (1963), 45 W.W.R. 161 (Alta. Dist. Ct.)

Roads on reserves are public highways if they are necessary for ordinary travel by provincial residents, and an Indian may be convicted of driving on one while his licence is suspended.

British Columbia

Dunstan v. Hell's Gate Enterprises Ltd. (1989), [1989] 2 C.N.L.R. 36 (B.C. C.A.)

An access road to river rafting which passed through the Tuckozap Reserve was not a public highway, because there had been no dedication.

R. v. Jules (1993), 48 M.V.R. (2d) 265, [1994] 3 C.N.L.R. 152 (B.C. S.C.)

The *Criminal Code* applies to a motor vehicle offence which occurs on a road passing through a reserve. Although the public had right of access, the First Nation claimed that it had not turned over the highway to anyone.

R. v. Charlie and Joe (1985), [1985] 4 W.W.R. 472, 32 M.V.R. 40, 19 D.L.R. (4th) 539, 19 C.C.C. (3d) 406 (B.C. C.A.)

The word **"operation"** should not be construed so broadly to include the administrative proscriptions of licensing and insurance.

Manitoba

R. v. Spence (1982), 6 Man. R. (2d) 48, [1982] 1 C.N.L.R. 115 (Co. Ct.)

The *Manitoba Highway Traffic Act*, C.C.S.M., c. H60, and the *Criminal Code*, R.S.C. 1970, c. C-34 [now R.S.C. 1985, c. C-46], apply on reserves in Manitoba under s. 6 of the *Indian Reserve Traffic Regulations*.

Nova Scotia

R. v. Maloney (1983), [1983] 2 C.N.L.R. 148, 51 N.S.R. 441, 102 A.P.R. 441 (C.A.)

The accused was charged with driving while his licence was suspended, when driving on a paved highway through the reserve. He was charged under the provincial legislation and convicted on appeal. The court held:

> The misconduct alleged here was driving while the required licence was suspended. There is no specific provision in the regulations dealing with such subject matter; therefore, in order for the respondent's position to prevail, s. 6 would have to be interpreted as an offence-creating section.

> To my mind, s. 6 does not go that far but rather is but a declaratory reminder that on roads on Indian reserves the conduct prescribed in the *Motor Vehicle Act* must be observed unless such is specifically covered by the regulations. [C.N.L.R. p. 150]

R. v. Marshall (1979), 31 N.S.R. (2d) 530, 52 A.P.R. 530 (C.A.)

Provincial motor vehicle acts apply where roads on reserves are provincial highways.

Ontario

Skerryvore Ratepayers' Assn. v. Shawanaga Indian Band (1993), 16 O.R. (3d) 390, 36 R.P.R. (2d) 23, 50 M.V.R. (2d) 9, 109 D.L.R. (4th) 449, [1994] 2 C.N.L.R. 61, 68 O.A.C. 69 (C.A.)leave to appeal to S.C.C. refused (1994), 17 O.R. (3d) xvii, 38 R.P.R. (2d) 245n, 2 M.V.R. (3d) 311n, [1994] 3 C.N.L.R. vin (S.C.C.)

A road which was used by the public, but which has not been surrendered, continues to belong to the First Nation.

R. v. Isaac (1974), 38 D.L.R. (3d) 349 (Ont. C.A.)

The regulations, under s. 6, incorporate the provisions of provincial laws into the regulations. In this case, where an Indian was charged in regard to the requirement for licensing and insurance, the court held that drivers of vehicles on reserves must comply with all provincial laws. The court held, at p. 352:

> It would appear that the fundamental purpose of Parliament in enacting s. 73 was to enable the control by Regulation of all elements of the operation of motor vehicles on Indian Reserves. This the Governor in Council has sought to do by the incorporation of all provincial laws relating to motor vehicles which are inconsistent with other Regulations under the *Indian Act*.

Saskatchewan

R. v. Bigeagle (1978), [1978] 6 W.W.R. 65, 43 C.C.C. (2d) 528 (Sask. C.A.)

A well maintained gravel road constructed for the use and benefit of a special group on the reserve is not a public highway and thus the accused did not require a licence to drive on such a road.

R. v. Daniels (1975), [1975] W.W.D. 181 (Sask. C.A.)

A road open to the public on a reserve is a public highway and all drivers must possess a driver's licence.

R. v. Thunderchild (1996), [1996] 1 C.N.L.R. 206 (Sask. Q.B.)

A road on the Thunderchild reserve was not a public highway because "its use was restricted to band members, their employees, and peace officers stationed on the reserve for the protection of band members and the preservation of the law." [C.N.L.R. at p. 209]

R. v. Johns (No.2) (1963), 45 W.W.R. 65, 41 C.R. 380 (Sask. Dist. Ct.)

A road on the reserve made by the Indians for their own use was not a public highway and the accused was not guilty of driving without a licence.

R. v. Wapach (1975), [1975] W.W.D. 134 (Sask. Mag. Ct.)

An Indian driving on a road on the reserve in which he is a member does not require a licence.

Indian Reserve Waste Disposal Regulations

Regulations respecting waste disposal in Indian reserves

C.R.C. 1978, c. 960

Short Title

1. These Regulations may be cited as the *Indian Reserve Waste Disposal Regulations.*

Interpretation

2. In these Regulations,

"Minister" means the Minister of Indian Affairs and Northern Development;

"permit" means a permit issued pursuant to section 5;

"reserve" means a reserve as defined in the *Indian Act*;

"waste" includes garbage, liquid and semi-liquid substances, landfill and scrap of all kinds and any combination of any of the foregoing.

Prohibitions Respecting the Disposal or Storage of Waste

3. No person shall

    (a) operate a garbage dump in a reserve, or

    (b) use any land in a reserve for the disposal or storage of waste

except under the authority of a permit issued pursuant to paragraph 5(a) or (b) and in the manner specified in the permit.

4. No Indian who is lawfully in possession of any lands in a reserve and no person to whom reserve lands have been leased or who lawfully occupies, uses, resides or otherwise exercises rights on land in a reserve shall permit any person to operate on that land a garbage dump or use any part of that land for the disposal or storage of waste unless a permit to carry on that action on that land has been issued pursuant to paragraph 5(a) or (b) and is still valid.

Permits

5. The Minister or the council of a band, if authorized by the Minister pursuant to section 8, may issue to any person a permit authorizing that person

    (a) to operate a garbage dump in a reserve;

    (b) to use land in a reserve for the disposal or storage of waste; or

(c) to burn waste on any land in a reserve.

6. A permit shall

(a) specify the land in respect of which the permit is issued; and

(b) specify the manner in which the activity authorized therein shall be exercised.

7. Subject to section 11, a permit shall expire on December 31st next following the date of issue thereof.

8. The Minister may, in writing, authorize the council of any band to issue a permit in respect of land in the reserve of that band and shall, in the authorization, specify the manner in which the activity to be authorized in the permit shall be exercised.

9. The revocation of an authorization given by the Minister pursuant to section 8 does not affect the validity of any permit issued under that authorization.

Burning of Waste Prohibited

10. No person shall burn any waste on any land in a reserve except under the authority of a permit issued pursuant to paragraph 5(c).

Orders and Cancellation of Permits

11. If the holder of a permit issued pursuant to section 5

(a) operates a garbage dump in a reserve,

(b) uses land in a reserve for the disposal or storage of waste, or

(c) burns waste on any land in a reserve other than in the manner specified in the permit, the Minister or the council of the band, whoever issued the permit, may cancel the permit and order the holder of the permit to close and clean up the garbage dump or to clean up the land in the reserve, as may be applicable, in a manner satisfactory to the Minister or the council.

Violation of Sections 3 and 10

12. Where a person is convicted of

(a) operating a garbage dump in a reserve or using land in a reserve for the disposal or storage of waste except under the authority of a permit issued pursuant to paragraph 5(a) or (b), or

(b) burning waste on land in a reserve except under the authority of a permit issued pursuant to section 5(c),

the Minister may order that person to close and clean up the garbage dump or to clean up the land, as may be applicable, in a manner satisfactory to the Minister.

Compliance with Orders

13. Any person who has been ordered by the Minister or the council of a band to do anything pursuant to section 11 or section 12 shall comply with that order without delay.

Penalties

14. Every person who violates these Regulations is liable on summary conviction to a fine not exceeding $100 or to imprisonment for a term not exceeding three months, or to both.

Indian Timber Regulations

Regulations in respect of the cutting of timber on Indian reserves and surrendered lands

C.R.C. 1978, c. 961, as am. SOR/93-244; SOR/94-690; SOR/95-531

Short Title

1. These Regulations may be cited as the *Indian Timber Regulations*.

SOR/93-244, Sched. I, s. 1.

Interpretation

2. In these Regulations,

"Act" means the *Indian Act*; (*Loi*)

"Department" means the Department of Indian Affairs and Northern Development; (*ministère*)

"dues" means any stumpage or royalty charges for the right or privilege of the cutting and removal of timber; (*droits*)

"licence" means any written authority or contract granted by the Minister for the cutting of timber on surrendered lands or reserve lands; (*permis*)

"limit" means the area included in a permit or licence; (*limite*)

"Minister" means the Minister of Indian Affairs and Northern Development; (*Ministre*)

"permit" means a licence granted to a band or to a member or group of members of a band for whose benefit the timber is being administered; (*licence*)

"person" includes corporation, syndicate, firm and partnership. (*personne*)

SOR/93-244, Sched. I, ss. 2, 14; SOR/95-531, s. 1.

Application

3. These Regulations apply to the cutting of timber on surrendered lands and on reserve lands.

SOR/93-244, Sched. I, s. 3; SOR/95-531, s. 2.

Prohibition

3.1 No person shall cut timber on surrendered lands or on reserve lands without a licence.

SOR/95-531, s. 2.

Permits for Indian Use

4. Permits to cut timber free of dues may be issued by the Minister to a band for band purposes, or to a member or group of members of a band, to cut timber and fuel wood for or their individual use.

SOR/93-244, Sched. I, s. 14.

Permits to Cut for Sale

5. (1) With the consent of the council of a band, permits to cut timber for sale may be issued by the Minister to a band or to a member or group of members of a band.

(2) Dues shall be charged at prevailing rates for timber cut on band land, and for timber harvested from individual locations or holdings of Indians the rate of dues may be reduced to one-half of such prevailing rates, and the rate of the dues shall be stated in the permit.

(3) [Repealed SOR/94-690, Sched., s. 1.]

6. All timber cut under permit shall be measured by a licensed scaler or by some competent person appointed by the superintendent,

(a) at the place of cutting or at a concentration point adjacent thereto; or

(b) in the Province of British Columbia, either at the place of cutting or at some point between such place and the mill.

SOR/93-244, Sched. I, s. 14.

7. Unless with the consent of the Minister, timber cut under permit shall not be

(a) manufactured, or

(b) except in the Province of British Columbia, removed from the place of cutting or concentration point adjacent thereto,

until it has been measured and dues paid thereon.

SOR/93-244, Sched. I, ss. 13, 14.

8. All timber permits expire on April 30th in the year next following the year of issue.

Licences

9. Subject to section 10, the Minister may grant licences for the right to cut timber

(a) on surrendered lands; or

(b) with the consent of the council of a band, on reserve lands.

SOR/93-244, Sched. I, s. 5.

10. Where it is estimated that the dues payable pursuant to a licence will exceed $2,500, the Minister shall invite tenders for the licence by public advertisement.

SOR/93-244, Sched. I, s. 5.

Renewals

11. (1) Timber licences expire on April 30 in the year that follows the year in which the licence was granted, unless otherwise specified in the licence.

(2) Application for renewal shall be made during the term of the licence and if the application is not made within 30 days following the date of expiration of the licence it shall thereupon determine, and in the discretion of the Minister any security given by the licensee may be declared forfeited.

(3) If a limit has not been worked during the licence year, the licensee shall, with his application for renewal, furnish a sworn statement of the reasons for his failure to operate and a renewal shall be granted only if the Minister is satisfied with such statement.

SOR/93-244, Sched. I, ss. 6, 13.

Ground Rent

12. Ground rent shall be paid for each licence year at the rate of $10 per square mile, except in the Province of British Columbia where the rate shall be $0.20 per acre, provided that in no case shall the rent for a licence year be less than $40.

13. [Revoked SOR/93-244, Sched. I, s. 7.]

Security Deposit

14. (1) It is a condition of every licence that the licensee shall deposit security in cash or bonds for the performance of the terms and conditions of the licence, in an amount equal to 15 per cent of the estimated dues payable under the licence.

SOR/94-690, Sched., s. 2.

(2) The Minister may convert the security deposit and apply it against dues in arrears, and in such event the licence shall not be renewed until the security deposit has been restored to the full amount.

(3) If a licensee fails to comply with any condition of his contract or to complete the operation in a satisfactory manner, the Minister may declare the security deposit forfeited to the Crown for the benefit of the band.

Scaling

15. Without the consent of the Minister, timber cut under licence shall not be

    (a) manufactured, or

    (b) except in the Province of British Columbia, removed from the place of cutting or concentration point adjacent thereto,

until it has been measured and dues paid thereon.

SOR/93-244, Sched. I, s. 13.

16. Failing any other provision in the licence, all timber cut from May 1st to November 30th in any year shall be scaled and paid for by January 31st of the year next following, and all timber cut from December 1st to April 30th in any licence year shall be scaled and paid for by June 30th next following the cutting.

17. A licensee shall at his expense supply scaler's returns verified by affidavit.

Fire Protection

18. The licensee shall pay all costs of fire protection service and of the suppression of any fire in the limit covered by his licence or occasioned by persons employed by him.

19. [Revoked SOR/93-244, Sched. I, s. 8.]

Records

20. (1) A licensee shall maintain a record of timber cut each month and, when required, shall furnish a copy of the record to the Minister.

(2) The Minister, or anyone authorized by him, shall at all times have free access to and be permitted to examine the books and memoranda kept by any licensee showing the quantity of timber in board measure sawn from logs and of other timber products cut under the licence, and failure to produce such books and memoranda when required so to do shall subject such licensee to a forfeiture of his rights under the licence.

SOR/93-244, Sched. I, s. 13.

Cancellation

21. It is a condition of every licence that, if the licensee fails to comply with the terms and conditions of the licence or with these Regulations, the Minister may cancel the licence.

SOR/93-244, Sched. I, s. 9.

Conservation

22. (1) With the consent of the licensee, the Minister may vary any licence in respect of one or more parts of a licensed area or in respect of any type, size or species of timber.

(2) Notwithstanding anything contained in a licence, the Minister may, for the purpose of forest management, watershed protection, fire protection or the preservation of the beauty of the landscape, game or game shelters, order the marking of such trees as are to be left standing or cut in the licensed area and order the licensee to pay the cost of such marking.

SOR/93-244, Sched. I, s. 13.

23. [Revoked SOR/93-244, Sched. I, s. 10.]

24. [Revoked SOR/93-244, Sched. I, s. 10.]

Compliance with Laws

25. Every licensee shall exercise the rights conferred by the licence in accordance with the laws of the province in which the licensee is operating under the licence regarding disposal of slash, prevention of fire hazard and the conduct of timber operations.

SOR/93-244, Sched. I, s. 10.

Seizure

26. (1) The Minister may seize and detain any timber and any product manufactured from timber, when he has reasonable grounds to believe that

(a) such timber or the timber from which such product was manufactured has not been measured or counted by a scaler as required by these Regulations;

(b) any charges in respect of such timber or on the timber from which such product was manufactured or in respect of the lands on which such timber was cut are in default; or

(c) such timber or the timber from which such product was manufactured was not cut under the authority of a licence or permit.

(2) Any timber or product that is seized under subsection (1) may be removed to such place as the Minister may deem proper for the protection of the timber or product, and if it is seized when in possession of a carrier it shall be removed by the carrier on behalf of the Minister to such place as the Minister may direct, provided that

(a) the Department may defray the costs of transportation and other charges incurred in consequence of the directions given by the superintendent, and all such costs shall be included in the costs of seizure; and

(b) such seizure shall not prejudice or affect any lien to which the carrier may be entitled in respect of the timber or product to the time of such seizure.

(3) Where timber within the meaning of this section has been made up with other timber into a crib, dam or raft, or in any other manner has been so mixed at a mill or elsewhere as to render it impossible or difficult to distinguish such timber from other timber with which it is mixed, the whole of the timber so mixed may be seized and detained until separated by the person claiming to be the owner thereof to the satisfaction of the Minister.

SOR/93-244, Sched. I, s. 13.

27. Seizure of timber or any product therefrom may be made by posting beside the timber or product a notice stating that the timber or product has been seized.

28. Where timber or any product manufactured therefrom has been seized and no claim to recover it has been made within 30 days from the date of the seizure, the timber or product is forfeited to the Crown.

SOR/93-244, Sched. I, s. 11.

Proceedings following Seizure

29. (1) Any person claiming to be the owner of timber, or any product manufactured therefrom, that has been seized under section 26 may, on at leat four days notice to the Minister, apply to a judge of a court of competent jurisdiction in the place in which the timber or product is held under seizure for an order for the release from seizure and delivery of the timber or product to that person.

(2) Upon receipt of a bond of the claimant, with two good and sufficient sureties in an amount not less than the market value of the timber or product and the costs of the seizure, to be forfeited to the Crown if the claimant is declared by the judge not to be the owner of the timber or product, the judge may order the timber or product to be released from seizure and to be delivered to the claimant.

(3) Upon the application of the Minister or the claimant, and upon at least 7 days notice, the judge shall determine the ownership of the timber or product whether or not it has been released and delivered to the claimant under subsection (2) and shall make an order

(a) declaring the claimant for charges, or

(i) free of any claim for charges, or

(ii) subject to payment of such dues, charges and expenses as he may find to be owing; or

(b) declaring the claimant not to be the owner and the bond, if any, forfeited to the Crown.

(4) The judge shall make such order as he may consider proper as to the costs of proceedings under this section and the costs of seizure.

(5) If the claimant is declared not to be the owner of the timber or product, it shall be disposed of in such manner as the Minister may determine.

SOR/93-244, Sched. I, ss. 12, 13.

Penalties

30. Every person who contravenes a provision of these Regulations is guilty of an offence and liable on summary conviction to a fine not exceeding one hundred dollars or to imprisonment for a term not exceeding three months, or to both.

SOR/95-531, s. 3.

DEPARTMENT OF INDIAN AFFAIRS AND NORTHERN DEVELOPMENT ACT

Department of Indian Affairs and Northern Development Act

R. S. C. 1985, c. I-6, as am. S.C. 1991, c. 50, s. 30; 1993, c. 28, s. 78 (Schedule III, items 75–77) (not in force at date of publication)

Short Title

1. Short title — This Act may be cited as the *Department of Indian Affairs and Northern Development Act.*

Establishment of the Department

2. (1) Department established — There is hereby established a department of the Government of Canada called the Department of Indian Affairs and Northern Development over which the Minister of Indian Affairs and Northern Development appointed by commission under the Great Seal shall preside.

(2) Minister — The Minister holds office during pleasure and has the management and direction of the Department.

3. Deputy head — The Governor in Council may appoint an officer called the Deputy Minister of Indian Affairs and Northern Development to hold office during pleasure and to be the deputy head of the Department.

Powers, Duties and Functions of the Minister

4. Powers, duties and functions of Minister — The powers, duties and functions of the Minister extend to and include all matters over which Parliament has jurisdiction, not by law assigned to any other department, board or agency of the Government of Canada, relating to

(a) Indian affairs;

(b) the Yukon Territory and the Northwest Territories and their resources and affairs; and

> (b) the Yukon Territory, and Northwest Territories and Nunavut and their resources and affairs; and
>
> [1993, c. 28, s. 78 (Schedule III, item 75). Not in force at date of publication.]

(c) Inuit affairs.

1993, c. 28, s. 78 (Schedule III, item 75).

5. Idem — The Minister shall be responsible for

(a) coordinating the activities in the Yukon Territory and the Northwest Territories of the several departments, boards and agencies of the Government of Canada;

(b) undertaking, promoting and recommending policies and programs for the further economic and political development of the Yukon Territory and the Northwest Territories; and

(a) coordinating the activities in the Yukon Territory, the Northwest Territories and Nunavut of the several departments, boards and agencies of the Government of Canada;

(b) undertaking, promoting and recommending policies and programs for the further economic and political development of the Yukon Territory, the Northwest Territories and Nunavut; and
[1993, c. 28, s. 78 (Schedule III, item 76). Not in force at date of publication.]

(c) fostering, through scientific investigation and technology, knowledge of the Canadian north and of the means of dealing with conditions related to its further development.

1993, c. 28, s. 78 (Schedule III, item 76).

6. Administration — The Minister has the administration of all lands situated in the Yukon Territory and the Northwest Territories belonging to Her Majesty in right of Canada except those lands that were immediately before October 1, 1966 under the management, charge and direction of any minister, department, branch or agency of the Government of Canada other than the Minister of Northern Affairs and National Resources or the Department of Northern Affairs and National Resources.

1991, c. 50, s. 30; 1993, c. 28, s. 78 (Schedule III, item 77).

6. The Minister has the administration of all lands situated in the Yukon Territory, the Northwest Territories and Nunavut belonging to Her Majesty in right of Canada except those lands that were immediately before October 1, 1966 under the management, charge and direction of any minister, department, branch or agency of the Government of Canada other than the Minister of Northern Affairs and National Resources or the Department of Northern Affairs and National Resources.
[1993, c. 28, s. 78 (Schedule III, item 77). Not in force at date of publication.]

Annual Report

7. Annual report — The Minister shall, on or before January 31 next following the end of each fiscal year or, if Parliament is not then sitting, on any of the first five days next thereafter that either House of Parliament is sitting, submit to Parliament a report showing the operations of the Department for that fiscal year.

CONSTITUTION ACTS

The Constitution Act, 1867

30 & 31 Victoria, c. 3 (Consolidated with amendments)

Powers of the Parliament

91. Legislative Authority of Parliament of Canada — It shall be lawful for the Queen, by and with the Advice and Consent of the Senate and House of Commons, to make Laws for the Peace, Order, and good Government of Canada, in relation to all Matters not coming within the Classes of Subjects by this Act assigned exclusively to the Legislatures of the Provinces; and for greater Certainty, but not so as to restrict the Generality of the foregoing Terms of this Section, it is hereby declared that (notwithstanding anything in this Act) the exclusive Legislative Authority of the Parliament of Canada extends to all Matters coming within the Classes of Subjects next hereinafter enumerated; that is to say, —

...

24. Indians, and Lands reserved for the Indians.

Commentary: The relationship between federal and provincial authority is very complex. The following is a very general summary of the main issues.

Federal authority

There is an area of exclusive federal authority which cannot be touched by provincial legislation. Reasons courts have found provincial laws invalid include: impairing the "status and capacities of Indians"; affecting "Indianness"; regulating Indians *qua* Indians; and regulating a matter which forms an integral part of the primary federal jurisdiction. (See, for example, *Derrikson v. Derrikson*)

The scope of federal authority is very wide, and includes authority over matters which would otherwise be in the legislative authority of the provinces. (See, for example, *Canada v. Canard*) All aboriginal rights are under exclusive federal authority and only the federal government can extinguish those rights. *(Delgamuukw v. British Columbia)*

Provincial authority

Provincial laws which attempt to legislate about Indians in the area of exclusive federal authority are not valid. (See for example, *R. v. Sutherland*). However, provincial laws which fall short of invading the area of exclusive federal authority may apply to Indians, unless those laws are inconsistent with a federal law. If there is an inconsistency, the federal law is paramount. (See for example *R. v. Francis*).

Provincial laws of general application which *do* invade the area of exclusive federal jurisdiction may be incorporated into federal law through s. 88 of the *Indian Act*. (See for example, *Dick v. R.* and the Commentary under s. 88)

Case Law:

Federal or Provincial Authority — Canada

Delgamuukw v. British Columbia ((December 11, 1997)), Doc. 23799 (S.C.C.)

The court held that all Aboriginal rights come under exclusive federal authority and only the federal government could extinguish those rights.

> The core of Indianness encompasses the whole range of aboriginal rights that are protected by s. 35(1). Those rights include rights in relation to land; that part of the core derives from s.

91(24)'s reference to "Lands reserved for the Indians". But those rights also encompass practices, customs and traditions which are not tied to land as well; that part of the core can be traced to federal jurisdiction over "Indians". Provincial governments are prevented from legislating in relation to both types of aboriginal rights. [at para.178]

R. v. Francis, [1988] 1 S.C.R. 1025, 5 M.V.R. (2d) 268, 85 N.B.R. (2d) 243, 217 A.P.R. 243, 51 D.L.R. (4th) 418, [1988] 4 C.N.L.R. 98, 41 C.C.C. (3d) 217, 85 N.R. 3

Even though provincial traffic laws were incorporated by reference as a federal law, the provincial law could also operate in its own right. Although Parliament could speak clearly enough to demand paramountcy, the intention to do so was not sufficiently clear in this case.

R. v. Simon, [1985] 2 S.C.R. 387, 24 D.L.R. (4th) 390, 71 N.S.R. (2d) 15, 171 A.P.R. 15, [1986] 1 C.N.L.R. 153, 23 C.C.C. (3d) 238, 62 N.R. 366

Derogation from rights recognized in treaties is in the exclusive power of Parliament.

Dick v. R., [1985] 2 S.C.R. 309, [1986] 1 W.W.R. 1, 69 B.C.L.R. 184, 23 D.L.R. (4th) 33, [1985] 4 C.N.L.R. 55, 22 C.C.C. (3d) 129, 62 N.R. 1

The first of three issues raised was whether British Columbia's *Wildlife Act* impaired the "Indianness" of the accused. In its reasoning, the court assumed, without deciding, that the provincial legislation on hunting did impair "Indianness".

Public Service Alliance of Canada v. St. Regis Indian Band Council, [1982] 2 S.C.R. 72, 139 D.L.R. (3d) 9, [1982] 4 C.N.L.R. 94, 82 C.L.L.C. 14, 208, 44 N.R. 136

Employees of a band council applied to the Canada Labour Relations Board for certification as a union. The Supreme Court of Canada held that, since the *Indian Act* provides for the creation of the band council with the powers to pass by-laws, the enforcement of which requires the hiring of staff, then the council is an employer for the purposes of the *Canada Labour Code*.

Four B. Manufacturing v. United Garment Workers of America, [1980] S.C.R. 1031, 80 C.L.L.C. 14,006, 102 D.L.R. (3d) 385, [1979] 4 C.N.L.R. 21 (S.C.C.)

Workers at a shoe factory located on reserve applied for certification under provincial labour legislation. The factory was owned by Indians and most, but not all, of the workers were Indians. The majority of the court held that labour relations was not related to "Indianness". Beetz, J. says at (C.N.L.R.) p. 25:

> ... neither Indian status is at stake nor rights so closely connected with Indian status that they should be regarded as necessary incidents of status such for instance as registrability, membership in a band, the right to participate in the election of Chiefs and Band Councils, reserve privileges, etc.

R. v. Sutherland, [1980] 2 S.C.R. 451, [1980] 5 W.W.R. 456, 113 D.L.R. (3d) 374, 7 Man. R. (2d) 289, 53 C.C.C. (2d) 289, 35 N.R. 361

Manitoba enacted s. 49 of its *Wildlife Act*, declaring certain provincial areas, including wildlife management areas, to be occupied Crown land to which Indians do not have a right of access for purposes of exercising any hunting rights under para. 13 of the Natural Resources Transfer Agreement. The Supreme Court of Canada held that this section was *ultra vires* the provincial legislature, since it was not of general application, and purported to limit a right of Indians.

Natural Parents v. Superintendent of Child Welfare, [1976] 2 S.C.R. 751, [1976] 1 W.W.R. 699, 21 R.F.L. 267, 60 D.L.R. (3d) 148, 6 N.R. 491

At issue was the applicability of provincial adoption legislation to an Indian child. The court found that provincial legislation applied, only through incorporation by the *Indian Act*. Laskin, J. said at (D.L.R.) p. 154:

> ... adoption legislation which would, if applicable as provincial legislation *simpliciter*, constitute a serious intrusion into the Indian family relationship. It is difficult to conceive what

would be left of exclusive federal power in relation to Indians if such provincial legislation was held to apply to Indians.

Canada (Attorney General) v. Canard, [1976] 1 S.C.R. 170, [1975] 3 W.W.R. 1, 52 D.L.R. (3d) 548, 4 N.R. 91

The court found that *Indian Act* provisions relating to testamentary dispositions by Indians were within federal authority. At (D.L.R.) p. 572, Beetz, J. says:

> ... I find myself in agreement with the general propositions that testamentary matters and causes with respect to deceased Indians come within the class of subjects of "Indians and Lands reserved for the Indians" and that Parliament can constitutionally oust the jurisdiction of provincial Courts in these as well as in other federal matters and vest it in a federal agency, subject perhaps to an obvious qualification: while Parliament has the power to establish Courts for the administration of the laws of Canada, it does not necessarily follow that it can clothe a Minister, or any official or board of a non-judicial nature, with all the functions of a superior Court; the powers of Parliament are limited by the wording of s. 101 of the *British North America Act, 1867*, as well as by the federal and fundamental nature of the Constitution which implies an inherent and entrenched jurisdiction in the Courts to adjudicate in constitutional matters.

Cardinal v. Alberta (Attorney General), [1974] S.C.R. 695, [1973] 6 W.W.R. 205, 40 D.L.R. (3d) 553, 7 C.N.L.C. 307, 13 C.C.C. (2d) 1

The majority held that provincial game laws do not relate to Indians *qua* Indians, and were applicable on reserves. Per Martland, J.:

> A provincial Legislature could not enact legislation in relation to Indians, or in relation to Indian reserves, but this is far from saying that the effect of s. 91(24) of the *British North America Act, 1867*, was to create enclaves within a Province within the boundaries of which provincial legislation could have no application. ... My point is that s. 91(24) enumerates classes of subjects over which the federal Parliament has the exclusive power to legislate, but it does not purport to define areas within a Province within which the power of a Province to enact legislation, otherwise within its powers, is to be excluded. [D.L.R. pp. 559-560]

Canada (Attorney General) v. Lavell (1973), [1974] S.C.R. 1349, 11 R.F.L. 333, 38 D.L.R. (3d) 481, 23 C.R.N.S. 197, 8 C.N.L.C. 236

The majority held that the Canadian Bill of Rights did not operate to strike down a provision of the former *Indian Act* which treated Indian women differently from Indian men. (The offending sections of the *Indian Act* were removed in 1985.) Ritchie, J. stated at (D.L.R.) p. 490:

> In my opinion the exclusive legislative authority vested in Parliament under s. 91(24) could not have been effectively exercised without enacting laws establishing the qualifications required to entitle persons to status as Indians and to the use and benefit of Crown "lands reserved for Indians". The legislation enacted to this end was, in my view, necessary for the implementation of the authority so vested in Parliament under the Constitution.

Canada (Attorney-General) v. Giroux (1916), 53 S.C.R. 172, 30 D.L.R. 123, 4 C.N.L.C. 147

Once land is surrendered, a purchaser who is an Indian is treated like any other purchaser. The *Indian Act* does not apply.

Sagkeeng Alcohol Rehab Centre Inc. v. Abraham, [1995] 1 C.N.L.R. 184, 79 F.T.R. 53 (T.D.)

An alcohol treatment centre was found to be a federal business or undertaking to which federal labour law applied:

> The fact that the rehabilitation centre is organized and operated primarily for Indians, governed solely by Indians, that its facilities and services are intended primarily for Indians, that its staff are specially trained under [the National Native Alcohol and Drug Abuse Program] and receive

First Nations training, and that its rehabilitation program, curriculum and materials are designed for Indians, all serve to identify the inherent "Indianness" of the centre and link it to Indians. [C.N.L.R. p. 190]

Qu'Appelle Indian Residential School Council v. Canada (Canadian Human Rights Commission) (1987), [1988] 2 F.C. 226, [1989] 2 C.N.L.R. 99, 14 F.T.R. 31, 10 C.H.R.R. D/5476 (T.D.)

In this case the union brought a complaint of sex discrimination to the Human Rights Commission, alleging that women on staff at the school were not being paid equally for performing work of equal value. The school council brought an application to prevent the Commission from commencing an inquiry, on the grounds that the school's operations fell under provincial jurisdiction and were thus not subject to federal labour relations laws. This application was dismissed. The court decided that

> ... the school Council's employees here are so directly involved in activities relating to Indian status, rights and privileges that their labour relations with the Council should be characterized as forming an integral part of the primary federal jurisdiction over Indians and Indian lands, under s. 91(24) of the *Constitution Act*, 1867. [C.N.L.R. p. 109]

— See also *Manitoba Teachers' Society v. Fort Alexander Band*, [1984] 1 F.C. 1109, [1985] 1 C.N.L.R. 172 (T.D.)

Otineka Development Corp. v. R., [1994] 2 C.N.L.R. 83, 94 D.T.C. 1234, [1994] 2 C.T.C. 2424 (T.C.C.)

It is within the legislative authority of Parliament in the context of its authority under s. 91(24) to create a municipality on lands reserved for Indians: the powers conferred upon and exercised by the band under ss. 81, 83 and 85.1 of the *Indian Act* have the effect of creating a form of self-government that is an essential aspect of a municipality within the ordinary meaning of the word. Corporations owned by the band were therefore exempt from taxation as owned by a Canadian municipality.

Federal or Provincial Authority — Alberta

R. v. Paul Band (Indian Reserve No. 133) (1984), 50 A.R. 190, 29 Alta. L.R. (2d) 310, [1984] 2 W.W.R. 540, [1984] 1 C.N.L.R. 87 (C.A.)

First Nation constables hired by the First Nation Council (Band Council) came under federal law. In this case, the activities performed by local constables formed an integral part of the main operations of the First Nation Council (Band Council). The First Nation had the power to administer First Nation affairs on the reserve, which power derived from the *Indian Act*, and thus fell within exclusive federal jurisdiction under s. 91(24). The labour relations between the council and the constables were therefore governed by federal legislation.

Auger v. Alberta (Workers' Compensation Board) (1989), 61 D.L.R. (4th) 660 (Alta. Q.B.)affirmed [1990], 111 A.R. 2, 76 Alta. L.R. (2d) 195, 33 C.C.E.L. 75, 73 D.L.R. (4th) 357 (C.A.), leave to appeal to S.C.C. refused (1992), 125 A.R. 160n, 83 Alta. L.R. (2d) lxvin, 86 D.L.R. (4th) viiin, 7 C.R.R. (2d) 384n (S.C.C.)

The court did not question the ability of Alberta workers compensation legislation to exclude "any industry carried on by an Indian or band on a reserve". (For a contrary result see *Isaac v. British Columbia (Workers' Compensation Board)*, [1995] 1 C.N.L.R. 26, [1994] 9 W.W.R. 263, 93 B.C.L.R. (2d) 291 (B.C. C.A.)

Federal or Provincial Authority — British Columbia

Isaac v. British Columbia (Workers' Compensation Board), [1994] 9 W.W.R. 245, 93 B.C.L.R. (2d) 273, [1995] 1 C.N.L.R. 26 (B.C. C.A.)

Isaac was a member of an Indian band and employed in its logging operations on reserve land. He died on reserve during a logging accident. British Columbia at that time had a policy which did not extend workers compensation to reserve operations unless a band had requested coverage and paid assessments. The Board distinguished *Auger v. Alberta (Workers' Compensation Board)* and held that the widow and children were entitled to benefits from the Workers' Compensation Board. It was held that (1) workers compensation legislation applies *ex proprio vigore*, and does not need to be brought in by s. 88, and (2) there is no problem with federal paramountcy because there is no conflict between the provisions of the *Indian Act* and the provincial legislation.

Rempel Brothers Concrete Ltd. v. Chilliwack (District), [1994] 5 W.W.R. 122, 88 B.C.L.R. (2d) 209, 19 M.P.L.R. (2d) 251 (C.A.)leave to appeal to S.C.C. refused (September 8, 1994), Doc. No. 24118 (S.C.C.)

A municipal by-law's pith and substance pertained to soil removal and road damage. The by-law had only an incidental effect, if any, on Indian lands from which gravel was being trucked, and was therefore *intra vires*. (The decision does not make clear whether the roads in question were public highways or reserve roads.)

R. v. White (1964), 52 W.W.R. 193, 50 D.L.R. (2d) 613 (B.C. C.A.)affirmed [1965] S.C.R. vi, 52 D.L.R. (2d) 481n

Provincial game laws could not take away treaty hunting rights. According to Davey, J.A. at (50 D.L.R.) p. 618:

> In my opinion, their peculiar rights of hunting and fishing over their ancient hunting grounds arising under agreements by which they collectively sold their ancient lands are Indian affairs over which Parliament has exclusive legislative authority, and only Parliament can derogate from those rights.

R. v. Morley (1932), 5 C.N.L.C. 446 (C.A.)

The application of provincial game laws to a non-Indian hunting on reserve did not conflict with federal legislation under s. 91(24) and was valid provincial legislation pertaining to property and civil rights in the province. (This case was decided before the enactment of s. 88 of the *Indian Act*.)

Westbank First Nation v. British Columbia (Labour Relations Board) (1996), 38 Admin. L.R. (2d) 89 (B.C. S.C.)

The court found that Pine Acres Home, an intermediate care facility, was controlled and operated by the Band Council. However, only 21%-32% of the residents were Aboriginal. The court followed *Four B Manufacturing Limited v. United Garment Workers of America* and found that in this case, the operation of the home was not a federal business. Consequently, provincial labour relations legislation applied.

R. v. Jim (1915), 22 B.C.R. 106, 26 C.C.C. 236 (S.C.)

Indians hunting on a reserve are a matter of federal jurisdiction and provincial hunting regulations do not apply. (This case was decided before the enactment of s. 88 of the *Indian Act*.)

Celtic Shipyards (1988) Ltd. v. Marine Workers' and Boilermakers' Industrial Union, Local 1 (1994), [1995] 3 C.N.L.R. 41, 94 C.L.L.C. 16,068 (B.C.L.R.B.)

The Board upheld the application of provincial labour legislation to a commercial fishing company owned by the Musqueam Band. The Board found that, in this case, the employer was the corporation, not the Band. There was nothing "Indian" about the company as it was engaged in ordinary industrial activity, and the company was not exercising Aboriginal rights to fish.

Federal or Provincial Authority — Manitoba

R. v. Campbell (1996), [1997] 1 C.N.L.R. 120, [1997] 2 W.W.R. 195, 112 C.C.C. (3d) 107, 41 C.R.R. (2d) 175, 5 C.R. (5th) 133, 142 D.L.R. 496 (Man. C.A.)

The accused lived off reserve. He was charged with violating a Moose Lake Indian Reserve by-law by being intoxicated on the reserve. The lawyer for the accused argued that the by-law was invalid because it was discriminatory. The court took the opposite view for three reasons.

1. The law was validly made pursuant to s.91(24) of the *Constitution Act, 1867*

2. The law was freely adopted by the residents of Moose Lake: it was not imposed on them through Parliament

3. "It does not authorize a band to make different laws for different people, but only to make an enforceable policy choice for the governance of all people on the reserve." [C.N.L.R. p. 125]

R. v. Rodgers, [1923] 2 W.W.R. 353, [1923] 3 D.L.R. 414, 33 Man. R. 139, 40 C.C.C. 51 (C.A.)

I do not think that the Provincial Legislature has any power to pass laws interfering with the rights of treaty Indians to hunt, fish and trap on their own reserves. If a treaty Indian leaves his reserve and takes up any calling or occupation outside of it, he comes under the control of the provincial laws as an ordianry citizen ... [D.L.R. pp. 415–416]

(This case was decided before the enactment of s. 88 of the *Indian Act*.)

Sanderson v. Heap (1909), 11 W.L.R. 238, 19 Man. R. 122, 3 C.N.L.C. 631 (K.B.)

An Indian's sale of land which was his individual property was not restricted by the *Indian Act* or by s. 91(24). Provincial law which related to property and civil rights, and which could not be said to be legislation concerning Indians, applied to the sale.

Federal or Provincial Authority — Nova Scotia

R. v. Gloade (1987), 72 N.S.R. (2d) 247, 173 A.P.R. 247, [1987] 1 C.N.L.R. 87 (C.A.)leave to appeal to S.C.C. refused (1986), 75 N.S.R. (2d) 270n, 186 A.P.R. 270n, 72 N.R. 160n (S.C.C.)

Provincial liquor control acts apply to Indians on a reserve without touching their "Indianness" and the provincial legislation therefore does not come within s. 88.

Federal or Provincial Authority — Ontario

Lovelace v. Ontario, [1997] O.J. No. 2313 (O.C.A.)

The province of Ontario entered into negotiations with First Nations in the province to establish a casino on reserve. The proceeds were to be shared among all of the First Nations in Ontario. Applicants representing Metis and Bands not recognized under the *Indian Act* commenced proceedings claiming a portion of the proceeds. At the trial stage, the judge found that there was discrimination under s. 15.

The Court of Appeal overturned the trial decision, finding that the scheme had been validly established under section 15(2). The court also found that this provincial scheme which dealt directly with "Indians" was valid because it did not impair "Indianness".

> ... it cannot be said that the Casino Rama project impairs the status or capacity of Indians. Casino Rama is a straightforward exercise of the provincial spending power. The First Nations Fund is a vehicle for the distribution of government monies and the monetary benefit can target reserves or Indian communities without the province legislating in relation to "Indians or lands reserved for Indians. [para. 98]

O.P.S.E.U. v. Ontario Métis & Non-Status Indians Assn., [1980] 3 Can. L.R.B.R. 328, [1980] O.L.R.B. Rep. 1304, [1982] 1 C.N.L.R. 83 (O.L.R.B.)

Provincial labour law applies to an off-reserve Aboriginal organization.

R. v. Martin (1917), 41 O.L.R. 79, 39 D.L.R. 635, 29 C.C.C. 189 (C.A.)

An Indian is punishable as other persons are for offences committed outside a reserve against provincial liquor laws.

R. v. Beboning (1908), 17 O.L.R. 23, 13 C.C.C. 405 (C.A.)

Stealing hay on an Indian reserve is none the less punishable under the Criminal Code because the circumstances disclose an offence under the *Indian Act*.

R. v. Hill (1907), 15 O.L.R. 406 (C.A.)

An Indian cannot practise medicine off the reserve except under the provisions of the *Ontario Medical Act*.

R. v. Hill, [1951] O.W.N. 824, 14 C.R. 266, 101 C.C.C. 343 (Co.Ct.)

Provincial game laws do not apply to Indians hunting on reserve. The Parliament of Canada has exclusive legislative power to regulate the conduct of Indians while on their reserves by virtue of s. 91(24).

Federal or Provincial Authority — Quebec

Delorimier v. Cross (1937), 5 C.N.L.C. 64 (Que. S.C.)

A dispute between two Indians over possession of reserve lands was governed by the *Indian Act* and not by the Quebec Civil Code. The Quebec Superior Court declined jurisdiction to hear this case.

Federal or Provincial Authority — Saskatchewan

Whitebear Band Council v. Carpenters Provincial Council (Saskatchewan), [1982] 3 W.W.R. 554, 135 D.L.R. (3d) 128, 15 Sask. R. 37, [1982] 3 C.N.L.R. 181 (C.A.)

The court held, at (W.W.R.) p. 565:

> ... the power generally to regulate the labour relations of a band council and its employees, engaged in those activities contemplated by the *Indian Act*, forms an integral part of primary federal jurisdiction in relation to "Indians, and Lands reserved for the Indians" pursuant to s. 91(24) of the *B.N.A. Act*.

R. v. Fiddler, [1993] 3 W.W.R. 594, 108 Sask. R. 5, [1994] 1 C.N.L.R. 121 (Q.B.)

As a general rule, provincial laws apply to Indians and Indian lands, with the exception of laws that seek to regulate Indians *qua* Indians, or regulate their use of reserve lands. Section 15(a) of the *Saskatchewan Prairie and Forest Fires Act*, which prohibited the starting of a fire without taking adequate precautions to control it, is a safety law of general application, and not an attempt to regulate the use of land. Even if s. 15(a) had touched the "Indianness" of the accused, s. 88 of the *Indian Act* would operate so as to make s. 15(a) applicable against him.

Lands Reserved for Indians — Privy Council

Ontario Mining Co. v. Seybold (1902), [1903] A.C. 73, 3 C.N.L.C. 203 (P.C.)

The Crown in right of Canada could only set aside lands which had been surrendered under Treaty No. 3, with the consent of the province. The Dominion had legislative authority over the lands in question, but not proprietary rights.

St. Catherines Milling and Lumber Co. v. R. (1888), 14 App. Cas. 46, 4 Cart. B.N.A. 107 (P.C.)

At the time of Confederation, reserve lands were vested in the Crown, subject to Indian title. Upon surrender to the Crown in the right of Canada, the beneficial interest in the lands, subject to any retained rights or privileges, is transmitted to the province.

Lands Reserved for Indians — Canada

Delgamuukw v. British Columbia ((December 11, 1997)), Doc. 23799 (S.C.C.)

The province argued that "Lands reserved for Indians" only included reserve lands. The Supreme Court rejected that argument stating that the federal government had jurisdiction over all lands held pursuant to Aboriginal title. Only the federal government could extinguish that title.

Canadian Pacific v. Paul, [1988] 2 S.C.R. 654, 1 R.P.R. (2d) 105, 91 N.B.R. (2d) 43, 232 A.P.R. 43, 53 D.L.R. (4th) 487, [1989] 1 C.N.L.R. 47, 89 N.R. 325

Provincial legislation on limitation periods does not apply to Indian lands.

Derrickson v. Derrickson, [1986] 1 S.C.R. 285, [1986] 3 W.W.R. 193, 1 B.C.L.R. (2d) 273, 50 R.F.L. (2d) 337, 26 D.L.R. (4th) 175, [1986] 2 C.N.L.R. 45, 65 N.R. 278

The court held that provincial legislation on the division of matrimonial property could not go so far as ordering the disposition of land on a reserve. However, the court could, pursuant to provincial legislation, order compensation to a spouse for the value of the property. The court states:

> The right to possession of lands on an Indian reserve is manifestly of the very essence of the federal exclusive legislative power under section 91(24) of the *Constitution Act, 1867.* [S.C.R. p. 296]

Paul v. Paul, [1986] 1 S.C.R. 306, [1986] 3 W.W.R. 210, 1 B.C.L.R. (2d) 290, 50 R.F.L. (2d) 355, 26 D.L.R. (4th) 196, [1986] 2 C.N.L.R. 74

The provincial law (*Family Relations Act*) could not be used for an order for interim occupancy of the family residence on the reserve to one spouse. Both possession and occupation are dealt with by the *Indian Act,* and an order under provincial law would be in conflict with this.

Smith v. R., [1983] 1 S.C.R. 554, 147 D.L.R. (3d) 237, [1983] 3 C.N.L.R. 161, 47 N.R. 132

Land was surrendered to the Crown in right of Canada to be held in trust for sale. The land was not sold, and the Crown brought an action for possession of a portion of this land occupied by a non-Indian. The court held that, once land is surrendered to the Crown in right of Canada, the beneficial ownership is restored to the province. The lands ceased to be under the legislative authority of Parliament.

Lands Reserved for Indians — Alberta

Western Industrial Contractors Ltd. v. Sarcee Developments Ltd. (1979), 15 A.R. 309, [1979] 3 W.W.R. 631, 98 D.L.R. (3d) 424 (C.A.)

Sarcee Developments was a Band-owned corporation. The Band surrendered reserve land to the federal government for 75 years, and the corporation leased the land back from the federal government. The court held that the corporation was not an Indian. Therefore, a provincial builder's lien could apply against the corporation and the corporation's interest in the lease. However, the provincial legislation could not apply to the Band's reversionary interest in the land, because that fell within "lands reserved for Indians."

Palm Dairies Ltd. v. R., [1979] 2 C.N.L.R. 43, 91 D.L.R. (3d) 665, [1979] 1 F.C. 531 (Fed. Ct. T.D.)

In the same fact situation as *Western Industrial,* the Federal Court held that these lands continued to be reserved for the Indians, and therefore within exclusive federal jurisdiction. The provincial *Builders' Lien Act* did not apply to such lands.

Lands Reserved for Indians — British Columbia

Re Park Mobile Sales Ltd. and Le Greely (1978), 85 D.L.R. (3d) 618, 9 C.N.L.C. 284 (B.C. C.A.)

Both the landlord and the tenant were non-Indians, but the property was located on reserve. The court found that a section of provincial tenancy legislation relating to rent increase applied to the situation.

Surrey v. Peace Arch (1970), 74 W.W.R. 380 (B.C. C.A.)

Municipal by-laws did not apply to non-Indian developers who had leased land on reserve.

> ... provincial or municipal legislation purporting to regulate the use of these "lands reserved for the Indians" is an unwarranted invasion of the exclusive legislative jurisdiction of Parliament ... [p. 383]

Simpson v. Ziprick (1995), 126 D.L.R. (4th) 754, 10 B.C.L.R. (3d) 41 (B.C. S.C.)

Members of the Okanagan Indian Band held a certificate of possession as joint tenants. One of the joint tenants applied for partition under the provincial *Partition of Property Act.* The court followed the Supreme Court of Canada in *Derrickson v. Derrickson* and found that the provincial statute was not made applicable by section 88. The court also found that if there were any common law right or English statute law right to partition, they were altered with the enactment of the *Indian Act.*

Matsqui Indian Band v. Bird, [1993] 3 C.N.L.R. 80 (B.C. S.C.)

The Chief and Council raised the rent for rental housing on reserve. The tenants attempted to use the provincial *Residential Tenancies Act* to oppose the eviction notice. The court, following *Derrickson v. Derrickson*, held that provincial statute did not apply to reserve housing. However, the common law of landlord and tenant applies to the interpretation of the lease agreement between the Band and the tenants.

Lands Reserved for Indians — Nova Scotia

Millbrook Indian Band v. Nova Scotia (Northern Counties Residential Tenancies Board) (1978), 3 R.P.R. 199, 84 D.L.R. (3d) 175 (N.S. T.D.)affirmed without reference to this point (1979), 93 D.L.R. (3d) 230, 28 N.S.R. (2d) 268, 43 A.P.R. 268, [1979] 4 C.N.L.R. 59 N.S. C.A.

The landlord was the band council, and the tenant a non-Indian. The provincial tenancies legislation does not apply because it relates to land, and lands reserved for Indians are under exclusive federal authority.

Lands Reserved for Indians — Ontario

Brantford (Township) v. Doctor (1995), [1996] 1 C.N.L.R. 49, 29 M.P.L.R. (2d) 300 (Ont. Gen. Div.)

Brantford Township attempted to apply the Ontario Building Code on construction in a trailer park owned by status Indians. Although there was no deed for the land, and its precise legal status was not clear, the court assumed that the lands were "Indian Lands". The court held then that the legislation should be enforced in this case because it applies to "conduct" and only "incidentally relates to land."

Lands Reserved for Indians — Quebec

Oka (Municipalité) c. Simon, [1993] R.J.Q. 2416 (C.S.)leave to appeal to C.A. granted (August 26, 1993), C.A. Montréal 500-09-001784-933 (Que. C.A.).

Land within the municipality of Oka was owned by the Crown, who had purchased it from the Suplicians in 1945. It was occupied by an Indian, who had obtained it from another Indian. This land did not constitute "lands reserved for the Indians" within the meaning of s. 91(24). A building erected on the land was therefore subject to municipal zoning and construction regulations.

Definition of "Indian" — Canada

Reference re Whether the term "Indians" in s. 91(24) of the B.N.A. Act, 1867, includes Eskimo Inhabitants of Quebec, [1939] S.C.R. 104, [1939] 2 D.L.R. 417

Eskimos are included in "Indians" for the purposes of 91(24).

Definitions of "Indian" — British Columbia

Delgamuukw v. British Columbia, [1993] 5 W.W.R. 97, 104 D.L.R. (4th) 470, [1993] 5 C.N.L.R. 1 (B.C. C.A.), leave to appeal to S.C.C. granted 1994 3 W.W.R. lxvin, 109 D.L.R. (4th) viin (S.C.C.)

Mr. Justice Macfarlane suggested:

> ... the application of the federal jurisdiction in s. 91(24) to the Métis people may well also involve special considerations. At least, the manner in which this jurisdiction applies to the Métis remains a question to be decided in future cases. [W.W.R. p. 147]

Definitions of "Indian" — Saskatchewan

R. v. Grumbo, [1996] 10 W.W.R. 170, [1996] 3 C.N.L.R. 122, 146 Sask. R. 286 (Q.B.)

John Grumbo was born in a tent at the Crescent Lake Metis Village in 1937. He trapped for a living since he was 12 or 13, and spoke Michif, English, Cree, Saulteaux, and French. He received a deer from his nephew Ken Pelltier, a registered Indian, and another deer from Debbie Pelltier who was also a registered Indian. Grumbo is not a registered Indian, and he was charged for having the deer, contrary to Saksatchewan's *Wildlife Act, 1979* which defined "Indian" as an individual registered under the *Indian Act*.

The court held that "Indian" under s. 12 of Saskatchewan's NRTA contemplated the same groups as "Indians" under s. 91(24) of the *Constitution Act, 1867*. The provincial Crown in this case conceded that Metis were "Indians" within s. 91(24). The judge concluded, then, that Metis were Indians within s. 12 of the NRTA. That being the case, the provincial legislation was *ultra vires* in attempting to restrict the definition of Indians to those who were registered under the *Indian Act*. Grumbo's conviction was quashed.

Manitoba Act, 1870

33 Victoria, c. 3 (Canada)

31. Provisions as to Indian title — And whereas, it is expedient, towards the ex-tinguishment of the Indian Title to the lands in the Province, to appropriate a portion of such ungranted lands, to the extent of one million four hundred thousand acres thereof, for the benefit of the families of the half-breed residents, it is hereby enacted, that, under regulations to be from time to time made by the Governor General in Council, the Lieutenant-Governor shall select such lots or tracts in such parts of the Province as he may deem expedient, to the extent aforesaid, and divide the same among the children of the half-breed heads of families residing in the Province at the time of the said transfer to Canada, and the same shall be granted to the said children respec-tively, in such mode and on such conditions as to settlement and otherwise, as the Gov-ernor General in Council may from time to time determine.

32. Quieting titles — For the quieting of titles, and assuring to the settlers in the Province the peaceable possession of the lands now held by them, it is enacted as fol-lows: —

(1) **Grants by H.B. Company** — All grants of land in freehold made by the Hud-son's Bay Company up to the eighth day of March, in the year 1869, shall, if required by the owner, be confirmed by grant from the Crown.

(2) **The same** — All grants of estates less than freehold in land made by the Hud-son's Bay Company up to the eighth day of March aforesaid, shall, if required by the owner, be converted into an estate in freehold by grant from the Crown.

(3) **Titles by occupancy with permission** — All titles by occupancy with the sanction and under the license and authority of the Hudson's Bay Company up to the eighth day of March aforesaid, of land in that part of the Province in which the Indian Title has been extinguished, shall, if required by the owner, be converted into an estate in freehold by grant from the Crown.

(4) **By peaceable possession** — All persons in peaceable possession of tracts of land at the time of the transfer to Canada, in those parts of the Province in which the Indian Title has not been extinguished, shall have the right of pre-emption of the same, on such terms and conditions as may be determined by the Governor in Council.

(5) **Lieut.-Governor to make provisions under Order in Council** — The Lieutenant-Governor is hereby authorized, under regulations to be made from time to time by the Governor General in Council, to make all such provisions for ascertaining and adjusting, on fair and equitable terms, the rights of Common, and rights of cutting Hay held and enjoyed by the settlers in the Province, and for the commutation of the same by grants of land from the Crown.

Commentary: Section 31 provides constitutional recognition that there existed a "half-breed" interest in the land

Case Law: *Dumont v. Canada* (1990), [1990] 2 C.N.L.R. 19, [1990] 1 S.C.R. 279, [1990] 4 W.W.R. 127, 67 D.L.R. (4th) 159, 65 Man. R. (2d) 182, 105 N.R. 228

Métis in Manitoba commenced an action in 1981 stating, among other things, that the intention of the *Manitoba Act* was to create a Métis land base. The Métis claimed that both the federal and provincial government had breached these constitutional provisions. Canada attempted to stop the proceedings by arguing that the statement of claim raised no justiciable issue. The Supreme Court of Canada disagreed, and allowed the action to proceed.

(For a subsequent decision on a motion for particulars, see *Dumont v. Canada (A.G.)* (1992), [1992] 2 C.N.L.R. 34, 75 Man. R. (2d) 273, 6 W.A.C. 273, 91 D.L.R. (4th) 654 (Man. C.A.).

British Columbia Terms of Union

R.S.C. 1985, Appendix II, No. 10

13. The charge of the Indians, and the trusteeship and management of the lands reserved for their use and benefit, shall be assumed by the Dominion Government, and a policy as liberal as that hitherto pursued by the British Columbia Government shall be continued by the Dominion Government after the Union.

To carry out such policy, tracts of land of such extent as it has hitherto been the practice of the British Columbia Government to appropriate for that purpose, shall from time to time be conveyed by the Local Government to the Dominion Government in trust for the use and benefit of the Indians on application of the Dominion Government; and in case of disagreement between the two Governments respecting the quantity of such tracts of land to be so granted, the matter shall be referred for the decision of the Secretary of State for the Colonies.

Case Law: *Jack v. R.* (1979), [1979] 2 C.N.L.R. 25, [1979] 5 W.W.R. 364, [1980] 1 S.C.R. 294, 48 C.C.C. (2d) 246, 100 D.L.R. (3d) 193, 28 N.R. 162

The Supreme Court considered the impact of this section on fishing rights. Dickson, J. stated,

> What protection, then, is afforded Indian fishing by article 13 of the Terms of Union? At a minimum, one can say that 'a policy as liberal' requires no discrimination against the Indian fishery as opposed to the commercial or sports fishery. I also think that one could go further — the Colony gave priority to the Indian fishery as an appropriate pursuit for the coastal Indians, primarily for food purposes and, to a lesser extent, for barter purposes with the white residents. Thus, when it comes time to take into consideration the emergence of commercial and sport fisheries, one could suggest that 'a policy as liberal' would require clear priority to Indian food fishing and some priority to limited commercial fishing over the competing demands of commercial and sport fishing. [C.N.L.R. at p.39]

Constitution Act, 1930

An Act to confirm and give effect to certain agreements entered into between the Government of the Dominion of Canada and the Governments of the Provinces of Manitoba, British Columbia, Alberta and Saskatchewan respectively

R.S.C. 1985, Appendix II, No. 26

Reproduced are sections 11, 12 and 13 of the Schedule (1) (Manitoba). These sections are identical to sections 10, 11 and 12 of Schedule (2) (Alberta) and Schedule (3) (Saskatchewan).

[10th July 1930]

Schedule (1.) — Manitoba — Memorandum of Agreement

Indian Reserves

11. All lands included in Indian reserves within the Province, including those selected and surveyed but not yet confirmed, as well as those confirmed, shall continue to be vested in the Crown and administered by the Government of Canada for the purposes of Canada, and the Province will from time to time, upon the request of the Superintendent General of Indian Affairs, set aside, out of the unoccupied Crown lands hereby transferred to its administration, such further areas as the said Superintendent General may, in agreement with the Minister of Mines and Natural Resources of the Province, select as necessary to enable Canada to fulfil its obligations under the treaties with the Indians of the Province, and such areas shall thereafter be administered by Canada in the same way in all respects as if they had never passed to the Province under the provisions hereof.

12. The provisions of paragraphs one to six inclusive and of paragraph eight of the agreement made between the Government of the Dominion of Canada and the Government of the Province of Ontario on the 24th day of March, 1924, which said agreement was confirmed by statute of Canada, fourteen and fifteen George the Fifth chapter forty-eight, shall (except so far as they relate to the *Bed of Navigable Waters Act*) apply to the lands included in such Indian reserves as may hereafter be set aside under the last preceding clause as if the said agreement had been made between the parties hereto, and the provisions of the said paragraphs shall likewise apply to the lands included in the reserves heretofore selected and surveyed, except that neither the said lands nor the proceeds of the disposition thereof shall in any circumstances become administrable by or be paid to the Province.

13. In order to secure to the Indians of the Province the continuance of the supply of game and fish for their support and subsistence, Canada agrees that the laws respecting game in force in the Province from time to time shall apply to the Indians within the boundaries thereof, provided, however, that the said Indians shall have the right, which the Province hereby assures to them, of hunting, trapping and fishing game and fish for food at all seasons of the year on all unoccupied Crown lands and on any other lands to which the said Indians may have a right of access.

Commentary: In 1930, the provinces of Alberta, Saskatchewan and Manitoba were transferred control over their natural resources through the Natural Resources Transfer Agreement (NRTA). Part of the agreement included these provisions relating to Indians. In *R. v. Horseman*, the Supreme Court of Canada found that the NRTA extinguished the right to commercial hunting, but in *R. v. Badger*, the same court held that the treaty right to hunt for food was modified, but not extinguished. *Badger* also held that the provincial conservation laws which infringed treaty rights had to be justified using the tests developed in *Sparrow*.

Case Law:

Natural Resources Transfer Agreement — Canada

R. v. Badger, [1996] 4 W.W.R. 457, 37 Alta. L.R. (3d) 153 (S.C.C.)

Three Treaty #8 Indians were charged with hunting on private property. The court provided guidance on the relationship between the Natural Resources Transfer Agreement and treaties.

1. The NRTA has amended the treaty right to hunt for food, but it has not extinguished the treaty right to hunt for food.

> Unless there is a direct conflict between the NRTA and a treaty, the NRTA will not have modified the treaty rights. Therefore, the NRTA language which outlines the right to hunt for food must be read in light of the fact that this aspect of the treaty right continues in force and effect. [W.W.R. p. 477]

2. Not all hunting on private land is prohibited.

> An interpretation of the Treaty properly founded upon the Indians' understanding of its terms leads to the conclusion that the geographical limitation on the existing hunting right should be based upon a concept of visible, incompatible land use. [W.W.R. p. 479]

3. The NRTA provides the basis for provincial conservation laws to apply to Indians.

> It follows that by the terms of both the Treaty and the NRTA, provincial game laws would be applicable to Indians so long as they were aimed at conserving the supply of game. However, the provincial government's regulatory authority under the Treaty and the NRTA did not extend beyond the realm of conservation. It is the constitutional provisions of s. 12 of the NRTA authorizing provincial regulations which make it unnecessary to consider s. 88 of the *Indian Act* and the general application of provincial regulations to Indians. [W.W.R. p. 486]

4. Provincial conservation laws had to be justified according to the tests set out in *Sparrow*.

> While [*Sparrow*] dealt with the infringement of aboriginal rights, I am of the view that these criteria should, in most cases, apply equally to the infringement of treaty rights. [W.W.R. p. 487]

R. v. Horseman, [1990] 1 S.C.R. 901, 108 A.R. 1, [1990] 4 W.W.R. 97, 73 Alta. L.R. (2d) 193, [1990] 3 C.N.L.R. 95, 55 C.C.C. (3d) 353, 108 N.R. 1

The hunting rights reserved to Indians by Treaty No. 8 included hunting for commercial purposes, but these rights have been limited to the right to hunt for food only — for sustenance for the individual

Indian or the Indian's family — by para. 12 of the Natural Resources Transfer Agreement. Horseman was convicted under the *Wildlife Act* for the sale, while in possession of a licence, of a bear-hide he had shot in an act of self-defence before obtaining a licence.

R. v. Horse, [1988] 1 S.C.R. 187, [1988] 2 W.W.R. 289, 47 D.L.R. (4th) 526, 65 Sask. R. 176, [1988] 2 C.N.L.R. 112, 39 C.C.C. (3d) 97, 82 N.R. 206

An Indian must have permission of the owner before he has the right to hunt on private land, even when the land is not posted to prohibit hunting or trespassing. (This case was distinguished in *R. v. Badger*)

R. v. Moosehunter, [1981] 1 S.C.R. 282, 123 D.L.R. (3d) 95, 9 Sask. R. 149, 59 C.C.C. (2d) 193, 36 N.R. 437

Where Indians had a limited right to hunt in and thus a right of access to a wildlife management area, an attempt by the province to limit Indian hunting for food to specified times of the year was held to be indirect derogation of the Natural Resources Agreement, and the conviction of the accused for hunting in a wildlife management area was quashed.

R. v. Sutherland, [1980] 2 S.C.R. 451, [1980] 5 W.W.R. 456, 113 D.L.R. (3d) 374, 7 Man. R. (2d) 289, 53 C.C.C. (2d) 289, 35 N.R. 361

Manitoba enacted s. 49 of its *Wildlife Act*, declaring certain provincial areas, including wildlife management areas, to be occupied Crown land to which Indians do not have a right of access for purposes of exercising any hunting rights under para. 13 of the Natural Resources Transfer Agreement. The supreme Court of Canada held that this section was *ultra vires* the provincial legislature, since it was not of general application, and purported to limit a right of Indians. The section was also *ultra vires* the province since it could not amend the Natural Resources Transfer Agreement without a concurrent statute by Parliament. In reply to the issue of the charge of hunting in the area, Dickson, J. stated at (W.W.R.) p. 463:

> The Indians' right to hunt for food under para. 13 is paramount and overrides provincial game laws regulating hunting and fishing. The province may deny access for hunting to Indians and non-Indians alike but if, as in the case at bar, limited hunting is allowed, then under para. 13 non-dangerous ... hunting for food is permitted to the Indians, regardless of provincial curbs on season, method or limit ...

Elk v. R., [1980] 2 S.C.R. 166, [1980] 4 W.W.R. 671, 16 C.R. (3d) 284, 114 D.L.R. (3d) 137, 5 Man. R. 400, 52 C.C.C. (2d) 382, 33 N.R. 516

The Natural Resources Transfer Agreements did not result in federal legislation concerning fishing ceasing to apply to Indians.

R. v. Mousseau, [1980] 2 S.C.R. 89, [1980] 4 W.W.R. 24 at 31, 111 D.L.R. (3d) 443, 3 Man. R. (2d) 338, 52 C.C.C. (2d) 140, 31 N.R. 620

A public highway is occupied Crown land, and provincial hunting regulations apply.

Frank v. R., [1978] 1 S.C.R. 95, 4 A.R. 271, [1977] 4 W.W.R. 294, 75 D.L.R. (3d) 481, 34 C.C.C. (2d) 209, 15 N.R. 487

The Natural Resources Transfer Agreements with the three western provinces provided that laws respecting game in the province shall apply to Indians within the boundaries of the province. This has been held to apply to all Indians regardless of their province of residence, and Indians may hunt in their treaty area even if it crosses provincial boundaries, and they may cross such borders to hunt.

In considering the right to hunt guaranteed by Treaty No. 6 and by para. 12 of the Alberta Natural Resources Agreement, the Supreme Court of Canada stated at (C.C.C.) p. 212:

> The essential differences, for present purposes, between the Treaty and the Agreement are (i) under the former the hunting rights were at large while under the latter the right is limited to

hunting for food and (ii) under the former the rights were limited to about one-third of the Province of Alberta, while under the latter they extended to the entire Province.

The right to hunt other than for food was limited by making that right subject to provincial legislation.

Myran v. R., [1976] 2 S.C.R. 137, [1976] 1 W.W.R. 196, 58 D.L.R. (3d) 1, 23 C.C.C. (2d) 73, 5 N.R. 551

Indians hunting with the use of a light at night near an occupied farm house were convicted of hunting without due regard for the safety of other persons in the vicinity under provincial legislation. The Supreme Court of Canada held that an Indian may hunt for food at any time of year on unoccupied Crown land or land to which he has access.

> But that is not to say that he has the right to hunt dangerously and without regard for the safety of other persons in the vicinity. [W.W.R. p. 200]

Cardinal v. Alberta (Attorney General), [1974] 2 S.C.R. 695, [1973] 6 W.W.R. 205, 40 D.L.R. (3d) 553, 13 C.C.C. (2d) 1

In considering the effect of the *Alberta Natural Resources Act*, 1930 (Alta.), c. 21, the Supreme Court of Canada held, in a 6 to 3 decision, that

> ... para. 12 of the Agreement made the provisions of the *Wildlife Act* applicable to all Indians, including those on reserves, and governed their activities throughout the Province, including reserves. [C.C.C. p. 12]

The accused was convicted under provincial legislation of trafficking in big game.

Daniels v. White, [1968] S.C.R. 517, 64 W.W.R. 385, 2 D.L.R. (3d) 1, [1969] 1 C.C.C. 299, 4 C.R.N.S. 176

The *Migratory Birds Convention Act* was not repealed or restricted by the Natural Resources Transfer Agreement.

Prince v. R., [1964] S.C.R. 81, 46 W.W.R. 121, 41 C.R. 403, 3 C.C.C. 2

The word **"hunt"** should be interpreted in its plain meaning and any restrictions placed on the word by statute shall not apply to Indians. Thus an Indian was acquitted of a charge of hunting with a "night light".

NRTA — Alberta

R. v. Gladue (1995), [1996] 1 C.N.L.R. 153, 130 D.L.R. (4th) 577, 36 Alta. L.R. (3d) 241, 103 C.C.C. (3d) 216 (C.A.)

A member of the Beaver Lake Indian Band appealed a conviction for selling fish without a license. The court found that Treaty #6 included the right to commercial fishing. However, following *R. v. Horseman*, the court held that the NRTA did not protect commercial fishing.

R. v. Alexson (1990), 107 A.R. 112, [1990] 4 W.W.R. 565, 73 Alta. L.R. (2d) 151, [1990] 4 C.N.L.R. 35 (C.A.)

Crown lands that were leased for grazing were not "unoccupied Crown Lands" within the meaning of the provincial *Wildlife Act*, which allowed natives to hunt on unoccupied Crown lands. The Act was to be strictly construed, as the legislation interfered with common law rights with respect to trespass, and prior consent to hunt on the land in question was required. [But now see *R. v. Badger*]

R. v. Machatis, 117 A.R. 281, 78 Alta. L.R. (2d) 153, [1991] 3 C.N.L.R. 109, 2 W.A.C. 281 (C.A.)

Provincial fishing regulations that do not restrict a licensee to fishing only for himself and his family and that are entirely permissive do not offend Aboriginal and treaty rights under s. 35(1).

R. v. Ominayak (1990), 108 A.R. 239, [1991] 1 C.N.L.R. 177 (C.A.)

A status Indian does not have the right of access pursuant to treaty exemptions to hunt on private, unoccupied lands without the landowner's consent. Access is determined by provincial law, and access without consent amounts to trespass under those laws. [But now see *R. v. Badger*]

R. v. Little Bear (1958), 26 W.W.R. 335, 122 C.C.C. 173 (Alta. C.A.)

The words **"right of access"** include the right to enter privately owned land with the consent of the owner. [But now see *R. v. Badger*]

R. v. Wesley, [1932] 2 W.W.R. 337, [1932] 4 D.L.R. 774, 58 C.C.C. 269 (Alta. C.A.)

Indians' right to hunt is protected by treaties, and remains undiminished until restrictive legislation is passed:

> The treaties with the Indians and the subsequent legislation treat with the rights of Indians to hunt, and until definite legislation is passed by a competent body, the Indian is, in my opinion, entitled to hunt on all "unoccupied Crown lands and on any other lands" to which he may have a right of access. [C.C.C. p. 273]

R. v. Desjarlais, [1996] 3 C.N.L.R. 113 (Alta. Q.B.)

Louise Desjarlais had relatives staying with her. She asked Kenneth Desjarlais and Frank Willier to bring back some game for the family. Kenneth was her natural born son. Frank Willier had lived with her since he was seven months old. Kenneth and Frank went hunting and succeeded in shooting a deer. Because neither of them were registered as Indians under the *Indian Act*, they were charged with hunting out of season.

The court found that the reference to "Indians" in s. 12 of the NRTA should be defined in reference to the *Indian Act* of 1927, which included "a person of Indian blood .... who follows the Indian mode of life.." (R.S.C. 1927, c. 98, s. 2(h)).

In this case, the judge rejected the Crown's contention that the individual must be of "predominantly Indian ancestry." He accepted that Kenneth, who was descended from Crees and Scots, had sufficient ancestry. Kenneth also passed the second part of the test — following an "Indian mode of life." He spoke Cree, learned to hunt with his father, described Indians as his own people, and hunted for food. The judge rejected the Crown's argument that "hunting, fishing and trapping has to play a significant role on an ongoing basis in order for a person to qualify." [C.N.L.R. p.119]

On the other hand, the judge found that Frank did not have evidence of sufficient ancestry. There was no information on his natural mother; and, although his natural father had lived on the Sucker Creek Indian Reserve, there was no evidence that his natural father was an Indian. The judge noted that Frank had not been formally adopted into the Desjarlais family.

R. v. Ferguson (1993), [1994] 1 C.N.L.R. 117 (Alta. Q.B.)

By virtue of his "Indian mode of life", Ferguson was a "non-treaty Indian" within the meaning of the *Indian Act, 1927*, and was therefore included in the term "Indian" in paragraph 12 of the Natural Resources Transfer Agreement, 1930. Without clear legislative disentitlement criteria, status as a "non-treaty Indian" and consequent hunting rights should not be jeopardized by casual or intermittent non-traditional pursuits.

R. v. Potts (1992), 132 A.R. 17, 4 Alta. L.R. (3d) 47, [1992] 3 C.N.L.R. 100 (Q.B.), leave to appeal to C.A. refused (1992), 131 A.R. 168, 4 Alta. L.R. (3d) 284 (C.A.), leave to appeal to S.C.C. refused (1992), 5 Alta. L.R. (3d) xlin, 147 N.R. 391n (S.C.C.)

Although Treaty No. 6 continued the right of Treaty No. 6 Indians to hunt commercially, that right was limited by the *Constitution Act* to the right to hunt only for personal consumption.

R. v. Arcand, 95 A.R. 173, [1989] 3 W.W.R. 635, 65 Alta. L.R. (2d) 326, [1989] 2 C.N.L.R. 110 (Q.B.)

A right that is regulated to the point of unenforceability does not necessarily cease to exist; it is merely rendered dormant until the regulation is repealed or altered. Treaty No. 6 hunting rights exist and are protected by s. 35(1) against the *Migratory Birds Regulations* prohibiting hunting ducks out of season.

R. v. Bretton, [1997] A.J. No. 715 (Alta. Q.B.)

The judge convicted Indians covered by Treaty #6 who hunted in a minesite. The area was posted as an area where the discharge of firearms was prohibited.

R. v. Daniels (1993), 146 A.R. 383, 13 Alta. L.R. (3d) 246, [1994] 3 C.N.L.R. 126 (Prov. Ct.)

The accused wounded a deer on reserve and followed the deer onto private property to complete the kill. He was convicted for hunting on private property.

R. v. Kootenay (1978), 6 Alta. L.R. (2d) 220 (Prov. Ct.)

Wildlife sanctuaries set aside to preserve wildlife in a reasonable area not prejudicial to normal hunting practices are areas excepted under treaties from Indian hunting rights, and Indians hunting in such areas are subject to conviction under provincial wildlife acts.

R. v. Norn, [1991] 3 C.N.L.R. 135 (Alta. Prov. Ct.)

Regulations requiring natives to obtain permits to hunt in national parks and limiting the discharge of firearms therein were held to be reasonable limits on the accused's treaty rights to hunt on park lands. The accused was entitled to a permit at no charge and accordingly the requirement did not adversely interfere with his right to hunt.

R. v. Cardinal, [1990] 4 C.N.L.R. 48 (Alta. Prov. Ct.)

The accused status Indian legally shot a deer, which then wandered into a farmer's field before dying. After retrieving the deer from the farmer's property, the accused was charged with hunting wildlife during a closed season, and acquitted. Although his treaty rights did not extend into the farmer's field, the deer was dead when retrieved, and "hunting" referred to living animals.

NRTA — Manitoba

R. v. Blais, [1996] M.J. No. 391 (Man. Prov. Ct.)

The accused were Métis. They were convicted of hunting in southern Manitoba in violation of the provincial *Wildlife Act*. The judge held that, among other things, the word "Indians" in the Manitoba NRTA did not include Metis.

R. v. Robinson, [1994] 4 C.N.L.R. 185 (Man. Prov. Ct.)

Provincial hunting regulations which prohibited hunting from a road were not contrary to the Natural Resources Transfer Agreement and were not contrary to rights under Treaty 5.

R. v. Flett, [1989] 6 W.W.R. 166, 60 Man. R. (2d) 294, [1989] 4 C.N.L.R. 128 (Q.B.)leave to appeal C.A. refused [1990] 5 W.W.R. lxxn, 68 Man. R. (2d) 159, [1990] 4 C.N.L.R. vin (C.A.)

When interpreting treaty rights one must look at the right as stated in the original treaty unless the right has been extinguished. The *Migratory Birds Convention Act* ("MBCA") did not extinguish Treaty No. 5 hunting rights. S. 35(1) therefore protects those rights against the MBCA's prohibition on hunting Canada geese out of season.

R. v. Daniels, [1990] 1 C.N.L.R. 108 (Man. Prov. Ct.)

The limitations on the possession of game as set out in the federal *Migratory Birds Convention Act* were never intended to apply to Indians hunting for food on unoccupied Crown lands. The right to hunt for food included the unfettered right to exceed possession limits unless these limits could be shown to be reasonable for conservation purposes.

NRTA — Saskatchewan

R. v. Sundown, [1997] S.J. No. 377 (Sask. C.A.)

Meadow Lake Provincial Park has commercial development, cottages, fenced off areas for grazing cattle, and hunting. John Sundown, a member of the Joseph Bighead First Nation, was charged with cutting trees and constructing a cabin in the park without a permit. Sundown had a right under the NRTA and Treaty #6 to hunt in the park, and used the cabin for hunting.

The Crown argued that constructing the cabin was not "reasonably necessary" for hunting, and therefore, should not be protected by the treaty. The court held that the test in *R. v. Simon* was that the activity had to be "reasonably incidental to the act of hunting itself." In this case, the court held that the right to hunt included the right to cut wood and construct a shelter from which to hunt.

R. v. McIntyre, [1992] 4 W.W.R. 765, 100 Sask. R. 255, [1992] 3 C.N.L.R. 113 (C.A.)leave to appeal to S.C.C. refused (1992), [1993] 1 W.W.R. lixn, 146 N.R. 400n (S.C.C.)

The province is constitutionally empowered, under the *Constitution Act, 1930*, to set aside reasonable and *bona fide* areas as game reserves in order to protect the supply of game. Section 35(1) of the *Constitution Act, 1982*, is not intended to apply to other provisions of the Constitution, such as the Natural Resources Transfer Agreement. That Agreement which forms part of the *Constitution Act, 1930*, is included in the Constitution pursuant to s. 52(2). Hence, an Indian in possession of game contrary to the provincial *Wildlife Act* is not protected from conviction by the operation of s. 35(1), which neither expanded nor contracted existing rights. Those existing rights were set out in para. 12 of the Transfer Agreement.

R. v. Baptiste (1986), 40 Sask. R. 250, [1986] 1 C.N.L.R. 61 (C.A.)leave to appeal to S.C.C. refused (1985), 40 Sask. R. 80n, 63 N.R. 320n (S.C.C.)

Indians must obtain permission, as do all hunters, to hunt on privately owned land. Shining a spotlight from the roadway onto private property constitutes hunting on that land. [But now see *R. v. Badger*]

R. v. Tobacco, [1981] 1 W.W.R. 545, 4 Sask. R. 380 (C.A.)

Hunters have a right of access to enclosed and occupied lands that have not been posted. This right is accorded to Indians in all seasons. [But now see *R. v. Badger*.]

R. v. Standingwater, [1983] 3 W.W.R. 766, 22 Sask. R. 78 (C.A.)

Public highways are occupied Crown lands.

R. v. Strongquill (1953), 8 W.W.R. 247, 16 C.R. 194, [1953] 2 D.L.R. 264, 105 C.C.C. 262 (Sask. C.A.)

A provincial statute cannot define what land is "unoccupied Crown land" and Indians may hunt for food in a forest reserve where other hunters who had a permit were allowed to hunt, and such legislation is *ultra vires* the province. A provincial legislature cannot, by unilateral action, alter the terms of the Natural Resources Transfer Agreement.

R. v. Smith, [1935] 2 W.W.R. 433, [1935] 3 D.L.R. 703, 64 C.C.C. 131 (C.A.)

"Unoccupied Crown land" means those areas that are "not put to use", "idle" or "not appropriated". Any Crown land that has been designated as an area for a specific present or continuing use is occupied.

The words "other purposes" can include the creation of a game preserve and thus Indians are not entitled to hunt on Crown land set aside as a game preserve. [But now see *R. v. Badger*.]

R. v. Grumbo, [1996] 10 W.W.R. 170, 3 C.N.L.R. 122, 146 Sask. R. 286 (Q.B.)

John Grumbo was born in a tent at the Crescent Lake Metis Village in 1937. He trapped for a living since he was 12 or 13, and spoke Michif, English, Cree, Saulteaux, and French. He received a deer from his nephew Ken Pelltier, a registered Indian, and another deer from Debbie Pelltier who was also a registered Indian. Grumbo is not a registered Indian, and he was charged for having the deer, contrary to Saksatchewan's *Wildlife Act, 1979* which defined **"Indian"** as an individual registered under the *Indian Act*.

The court held that "Indian" under s. 12 of Saskatchewan's NRTA contemplated the same groups as "Indians" under s. 91(24) of the *Constitution Act, 1867*. The provincial Crown in this case conceded that

Metis were "Indians" within s. 91(24). The judge concluded, then, that Metis were Indians within s.12 of the NRTA. That being the case, the provincial legislation was *ultra vires* in attempting to restrict the definition of Indians to those who were registered under the *Indian Act*. Grumbo's conviction was quashed.

R. v. Bill (1996), 151 Sask. R. 174 (Q.B.)

The accused who were covered by Treaty #6, appealed from convictions for violations of the provincial *Wildlife Act*. The Queen's Bench ordered a new trial to take into account the decision of the Supreme Court of Canada in *R. v. Badger*.

R. v. Custer (1995), 127 Sask. R. 210 (Q.B.)

A road corridor game preserve is occupied Crown land.

Saskatchewan (Minister of Natural Resources) v. Iron (1993), 111 Sask. R. 114, [1994] 2 C.N.L.R. 181 (Q.B.)

Indians occupying provincial land to protest logging as a threat to their hunting, trapping and fishing rights under Treaty No. 10 and the Natural Resources Transfer Agreement were required to vacate the land because their occupation was not connected with the direct exercise of any right to hunt, trap or fish.

R. v. Bellegarde, [1984] 2 W.W.R. 425, 30 Sask. R. 47, [1984] 1 C.N.L.R. 98 (Q.B.)

Indians may hunt for food on occupied land including provincial parks to which they have a right of access, unless all persons are prohibited from hunting.

R. v. Saskamoose, [1997] S.J. No. 168 (Sask. Prov. Ct.)

Saskamoose, a member of Sandy Lake Indian Reserve, was charged with selling fish to an undercover agent. The court held that even though Treaty #6 contemplated commercial fishing, commercial fishing rights were extinguished by the NRTA.

R. v. Couillonneur (1996), [1997] 1 C.N.L.R. 130 (Sask.Prov.Ct.)

The members of Canoe Lake First Nation are covered under Treaty #10. Pierre Couillonneur, a member of the First Nation, was charged with fishing with a small mesh gill net, contrary to the federal *Fisheries Act*. The court finds that there is an infringement of the treaty right, but that the infringement is justified. There was evidence that the prohibition of the small mesh net had succeeded in maintaining a healthy population of fish, and that there was Aboriginal priority in the fishery.

R. v. Janvier, [1995] 4 C.N.L.R. 29 (Sask. Prov. Ct.)

Members of the Cold Lake First Nation, signatories to Treaty #6, were acquitted of charges under the *Wildlife Act*. They had been hunting on land that was subject to leases to TransGas Utilities and for grazing, but not actually nor observedly in use.

> In my opinion, a blanket rule that says that leased Crown land that is not actually in use is occupied Crown land within the meaning of s. 12 of the Natural Resources Transfer Agreement seems to violate the solemn assurances and promises made by successive British, Canadian, federal and provincial governments to Indian people to allow them to pursue their avocation of hunting so long as this does not interfere or constitute a dangerous activity or does not interfere with legitimate government policies for settlement, mining, lumbering or other valid *bona fide* purposes. [C.N.L.R. p. 37]

R. v. Lerat (1993), [1994] 2 C.N.L.R. 126 (Sask. Prov. Ct.)

"Avocation" in Treaty No. 4 means the right to fish for food, and does not include a right to fish commercially as the evidence did not establish commercial fishing as integral to traditional Indian culture. Safety and conservation regulations were reasonable and justifiable.

R. v. Glessing, [1990] 2 C.N.L.R. 144 (Sask. Prov. Ct.)

Native guides escorting non-resident sports hunters into an Indian reserve closed to non-resident hunters were held to be guilty of hunting in a prohibited zone. Their actions were integral to the hunt, and the purpose of the hunt was not directly related to obtaining food for themselves or their family.

Constitution Act, 1982

R.S.C. 1985, Appendix II, No. 44 En. Canada Act 1982 (U.K.), c. 11 Am. Constitution Amendment Proclamation, 1983, SI/84-102, Schedule

Equality Rights

15. (1) **Equality before and under law and equal protection and benefit of law** — Every individual is equal before and under the law and has the right to the equal protection and equal benefit of the law without discrimination and, in particular, without discrimination based on race, national or ethnic origin, colour, religion, sex, age or mental or physical disability.

(2) **Affirmative action programs** — Subsection (1) does not preclude any law, program or activity that has as its object the amelioration of conditions of disadvantaged individuals or groups including those that are disadvantaged because of race, national or ethnic origin, colour, religion, sex, age or mental or physical disability.

Commentary: Other sections related to equality between male and female persons are section 28 of the Charter and section 35(4).

Case Law:

Canada

Native Women's Assn. of Canada v. R., [1994] 3 S.C.R. 627, 119 D.L.R. (4th) 224, [1995] 1 C.N.L.R. 47, 24 C.R.R. (2d) 233, 173 N.R. 241, 84 F.T.R. 240

During the national constitutional talks which eventually resulted in the Charlottetown Accord of 1992, the federal government provided funding for four national Aboriginal organizations to participate fully in those talks. The Native Women's Association of Canada said that its constituents were not represented, and claimed that there was a violation of their freedom of expression (s. 2(b)), their equality rights (s. 28 and s. 15) and their rights as Aboriginal women (s. 35(4)). The Supreme Court of Canada found that the evidence did not indicate any violation of the provisions of the Charter, nor of s. 35(4).

Corbiere v. Canada (Minister of Indian & Northern Affairs) (1996), [1997] 1 F.C. 689, 41 C.R.R. (2d) 1, 122 F.T.R. 319 (note), 206 N.R. 85, 142 D.L.R. (4th) 122leave to appeal to SCC granted (April 24, 1997), Doc 25708 (S.C.C.) (Judgement stayed, pending appeal to Supreme Court of Canada [1996] F.C.J. 1620)

The issue in this case was the validity of the *Indian Act* requirement under s.77, that only Band members ordinarily resident on reserve could vote in elections held under s. 74. The Batchewana Band had almost 70% of its membership living off reserve, most of whom had been re-registered after the changes to the *Indian Act* made in 1985 by Bill C-31.

The court found that the off reserve members were denied benefits because the *Indian Act* did not allow them to vote for Chief and Council. While they were not a minority, they constituted an "analogous ground" for finding of discrimination.

> On the facts of this case, it can be concluded that non-resident Band members suffer from exactly the kind of political powerlessness to which the protection of the analogous grounds is aimed. Although non-resident Band members are not now a minority in relation to Band mem-

bers living on the reserve, their disenfranchisement guarantees that they are powerless to hold accountable the elected officials of the Band who govern them. [D.L.R. p. 147]

Chippewas of the Nawash First Nation v. Canada (Minister of Indian and Northern Affairs), [1997] 1 C.N.L.R. 1 (F.C.T.D.)

The federal government, pursuant to the *Access to Information Act*, proposed to released two Band Council Resolutions (B.C.R.'s) from the First Nation to an individual. The B.C.R.'s dealt with a federal Bill which would have changed the land regime under the *Indian Act*. The First Nation objected to the release of the information. The court rejected the First Nation's arguments based on a breach of fiduciary duty, and on a breach of section 15 of the *Charter of Rights and Freedoms*.

On the issue of s. 15, the First Nation argued that the discrimination resulted from the fact that communications from provincial municipalities were exempt from disclosure, whereas communications from *Indian Act* Bands were not exempt. The judge held that s. 15 could not be invoked in this case because, among other things, the judge could not see how the *Access to Information Act*, distinguished between the Band councils and other groups based on personal characteristics.

Moore v. Canada, [1997] T.C.J. No. 953 (T.C.C.)

Moore is a chartered accountant living in Victoria. He argued that he should get the same tax exemption that Indians get under the *Indian Act*. The Tax Court dismissed his appeal saying,

> The Appellant's argument is so devoid of merit that giving further reasons would only lend legitimacy to his position. [para. 9]

Brant v. Minister of National Revenue (1992), 92 D.T.C. 2274, [1992] 2 C.T.C. 2633 (T.C.C.)

There is no violation of this section because a taxpayer who lives on reserve, but works off reserve, is not exempt from tax.

Alberta

Willier v. Alberta (Liquor Control Board) (1995), [1996] 3 C.N.L.R. 233, 36 Alta. L.R. (3d) 382 (Liquor Licensing Appeal Council)

Although Willier fulfilled all of the requirements for a Retail Liquor Store License for a store on the Sucker Creek Indian Reserve, Willier was refused by the Liquor Control Board. Between the first hearings, and the date of the refusal, the Board instituted a policy which effectively prevented granting licenses to stores on reserves.

The Appeal Council found that the Board's policy breached the equality provisions of s.15 of the *Charter of Rights and Freedoms*.

Manitoba

R. v. Campbell, [1997] 1 C.N.L.R. 120 (Man. C.A.)

The accused lived off reserve. He was charged with violating a Moose Lake Indian Reserve by-law by being intoxicated on the reserve. The lawyer for the accused argued that the by-law was invalid because it was discriminatory. The court took the opposite view for three reasons.

> 1. The law was validly made pursuant to s.91(24) of the *Constitution Act, 1867*

> 2. The law was freely adopted by the residents of Moose Lake: it was not imposed on them through Parliament

> 3. "It does not authorize a band to make different laws for different people, but only to make an enforceable policy choice for the governance of all people on the reserve." [C.N.L.R. p.125]

Nova Scotia

R. v. Penney (A.) (1996), 157 N.S.R. (2d) 108, 462 A.P.R. 108 (N.S.S.C.)

The accused was non-native. He was convicted by a trial court of violations of the *Fisheries Act*. He complained that he was discriminated against because he could not have the charges dealt with through an alternative process which was available to members of the Native Council of Nova Scotia through a Protocol with the Department of Fisheries.

The court found that the accused had been denied the benefit of a Protocol process and had been treated differently. However, this did not amount to discrimination within s. 15 because the accused was not a member of a historically disadvantaged group.

> The reasons for his being denied this benefit are that he is a member of the powerful non-native majority and that he is a member of a select group of Canadians licensed to fish commercially, neither of which, in my opinion, is a disadvantaged group. [para.35]

Ontario

Lovelace v. Ontario, [1997] O.J. No. 2313 (O.C.A.)

The province of Ontario entered into negotiations with First Nations in the province to establish a casino on reserve, and share the proceeds among all of the First Nations. Applicants representing Metis and other Bands not recognized under the *Indian Act* commenced proceedings claiming a portion of the proceeds. At the trial stage, the judge found that there was discrimination under s. 15.

The Court of Appeal overturned the trial decision, finding that the scheme was validly established under s. 15(2). The court held that the objective of the section was not to benefit all Aboriginal peoples: it was only to benefit First Nations recognized under the *Indian Act*.

R. v. Perry, [1997] O.J. No. 2314 (O.C.A.)

Ontario had developed an Interim Enforcement Policy which provided guidance on the laying of hunting and fishing charges against registered Indians. A native person who was not registered under the *Indian Act* challenged this Policy as being discriminatory. Before the trial proceedings were completed, the provincial government withdrew the Interim Enforcement Policy completely. The trial judge ordered, among other things, that the Policy be reinstated to include Metis and non-status Indians, and that the province enter into negotiations with these peoples.

The Ontario Court of Appeal overturned this decision. They held that the Policy could be withdrawn any time without consultation with the Aboriginal people. They also held that the fact that Metis and non-status Indians were treated differently than registered Indians was not a violation of s. 15 of the *Charter of Rights and Freedoms*.

Six Nations of the Grand River Band Council v. Henderson (1996), [1997] 1 C.N.L.R. 202 (Ont. Gen. Div.)

The Band Council passed a by-law which prohibited non-Indian spouses from residing on reserve. The court found that this by-law contravened section 15(1) of the *Charter of Rights and Freedoms*. However, the judge was persuaded that the socio-economic circumstances of the Band and the over crowding on the reserve were sufficient to justify the by-law under section 1 of the *Charter*.

R. v. Willocks (1995), 22 O.R. (3d) 552, 37 C.R. (4th) 131 (Gen. Div.)

In Toronto, there is an alternative justice program for Aboriginal people which permits some cases to be diverted from the courts to an Aboriginal community council. A Jamaican Canadian claimed that there was a breach of the Charter because he did not have access to the Aboriginal community council or a similar program. The court held that there was no breach of section 15(1). In the alternative, the Aboriginal program was an affirmative action program under section 15(2).

R. v. Goulais, [1988] 3 C.N.L.R. 125, 30 O.A.C. 5 (Dist. Ct.)

There is no violation resulting from the uneven application across the country of regulations made under the federal *Fisheries Act*.

R. v. LaForme, [1996] 1 C.N.L.R. 193 (Ont. Prov. Div.)

Accused were selling intoxicants contrary to a by-law passed under section 85.1 of the *Indian Act*. The court found that the by-law did not contravene section 15 of the Charter.

Saskatchewan

R. v. Bob (1991), 3 C.R. (4th) 348, [1991] 2 C.N.L.R. 104, 88 Sask. R. 302, 6 C.R.R. (2d) 144 (C.A.)

Members of an Indian band were charged with conducting a bingo on reserve for charitable purposes without a provincial licence. The court found that, in other respects, the bingo would have complied with the conditions of a licence, had one been issued. The province cancelled the licence when the band refused to pay a fee of 2 per cent of the prizes awarded. The court found that the "2 per cent fee" was, in fact, a tax, and therefore exempt under s. 87 of the *Indian Act*.

The Court of Appeal reasoned that, in order to obtain a licence, the band would have had to give up its tax exemption right under the *Indian Act*. This requirement would constitute a violation of s. 15 based on race, because no other group would have had to make similar concessions in order to obtain a licence.

R. v. Partridge, [1988] 4 C.N.L.R. 102, 70 Sask. R. 1 (Q.B.)

An Indian was charged with snaring fish in contravention of *Fisheries Regulations*. The trial court found that such Regulations were not uniform across the country, and therefore, there was a violation of s. 15. On appeal, the court found that the violation was justified under s. 1 of the Charter.

25. Aboriginal rights and freedoms not affected by Charter — The guarantee in this Charter of certain rights and freedoms shall not be construed so as to abrogate or derogate from any aboriginal treaty or other rights or freedoms that pertain to the aboriginal peoples of Canada including

> **(a) any rights or freedoms that have been recognized by the Royal Proclamation of October 7, 1763; and**

> **(b) any rights or freedoms that now exist by way of land claims agreements or may be so acquired.**

Commentary: This section is a "shield" in the sense that it protects rights of Aboriginal peoples from the operation of the other sections of the Charter. Note that, in addition to aboriginal and treaty rights, this section includes "other rights or freedoms".

Case Law: *Corbiere v. Canada (Minister of Indian & Northern Affairs)* (1996), [1997] 1 F.C. 689, 41 C.R.R. (2d) 1, 122 F.T.R. 319 (note), 206 N.R. 85, 142 D.L.R. (4th) 122 (C.A.)leave to appeal to S.C.C. granted (April 24, 1997), Doc. 25708 (S.C.C.) (Judgement stayed, pending appeal to Supreme Court of Canada [1996] F.C.J. 1620)

The issue in this case was the validity of the *Indian Act* requirement under s. 77, that only Band members ordinarily resident on reserve could vote in elections held under s. 74. The trial court had found that this provision discriminated against off reserve members, and violated s. 15 of the *Charter of Rights and Freedoms*. The Band argued, among other things, that s. 25 should operate to protect the restriction, because the provision was an "other right or freedom" within the ambit of s. 25.

The court rejected this argument. Although some provisions of the *Indian Act* which affirmed Aboriginal difference might be within s. 25, the provisions in issue did not meet that test.

> The purpose of section 25 is to protect those rights which belong to aboriginal peoples *as aboriginal peoples*. As our section 35(1) analysis of the residency requirement reveals there is insufficient evidence on this appeal to establish that the exclusion of non-resident Band members from decision-making reflects the distinctive aboriginal culture of the Band. Although the central thrust of the *Indian Act* is to accommodate and affirm aboriginal different, not all of its provisions are aimed at achieving this purpose. One commentator suggests that "[t]he protection afforded to Aboriginal rights by s. 25 may be particularly important to traditional forms of

Aboriginal government which do not necessarily fall into the current western understanding of 'democratic'. Some traditional forms of Aboriginal government rely on hereditary chiefs or government based upon consensus, not necessarily relying upon democratic elections for legitimacy". Some *Indian Act* provisions enacted to assist in the accommodation and implementation of such objectives may well be suitable for section 25 protection. Here, however, the *Indian Act* has imposed a system of democratic election. This system is not aimed at protecting and affirming aboriginal difference. [D.L.R. p. 136]

R. v. Nicholas (1988), [1989] 2 C.N.L.R. 131, 91 N.B.R. (2d) 248, 232 A.P.R. 248 (Q.B.)

The accused were members of the Maliseet Band, charged with various offences against the federal *Fisheries Act*. The court stated that they could not rely on s. 25 to assert Aboriginal or treaty rights.

I do point out that s. 25 of the *Constitution Act*, 1982 confers no new substantive rights or freedoms other than the right not to have aboriginal rights or freedoms other than the right not to have aboriginal rights or freedoms derived from a treaty or otherwise abrogated or derogated from by any other guarantee, of general application, contained in the Charter. In my view what Parliament was saying in enacting s. 25 was that, even though aboriginal and treaty rights then existing and recognized under s. 35 might offend against, say, s. 15(1) of the Charter, which provides for equality before and under the law, s. 15(1) cannot serve to abrogate or derogate from such rights. [C.N.L.R. p.134]

Part II — Rights of the Aboriginal Peoples of Canada

35. (1) Recognition of existing aboriginal and treaty rights — The existing aboriginal and treaty rights of the aboriginal peoples of Canada are hereby recognized and affirmed.

(2) Definition of "aboriginal peoples of Canada" — In this Act, "aboriginal peoples of Canada" includes the Indian, Inuit and Métis peoples of Canada.

(3) Land claims agreements — For greater certainty, in subsection (1) "treaty rights" includes rights that now exist by way of land claims agreements or may be so acquired.

(4) Aboriginal and treaty rights are guaranteed equally to both sexes — Notwithstanding any other provision of this Act, the aboriginal and treaty rights referred to in subsection (1) are guaranteed equally to male and female persons.

Commentary: This section protects rights which were existing as of April 17, 1982, when this section came into force. Although some rights were extinguished before that date, rights which were merely regulated continue to exist (see *R. v. Sparrow*).

Aboriginal rights which are protected by this section are identified through a two stage test articulated in *R. v. Van der Peet*.

This section articulates a fiduciary relationship between the Crown and Aboriginal peoples, and restricts the ability of Parliament to infringe Aboriginal and treaty rights to circumstances when infringement is justified. The test for infringement is found in *R. v. Sparrow*.

Cases dealing with treaties which are listed under s. 88 of the *Indian Act* may be relevant to the discussion of treaties in this section. The hunting and fishing cases on treaties from Alberta, Manitoba and

Saskatchewan are affected by the Natural Resources Transfer Agreements. Those cases are listed under the Constitution Act, 1930.

Case Law:

Extinguishment — Canada

Delgamuukw v. British Columbia (December 11, 1997), Doc. 23799 (S.C.C.)

Under section 91(24) of the *Constitution Act, 1867*, the federal government has authority over "Indians and Lands reserved for Indians." This brings all aboriginal rights under exclusive federal authority and only the federal government can extinguish those rights.

> The core of Indianness encompasses the whole range of aboriginal rights that are protected by s. 35(1). Those rights include rights in relation to land; that part of the core derives from s. 91(24)'s reference to "Lands reserved for the Indians". But those rights also encompass practices, customs and traditions which are not tied to land as well; that part of the core can be traced to federal jurisdiction over "Indians". Provincial governments are prevented from legislating in relation to both types of aboriginal rights. [at para.178]

The province argued that "Lands reserved for Indians" only included reserve lands. The Supreme Court rejected that argument stating that the federal government had jurisdiction over all lands held pursuant to Aboriginal title. Only the federal government could extinguish that title. [at para. 174]

R. v. Adams, [1996] 3 S.C.R. 101, [1996] 4 C.N.L.R. 1, 110 C.C.C. (3d) 97, 138 D.L.R. (4th) 657, 202 N.R. 89

George Adams is a Mohawk living on Akwesasne Territory. He was fishing during the spawning season in a marsh on the St. Lawrence River. He caught perch with a seine net made of fine mesh, several hundred feet in length. He did not have a license under the federal *Fisheries Act*. Adams argued that he had an Aboriginal right to fish in that area.

In 1845 lands which were the fishing area were flooded to create a canal, and in 1888, the lands around the fishing area were surrendered by the Mohawks. Quebec argued that these events indicated that any right to fish was extinguished before 1982. The court rejected this argument, saying,

> While these events may be adequate to demonstrate a clear and plain intention in the Crown to extinguish any aboriginal *title to the lands* of the fishing area, neither is sufficient to demonstrate that the Crown had the clear and plain intention of extinguishing the appellant's aboriginal *right to fish for food* in the fishing area. The enlargement of the body of water on which the appellant has the aboriginal right to fish for food does not relate to the existence of that right, let alone demonstrate a clear and plain intention to extinguish it. The surrender of lands, because of the fact that title to land is distinct from the right to fish in the waters adjacent to those lands, equally does not demonstrate a clear and plain intention to extinguish a right. The surrender agreement dealt only with the Mohawks proprietary interest to the lands in question; it did not deal with the free-standing aboriginal right to fish for food which existed in the waters adjacent to those lands. There is no evidence to suggest what the parties to the surrender agreement, including the Crown, intended with regards to the right of the Mohawks to fish in the area; absent such evidence the *Sparrow* test for extinguishment cannot be said to have been met. [C.N.L.R. p.20]

R. v. Coté, [1996] 3 S.C.R. 139, [1996] 4 C.N.L.R. 26, 110 C.C.C. (3d) 122, 138 D.L.R. (4th) 385, 202 N.R. 161

Franck Coté, a member of the Desert River Band, took a group of young people to educate them about traditional fishing in their traditional fishing territory. The territory was now a provincially designated "zone d'exploitation controlee", or "Z.E.C." ("Controlled Harvest Zone"). Cote was charged with entering the zone without paying a fee for the motor vehicle and fishing without a license. Cote argued that he had an Aboriginal right.

Quebec argued, among other things, that there could be no Aboriginal rights or Aboriginal title in New France because France did not recognize Aboriginal title when it came to North America. The court rejected this argument, saying,

> Section 35(1) would fail to achieve its noble purpose of preserving the integral and defining features of distinctive aboriginal societies if it only protected those defining features which were fortunate enough to have received the legal recognition and approval of European colonizers. I should stress that the French Regime's failure to recognize legally a specific Aboriginal practice, custom or tradition (and indeed the French Regime's tacit toleration of a specific practice, custom or tradition) clearly cannot be equated with a clear and plain intention to extinguish such practices under the extinguishment test of s. 35(1). [C.N.L.R. p. 48]

R. v. Badger, [1996] 4 W.W.R. 457, 37 Alta. L.R. (3d) 153, 195 N.R. 1, 105 C.C.C. (3d) 289, 133 D.L.R. (4th) 324, [1996] 2 C.N.L.R. 77 (S.C.C.)

The court held that the onus of proving that a treaty or aboriginal right has been extinguished lies upon the Crown. There must be "strict proof of the fact of extinguishment" and evidence of a clear and plain intention on the part of the government to extinguish treaty rights.

Although the NRTA disallowed commercial hunting rights, food hunting rights continued.

> Unless there is a direct conflict between the NRTA and a treaty, the NRTA will not have modified the treaty rights. Therefore, the NRTA language which outlines the right to hunt for food must be read in light of the fact that this aspect of the treaty right continues in force and effect. [W.W.R. p. 477]

R. v. Howard, [1994] 2 S.C.R. 299, 18 O.R. (3d) 384n, [1994] 3 C.N.L.R. 146, 90 C.C.C. (3d) 131, 166 N.R. 282, 71 O.A.C. 278

Fishing and hunting rights were surrendered by the 1923 Williams Treaty.

Ontario (Attorney General) v. Bear Island Foundation, [1991] 2 S.C.R. 570, 4 O.R. (3d) 133n, 20 R.P.R. (2d) 50, 83 D.L.R. (4th) 381, [1991] 3 C.N.L.R. 79, 127 N.R. 147, 46 O.A.C. 396

An Aboriginal right to land could be surrendered, even though the Indians did not actually sign the treaty, by "arrangements subsequent to that treaty by which the Indians adhered to the treaty in exchange for treaty annuities and a reserve." (C.N.L.R. p. 81)

R. v. Horseman, [1990] 1 S.C.R. 901, 108 A.R. 1, [1990] 4 W.W.R. 97, 73 Alta. L.R. (2d) 193, [1990] 3 C.N.L.R. 95, 55 C.C.C. (3d) 353, 108 N.R. 1

The treaty right to hunt for commercial purposes was taken away by the Natural Resources Transfer Agreement. The rights under the treaty were merged and consolidated under the Agreement.

R. v. Sparrow, [1990] 1 S.C.R. 1075, [1990] 4 W.W.R. 410, 46 B.C.L.R. (2d) 1, 70 D.L.R. (4th) 385, [1990] 3 C.N.L.R. 160, 56 C.C.C. (3d) 263, 111 N.R. 241 (S.C.C.)

The test of extinguishment requires that the Sovereign's intention be clear and plain. Rights which were merely regulated (in this case through the *Fisheries Act*) were not extinguished. Section 35(1) does not revive rights which had been extinguished before the *Constitution Act*, 1982 came into effect.

Extinguishment — Saskatchewan

R. v. Morin, [1997] S.J. No. 529 (Sask.Q.B.)

The two accused were Métis who were ice fishing without a license. The trial judge found that the Métis people in northwest Saskatchewan continued to live "as a community and basically off the land as they have since the early 1800's."

The Queen's Bench upheld the trial judge's finding that scrip did not result in the extinguishment of the right to hunt and fish.

The court did not have to decide whether scrip resulted in the surrender of aboriginal title.

Infringement and Justification — General Principles — Canada

Delgamuukw v. British Columbia (December 11, 1997), Doc. 23799 (S.C.C.)

In *Delgamuukw* the *Sparrow* approach is used, but the tests are varied to apply to Aboriginal title.

The list of legitimate legislative objectives are very wide.

> In my opinion, the development of agriculture, forestry, mining, and hydroelectric power, the general economic development of the interior of British Columbia, protection of the environment or endangered species, the building of infrastructure and the settlement of foreign populations to support those aims, are the kinds of objectives that are consistent with this purpose and, in principle, can justify the infringement of aboriginal title. Whether a particular measure or government act can be explained by reference to one of those objectives, however, is ultimately a question of fact that will have to be examined on a case-by-case basis. [at para.165]

If the legislative objectives were valid, the Crown must fulfill its fiduciary duty. Chief Justice Lamer outlines how the fiduciary duty could be discharged in relation to three features of Aboriginal title.

(i) The right to exclusive use and occupation of land

If the right to exclusive use is to be infringed, the Crown must take into account the priority of Aboriginal people in a variety of ways.

> ... this might entail, for example, that governments accommodate the participation of aboriginal peoples in the development of the resources of British Columbia, that the conferral of fee simples for agriculture, and of leases and licences for forestry and mining reflect the prior occupation of aboriginal title lands, that economic barriers to aboriginal uses of their lands (e.g., licensing fees) be somewhat reduced. This list is illustrative and not exhaustive. [at para. 167]

(ii) The right to choose uses for the land - consultation and consent

The fiduciary duty may be satisfied by addressing the right to choose through consultation. The degree of consultation would depend on the circumstances.

> In occasional cases, when the breach is less serious or relatively minor, it will be no more than a duty to discuss important decisions that will be taken with respect to lands held pursuant to aboriginal title. Of course, even in these rare cases when the minimum acceptable standard is consultation, this consultation must be in good faith, and with the intention of substantially addressing the concerns of the aboriginal peoples whose lands are at issue. In most cases, it will be significantly deeper than mere consultation. Some cases may even require the full consent of an aboriginal nation, particularly when provinces enact hunting and fishing regulations in relation to aboriginal lands. [at para. 168]

(iii) The economic component of the land

The Chief Justice states that the Crown will have to address the economic component through "fair compensation". [at para. 169].

R. v. Adams, [1996] 3 S.C.R. 101, [1996] 4 C.N.L.R. 1, 110 C.C.C. (3d) 97, 138 D.L.R. (4th) 657, 202 N.R. 89

George Adams was a Mohawk living on Akwesasne Territory. He was fishing during the spawning season in a marsh on the St. Lawrence River. He caught perch with a seine net made of fine mesh, several hundred feet in length. He did not have a license under the federal *Fisheries Act*. Adams argued that he had an Aboriginal right to fish in that area.

In this case, the *Quebec Fisheries Regulations*, made under the *Fisheries Act*, provided that the Minister, at his discretion, could provide a special permit to fish for subsistence to an individual Indian or Inuk. The court found that such a wide discretionary power infringed the Aboriginal right.

> In light of the Crown's unique fiduciary obligations towards aboriginal peoples, Parliament may not simply adopt an unstructured discretionary administrative regime which risks infringing Aboriginal rights in a substantial number of applications in the absence of some explicit guidance. If a statute confers an administrative discretion which may carry significant consequences for the exercise of an aboriginal right, the statute or its delegate regulations must outline specific criteria for the granting or refusal of that discretion which seek to accommodate the existence of aboriginal rights. In the absence of such specific guidance, the statute will fail to provide representatives of the Crown with sufficient directives to fulfil their fiduciary duties, and the statute will be found to represent an infringement of aboriginal rights under the *Sparrow* test. [C.N.L.R. p. 21]

The Crown failed to provide sufficient justification for this infringement. It appeared that no permits for fishing for food were being issued, whereas sports fishing was encouraged.

R. v. Coté, [1996] 3 S.C.R. 139, [1996] 4 C.N.L.R. 26, 110 C.C.C. (3d) 122, 138 D.L.R. (4th) 385, 202 N.R. 161

Franck Cote, a member of the Desert River Band, took a group of young people to educate them about traditional fishing in their traditional fishing territory. The territory was now a provincially designated "zone d'exploitation controlée", or "Z.E.C." ("Controlled Harvest Zone"). Coté was charged with entering the zone without paying a fee for the motor vehicle and fishing without a license.

The requirement to obtain a fishing licence was based on the same regulation as in *Adams*. While a licence requirement was not an infringement in itself (see *R. v. Nikal*), in this case, it was an infringement because there were no guidelines on the discretion to grant the license, and no provision for Aboriginal priority. (see *Adams*).

The requirement for paying a motor vehicle fee to enter into the Z.E.C. was based on a provision in provincial statute. A fee was not charged for people entering by foot or by snowmobile. The court found that, as the small fee for motor vehicles was used to improve the roads, there was no infringement.

> I accept the general proposition that a regulation may infringe an Aboriginal or treaty right under the *Sparrow* test by conditioning the exercise of such a right upon the payment of a user fee to the state. But in light of the surrounding circumstances of this case, I am persuaded that the financial burden in this instance does not amount to an infringement of the appellants' ancestral right to fish for food. [C.N.L.R. p. 57]

R. v. Badger, [1996] 4 W.W.R. 457, 37 Alta. L.R. (3d) 153, [1996] 2 C.N.L.R. 77 (S.C.C.)

Legislation which infringes treaty rights must be justified using the tests set out in *Sparrow*.

> In my view, it is equally if not more important to justify *prima facie* infringements of treaty rights. The rights granted to Indians by treaties usually form an integral part of the consideration for the surrender of their lands. [W.W.R. p. 488]

— See also *R. v. Little* (1995), 131 D.L.R. (4th) 220, 16 B.C.L.R. (3d) 253 (C.A.); *R. v. Bombay*, [1993] 1 C.N.L.R. 92, 61 O.A.C. 312 (C.A.)

R. v. Gladstone, [1996] 2 S.C.R. 723, [1996] 4 C.N.L.R. 65, 23 B.C.L.R. (3d) 155, 50 C.R. (4th) 111, [1996] 9 W.W.R. 147, 109 C.C.C. (3d) 193, 137 D.L.R. (4th) 648, 200 N.R. 189, 79 B.C.A.C. 161, 129 W.A.C. 161

Donald and William Gladstone were charged with attempting to sell 4,200 pounds of herring spawn on kelp, which they had harvested under an Indian food fishing license. The accused were members of the Heiltsuk First Nation and claimed an Aboriginal right to commercial fishing. After reviewing historical evidence of extensive intertribal trade involving tons of spawn, the Supreme Court agreed that the "exchange of herring spawn on kelp for money or other goods was a central, significant and defining feature of the culture of the Heiltsuk prior to contact." [C.N.L.R. p. 76] In addition, the court found that this exchange occurred on a scale which today could be called large scale commercial.

While affirming the absolute priority (after conservation) of Aboriginal food requirements articulated in *Sparrow*, the court indicated that a modified priority would be acceptable in the case of commercial fishing. In light of the existence of the Aboriginal right in this case, Chief Justice stressed that the Heiltsuk should have priority in commercial fishing, but he did not feel that they should have exclusive use of the resource. He cited the importance of recognizing the rights of other Aboriginal users and the common law rights of non-Aboriginal users.

The majority of the Supreme Court agreed on examples of factors which could be relevant in determining the appropriate priority:

> Questions relevant to the determination of whether the government has granted priority to aboriginal rights holders are those enumerated in *Sparrow* relating to consultation and compensation, as well as questions such as whether the government has accommodated the exercise of the aboriginal right to participate in the fishery (through reduced licence fees, for example), whether the government's objectives in enacting a particular regulatory scheme reflect the need to take into account the priority of aboriginal right holders, the extent of the participation in the fishery of aboriginal rights holders relative to their percentage of the population, how the government has accommodated different aboriginal rights in a particular fishery (food versus commercial rights, for example), how important the fishery is to the economic and material well-being of the band in question, and the criteria taken into account by the government in, for example, allocating commercial licences amongst different users. [C.N.L.R. p. 93]

The Chief Justice also took this opportunity to clarify some confusion about the interpretation of the infringement test in *Sparrow*.

> The *Sparrow* test for infringement might seem, at first glance, to be internally contradictory. On the one hand, the test states that the appellants need simply show that there has been a *prima facie* interference with their rights in order to demonstrate that those rights have been infringed, suggesting thereby that any meaningful diminution of the appellants' rights will constitute an infringement for the purpose of this analysis. On the other hand, the questions the test directs courts to answer in determining whether an infringement has taken place incorporate ideas such as unreasonableness and "undue" hardship, ideas which suggest that something more than meaningful diminution is required to demonstrate infringement. This internal contradiction is, however, more apparent than real. The questions asked by the Court in *Sparrow* do not define the concept of *prima facie* infringement; they only point to factors which will indicate that such an infringement has taken place. Simply because one of those questions is answered in the negative will not prohibit a finding by a court that a *prima facie* infringement has taken place; it will just be one factor for a court to consider in its determination of whether there has been a *prima facie* infringement. [C.N.L.R. p. 85]

R. v. Sparrow, [1990] 1 S.C.R. 1075, [1990] 4 W.W.R. 410, 46 B.C.L.R. (2d) 1, 70 D.L.R. (4th) 385, [1990] 3 C.N.L.R. 160, 56 C.C.C. (3d) 263, 111 N.R. 241 (S.C.C.)

There are two stages to the test for infringement and justification.

1. The individual or group challenging the legislation has the onus of proving *prima facie* infringement. Among the questions to be asked are:

> First, is the limitation unreasonable? Second, does the regulation impose undue hardship? Third, does the regulation deny to the holders of the right their preferred means of exercising that right? [C.N.L.R. at p. 182]

2. The government bears the burden of justifying the infringement. There are two questions in the justification stage.

> First, is there a valid legislative objective? Here the court would inquire into whether the objective of Parliament in authorizing the department to enact regulations regarding fisheries is valid. The objective of the department in setting out the particular regulations would also be scrutinized. [C.N.L.R. at p. 183]

> If a valid legislative objective is found, the analysis proceeds to the second part of the justification issue. ... That is, the honour of the Crown is at stake in dealings with Aboriginal peoples. The special trust relationship and the responsibility of the government vis-a-vis aboriginals must be the first consideration in determining whether the legislation or action in question can be justified. [C.N.L.R. at p. 183–184]

> ... there are further questions to be addressed, depending on the circumstances of the inquiry. These include the questions of whether there has been as little infringement as possible in order to effect the desired result; whether, in a situation of expropriation, fair compensation is available; and, whether the aboriginal group in question has been consulted with respect to the conservation measures being implemented. The aboriginal peoples, with their history of conservation-consciousness and interdependence with natural resources, would surely be expected, at the least, to be informed regarding the determination of an appropriate scheme for the regulation of the fisheries. [C.N.L.R. at p. 187]

Infringement and Justification — General Principles — British Columbia

R. v. Jack (1995), 131 D.L.R. (4th) 165, 16 B.C.L.R. (3d) 201, 103 C.C.C. (3d) 385 (C.A.)

The court made several general comments on the standard of consultation required to justify interference with an Aboriginal right to fish. These include:

> [The Department of Fisheries and Oceans] did not cover all of the conservation measures which were implemented and which affected the availability of chinook at the mouth of the Leiner River. In particular, there was no discussion of the conservation measures dealing with the restrictions on sport fishing for chinook ... We consider that there was a duty on the DFO to ensure that the Indian band was provided with full information on the conservation measures and their effect on the Indians and other user groups. The DFO had a duty to fully inform itself of the fishing practices of the aboriginal groups and their views of the conservation measures. [D.L.R. at p. 188]

As well, the court indicated that the unilateral imposition of the regulations did not reflect the trust-like relationship between the First Nations and the Crown.

R. v. Little (1995), 131 D.L.R. (4th) 220, 16 B.C.L.R. (3d) 253, 103 C.C.C. (3d) 440 (C.A.)

The court found that the Department of Fisheries and Oceans could not justify a complete prohibition of food fishing in the Nanaimo Band's traditional area.

Although the court did not have to decide whether there had been sufficient consultation in this case, it commented,

> The fact that there were discussions between the [Department of Fisheries and Oceans] and the band, however, does not eliminate or diminish the constitutional requirement to adhere to the priorities mandated by *Sparrow*, and the need to disclose to the band the steps being taken to arrive at that allocation. [D.L.R. at p. 247]

R. v. Sampson (1995), 131 D.L.R. (4th) 192, 16 B.C.L.R. (3d) 226, 103 C.C.C. (3d) 411 (C.A.)

The trial level judge, in attempting to apply the *Sparrow* analysis, asked questions relating to the second stage of the inquiry (justification) in analyzing the first issue of *prima facie* infringement. The Court of Appeal confirms that the two stages of the *Sparrow* analysis must be kept distinct.

> The purpose of the three questions posed in the first stage of the test (is the limitation unreasonable; does the regulation impose undue hardship; and does the regulation deny to the holders of the right their preferred means of exercising that right) is, in our view, to ensure that only meritorious claims are considered. The onus on the applicant is not heavy. The establishment of an infringement on a *prima facie* basis is sufficient. To include consideration of such factors as priority and consultation — factors which are relevant to the second stage of the test — would adversely affect the onus of proof resting upon the applicant. It would diminish the safeguard for aboriginal rights established by s. 35(1) as interpreted by the Supreme Court in *Sparrow*. [D.L.R. at p. 207]

Infringement and Justification — General Principles — Northwest Territories

R. v. Noel, [1995] 4 C.N.L.R. 78 (N.W.T. Terr. Ct.)

The Northwest Territories government established a no-hunting zone citing safety as the reason. The court found that there was a *prima facie* infringement, and that such in fringement was not justified. On the issue of consultation, the court noted that there had been only one meeting with the band, and stated,

> ... the government was made aware of the objections of the representatives of the Aboriginal people to be affected. Other alternatives were suggested which the government representatives either ignored or did not consider seriously. In my view this does not amount to meaningful consultation or a deliberation of people on a subject. The priority that must be given to the constitutionally protected Aboriginal right in question does not seem to have been recognized on the part of the government. Consultation must require the government to carry out meaningful and reasonable discussions with the representatives of Aboriginal people involved. [C.N.L.R. at p. 95]

Infringement and Justification — General Principles — Ontario

R. v. Bombay, [1993] 1 C.N.L.R. 92, 61 O.A.C. 312

In this case, there were violations against federal fisheries legislation. The treaty provided that fishing rights were to be "subject to such regulation as may from time to time be made by Her Government ...". The court found that such regulations had to be justified under the *Sparrow* tests.

Aboriginal Rights — Canada

Delgamuukw v. British Columbia (December 11, 1997), Doc. 23799 (S.C.C.)

The Gitskan and Wet'suwet'en First Nations claimed aboriginal title over 58,000 square kilometres in British Columbia.

Oral histories

The Supreme Court ordered a new trial because the trial judge had erred in refusing to admit, or in giving no independent weight to oral histories. Chief Judge Lamer affirmed the importance of considering oral histories on equal footing with other types of historical evidence.

Content of Aboriginal title

Chief Justice Lamer sets out two propositions to describe the content of Aboriginal title.

1. Aboriginal title provides exclusive use and occupation of the land for a variety of purposes.

> Aboriginal title encompasses the right to use the land held pursuant to that title for a variety of purposes, which need not be aspects of those aboriginal practices, cultures and traditions which are integral to *distinctive aboriginal cultures*. [para. 117]

2. The uses of Aboriginal title land must be consistent with the group's attachment to the land.

> ... there will exist a special bond between the group and the land in question such that the land will be part of the definition of the group's distinctive culture. It seems to me that these elements of aboriginal title create an inherent limitation on the uses to which the land, over which such title exists, may be put. For example, if occupation is established with reference to the use of the land as a hunting ground, then the group that successfully claims aboriginal title to that land may not use it in such a fashion as to destroy its value for such a use (e.g., by strip mining it). Similarly, if a group claims a special bond with the land because of its ceremonial or cultural significance, it may not use the land in such a way as to destroy that relationship (e.g., by developing it in such a way that the bond is destroyed, perhaps by turning it into a parking lot.) [at para. 128]

Proof of Aboriginal title

Chief Justice Lamer outlines three criteria for establishing the existence of Aboriginal title.

1. The land must have been occupied prior to the assertion of British sovereignty.

The point in time for establishing the existence of an Aboriginal practice or custom was the *point of contact* with the Europeans (*R. v. Van der Peet*). In the case of Aboriginal title, the point in time is the date of the assertion of British sovereignty. However, there may be circumstances, such as in the case of dispossession after the arrival of the Europeans, where possession after the assertion of sovereignty may be relevant in establishing Aboriginal title. [para. 145]

In order to establish occupation, courts should take into account both the physical occupation required at common law as well as relevant Aboriginal laws which "might include, but are not limited to, a land tenure system or laws governing land use." [para. 148]

2. There must be continuity in the possession between the present and the pre-sovereignty occupation.

While present occupation could be used to support a claim for pre-sovereignty occupation, the court attempts to ensure that the requirement is somewhat flexible. There need not be an "unbroken chain of continuity", and a change in the nature of the occupation would not preclude a claim. [para. 153]

3. The occupation must be exclusive.

Chief Justice Lamer, however, appears to use the term in an expansive way, underscoring the importance of Aboriginal laws which delineate boundaries between Aboriginal nations for various purposes. Using this approach, then, the Chief Justice is able to allow room for the possibility of joint title among Aboriginal nations using the same territory. [para.158]

R. v. Adams, [1996] 3 S.C.R. 101, [1996] 4 C.N.L.R. 1, 110 C.C.C. (3d) 97, 138 D.L.R. (4th) 657, 202 N.R. 89

George Adams was a Mohawk living on Akwesasne Territory. He was fishing during the spawning season in a marsh on the St. Lawrence River. He caught perch with a seine net made of fine mesh, several hundred feet in length. He did not have a license under the federal *Fisheries Act.*

Lamer, C.J., writing for the majority of the court, held that Aboriginal title was one manifestation of the doctrine of Aboriginal rights. Therefore it was not necessary to establish Aboriginal title in order to assert Aboriginal rights.

> Where an aboriginal group has shown that a particular activity, custom or tradition taking place on the land was integral to the distinctive culture of that group then, *even if they have not shown that their occupation and use of the land was sufficient to support a claim of title to the land*, they will have demonstrated that they have an aboriginal right to engage in that practice, custom or tradition. [C.N.L.R. p.11]

In this case, the court found that the Mohawks fished in the area at the point of contact with Europeans, and that there was sufficient continuity in the practice to establish an existing Aboriginal right, even if there was not sufficient evidence to establish Aboriginal title. Having found that there was an infringement which was not justified, Adams was acquitted.

R. v. Coté, [1996] 3 S.C.R. 139, [1996] 4 C.N.L.R. 26, 110 C.C.C. (3d) 122, 138 D.L.R. (4th) 385, 202 N.R. 161

Franck Coté, a member of the Desert River Band, took a group of young people to educate them about traditional fishing in their traditional fishing territory. The territory was now a provincially designated "zone d'exploitation controlée", or "Z.E.C." ("Controlled Harvest Zone"). Coté was charged with entering the zone without paying a fee for the motor vehicle and fishing without a license.

The court, applying the *Van der Peet* analysis, found that there was an Aboriginal right. According to Lamer, C.J., the evidence

> ... [was] sufficient to support the inference that fishing for food within the lakes and rivers of the territory of the Z.E.C. and in particular, Desert Lake, was a significant part of the life of the Algonquins from a time dating from at least 1603 and the arrival of French explorers and missionaries into the area. Fishing was significant to the Algonquins, as it represented the predominant source of subsistence during the season leading up to winter. [C.N.L.R. p. 54]

In this case, while Coté was not actually fishing for food, the court found that education was incidental to the Aboriginal right.

> In the aboriginal tradition, societal practices and customs are passed from one generation to the next by means of oral description and actual demonstration. As such, to ensure the continuity of aboriginal customs and traditions, a substantive aboriginal right will normally include the incidental right to teach such a practice, custom and tradition to a younger generation. [C.N.L.R. p. 49]

R. v. Vanderpeet, [1996] 2 S.C.R. 507, [1996] 4 C.N.L.R. 177, 23 B.C.L.R. (3d) 1, 50 C.R. (4th) 1, [1996] 9 W.W.R. 1, 109 C.C.C. (3d) 1, 137 D.L.R. (4th) 289, 200 N.R. 1, 80 B.C.A.C. 81, 130 W.A.C. 81, application for rehearing refused (January 16, 1997), Doc. 23803 (S.C.C.)

Dorothy Van der Peet, a member of the Sto:lo, was charged under the federal *Fisheries Act* with selling 10 salmon caught under a food fishing license.

Chief Justice Lamer stated that "in order to be an aboriginal right an activity must be an element of a practice, custom or tradition integral to the distinctive culture of the aboriginal group claiming the right." [para.46] He set out ten factors which must be considered to establish Aboriginal rights.

> 1. Courts must take into account the perspective of aboriginal peoples themselves

> 2. Courts must identify precisely the nature of the claim being made in determining whether an aboriginal claimant has demonstrated the existence of an aboriginal right

> 3. In order to be integral a practice, custom or tradition must be of central significance to the aboriginal society in question

> 4. The practices, customs and traditions which constitute aboriginal rights are those which have continuity with the traditions, customs and practices that existed prior to contact

> 5. Courts must approach the rules of evidence in light of the evidentiary difficulties inherent in adjudicating aboriginal claims

> 6. Claims to aboriginal rights must be adjudicated on a specific rather than general basis

> 7. For a practice, tradition or custom to constitute an aboriginal right it must be of independent significance to the aboriginal culture in which it exists

> 8. The integral to a distinctive culture test requires that a practice, custom or tradition be distinctive; it does not require that practice, custom or tradition be distinct

9. The influence of European culture will only be relevant to the inquiry if it is demonstrated that the practice, custom or tradition is only integral because of that influence

10. Courts must take into account both the relationship of aboriginal peoples to the land and the distinctive societies and cultures of aboriginal peoples

A two stage process is used to make the determination. First, the court must identify the precise nature of the claim for recognition as an Aboriginal right. In this case, the activity in issue was "an Aboriginal right to exchange fish for money or for other goods." Given the scale of the sale, the transaction could not be characterized as "commercial fishing". [S.C.R. p. 563]

Second, the court must answer the following question:

Was the practice of exchanging fish for money or other goods an integral part of the specific distinctive culture of the Sto:lo prior to contact with Europeans? [S.C.R. p. 564]

The court finds, in this case, that fishing for food and ceremonial purposes was integral to the culture, but the exchange of fish was merely incidental and therefore not protected by s. 35(1).

R. v. Gladstone, [1996] 2 S.C.R. 723, [1996] 4 C.N.L.R. 65, 23 B.C.L.R. (3d) 155, 50 C.R. (4th) 111, [1996] 9 W.W.R. 149, 109 C.C.C. (3d) 193, 137 D.L.R. (4th) 648, 200 N.R. 189, 79 B.C.A.C. 161, 129 W.A.C. 161

Donald and William Gladstone were charged with attempting to sell 4,200 pounds of herring spawn on kelp, which they had harvested under an Indian food fishing license. The accused were members of the Heiltsuk First Nation and claimed an Aboriginal right to commercial fishing. After reviewing historical evidence of extensive intertribal trade involving tons of spawn, the Supreme Court agreed that the "exchange of herring spawn on kelp for money or other goods was a central, significant and defining feature of the culture of the Heiltsuk prior to contact." [para. 26] In addition, the court found that this exchange occurred on a scale which today could be called large scale commercial.

While this commercial right had been regulated, it had not extinguished, and the *Fisheries Act* infringed this right by limiting the catch. Since no evidence was adduced on whether there was justification for the *Fisheries Act* limitation, the matter was sent back to trial on that issue.

R. v. N.T.C. Smokehouse, [1996] 4 C.N.L.R. 130, [1996] 9 W.W.R. 114, 23 B.C.L.R. (3d) 114, 50 C.R. (4th) 181, 137 D.L.R. (4th) 528, 109 C.C.C. (3d) 129, 200 N.R. 321, [1996] 2 S.C.R. 672

N.T.C. Smokehouse owns a food processing plant near Port Albierni, British Columbia. It was charged under the federal *Fisheries Act* with purchasing and selling salmon caught by members of the Sheshaht and Opetchesaht Indian Bands under Indian food fishing licenses.

Chief Justice Lamer characterized this as large scale commercial activity involving more than 119,000 pounds of salmon. Unlike the situation in *Gladstone* the First Nations in this case did not provide evidence that large scale commercial fishing was an Aboriginal right. He found that the exchange of fish was only incidental to other activities of the First Nations.

Potlatches and other ceremonial occasions may well be integral features of the Sheshaht and Opetchesaht cultures and, as such, recognized and affirmed as Aboriginal rights under s. 35(1); however, the exchange of fish incidental to these occasions is not, itself, a sufficiently central, significant or defining feature of these societies so as to be recognized as an aboriginal right under s. 35(1). The exchange of fish, when taking place apart from the occasion to which such exchange was incidental, cannot, even if that occasion was an integral part of the aboriginal society in question, constitute an aboriginal right. [C.N.L.R. p. 141–142]

R. v. Nikal (April 24, 1996), Doc. 23804 (1996) (S.C.C.)

A member of the Moricetown First Nation was charged with fishing without a license on the Bulkley River, which flowed through his reserve. The court found that his aboriginal rights to fish included,

(i) the right to determine who within the band will be the recipients of the fish for ultimate consumption;

(ii) the right to select the purpose for which the fish will be used; i.e. food, ceremonial, or religious purposes;

(iii) the right to fish for steelhead;

(iv) the right to choose the period of time to fish in the river (S.C.R. para 104)

(v) the right to determine when fishing will occur and the method and manner of fishing. (S.C.R. para. 106)

Nikal had refused to get a license based on instructions from his elders. The court held that a license by itself was not an infringement of aboriginal rights. However, the court noted,

This is not to say that there are not conditions of the license which could constitute infringements of s. 35 rights. Even a simple license could constitute an infringement if it could only be obtained with great difficulty or expense. (S.C.R. para. 97)

In this case, the court found that the aboriginal rights to fish were infringed by several of the conditions. Nikal was acquitted because the Crown had not provided evidence which justified those infringements.

R. v. Pamajewon, [1996] S.C.J. No. 20

The Shawanaga First Nation and the Eagle Lake First Nation conducted bingos on reserve to raise money for community purposes. They did not obtain provincial licenses. Convictions were affirmed for holding bingos contrary to the *Criminal Code*. While the court was prepared to assume, without deciding, that there was a right of self-government within s. 35(1), Mr. Justice Lamer held that self-government was not the issue in this case. Following the analysis in *Van Der Peet*, he characterized the issue as the existence of gambling or the regulation of gambling as an Aboriginal right. The facts of this case did not support the existence of such a right.

Native Women's Assn. of Canada v. R., [1994] 3 S.C.R. 627, 119 D.L.R. (4th) 224, [1995] 1 C.N.L.R. 47, 24 C.R.R. (2d) 233, 173 N.R. 241, 84 F.T.R. 240

During the national constitutional talks which eventually resulted in the Charlottetown Accord of 1992, the federal government provided funding for four national Aboriginal organizations to participate fully in those talks. The Native Women's Association of Canada was not one of the four organizations, and did not get equal funding nor equal participation in the constitutional talks.

The court stated, at (S.C.R.) p. 665:

The right of the Aboriginal people of Canada to participate in constitutional discussions does not derive from any existing Aboriginal or treaty right protected under s. 35. Therefore, s. 35(4) ... which guarantees Aboriginal and treaty rights referred to in s. 35(1) equally to male and female persons, is of no assistance to the respondents.

R. v. Sparrow, [1990] 1 S.C.R. 1075, [1990] 4 W.W.R. 410, 46 B.C.L.R. (2d) 1, 70 D.L.R. (4th) 385, [1990] 3 C.N.L.R. 160, 56 C.C.C. (3d) 263, 111 N.R. 241 (S.C.C.)

Section 35(1) is to be construed generously and liberally. "Existing aboriginal rights" must be interpreted flexibly so as to permit their evolution over time. The phrase does not freeze the right in the specific manner in which it was regulated before 1982. In this case, fishing for food by a member of the

Musqueam First Nation was found to be an aboriginal right. Any allocation of priorities after valid conservation measures have been implemented must give top priority to the Aboriginal right.

> [Aboriginal] fishing rights are not traditional property rights. They are rights held by a collective and are in keeping with the culture and existence of that group. [C.N.L.R. p. 182]

Wewayakum Indian Band v. Canada, [1989] 1 S.C.R. 322, 3 R.P.R. (2d) 1, 35 B.C.L.R. (2d) 1, [1989] 3 W.W.R. 117, (sub nom. *Roberts v. Canada*) 25 F.T.R. 161, 57 D.L.R. (4th) 197, [1989] 2 C.N.L.R. 146, 92 N.R. 241

The *Indian Act* and the common law of Aboriginal title are "laws of Canada" within the meaning of s. 101 of the *Constitution Act*, 1982. Hence, it is within the jurisdiction of the Federal Court of Canada to determine a dispute between Indian bands with conflicting claims to an obligation owed by the federal Crown. In this instance, the plaintiff band sought a declaration that its land had been unlawfully granted to the defendant Indian band.

Sawridge Band v. Canada, [1997] F.C.J. No. 794 (F.C.A.)

Three bands in Treaties 6,7 and 8 challenged amendments (made under Bill C-31 in 1985) which reinstated Indian women who had lost status when they had married non-Indian men. The Bands claimed that they had a "woman follows man" custom which meant that women marrying non-Band members left the Band. It was argued that the *Indian Act* amendments violated this custom by requiring that these women be reinstated to the Band list. The Band was unsuccessful at trial, and appealed, citing in part, a reasonable apprehension of bias on part of the trial judge, Muldoon, J.

The Court of Appeal cited many examples of "critical, perjorative language" by Muldoon, J. about constitutional and statutory provisions relating to Aboriginal peoples. Comments included comparing Indians to adolescents, referring to Aboriginal rights as racist, and making derogatory comments about the recognition of Metis in the Constitution. The Court of Appeal found that there was a reasonable apprehension of bias and sent the matter back for a new trial.

Corbiere v. Canada (Minister of Indian & Northern Affairs) (1996), [1997] 1 F.C. 689, 41 C.R.R. (2d) 1, 122 F.T.R. 319 (note), 206 N.R. 85, 142 D.L.R. (4th) 122 (C.A.)leave to appeal to S.C.C. granted (April 24, 1997), Doc. 25708 (S.C.C.) (Judgement stayed, pending appeal to Supreme Court of Canada [1996] F.C.J. 1620)

The issue in this case was the validity of the *Indian Act* requirement under s. 77 that only Band members ordinarily resident on reserve could vote in elections held under s. 74 of the *Indian Act*. The trial court had found that this provision discriminated against off reserve members, and violated s. 15 of the *Charter of Rights and Freedoms*.

The Court of Appeal rejected the argument that the Batchewana First Nation had an Aboriginal right to exclude non-residents from voting in Band elections. The court found no evidence of such a practice prior to contact: in fact, until 1902, the Chief was a hereditary position.

Mohawk Council of Akwesasne v. Canada (Minister of National Revenue), [1997] F.C.J. No. 882 (F.C.T.D.)

Akwesasne is a Mohawk reserve which straddles the Canada-U.S.A. border as well as the Ontario-Quebec border. In 1988, Chief Mike Mitchell crossed the border with one washing machine, 10 blankets, 20 Bibles, various articles of used clothing, one case of lubricating motor oil, 10 loaves of bread, two pounds of butter, four gallons of whole milk, six bags of cookies and 12 cans of soup. He told customs officials that these were gifts for a ceremonial dinner at the neighboring Mohawk reserve of Tyendinaga to commemorate the renewal of trade ties with that community. Chief Mitchell refused to pay the duty of $361.64 claiming an Aboriginal right, and rights under the Jay Treaty.

After reviewing the history of the Mohawks, and the place trade played in their society, the court found that there was an existing Aboriginal right to the following:

> . . . to pass and repass freely across what is now the Canada-United States boundary including the right to bring goods from the United States into Canada for personal and community use without having to pay customs duties on those goods. Goods for personal and community use includes goods used for sustenance, household goods and goods used for First Nations' custom. The aboriginal right includes the right to bring these goods from the United States into Canada for non-commercial scale trade with other First Nations.
>
> As the plaintiff has explained, the aboriginal right does not include the right to bring into Canada any form of firearm, restricted or prohibited drug, alcohol, plants and the like. The aboriginal right is also limited to the extent that any Mohawk of Akwesasne entering Canada with goods from the United States will be subject to search and declaration procedures at Canadian Customs. [para. 299]

As his Aboriginal right was infringed by the requirement to pay duty, and as the Crown had not introduced evidence of justification, the *Customs Act* was found to be of no force or effect to the extent that it was inconsistent with the Aboriginal right.

Watt v. Canada (Immigration Act, Adjudicator), [1995] 1 C.N.L.R. 230, 82 F.T.R. 57 (T.D.)

A member of a tribe whose traditional territory straddled the border between Canada and the United States did not have an Aboriginal right to come to Canada. His rights were described in the *Immigration Act*, which required that he be a citizen of Canada or a registered Indian.

Reid v. Canada, [1993] 2 C.N.L.R. 188, 59 F.T.R. 308 (T.D.)

The evidence did not establish an aboriginal right to commercial herring roe harvesting on kelp. Historically Heiltsuk peoples collected herring roe on bough and not on kelp. Some exchange, with friends and relatives, of herring roe did not constitute a recognizable commercial activity.

Aboriginal Rights — Alberta

Manychief v. Poffenroth (1994), 164 A.R. 161, [1995] 3 W.W.R. 210, 25 Alta. L.R. (3d) 393, [1995] 2 C.N.L.R. 67 (Alta. Q.B.)

The provincial *Fatal Accidents Act* provided rights to wives of deceased, but did not recognize common law relationships. The plaintiff had lived with the deceased for eight years and they had a child, but the couple did not have a "church wedding". The plaintiff made a claim under the provincial *Fatal Accidents Act* as a wife by customary Blood marriage. The judge found that there was an existing Aboriginal right to customary marriage but that in this case the relationship was a common law relationship like those found in the non-native community, and therefore was not covered by the statute.

Aboriginal Rights — British Columbia

Haida Nation v. British Columbia (Minister of Forests), [1997] B.C.J. No. 2480 (C.A.)

The province issued a tree farm license for cutting timber over land included in Haida Gwaii (Queen Charlotte Islands). Under the provincial *Forest Act*, a license could only issue on land which was "not otherwise encumbered." The parties agreed that *Delgamuukw v. British Columbia* had settled that aboriginal rights were an "encumbrance" on Crown title, but the province argued that aboriginal rights were not an "encumbrance" within the meaning of the *Forest Act*.

The Court of Appeal disagreed with the province, holding that aboriginal title was an encumbrance which prevented the issuing of a forestry license.

R. v. Johnnie, 18 B.C.L.R. (3d) 73, [1996] 6 W.W.R. 112, 69 B.C.A.C. 304, 113 W.A.C. 304 (C.A.)

Johnnie was a member of the Cowichan First Nation. He shot an elk in closed season. Some of the meat he froze for his family, and some he gave to a friend. He sold a hind quarter to a non-native person for $75.00.

The Court of Appeal ordered a new trial on all counts, including the trafficking charge because the courts below had not taken into account new cases on Aboriginal rights. The Court of Appeal commented,

> Although both judges below firmly rejected any aboriginal right to sell meat taken by hunting, I am not satisfied that the conclusion was reached by the proper route. A trial judge may arrive at a different result after analyzing the evidence pertaining to all the rights claimed according to the contemporary rules. [B.C.L.R. p. 84]

R. v. Sampson (1995), 131 D.L.R. (4th) 192, 16 B.C.L.R. (3d) 226, 103 C.C.C. (3d) 411 (C.A.)

Two young men who were members of the Chemainus Band were caught early in the morning with 27 chum and 8 coho salmon taken in nets. The court found that there was a *prima facie* infringement of their aboriginal right to fish because regulations prohibited them from their preferred method of fishing — in this case, by a gill-net — within their traditional fishing area.

The court then found that the infringement failed to be justified by the Department of Fisheries and Oceans (DFO) because sufficient priority was not given to the Indian food fishery. Noting that sports and commercial fishers had depleted the stocks of salmon, the court stated,

> While prohibiting members of the Chemainus Band from fishing by gill-net in Ladysmith Harbour, the DFO nevertheless allowed sport fishers to troll for salmon throughout the calendar year within the Ladysmith Harbour and also beyond the entrance to Ladysmith Harbour. [D.L.R. at p. 216]

R. v. Jack (1995), 131 D.L.R. 165, 16 B.C.L.R. (3d) 201, 103 C.C.C. (3d) 385 (C.A.)

Mr. Jack was a hereditary chief of the Mowachaht Band. He was fishing with distant kin from the Ehattesaht Band in his traditional territory to catch fish for his son's wedding. Noting that the aboriginal right extended to ceremonial purposes, the court stated,

> Mr. Jack, as head of a family group, possesses a hereditary compendium of rights, assets and responsibilities known as "hahuujli". His aboriginal right to fish included the right to invite kinsmen to assist him in fishing. [D.L.R. at p. 174]

There was *prima facie* infringement because he was denied his preferred means of fishing (with a hand seine net) in his hereditary territory. The infringement was not justified because the Indian food fishery was not accorded the appropriate priority.

> In our opinion, the DFO failed to give priority to Mr. Jack's aboriginal right when it prohibited any fishing for chinook at the mouth of the Leiner River but at the same time allowed sport fishers a daily limit of two chinook per person in the entrances to Esperanza and Nootka Inlets. [D.L.R. at p. 185]

R. v. Jim (1995), [1996] 1 C.N.L.R. 160, 66 B.C.A.C. 105, 108 W.A.C. 105, 14 B.C.L.R. (3d) 350, [1996] 3 W.W.R. 30 (C.A.)

A Wet'suwet'en person was charged with gaming without a provincial license. In this case, the evidence did not establish an Aboriginal right of gaming. Therefore, section 35(1) did not provide a defence to the charge under the Criminal Code.

Oregon Jack Creek Indian Band v. Canadian National Railway, 34 B.C.L.R. (2d) 344, 56 D.L.R. (4th) 404, [1990] 2 C.N.L.R. 85 (C.A.)affirmed [1989] 2 S.C.R. 1069, 43 B.C.L.R. (2d) xxxvin, 63 D.L.R. (4th) 607, [1990] 2 C.N.L.R. 96, application for rehearing refused [1990] 1 S.C.R. 117, 43 B.C.L.R. (2d) xxxvin, 68 D.L.R. (4th) 478, 103 N.R. 23

> It is a mistake, in my view, to conclude that aboriginal rights vest in an entity (which clearly does not exist today) and to ignore the historical fact that the rights are communal, and that they are possessed today by the descendants of the persons who originally held them. They are not personal rights in the sense that they exist independently of the community, but are per-

sonal in the sense that a violation of the communal rights affect the individual member's enjoyment of those rights. [C.N.L.R. p. 89]

Casimel v. Insurance Corp. of British Columbia (1993), 82 B.C.L.R. (2d) 387, 18 C.C.L.I. (2d) 161, 106 D.L.R. (4th) 720, [1994] 2 C.N.L.R. 22 (C.A.)

Customary adoption of a biological grandchild was an integral part of the distinctive culture of the band, and therefore constituted an aboriginal right within the meaning of s. 35(1). The status of parent conferred by customary adoption entitled the grandparents to death benefits as "dependent parents" under the *Insurance (Motor Vehicle) Regulations.*

R. v. Alphonse, [1993] 5 W.W.R. 401, 80 B.C.L.R. (2d) 17, [1993] 4 C.N.L.R. 19, 83 C.C.C. (3d) 417 (C.A.)

The shooting of a deer on unoccupied, unfenced and uncultivated private land, although contrary to s. 27(1)(c) of the *Wildlife Act,* was accomplished pursuant to the exercise of an unextinguished Aboriginal right. Accordingly, s. 27(1)(c) constituted a *prima facie* infringement of that right, and was inconsistent with s. 35(1) of the *Constitution Act,* 1982.

R. v. Dick, [1993] 5 W.W.R. 446, 80 B.C.L.R. (2d) 62, [1993] 4 C.N.L.R. 63 (C.A.)

Sections 17(1) and 34(2) of the *B.C. Wildlife Act,* which regulated the issuance of hunting permits through lottery and other randoms means of selection, and prohibited possession of dead wildlife without a permit, were of no force or effect with respect to Aboriginals. The provisions constituted a *prima facie* infringement of Aboriginal rights, and were therefore inconsistent with s. 35(1) of the *Constitution Act,* 1982. The legislative scheme was not sensitive to the needs of Aboriginal hunters, made no attempt to allocate priorities, and gave no indication that the conservation strategy infringed as little as possible on Aboriginal rights.

R. v. Williams, [1995] 2 C.N.L.R. 229 (B.C. C.A.)leave to appeal to S.C.C. refused.

The Aboriginal applicants argued that the provincial court had no jurisdiction over them because their lands had not been ceded or purchased by the Crown. The court rejected the argument that Aboriginal people remained sovereign over their territory.

Delgamuukw (Uukw) v. British Columbia (1987), 37 D.L.R. (4th) 408, [1987] 6 W.W.R. 240, 16 B.C.L.R. (2d) 145, [1988] 1 C.N.L.R. 173 (C.A.)

First Nations obtained certificates of *lis pendens* for land subject to aboriginal title litigation. The court held the *lis pendens* was not capable of registration under the provincial *Land Titles Act.*

R. v. Seward, [1997] B.C.J. No. 1691 (B.C.S.C.)

Dean Thomas required fresh meat for a burning ceremony. He went hunting at night with Joe Seward and Ken Thomas, and used halogen lamps. All three were members of the Penelakut Band. The accused claimed that there was an Aboriginal right to hunt.

The court found that conservation and safety were concerns in the Copper Canyon area where they were hunting, and entered convictions.

Westbank First Nation v. British Columbia, [1997] 2 C.N.L.R. 229 (B.C.S.C.)

The First Nation attempted to get an interim injunction against logging claiming that there was an Aboriginal right to trap marten on the lands in question. The province, they argued, could not infringe those Aboriginal rights by issuing logging permits.

The court held that there was a fair issue to go to trial on the existence of an Aboriginal right, and on an apprehended breach of that right. Until the merits of the issue were decided in a full trial, however, the court held that the balance of convenience favoured allowing the cutting for 1996. The court left open the possibility of reconsidering the situation based on anticipated logging in 1997 and 1998.

Tsay Keh Dene Band v. British Columbia (Minister of Environment, Land & Parks), [1997] B.C.J. No. 1482 (B.C. S.C.)

The Tsay Keh Dene Band applied for an interim injunction to stop Kemess Mines from cutting timber on traditional lands which were part of a land claim. The court refused the injunction, partly because there would not be any irreparable harm. One of the reasons the court came to the conclusion that there would be no irreparable harm to the Band, was the court's understanding that the Band only wanted monetary compensation.

R. v. Pike (1993), [1994] 1 C.N.L.R. 160 (B.C. S.C.)

Aboriginal fishing rights are held by a collective and by the individuals who make up that collective. Aboriginal rights may not be exercised by non-Aboriginal persons. An Aboriginal person did not have the right to appoint her non-Aboriginal husband to exercise her fishing rights on her behalf.

Yale Indian Band v. Lower Fraser Fishing Authority (1992), [1993] 1 C.N.L.R. 182 (B.C. S.C.)

An application for an interlocutory injunction was brought by a band to prevent other Indian bands from fishing pursuant to a communal licence issued by the Crown. The band claimed that they had historically controlled the fishing in that part of the river. The application was refused. The communal licence was part of a pilot project to help create a co-operative relationship between the federal government and Indian fishermen in an area where fishing rights had been disputed for years. There was no status quo to protect, the risk of irreparable harm to the respondents was substantial, and the injunction would threaten the cooperation between the federal government and the bands.

R. v. Hopkins (1992), [1993] 1 C.N.L.R. 123 (B.C. S.C.)

A ban on clam fishing in an area closed due to contamination was reasonable. Its objective was to protect people, including band members, from eating contaminated fish, and clams could be harvested in from a nearby area. Although the accused argued that the clams were caught for ceremonial burning purposes, the evidence did not clearly establish that none of the clams were to be eaten. A *prima facie* infringement of s. 35(1) was not established.

Thomas v. Norris, [1992] 2 C.N.L.R. 139 (B.C. S.C.)

Thomas was a member of the Lyackson Band, but had resided most of his life off reserve in Duncan. When he and his common law wife encountered marital difficulties, she asked elders to initiate Thomas into the Spirit Dance in the Coast Salish Big House Tradition. He was forcibly removed from his home and confined for four days where he was physically assaulted and deprived of food.

The court found that there was insufficient evidence to prove that spirit dancing was an Aboriginal right. The court also commented, "If spirit dancing generally was in existence in April of 1982 when the *Constitution Act, 1982* came into force, the impugned aspects of it, to which I have referred, had been expressly extinguished." [C.N.L.R., p. 160]

R. v. Archie, [1991] 4 C.N.L.R. 107 (B.C. S.C.)

A closure of a fishery was not justified because the Department of Fisheries did not respond in a timely manner to indications that there were more salmon than originally estimated.

R. v. Joseph, [1990] 4 C.N.L.R. 59 (B.C. S.C.)

A reduction in fishing quotas for conservation purposes which is borne equally by all user groups — native, sport and commercial — without special consideration of Indian food needs, violates native food fishing rights under s. 35 of the *Constitution Act*, 1982.

R. v. Watts, [1989] 3 C.N.L.R. 176 (B.C. Co. Ct.)An appeal by the Crown to the British Columbia Court of Appeal was dismissed as abandoned, September 13, 1993, [1994] 3 C.N.L.R. vin.

A fishery quota allocation made by the Department of Fisheries resulted in the closure of an Indian food fishery. The defendant band members were subsequently convicted of unlawfully fishing without a permit. On appeal, it was held that the quota allocation was arbitrary and failed to take into account the food and societal needs of the Indian band, and acquittals were entered.

R. v. Sam, [1989] 3 C.N.L.R. 162 (B.C. Co. Ct.)

The constitutionally protected right of Indians to fish supersedes the considerations to be given to sports fisheries. In this instance, a federal Department of Fisheries regulation that ran contrary to proper conservation and management practices and that had the effect of favouring a sports fishery over the Indian fishery, was not enforced.

R. v. Ned, [1997] 3 C.N.L.R. 251 (B.C. Prov. Ct.)

The Pavilion, Fountain and Bridge River Bands are part of the Stl'atl'imx Nation. Members of the Pavilion and Fountain Bands were charged with sport fishing on part of a river which passed through the Bridge River Reserve. The Bridge River Band and the Department of Fisheries considered that part of the river closed to sport and food fishing as a conservation measure. The court held that the Bridge River Band did not have exclusive right to the fishery, and that members of the Pavilion and Fountain Bands had a right to fish for food in that area. The accused were acquitted because they were fishing for food.

R. v. Quipp, [1997] B.C.J. No. 1205 (B.C. Prov. Ct.)

Two members of the Sto:lo Nation were charged after shooting a cow elk in closed season. They were hunting, not on Sto:lo lands, but on the territory of the Thompson or Okanagan First Nations. The accused were convicted because they did not show that they had Aboriginal rights to hunt in that territory without prior permission from those nations.

R. v. Dick, [1993] 2 C.N.L.R. 137, 15 C.R.R. (2d) 160 (B.C. Prov. Ct.)

The Lekwiltok tribe had neither exclusive nor indefinite occupation of the waters in question at the time British sovereignty was asserted; barter was incidental to the lives and culture of the Lekwiltok; there was no proof of a deep water fishery. Therefore, no Aboriginal right to fish commercially existed. If such a right once existed, it had been extinguished by the intended consequences of legislation. If it had not been extinguished, closure of the area was justified for conservation.

R. v. Bones, [1990] 4 C.N.L.R. 37 (B.C. Prov. Ct.)

The government is required to justify legislation that has a negative impact on Aboriginal rights protected by s. 35(1) of the *Constitution Act, 1982*. In this instance, regulations that restricted licensing, quotas and the time during which the fisheries were open were found to be unjustified.

R. v. Cunningham, [1990] 2 C.N.L.R. 110 (B.C. Prov. Ct.)

The accused was charged with fishing without a licence while fishing with his wife, a status Indian who held a legitimate licence. An acquittal was registered, as the accused was helping his wife exercise a constitutional right, and was entitled to assist her to minimize her exposure to danger.

Re Family & Child Service Act (British Columbia), [1990] 4 C.N.L.R. 14 (B.C. Prov. Ct.)

The provincial *Family and Child Service Act* applies to Aboriginal children in the care of residents on a reserve. The right to determine whether children are in need of protection, and the power to implement remedies, are not Aboriginal rights protected by s. 35 of the *Constitution Act, 1982*.

Aboriginal Rights — Manitoba

R. v. McPherson, [1994] 2 W.W.R. 761, 111 D.L.R. (4th) 278, [1994] 2 C.N.L.R. 137, 90 Man. R. (2d) 290 (Man. Q.B.)

The hunters charged were Métis. Provincial regulations which unjustifiably infringe an Aboriginal right should be read down so as not to apply to aboriginal persons and to preserve their rights. The court did not overturn acquittals entered at trial, based on the finding that the Métis had a common law right to hunt moose out of season.

Aboriginal Rights — New Brunswick

R. v. Francis (1996), 21 C.E.L.R. (N.S.) 89, 177 N.B.R. (2d) 155, 449 A.P.R. 155 (Q.B.)

It was agreed by the parties that the accused had an Aboriginal or treaty right to take lobster for food, social and ceremonial purposes. In this case, charges were laid because the accused had in their possession undersized lobster, in contravention of the *Atlantic Fisheries Regulations.* The court found that there was an infringement of the right, but that the regulation was aimed at conservation, and so the infringement was justified.

Aboriginal Rights — Nova Scotia

R. v. Murdock (1996), 38 C.R.R. (2d) 15, 154 N.S.R. (2d) 1, 452 A.P.R. 1, [1997] 2 C.N.L.R. 103 (N.S. C.A.) [For a related case, which followed this case, see *R. v. Johnson (S.G.)*, 156 N.S.R. (2d) 71, 461 A.P.R. 71, [1997] 3 C.N.L.R. 206 (N.S. C.A.)]

Johnson, a Mi'kmaq from the Millbrook Reserve bought tobacco from Murdock, a Mohawk from Six Nations. Johnson sold the tobacco to both members of the Band and to non-natives. The court found that there were no Aboriginal rights in this case.

The appellants, if anything, may have established an existing aboriginal right to use tobacco for personal consumption and for ceremonial purposes although the trial judge did not make such a finding.

> Even if one were to conclude that this use of tobacco constitutes an aboriginal right of some sort, in the absence of evidence, the appellants have failed to prove that the scope of the aboriginal right to use tobacco extends to include Mi'kmaq Indians dealing, or trading in tobacco between different Indians or Indian Bands in different parts of Canada. And it clearly would not involve selling tobacco to nonnatives. [N.S.R. p. 56]

R. v. Denny (1990), 94 N.S.R. (2d) 253, 247 A.P.R. 253, [1990] 2 C.N.L.R. 115, 55 C.C.C. (3d) 322 (C.A.)

Aboriginal rights under s. 35(1), while subject to valid federal regulation, are subordinate only to conservation measures. Natives were therefore entitled to limited immunity from prosecution for fishing contrary to the fishery regulations, and were entitled to priority in the allocation of a surplus of fish where it existed.

Aboriginal Rights — Ontario

R. v. Jones, 14 O.R. (3d) 421, [1993] 3 C.N.L.R. 182 (Prov. Div.)

Commercial fishing for band sustenance (as opposed to profit) was protected as an Aboriginal or treaty right. Evidence showed commercial fishing was a community-based, collective activity directed to the subsistence of the group as a whole. A quota on preferred species caused undue hardship by curtailing income to a subsistence economy, and increasing unemployment and poverty. Once conservation objectives have been met, the Saugeen Ojibway Nation has priority over other user groups, a priority which the existing regulatory scheme failed to accommodate. Regulations transferring the economic benefit of the fishery to tourism and non-Aboriginal commercial fishers are tantamount to expropriation, and the absence of fair compensation weighs against the Crown. Prohibition against purchase of fish from band members pending negotiations and a new arrangement would also be unconstitutional.

Aboriginal Rights — Saskatchewan

James Smith Indian Band v. Saskatchewan (Master of Titles), [1995] 6 W.W.R. 158, 123 D.L.R. (4th) 280, 131 Sask. R. 60, 95 W.A.C. 60, [1995] 3 C.N.L.R. 100 (C.A.)

The court upheld the refusal of the Master of Titles to register a caveat on lands claimed by the First Nation. The majority of judges held that a decision should be made case by case on whether an Aboriginal interest in land could be protected by a caveat.

R. v. Morin, [1997] S.J. No. 529 (Sask. Q.B.)

The two accused were Metis who were ice fishing without a license. The trial judge found that the Metis people in northwest Saskatchewan continued to live "as a community and basically off the land as they have since the early 1800's."

The Queen's Bench found that there was an existing Aboriginal right to hunt and fish. These Metis rights were infringed in three ways. First, the license issued for domestic fishing issued was discretionary, and was invalid for the same reason that a discretionary fishing license was found to be invalid by the Supreme Court of Canada in *R. v. Adams*. Second, the $5 fee, which did not apply to Indians, was a hardship.

And third, the court found that a provincial policy which gave preferential treatment to status Indians over Metis was an infringement of Metis rights.

> In any one situation, Metis persons could be denied the right to fish for food in the interests of conservation while treaty Indian persons might continue to fish. As noted above, there is no basis to distinguish between Indian and Metis aboriginal groups with respect to the right to fish for food. [at para 58]

R. v. Bear Claw Casino Ltd., [1994] 4 C.N.L.R. 81 (Sask. Prov. Ct.)

The accused were acquitted of operating gaming on reserve contrary to the Criminal Code because they held an honest belief that they did not surrender their right to self-government. The judge also noted (at p. 93):

> In reference to defence argument that the White Bear First Nation has the right and ability to control gaming on the reserve because they have the right to self-government by virtue of s. 35(1) of the *Constitution Act, 1982* and s. 91(24) of the *Constitution Act, 1867*, I have read and studied counsel's Written Arguments and presentations including case law referred to and agree that they have a good argument in that regard ....

Aboriginal Rights — Yukon

R. v. Joseph, [1991] N.W.T.R. 263 (Yukon Terr. Ct.)

The angling and fishing licence requirement imposed on members of the Han Owitch'in Indian people by s. 4 of the *Yukon Territory Fishery Regulations* infringes on their Aboriginal rights as protected by s. 35 of the *Constitution Act*, 1982. The infringement is not justifiable and is of no force and effect in relation to native persons who angle for food fish.

Treaty Rights — Canada

R. v. Coté, [1996] 3 S.C.R. 139, [1996] 4 C.N.L.R. 26, 110 C.C.C. (3d) 122, 138 D.L.R. (4th) 385, 202 N.R. 161

Franck Coté was an Algonquin, a member of the Desert River Band, located in Quebec. He was charged with fishing without a license, contrary to the federal *Fisheries Regulations*. He was also charged with entering a "zone d'exploitation controlée', or "Z.E.C." ("Controlled Harvest Zone") without paying a motor vehicle fee, contrary to a provincial statute. He relied on an Aboriginal right to fish (see annotations under "Aboriginal rights") and on a treaty right.

The Quebec Court of Appeal found that the Algonquins had signed a treaty at Swegatchy in 1760 which protected their right to fish for food. At the Supreme Court of Canada, Lamer, C.J., assumed, without deciding, that there was such a treaty right. However, he then found that the requirement for a motor vehicle fee to enter the Z.E.C. did not infringe that treaty right.

R. v. Badger, [1996] 4 W.W.R. 457, 37 Alta. L.R. (3d) 153, 195 N.R. 1, 105 C.C.C. (3d) 289, 133 D.L.R. (4th) 324, [1996] 2 C.N.L.R. 77 (S.C.C.)

The court set down several guidelines relating to the interpretation of treaties.

> First, it must be remembered that a treaty represents an exchange of solemn promises between the Crown and the various Indian nations. It is an agreement whose nature is sacred ...

> Second, the honour of the Crown is always at stake in its dealing with Indian people. Interpretations of treaties and statutory provisions which have an impact upon treaty or aboriginal rights must be approached in a manner which maintains the integrity of the Crown. It is always assumed that the Crown intends to fulfil its promises. No appearance of "sharp dealing" will be sanctioned ...

Third, any ambiguities or doubtful expressions in the wording of the treaty or document must be resolved in favour of the Indians. A corollary to this principle is that any limitations which restrict the rights of Indians under treaties must be narrowly construed ...

Fourth, the onus of proving that a treaty or aboriginal right has been extinguished lies upon the Crown. There must be "strict proof of the fact of extinguishment" and evidence of a clear and plain intention on the part of the government to extinguish treaty rights. [W.W.R. p. 474-475]

The court indicated that verbal promises were an important source of information in interpreting treaties.

In addition, when considering a treaty, a court must take into account the context in which the treaties were negotiated, concluded and committed to writing. The treaties, as written documents, recorded an agreement that had already been reached orally and they did not always record the full extent of the oral agreement ... As a result, it is well settled that the words in the treaty must not be interpreted in their strict technical sense nor subjected to rigid modern rules of construction. Rather, they must be interpreted in the sense that they would naturally have been understood by the Indians at the time of the signing. [W.W.R. p. 478]

The Indian people made their agreements orally and recorded their history orally. Thus, the verbal promises made on behalf of the federal government at the times the treaties were concluded are of great significance in their interpretation. [W.W.R. p. 479]

R. v. Howard, [1994] 2 S.C.R. 299, 18 O.R. (3d) 384n, [1994] 3 C.N.L.R. 146, 90 C.C.C. (3d) 131, 166 N.R. 282, 71 O.A.C. 278

The court found that fishing rights had been surrendered by the treaty, and observed, at (C.C.C.) p. 137:

The 1923 Treaty does not raise the same concerns as treaties signed in the more distant past or in more remote territories where one can legitimately question the understanding of the Indian parties ... The 1923 Treaty concerned lands in close proximity to the urbanized Ontario of the day. The Hiawatha signatories were businessmen, a civil servant and all were literate. In short, they were active participants of the economy and society of their province.

The treaty was valid even though it had not been ratified by an Order in Council from Canada.

Sioui v. Quebec (Attorney General), [1990] 1 S.C.R. 1025, 70 D.L.R. (4th) 427, [1990] 3 C.N.L.R. 127, 56 C.C.C. (3d) 225, 109 N.R. 22, 30 Q.A.C. 280

An agreement between the Hurons and General Murray in 1760 constitutes a treaty, both parties having had the intention to create mutually binding obligations. The treaty reads as follows:

These are to certify that the Chief of the Huron tribe of Indians, having come to me in the name of his Nation, to submit to His Britannick Majesty, and make Peace, has been received under my Protection, with his whole Tribe, and henceforth no English Officer or party is to molest, or interrupt them in returning to their Settlement at Lorette; and they are received upon the same terms with the Canadians, being allowed the free Exercise of their Religion, their Customs, and Liberty of trading with the English: — recommending it to the Officers commanding the Posts, to treat them kindly.

Given under my hand at Longueuil, this 5th day of September, 1760.

> By the Genl's Command,
> John Cosnan, Ja. Murray
> Adjut. Genl.

The treaty protects the exercise of Huron religion, and has not been extinguished by historical events. Non-user does not extinguish treaty rights. Cutting down trees, camping, and making fires in the exercise of Huron rites and customs was not incompatible with Crown occupancy of the land as a provincial park. These activities were therefore exempt from the application of provincial legislation.

> ... we can conclude from the historical documents that both Great Britain and France felt that the Indian nations had sufficient independence and played a large enough role in North America for it to be good policy to maintain relations with them very close to those maintained between sovereign nations.

> The mother countries did everything in their power to secure the alliance of each Indian nation and to encourage nations allied with the enemy to change sides. When these efforts met with success, they were incorporated in treaties of alliance or neutrality. This clearly indicates that the Indian nations were regarded in their relations with the European nations which occupied North America as independent nations. [C.N.L.R. p. 145]

(Note that this case was actually interpreting s. 88 of the *Indian Act*.)

R. v. Simon, [1985] 2 S.C.R. 387, 71 N.S.R. (2d) 15, 171 A.P.R. 15, 24 D.L.R. (4th) 390, [1986] 1 C.N.L.R. 153, 23 C.C.C. (3d) 238, 62 N.R. 366

Indian treaties are not the same as treaties between independent countries; they are *sui generis*. Section 88 of the *Indian Act* operates to exempt Indians from provincial legislation which restricts or contravenes treaty terms. Although a treaty right to hunt was not absolute, to be effective it had to include reasonably incidental activities such as travelling with the necessary equipment to the hunting grounds and possessing a hunting rifle and ammunition in a safe manner.

Nowegijik v. R., [1983] 1 S.C.R. 29, 144 D.L.R. (3d) 193, [19830 2 C.N.L.R. 89, [1983] C.T.C. 20, 83 D.T.C. 5041

> ... treaties and statutes relating to Indians should be liberally construed and doubtful expressions resolved in favour of the Indians ... In *Jones v. Meehan*, 175 U.S. 1 (1899), it was held that Indian treaties "must ... be construed, not according to the technical meaning of [their] words ... but in the sense in which they would naturally be understood by the Indians. [S.C.R. p. 36]

Beattie v. Canada (Minister of Indian Affairs & Northern Development) (1996), 119 F.T.R. 123

Mr. and Mrs. Beattie were members of the Fort Good Hope Indian Band which was covered by Treaty #11. However, they resided outside of the treaty area near the city of Merritt, British Columbia.

Treaty #11, signed in 1921, contained a provision addressing education which reads as follows:

> Further, His Majesty agrees to pay the salaries of teachers to instruct the children in such a manner as His Majesty's government may deem advisable.

The Beatties claimed tax deductions for education expenses for their children, and objected to paying school taxes in their district. The court held that the treaty provision only applied within the treaty area.

Mohawk Council of Akwesasne v. Canada (Minister of National Revenue), [1997] F.C.J. No. 882 (F.C.T.D.)

Akwesasne is a Mohawk reserve which straddles the Canada-U.S.A. border as well as the Ontario-Quebec border. In 1988, Chief Mike Mitchell crossed the border with one washing machine, 10 blankets, 20 Bibles, various articles of used clothing, one case of lubricating motor oil, 10 loaves of bread, two pounds of butter, four gallons of whole milk, six bags of cookies and 12 cans of soup. He told customs officials that these were gifts for a ceremonial dinner at the neighbouring Mohawk reserve of Tyendinaga to commemorate the renewal of trade ties with that community. Chief Mitchell refused to pay the duty of $361.64 claiming an Aboriginal right, and rights under the Jay Treaty.

Although the court found that an existing Aboriginal right exempted Mitchell from paying duty on those items, it did not find that the Jay Treaty was applicable. The court noted that legislation was necessary in order to implement international treaties, and no legislation has existed with respect to the Jay Treaty since 1824. The court also held that s. 35(1) of the *Constitution Act, 1982*, contemplated treaties between the Crown and Aboriginal peoples. It did not contemplate international treaties such as the Jay Treaty, signed between Canada and other states.

Treaty Rights — Alberta (For treaty hunting and fishing cases, see annotations under the Constitution Act, 1930)

R. v. Arcand, 95 A.R. 173, [1989] 3 W.W.R. 635, 65 Alta. L.R. (2d) 326, [1989] 2 C.N.L.R. 110 (Q.B.)

A right that is regulated to the point of unenforceability does not necessarily cease to exist; it is merely rendered dormant until the regulation is repealed or altered. Treaty No. 6 hunting rights exist and are protected by s. 35(1) against the *Migratory Birds Regulations* prohibiting hunting ducks out of season.

Treaty Rights — British Columbia

R. v. Little (1995), 131 D.L.R. (4th) 220, 16 B.C.L.R. (3d) 253, 103 C.C.C. (3d) 440 (C.A.)

The Douglas Treaty of 1854 provided that Indians of the Nanaimo Band were to have the "liberty ... to carry on fisheries as formerly." The court stated that the word fisheries "... may be used to denote not only the right to catch the fish but also the place where the right can be exercised". [D.L.R. at p. 236]

In this case, the individual was fishing for food with a gill net in his traditional fishing area. The area had been closed to salmon for conservation measures. There was no dispute that this was a *prima facie* infringement, and the court focused on justification. While conservation was a valid legislation objective, the court found that:

> In this case, the evidence called by the Crown ... does not support the conclusion that, after conservation, the Indian food fishing requirements were given priority over the commercial and sports fisheries. Instead, any aboriginal fishery in the fall chinook salmon run in the Nanaimo River was completely prohibited, although a different allocation to meet escapement targets would have permitted a limited and restricted aboriginal fishery on that run. [D.L.R. at p. 245]

Claxton v. Saanichton Marina Ltd., [1989] 3 C.N.L.R. 46, 36 B.C.L.R. (2d) 79, [1989] 5 W.W.R. 82, 57 D.L.R. (4th) 161 (C.A.)

The Tsawout Indian Band objected to the construction of a marina at Saanichton Bay on Vancouver Island. A treaty of 1852 recognized rights to a fishery which would have been interfered with if the marina had been constructed. The court prohibited the construction of the marina. Following *R. v. Simon*, the court held that the treaty right included incidental rights, including the right to travel to and from the fishery.

R. v. Bartleman (1984), 55 B.C.L.R. 78, [1984] 3 C.N.L.R. 114 (C.A.)

A member of the Tsarlip First Nation was hunting on private land outside of his treaty area, but within his traditional hunting area. The treaty relied upon in this case was the North Saanich Treaty of 1852. In attempting to interpret the treaty, the court took into consideration the "historical factual matrix" and the oral traditions. In this case, a blank sheet had been presented to the Indians at the time of making the treaty, to which the text of the treaty was added later, and it appeared that the names and the "x"'s were all made by the same individual.

The court held first, that the understandings of the Indians of the time was that hunting could occur on unoccupied land throughout their traditional territory (not just in the area covered by the treaty). Second, hunting was permitted on private land, but it must take place "on land that is unoccupied in the sense that the particular form of hunting that is being undertaken does not interfere with the actual use and enjoyment of the land by the owner or occupier." [C.N.L.R. p. 131]

Halfway River First Nation v. British Columbia (Ministry of Forests, [1997] B.C.J. No. 1494 (B.C. S.C.)

A District Manager of the Ministry of Forests gave a permit to a forestry company, Canfor, to cut trees on land which was the subject of a claim under Treaty #8. The First Nation challenged the decision of the District Manager.

One of the arguments made by the forestry company was that according to Treaty #8, hunting and fishing rights were only recognized on land which was not "required, or taken up from time to time for settlement, lumbering, trading or other purposes." As the permit served to "take up the land", there were no treaty rights. The court rejected this contention, saying

> this submission is not compatible with the statements made in the Report of the Commissioners, considered by Cory J in *Badger*, supra, to be relevant to the interpretation of Treaty 8 rights. These statements suggest that any interference with the right to hunt, fish or trap constitutes a *prima facie* infringement of Treaty 8 rights. [para. 101]

The court concluded, therefore, that there was an infringement of a treaty right. This infringement could not be justified because there had not been any consultation with the First Nation.

R. v. Ellsworth, [1992] 4 C.N.L.R. 89 (B.C. S.C.)

While Indian treaty rights do not entitle native Indians to fish unencumbered by regulation, any such regulation must be consistent with those rights. The allocation of priorities after valid conservation provisions have been implemented must give precedence to Indian food fishing, at the expense of the sport and commercial fisheries. The availabilty to natives of licences to fish another species of fish is not relevant in weighing the effect of the regulation.

R. v. Wolfe, [1997] 1 C.N.L.R. 171 (B.C.Prov.Ct.)

Frank Wolfe was 63 years old. He had rights to hunt under Treaty #3 in Ontario, and hunted to provide food for his family of 14 children. His health was deteriorating and he moved to British Columbia to live with one of his daughters. His daughter's husband was not a registered Indian, but had a trapline in the Treaty #8 territory. Wolfe killed an elk and two deer for food while trapping with his son in law. Wolfe was acquitted of charges under the provincial *Wildlife Act*.

R. v. Hunt, [1995] 3 C.N.L.R. 135 (B.C. Prov. Ct.)

Salmon were caught and sold by the Kwakiutl First Nation and the money used for a Native Brotherhood convention. The court found that the Douglas Treaties did not protect the commercial fishery, even if the proceeds were used for community purposes.

Treaty Rights — Manitoba (For treaty hunting and fishing cases, see annotations under the Constitution Act, 1930)

R. v. Flett, [1989] 6 W.W.R. 166, 60 Man. R. (2d) 294, [1989] 4 C.N.L.R. 128 (Q.B.)leave to appeal C.A. refused [1990] 5 W.W.R. lxxn, 68 Man. R. (2d) 159, [1990] 4 C.N.L.R. vin (C.A.)

When interpreting treaty rights one must look at the right as stated in the original treaty unless the right has been extinguished. The *Migratory Birds Convention Act* ("MBCA") did not extinguish Treaty No. 5 hunting rights. S. 35(1) therefore protects those rights against the MBCA's prohibition on hunting Canada geese out of season.

Treaty Rights — New Brunswick

R. v. Paul (1993), 110 D.L.R. (4th) 382, 142 N.B.R. (2d) 55, 364 A.P.R. 55, [1994] 2 C.N.L.R. 167 (C.A.)*R. v. McCoy* (1993), 109 D.L.R. (4th) 433, 141 N.B.R. (2d) 185, 361 A.P.R. 185, [1994] 2 C.N.L.R. 129 (C.A.)

Treaty rights exercised in an unsafe manner were not exempt from the application of provincial law.

R. v. Paul, [1997] N.B.J. No. 439 (Q.B.)

Paul was a Micmac resident on the Papineau Reserve. He was charged under a provincial statute with taking logs from Crown land without a license. Paul hoped to sell the bird's eye maple for $1,000 -

$3,000. The trees were in an area covered by a provincial license granted to Stone Consolidated (Canada) Inc.

The court held that the Dummer's Treaty of 1725-1726 did not cede Indian land to the English. Rather, the treaty confirmed land rights and rights to harvest trees by Micmacs in New Brunswick. The land and harvesting rights are not exclusive, but the judge holds:

> I am of the opinion the Indians in New Brunswick can harvest any and all trees they wish on Crown lands as an appurtenance of their land rights under Dummer's Treaty. [para. 20]

Paul was acquitted.

R. v. Pelletier, [1996] N.B.J. No. 181 (Q.B.)

Two Maliseets were acquitted of fishing on a portion of the Restigouche River which flowed beside lands which had been granted to a private individual by a Crown grant. The Crown had argued that the private individual had been granted rights to the middle of the river. The court held that a grant from the Crown extended to the middle of non-tidal rivers. Since the Crown failed to prove that this was a non-tidal river, the Crown failed to prove that the grant extended to the middle of the river. Consequently, the treaty rights to fish had not been extinguished.

R. v. Fullerton (1996), 182 N.B.R. (2d) 138, 463 A.P.R. 138 (Prov. Ct.)

Fullerton was charged under a provincial law for taking a Bird's Eye Maple logs without a license. He went to cut the maple with three Maliseet who were not charged. Fullerton was not native, although he was married to a native woman from the reserve. The court found that Fullerton could not benefit from any treaty rights, and was convicted. (See *R. v. Paul* above for a related case)

R. v. Fowler, [1993] 3 C.N.L.R. 178, 134 N.B.R. (2d) 361, 342 A.P.R. 361 (Prov. Ct.)

The accused was not a registered Indian, but could show ancestry to treaty signatories. The court found that he was protected by the treaty.

Treaty Rights — Northwest Territories

R. v. Noel, [1995] 4 C.N.L.R. 78 (N.W.T. Terr. Ct.)

A member of the Yellowknives Dene Band was charged with hunting in a year round no-hunting zone. He was covered by Treaty #8. The court found that there had been a *prima facie* infringement which was not justified because "... there were other alternatives available that were either considered and rejected or just rejected out of hand."

Treaty Rights — Nova Scotia

R. v. Marshall (1997), 146 D.L.R. (4th) 257, [1997] 3 C.N.L.R. 209 (N.S. C.A.)

Donald Marshall was charged with catching eels and selling them without a license. He was a Mi'kmaq member of the Membertou reserve. He claimed protection of treaties signed in 1760–61, and in particular the following "truck house" clause contained in the treaty.

> And I do further engage that we will not traffic, barter or Exchange any Commodities in any manner but with such persons or the managers of such Truck houses as shall be appointed or Established by His Majesty's Governor at Lunenbourg or Elsewhere in Nova Scotia or Accadia.

The court interpreted this clause to say that the treaty required the Mi'kmaq to trade only at British truck houses; but the treaty did not recognize a general right of Mi'kmaq to trade without regulation. Marshall's conviction was upheld on the appeal.

Treaty Rights — Ontario

R. v. Fox, [1994] 3 C.N.L.R. 132, 71 O.A.C. 50 (C.A.)

The accused was charged with wrongfully discharging a firearm, contrary to Ontario's *Game and Fish Act*. Both sides agreed that this provision infringed a right to hunt under Treaty No. 9. However, the

Crown argued that the provision was justified for safety reasons. The court dismissed the Crown's argument pointing out that disabled persons could be allowed to shoot from moving motor boats, so that the provision could not be related to safety.

R. v. Vincent, 12 O.R. (3d) 397 (Fr.), 12 O.R. (3d) 427 (Eng.), [1993] 2 C.N.L.R. 165, 80 C.C.C. (3d) 256, 61 O.A.C. 371 (C.A.)leave to appeal to S.C.C. refused, 15 O.R. (3d) xvin, [1994] 4 C.N.L.R. vin 83 C.C.C. (3d) viin, 163 N.R. 239n, 68 O.A.C. 239n (S.C.C.)

"Treaty rights" refers to rights that belong to Aboriginal peoples and which stem from treaties concluded with Aboriginal peoples. The Jay Treaty is an international treaty, and cannot confer rights on an individual or group of individuals. It is not a treaty within the meaning of s. 35(1) of the *Constitution Act, 1982*, and does not confer a right to import commercial goods duty free. If it were a treaty within the meaning of s. 35(1), any rights contained therein were probably extinguished before April 17, 1982.

R. v. Agawa, 65 O.R. (2d) 505, 53 D.L.R. (4th) 101, [1988] 3 C.N.L.R. 73, 43 C.C.C. (3d) 266 (C.A.)

The treaty fishing right included commercial fishing. However, a commercial licensing scheme serves a valid conservation purpose and constitutes a reasonable limit on the band's treaty right to fish, and therefore does not infringe s. 35(1).

R. v. Corbiere (1996), 38 C.R.R. (2d) 155 (Ont. Gen. Div.)

The accused were members of the West Bay First Nation. They had hunting and fishing rights on Manitoulin Island under the Bond Head Treaty of 1836.

The accused were charged after hunting at night on a private property. The court found that the accused had failed to provide evidence supporting a treaty right to hunt at night, and they were convicted. In the course of his reasons, the judge commented that when there were safety and conservation concerns, the burden should be on the Crown to justify infringements to treaty or Aboriginal rights in the second stage of the *Sparrow* test. In other words, conservation and safety concerns do not automatically mean that there is no infringement.

> I have grave doubts that where a regulation or a provision in a statute is directed solely to conservation or has both a conservation and safety component that fact alone will nullify an aboriginal right at the infringement stage. In my view legislation that has both a public safety and conservation component is more appropriately left to be dealt with during the justification analysis. Most laws with a public safety and conservation component will be found to be reasonable at the initial stage. It is during the justification analysis that the entire statute is looked at to determined whether aboriginal priority has been considered and whether, if public safety is the issue, there has been as little infringement of the aboriginal right as possible. On the other hand laws directed solely at public safety, such as careless hunting, will usually be found to be constitutional. [C.R.R. p. 183]

The accused were also charged with angling during spawning season for rainbow trout. The judge fond that the accused failed to establish that there was a right to fish during that season, and noted that the Chief of the First Nation agreed to the laying of the charges. The accused were convicted on these charges as well.

R. v. Pine, [1997] O.J. No. 1004 (Ont. Gen. Div.)

Darwin Pine was a member of the Garden River First Nation. He was charged with taking three fish for food from the Bar River Fish Sanctuary, contrary to the federal *Fisheries Act*. The existence of the Sanctuary, which was established to protect walleye, was supported by the Chief of the First Nation.

The court found that this case was not about allocation, because all fishing was prohibited. Moreover, it was agreed that if conservation efforts were successful, top priority would be given to the Indian food fishery. In this case, the regulation was justified on grounds of conservation, and Pine was convicted.

Chippewas of Kettle & Stony Point v. M.M. Dillon Ltd., [1996] 1 C.N.L.R. 99 (Ont. Gen. Div.)

A reserve established under Treaty No. 29 of 1827 could be appropriated under the *War Measures Act*.

R. v. Chevrier (1988), [1989] 1 C.N.L.R. 128 (Ont. Dist. Ct.)

The accused was not a registered Indian, and was charged with a hunting offence under provincial stat-ute. The judge found that he had ancestors who were signatories to the Robinson-Superior Treaty, and therefore had treaty rights to hunt.

R. v. Buckner, [1997] O.J. No. 1165 (Ont. Prov. Div.)

The accused lived in the Treaty #3 area in northwestern Ontario, but his Aboriginal lineage orginated from Micmacs in New Brunswick. He had a membership card from the Metis Nation of Ontario which defined a Metis as:

> Anyone of aboriginal ancestry who self-identifies as Métis; is distinct from Indian or Inuit; has at least one grandparent who is aboriginal and who is accepted by the Métis Nation of Ontario.

The court accepted that Buckner was a Metis and found that he had the benefit of the "Half-breed Adhesion" to Treaty #3, which provided for hunting and fishing rights. He was acquitted of the charge of hunting moose without a license.

R. v. Machimity, [1996] O.J. No. 4365 (Ont. Prov. Div.)

Ed Machimity was a member of the Ojibway Nation of Saugeen covered by Treaty #3, which provided that the Indians

> ... shall have the right to pursue their avocations of hunting and fishing throughout the tract surrendered as hereinbefore described .. saving and excepting such tracts as may, from time to time, be required or taken up for settlement, mining, lumbering or other purposes by Her said Government of the Dominion of Canada, or by any of the subjects thereof duly authorized therefor by the said Government.

He was charged after shooting at a moose decoy at night from the shoulder of the highway.

The Crown argued that the shoulder of the highway was land "taken up" and therefore, no treaty rights could be exercised on that land. The court found that the non-natives were allowed to shoot from the shoulder of the highway, and that "the hunting rights guaranteed in Treaty No. #3 must at least give the defendant equal hunting rights to non-Indians".

With respect to the night hunting, the Crown argued that it was inherently dangerous and should not be protected by the treaty. The court found that the Ontario regulations allow night hunting by non-natives under some circumstances. Consequently, the issue was not whether the hunting occurred at night, but whether, in the particular instance, hunting was carried on in a safe manner. On the facts of this case, the court held that safety was not an issue.

Chief Machimity was acquitted.

R. v. Jones, 14 O.R. (3d) 421, [1993] 3 C.N.L.R. 182 (Prov. Div.)

See discussion of this case above under "Aboriginal Rights".

R. v. Major, [1993] 1 C.N.L.R. 131 (Ont. Prov. Div.)

A registered Indian who was hunting co-operatively with non-Indians was acquitted of violating provin-cial law.

R. v. Jackson, [1992] 4 C.N.L.R. 121 (Ont. Prov. Div.)

A 1979 fishing limit imposed by the Ontario Ministry of Natural Resources did not apply to members of an Indian band accused of fishing with a gill net without a licence, and failing to return fish caught without a licence. The accused's rights to fish were preserved by the Royal Proclamation of 1763, the Treaty of 1827, and s. 35 of the *Constitution Act*. There was no formal recognition, acknowledgment or consent by or on behalf of the band to the fishing limits, and the boundaries imposed were arbitrary.

Treaty Rights — Quebec

Quebec (Deputy Minister of Revenue) v. Sioui (1996), 142 D.L.R. (4th) 742 (Que.C.A.)

A member of the Lorette Huron Band had a commercial business on the Lorette reserve. He refused to collect provincial taxes, and the Quebec government applied for an injunction to close his business. One of his defences was that the Murray Treaty of 1760 guaranteed the Hurons autonomy in their own territory, so that he was not under an obligation to collect taxes for the Quebec government. He relied on the statement in the treaty which allowed the Hurons free exercise of their "customs" (See *R. v. Sioui* above, for text of the treaty).

The court of appeal upheld the conviction at trial, saying that "customs" only referred to a way of life, cultural habits, traditional hunting or fishing, etc.

Treaty Rights — Saskatchewan (For treaty hunting and fishing cases, see annotations under the Constitution Act, 1930)

R. v. Poitras, [1994] 7 W.W.R. 686, [1994] 3 C.N.L.R. 157 (Sask. Q.B.)

Treaty No. 4 does not contain a provision which would result in an exemption from customs and excise tax. Members of the Peepeekisis Band were convicted of selling tobacco illegally.

Fiduciary Duty

Delgamuukw v. British Columbia (December 11, 1997), Doc. 23799 (S.C.C.)

In this case, we see the strongest statement to come out of the Supreme Court on the duty of the Crown to negotiate in good faith.

> ... the Crown is under a moral, if not a legal, duty to enter into and conduct those negotiations in good faith. Ultimately, it is through negotiated settlements, with good faith and give and take on all sides, reinforced by the judgments of this Court, that we will achieve what I stated in *Van der Peet*, ... to be a basic purpose of s. 35(1) — "the reconciliation of the pre-existence of aboriginal societies with the sovereignty of the Crown". Let us face it, we are all here to stay. [para. 186]

R. v. Adams, [1996] 4 C.N.L.R. 1, 202 N.R. 89, 138 D.L.R. (4th) 657, 110 C.C.C. (3d) 97 (S.C.C.)

George Adams is a Mohawk living on Akwesasne Territory. He was fishing during the spawning season in a marsh on the St. Lawrence River. He caught perch with a seine net made of fine mesh, several hundred feet in length. He did not have a license under the federal *Fisheries Act*. Adams argued that he had an Aboriginal right to fish in that area.

In this case, the *Quebec Fisheries Regulations*, made under the *Fisheries Act*, provided that the Minister, at his discretion, could provide a special permit to fish for subsistence to an individual Indian or Inuk. The court found that such a wide discretionary power infringed the Aboriginal right.

> In light of the Crown's unique fiduciary obligations towards aboriginal peoples, Parliament may not simply adopt an unstructured discretionary administrative regime which risks infringing aboriginal rights in a substantial number of applications in the absence of some explicit guidance. If a statute confers an administrative discretion which may carry significant consequences for the exercise of an aboriginal right, the statute or its delegate regulations must outline specific criteria for the granting or refusal of that discretion which seek to accommodate the existence of aboriginal rights. In the absence of such specific guidance, the statute will fail to provide representatives of the Crown with sufficient directives to fulfil their fiduciary duties, and the statute will be found to represent an infringement of aboriginal rights under the *Sparrow* test. [C.N.L.R. p. 21]

R. v. Lewis, [1996] 5 W.W.R. 348, 19 B.C.L.R. (3d) 244, 105 C.C.C. (3d) 523, 133 D.L.R. (4th) 700, 196 N.R. 165, [1996] 1 S.C.R. 921, [1996] 3 C.N.L.R. 131

The First Nation argued that the Crown had a fiduciary duty to set secure access to the fishery in the Squamish River. The court held that, if there were a fiduciary duty, which was not decided, any obligation had been honoured by providing fishing stations for access to the river. (S.C.R. at para. 52)

Blueberry River Indian Band v. Canada (Department of Indian Affairs & Northern Development) (1995), 130 D.L.R. (4th) 193, [1995] 4 S.C.R. 344, 190 N.R. 89, 102 F.T.R. 160(n) (S.C.C.)

Indian Affairs had a duty, after a surrender of reserve lands, to act in the best interests of the Band. The usual Department practice at the time of the surrender was to lease mineral rights for the benefit of the Band. In this case, however, without any mandate from the band, the land was sold to the Department of Veteran's Affairs. The court found that there was a breach of a fiduciary duty when the mineral rights were sold rather than being leased.

Quebec (Attorney General) v. Canada (National Energy Board), [1994] 1 S.C.R. 159, 112 D.L.R. (4th) 129, [1994] 3 C.N.L.R. 49, 14 C.E.L.R. (N.S.) 1, 163 N.R. 241 (S.C.C.)

The National Energy Board, in its quasi-judicial function, does not owe a fiduciary duty to the Grand Council of the Crees of Quebec. (Any possible impact of provisions of the James Bay and Northern Quebec Agreement were not considered in this proceeding.)

R. v. Sparrow, [1990] 3 C.N.L.R. 160, [1990] 1 S.C.R. 1075, 70 D.L.R. (4th) 385

This is a leading case on the fiduciary duty of the Crown to Aboriginal peoples. The duty extends to the enactment of legislation, requiring the Crown to justify laws which infringe existing Aboriginal and treaty rights. (For a description of the test, see the heading "Infringement and justification — General Principles — Canada" in the annotations under section 35(1) of the *Constitution Act, 1982*). The court made this general statement of the fiduciary relationship.

> ... the Government has the responsibility to act in a fiduciary capacity with respect to aboriginal peoples. The relationship between the Government and aboriginals is trust-like, rather than adversarial, and contemporary recognition and affirmation of aboriginal rights must be defined in light of this historic relationship. [C.N.L.R. p. 180]

Guerin v. R., [1984] 2 S.C.R. 335, [1984] 6 W.W.R. 481, [1985] 1 C.N.L.R. 120

In this case, the agents of the federal government obtained a surrender from the Musqueam Band. The Crown then leased the land to a golf club at terms which were unfavourable to the Band and which were counter to the instructions of the Band. The court found that there was a breach of fiduciary duty, and ordered damages of $10 million against the federal Crown. Dickson, C.J., commented on the relationship of the surrender provisions to the fiduciary duty. (See more quotes from this decision under section 18 of the *Indian Act*.)

> The fiduciary relationship between the Crown and the Indians has its roots in the concept of aboriginal, native or Indian title. The fact that Indian Bands have a certain interest in lands does not, however, in itself give rise to a fiduciary relationship between the Indians and the Crown. The conclusion that the Crown is a fiduciary depends upon the further proposition that the Indian interest in the land is inalienable except upon surrender to the Crown. [S.C.R. at p. 376] (Note that this case was decided without reference to section 35(1))

Samson Indian Band v. Canada, [1997] F.C.J. No. 1449 (Fed. C.A.)

The Enoch Band, the Samson Band and the Ermineskin Band brought an action against the federal government relating to the management of lands surrendered in the 1940's. As part of the litigation, the Bands sought disclosure of legal advice obtained by the Crown relating to the matters in dispute. The Court of Appeal approved the disclosure related to the Crown's role as trustee, and cited with approval the following statement made by the trial judge:

> That production will treat the plaintiff bands and nations much like beneficiaries of a private trust, entitled to access to legal advice obtained by the Crown as "trustee". This is because, as beneficiaries of a variation of a trust in Indian land, the plaintiffs share an interest in that advice with the Crown, which is responsible for administration and management of the mineral assets and revenues therefrom for the benefit exclusively of the plaintiff bands and nations. [para. 24]

Semiahmoo Indian Band v. Canada (1997), 148 D.L.R. (4th) 523, 215 N.R. 241 (Fed. C.A.)

The reserve of the Semiahmoo First Nation is located near the border between British Columbia and the United States. In 1951, the federal government requested that the Band surrender 22.4 acres of its 382 acre reserve. The Band reluctantly voted for an absolute surrender knowing that the government could expropriate the land (as it had done previously with a different parcel of the reserve). The land was never developed, and no plans were made for use of the land until 1992 after the Band began a court case.

The court held that there had been a breach of a pre-surrender fiduciary duty by the Crown in 1951, because of the failure to ensure that the land was going to be used for a public purpose. Although a claim for this breach of fiduciary duty was barred by the British Columbia limitation period, there were two breaches of two other post-surrender fiduciary duties.

First, the Crown should have made the surrender conditional, or at least provide for a reversionary interest once the land was no longer needed for public purposes. The Crown failed to correct this error after the surrender, and so breached its fiduciary duty.

Second, in 1969, when the Band asked for return of the land, the Crown should have returned the land because it had not been used.

Begetikong Anishnabe v. Canada (Minister of Indian Affairs & Northern Development), [1997] F.C.J. No. 1434 (T.D.)

The Begetikong Anishnabe (also known as the Ojibways of Pic River) received a letter from the Minister of Indian Affairs denying their land claim. The First National argued that there was a fiduciary duty on the part of the Crown to make available the legal opinion on which the decision of the Minister was based. The Trial Division found that there was no fiduciary duty which would compel the Crown to disclose the opinion. [Note that this decision was made before the decision of the Federal Court of Appeal in *Samson Indian Band v. Canada*, above.]

Chippewas of Nawash First Nation v. Canada (Minister of Indian & Northern Affairs), [1997] 1 C.N.L.R. 1, 41 Admin. L.R. (2d) 232, 116 F.T.R. 37 (T.D.)

The federal government, pursuant to the *Access to Information Act*, proposed to release two Band Council Resolutions (B.C.R.'s) from the First Nation to an individual. The B.C.R.'s dealt with a federal Bill which would have changed the land regime under the *Indian Act*. The First Nation objected to the release of the information. The court rejected the First Nation's arguments based on a breach of fiduciary duty, and on a breach of s. 15 of the *Charter of Rights and Freedoms*.

On the issue of the fiduciary duty, the court held that the federal duty did not extend to keeping Band Council resolutions secret.

Halfway River First Nation v. British Columbia (Ministry of Forests), [1997] B.C.J. No. 1494 (B.C. S.C.)

A District Manager of the Ministry of Forests permitted a forestry company, Canfor to cut trees on land which was the subject of a claim under Treaty 8. The court overturned the decision of the District Manager.

The provincial Crown had a fiduciary duty to consult with the Band, and in this case, failed to make all reasonable efforts to fully inform itself respecting Aboriginal and treaty rights in the region.

> ... the Crown has an obligation to undertake reasonable consultation with a First Nation which may be affected by its decision. In order for the Crown to consult reasonably, it must fully inform itself of the practices and of the views of the Nation affected. In so doing, it must ensure that the group affected is provided with full information with respect to the proposed legislation or decision and its potential impact on aboriginal rights. [para. 133]

R. v. Seward, [1997] 1 C.N.L.R. 139 (B.C. Prov. Ct.), reversed on other grounds [1997] B.C.J. No. 1691 (B.C. S.C.)

The judge in this case commented on the adversarial position taken by the Crown Attorney.

> I consider the Crown position in contesting that the Penelakut Band constituted an organized society at the time of the assertion of British sovereignty to be egregious and opportunistic, and not in strict keeping with its obligation to take a trust-like approach as opposed to an adversarial approach. If the Crown is going to take the position that selected tribes must prove that they constituted an organized society in 1846, the Indian tribes that will suffer are those that have not been litigious in the past or near future, because clearly it will become more and more difficult to prove that fact as time goes by and the memories of the elders are not available to assist us. [C.N.L.R. p. 143]

R. v. Jones, 14 O.R. (3d) 421, [1993] 3 C.N.L.R. 182 (Prov.Div.)

The judge in this case found that the Ministry of Natural Resources favoured sports fishermen over the subsistence requirements of the members of the First Nation.

> What should be stated, however, is that a high-handed and adversarial stance on the part of the Ministry [of Natural Resources] will neither meet the constitutional requirements with which, one would expect, it would consider itself duty-bound to comply, nor will it provide an enforceable regulatory scheme capable of achieving the conservation goals which it seeks. It is self-evident, I think, that s. 35(1) of the *Constitution Act, 1982*, particularly after the judgment of the Supreme Court of Canada in *Sparrow*, dictated that a new approach be taken by the government to ensure that its policies discharge the obligations assumed by its constitutional agreement. I do not think it was ever suggested that there would necessarily be no adjustments required or no costs attached. [C.N.L.R. p. 208]

R. v. Jackson, [1992] 4 C.N.L.R (Ont. Prov. Div.)

Members of the Kettle Point First Nation who were fishing were arrested one morning by three boatfuls of law enforcement officers carrying sidearms and shotguns, and charged with fishing offences. When the case went to court, the judge found that the province had created arbitrary boundaries for Aboriginal fishing and that there was no evidence to support the conclusion that the accused people were fishing for commercial purposes. All the accused were acquitted.

> In my judgment, the time has long since passed when the Crown should seek to determine its relationship by way of regulation of Indian fishing and hunting rights through the use of the courts, particularly in the manner utilized in this case. Surely the matter of receiving a complaint from the Bluewater Angler's Association, entering upon an investigation of such complaint to the extent of conscripting members of the Ontario Provincial Police, officers of the Department of Natural Resources of the State of Michigan, together with officers of the Ministry of Natural Resources, organizing a pre-dawn raid with boats pursuing and intercepting persons engaged in fishing activities, approaching with guns drawn and boarding and seizing the nets and gear scarely can be construed as an activity in which the government's relationship is trust-like rather than adversarial.

> Surely the honour of the Crown in so proceeding is not much in evidence. In that sense I would echo the observation of counsel for the accused, "we are here for all the wrong reasons, we should not be doing what we are doing, the way we are doing it." [C.N.L.R. p. 138]

Metis rights

Metis rights — Canada

R. v. Vanderpeet, [1996] 2 S.C.R. 507, [1996] 2 C.N.L.R. 177, 23 B.C.L.R. (3d) 1, 50 C.R. (4th) 1, [1996] 9 W.W.R. 1, 109 C.C.C. (3d) 1, 137 D.L.R. (4th) 289, 200 N.R. 1, 85 B.C.A.C. 81, 130 W.A.C. 81 (S.C.C.)application for re-hearing refused (January 16, 1997), Doc. 23803 (S.C.C.)

Mr. Justice Lamer indicated that Metis rights may be considered on a different basis from Indian rights.

Although s. 35 includes the Métis within its definition of "aboriginal peoples of Canada", and thus seems to link their claims to those of other aboriginal peoples under the general heading of "aboriginal rights", the history of Métis, and the reasons underlying their inclusion in the protection given by s. 35, are quite distinct from those of other aboriginal peoples in Canada. As such, the manner in which the aboriginal rights of other aboriginal peoples are defined is not necessarily determinative of the manner in which the aboriginal rights of the Métis are defined. At the time when this Court is presented with a Métis claim under s. 35 it will then, with the benefit of the arguments of counsel, a factual context and a specific Métis claim, be able to explore the question of the purposes underlying s. 35's protection of the aboriginal rights of Métis people, and answer the question of the kinds of claims which fall within s. 35(1)'s scope when the claimants are Métis. The fact that, for other aboriginal peoples, the protection granted by s. 35 goes to the practices, customs and traditions of aboriginal peoples prior to contact, is not necessarily relevant to the answer which will be given to that question. It may, or it may not, be the case that the claims of the Métis are determined on the basis of the pre-contact practices, traditions and customs of their aboriginal ancestors; whether that is so must await determination in a case in which the issue arises. [S.C.R. p. 558]

Metis rights — Alberta

R. v. Desjarlais, [1996] 3 C.N.L.R. 113 (Alta. Q.B.)

Louise Desjarlais had relatives staying with her. She asked Kenneth Desjarlais and Frank Willier to bring back some game for the family. Kenneth was her natural born son. Frank Willier had lived with her since he was seven months old. Kenneth and Frank went hunting and succeeded in shooting a deer. Because neither of them were registered as Indians under the *Indian Act*, they were charged with hunting out of season.

The court found that the reference to "Indians" in s. 12 of the NRTA should be defined in reference to the *Indian Act* of 1927, which included "a person of Indian blood. ... who follows the Indian mode of life." (R.S.C. 1927,c.98,s.2(h)).

In this case, the judge rejected the Crown's contention that the individual must be of "predominantly Indian ancestry." He accepted that Kenneth, who was descended from Crees and Scots, had sufficient ancestry. Kenneth also passed the second part of the test — following an "Indian mode of life". He spoke Cree, learned to hunt with his father, described Indians as his own people, and hunted for food. The judge rejected the Crown's argument that "hunting, fishing and trapping has to play a significant role on an ongoing basis in order for a person to quality." [C.N.L.R. p. 119]

On the other hand, the judge found that Frank did not have evidence of sufficient ancestry. There was no information on his natural mother; and, although his natural father had lived on the Sucker Creek Indian Reserve, there was no evidence that his natural father was an Indian. The judge noted that Frank had not been formally adopted into the Desjarlais family.

R. v. Ferguson (1993), [1994] 1 C.N.L.R. 117 (Alta. Q.B.)

By virtue of his "Indian mode of life", Ferguson was a "non-treaty Indian" within the meaning of the *Indian Act*, 1927, and was therefore included in the term "Indian" in paragraph 12 of the Natural Resources Transfer Agreement, 1930. Without clear legislative disentitlement criteria, status as a "non-treaty Indian" and consequent hunting rights should not be jeopardized by casual or intermittent non-traditional pursuits.

Metis rights — Manitoba

R. v. McPherson, [1994] 2 C.N.L.R. 137, [1994] 2 W.W.R. 761, 111 D.L.R. (4th) 278, 90 Man. R. (2d) 290 (Q.B.)

The hunters charged were Metis. Provincial regulations which unjustifiably infringe an Aboriginal right should be read down so as not to apply to Aboriginal persons and to preserve their rights. The court did not overturn an acquittal at trial, based on the finding that the Metis had a common law right to hunt moose out of season.

R. v. Blais, [1996] M.J. No. 391 (Man. Prov. Ct.)

The accused Metis were convicted of hunting in southern Manitoba, in violation of the provincial *Wildlife Act*. The judge held that, among other things, the word "Indians" in the Manitoba NRTA did not include Metis.

The question of whether these individuals were Metis was not at issue. However, the court commented that an appropriate definition might be taken from the wording of the Metis Nation Accord which was accepted by federal, provincial and Aboriginal leaders in 1992 as part of the larger constitutional amendment agreement package referred to as the Charlottetown Accord. Although the Charlottetown Accord was rejected in a national referendum, and was not legally binding, the judge felt that the following definition contained in the Metis Nation Accord should be pursuasive as a political definition leaders in 1992 as part of the larger constitutional amendment agreement referred to as the Charlottetown Accord. Although the Charlottetown Accord was rejected in a national referendum, and was not legally binding, the judge felt that the following definition contained in the Metis Nation Accord should be persuasive as a political answer to a political question.

> For the purposes of the Metis nation and this Accord:
>
> > (a) Metis means an aboriginal person who self-identifies as Metis who is distinct from Indian and Inuit and is a descendant of those Metis who received or were entitled to receive land grants and/or Scrip under the provisions of the *Manitoba Act 1870* or the *Dominion Lands Act* as enacted from time to time. [para.26]

Metis rights — New Brunswick

R. v. Fowler, [1993] 3 C.N.L.R. 178, 134 N.B.R. (2d) 361, 342 A.P.R. 361 (Prov. Ct.)

The accused was not a registered Indian, but could show ancestry to treaty signatories. The court found that he was protected by the treaty.

Metis rights — Ontario

R. v. Perry, [1997] O.J. No. 2314 (O.C.A.)

Ontario had developed an Interim Enforcement Policy which provided guidance on the laying of hunting and fishing charges against registered Indians. A native person who was not registered under the *Indian Act* challenged this Policy as being discriminatory. Before the trial proceedings were completed, the provincial government withdrew the Interim Enforcement Policy completely. The trial judge ordered, among other things, that the Policy be reinstated to include Metis and non-status Indians, and that the province enter into negotiations with these peoples.

The Ontario Court of Appeal overturned this decision. They held that the Policy could be withdrawn any time without consultation with the Aboriginal people. They also held that the fact that Metis and non-status Indians were treated differently than registered Indians was not a violation of s. 15 of the *Charter of Rights and Freedoms*.

Lovelace v. Ontario, [1997] O.J. No. 2313 (O.C.A.)

The province of Ontario entered into negotiations with First Nations in the province to establish a casino on reserve, and share the proceeds among all of the First Nations. Applicants representing Metis and other Bands not recognized under the *Indian Act* commenced proceedings claiming a portion of the proceeds. At the trial stage, the judge found that there was discrimination under s. 15.

The Court of Appeal overturned the trial decision, finding that the scheme was validly established under s. 15(2). The court held that the objective of the section was not to benefit all Aboriginal peoples: it was only to benefit First Nations recognized under the *Indian Act*.

R. v. Buckner, [1997] O.J. No. 1165 (Prov.Ct.)

The accused lived in the Treaty #3 area in northwestern Ontario, but his aboriginal lineage originated from Micmacs in New Brunswick. He had a membership card from the Metis Nation of Ontario which defined a Metis as:

> Anyone of aboriginal ancestry who self-identifies as Métis; is distinct from Indian or Inuit; has at least one grandparent who is aboriginal and who is accepted by the Métis Nation of Ontario.

The court accepted that Buckner was a Metis and found that he had the benefit of the "Half-breed Adhesion" to Treaty #3, which provided for hunting and fishing rights. He was acquitted of the charge of hunting moose without a license.

R. v. Chevrier (1988), [1989] 1 C.N.L.R. 128 (Ont. Dist. Ct.)

The accused was not a registered Indian, and was charged with a hunting offence under provincial statute. The judge found that he had ancestors who were signatories to the Robinson-Superior Treaty, and therefore had treaty rights to hunt.

Metis rights — Saskatchewan

R. v. Morin, [1997] S.J. No. 529 (Sask. Q.B.)

The two accused were Métis who were ice fishing without a license. The trial judge found that the Métis people in northwest Saskatchewan continued to live "as a community and basically off the land as they have since the early 1800's."

The Queen's bench upheld the trial judge's finding that scrip did not result in the extinguishment of the right to hunt and fish. The court did not have to decide whether scrip resulted in the surrender of aboriginal title.

The Queen's Bench found that there was an existing Aboriginal right to hunt and fish. These Metis rights were infringed in three ways. First, the license for domestic fishing issued was discretionary, and was invalid for the same reason that a discretionary fishing license was found to be invalid by the Supreme Court of Canada in *R. v. Adams*. Second, the $5 fee, which did not apply to Indians, was a hardship.

And third, the court found that a provincial policy which gave preferential treatment to status Indians over Metis was an infringement of Metis rights.

> In any one situation, Metis persons could be denied the right to fish for food in the interests of conservation while treaty Indian persons might continue to fish. As noted above, there is no basis to distinguish between Indian and Metis aboriginal groups with respect to the right to fish for food. [para. 58]

R. v. Grumbo, [1996] 3 C.N.L.R. 122 (Sask.Q.B.)

John Grumbo was born in a tent at the Crescent Lake Metis Village in 1937. He trapped for a living since he was 12 or 13, and spoke Michif, English, Cree, Saulteaux, and French. He received a deer from his nephew Ken Pelltier, a registered Indian, and another deer from Debbie Pelltier who was also a registered Indian. Grumbo is not a registered Indian, and he was charged for having the deer, contrary to Saskatchewan's *Wildlife Act, 1979* which defined "Indian" as an individual registered under the *Indian Act*.

The court held that "Indian" under s. 12 of Saskatchewan's NRTA contemplated the same groups as "Indians" under s. 91(24) of the *Constitution Act, 1867*. The provincial Crown in this case conceded that Metis were "Indians" within s. 91(24). The judge concluded, then, that Metis were Indians within s.12 of the NRTA. That being the case, the provincial legislation was *ultra vires* in attempting to restrict the definition of Indians to those who were registered under the *Indian Act*. Grumbo's conviction was quashed.

Section 35(4) — Equality

Native Women's Assn. of Canada v. Canada, [1995] 1 C.N.L.R. 47, 119 D.L.R. (4th) 224, [1994] 3 S.C.R. 627, 84 F.T.R. 240

The Native Women's Association did not receive funding to participate in the constitutional talks that lead to the Charlottetown Accord of 1982. The court stated

> The right of the Aboriginal people of Canada to participate in constitutional discussions does not derive from any existing Aboriginal or treaty right protected under s. 35. Therefore, s. 35(4) ... which guarantees Aboriginal and treaty rights referred to in s. 35(1) equally to male and female persons, is of no assistance to the respondents. [C.N.L.R. at p. 73]

35.1 Commitment to participation in Constitutional conference — The government of Canada and the provincial governments are committed to the principle that, before any amendment is made to Class 24 of section 91 of the *"Constitution Act, 1867"*, to section 25 of this Act or to this Part,

(a) a constitutional conference that includes in its agenda an item relating to the proposed amendment, composed of the Prime Minister of Canada and the first ministers of the provinces, will be convened by the Prime Minister of Canada; and

(b) the Prime Minister of Canada will invite representatives of the aboriginal peoples of Canada to participate in the discussions on that item.

Commentary: Representatives of the Aboriginal peoples were not invited to participate in the First Ministers' Conferences leading to the Meech Lake Accord of 1987. Representatives of the Assembly of First Nations, the Inuit Tapirisat of Canada, the Metis National Council and the Native Council of Canada (now, The Congress of Aboriginal Peoples), participated in the First Ministers' Conferences leading to the Charlottetown Accord of 1992.

The Jay Treaty, 1794 — Treaty of Amity Commerce and Navigation

Concluded November 19, 1794; ratification advised by the senate with amendment June 24, 1795; ratified by the President; ratifications exchanged October 28, 1795; proclaimed February 29, 1796.

His Britannic Majesty and the United States of America, being desirous, by a treaty of amity, commerce and navigation, to terminate their difference in such a manner, as, without reference to the merits of their respective complaints and pretentions, may be the best calculated to produce mutual satisfaction and good understanding; and also to regulate the commerce and navigation between their respective countries, territories and people, in such a manner as to render the same reciprocally beneficial and satisfactory; they have, respectively, named their Plenipotentiaries,

Who have agreed on and concluded the following articles:

Article III

It is agreed that it shall at all times be free to His Majesty's subjects, and to the citizens of the United States, and also to the Indians dwelling on either side of the said boundary line, freely to pass and repass by land or inland navigation, into the respective territories and countries of the two parties, on the continent of America, (the country within the limits of the Hudson's Bay Company only excepted.) and to navigate all the lakes, rivers and waters thereof, and freely to carry on trade and commerce with each other. But it is understood that this article does not extend to the admission of vessels of the United States into the sea-ports, harbours, bays or creeks of His Majesty's said territories; nor into such parts of the rivers in His Majesty's said territories as are between the mouth thereof, and the highest port of entry from the sea, except in small vessels trading bona fide between Montreal and Quebec, under such regulations as shall be established to prevent the possibility of any frauds in this respect. Nor to the admission of British vessels from the sea into the rivers of the United States, beyond the highest ports of entry for foreign vessels from the sea. The river Mississippi shall, however, according to the treaty of peace, be entirely open to both parties; and it is further agreed, that all the ports and places on its eastern side, to whichsoever of the parties belonging, may freely be resorted to and used by both parties, in as ample a manner as any of the Atlantic ports or placed of the United States, or any of the ports or places of His Majesty in Great Britain.

. . . . .

No duty of entry shall ever be levied by either party on peltries brought by land or inland navigation into the said territories respectively, nor shall the Indians passing or repassing with their own proper goods and effects of whatever nature, pay for the same any impost or duty whatever. But goods in bales, or other large packages, unusual among Indians, shall not be considered as goods belonging bona fide to Indians.

Commentary:

An explanatory Article was signed at Philadelphia on 4th May 1796, to clarify Article 3. This explanatory Article stated:

> ... no stipulations in any treaty subsequently concluded by either of the contracting parties with any other State or Nation, or with any Indian tribe, can be understood to derogate in any manner from the rights of free intercourse and commerce secured by the aforesaid third Article of the treaty of Amity, commerce and navigation, to the subjects of his Majesty and to the Citizens of the United States and to the Indians dwelling on either side of the boundary-line aforesaid; but that all the said persons shall remain at full liberty freely to pass and repass by land or inland navigation, into the respective territories and countries of the contracting parties, on either side of the said boundary-line, and freely to carry on trade and commerce with each other, according to the stipulations of the said third Article of the treaty of Amity, Commerce and Navigation.

This reiterates the Indians' right to cross the border, but does not reaffirm the non-payment of duty on goods carried. This omission does not diminish, however, the protection from paying a duty on Indians' own property carried over the border.

Case Law:

Francis v. R., [1956] S.C.R. 618, 3 D.L.R. (2d) 641, 56 D.T.C. 1077

The Supreme Court of Canada, in a unanimous decision, held that the Jay Treaty did not exempt Indians from the payment of customs duty on goods imported into Canada. The appellant was an Indian who lived on a reserve which adjoined a reserve in the United States. He purchased three large appliances in the United States and took them to his home in Canada. These were later placed under customs detention and a duty was assessed. The appellant appealed against this.

The court held that a treaty such as the Jay Treaty was not enforceable as a law of the country without legislation. Rand J. stated this at (S.C.R.) p. 626:

> ... treaty provisions affecting matters within the scope of municipal law, that is, which purport to change existing law or restrict the future action of the legislature ... and in the absence of a constitutional provision declaring the treaty itself to be law of the state, as in the United States, must be supplemented by statutory action ... To the enactment of fiscal provisions, certainly in the case of a treaty not a peace treaty, the prerogative does not extend, and only by legislation can customs duties be imposed or removed or can the condition under which goods may be brought into this country be affected ... legislation was necessary to bring within municipal law the exemption of the clause in question.

And at p. 627:

> For over a century, then, there has been no statutory provision in this country giving effect to that clause of the article.

It was also held that s. 87 of the *Indian Act* did not give an exemption from custom duties. See the discussion under that section.

Mohawk Council Akwesasne v. Canada (Minister of National Revenue), [1997] F.C.J. No. 882 (Fed. T.D.)

Akwesasne is a Mohawk reserve which straddles the Canada-U.S.A. border as well as the Ontario-Quebec border. In 1988, Chief Mike Mitchell crossed the border with one washing machine, 10 blankets, 20 Bibles, various articles of used clothing, one case of lubricating motor oil, 10 loaves of bread, two pounds of butter, four gallons of whole milk, six bags of cookies and 12 cans of soup. He told customs officials that these were gifts for a ceremonial dinner at the neighbouring Mohawk reserve of

Tyendinaga to commemorate the renewal of trade ties with that community. Chief Mitchell refused to pay the duty of $361.64 claiming an Aboriginal right, and rights under the Jay Treaty.

Although the court found that an existing Aboriginal right exempted Mitchell from paying duty on those items, it did not find that the Jay Treaty was applicable. The court noted that legislation was necessary in order to implement international treaties, and no legislation has existed with respect to the Jay Treaty since 1824. The court also held that s. 35(1) of the *Constitution Act, 1982*, contemplate treaties between the Crown and Aboriginal peoples. It did not contemplate international treaties such as the Jay Treaty, signed between Canada and other states.

R. v. Vincent (1993), 12 O.R. (3d) 397 (Fr.), 12 O.R. (3d) 427 (Eng.), [1993] 2 C.N.L.R. 165, 80 C.C.C. (3d) 256, 61 O.A.C. 371 (C.A.)leave to appeal to S.C.C. refused, 15 O.R. (3d) xvin, [1994] 4 C.N.L.R. vin, 83 C.C.C. (3d) viin, 163 N.R. 239n, 68 O.A.C. 239n (S.C.C.)

"Treaty rights" refers to rights that belong to Aboriginal peoples and which stem from treaties concluded with Aboriginal peoples. The Jay Treaty is an international treaty, and cannot confer rights on an individual or group of individuals. It is not a treaty within the meaning of s. 35(1) of the *Constitution Act, 1982*, and does not confer a right to import commercial goods duty free. If it were a treaty within the meaning of s. 35(1), any rights contained therein were probably extinguished before April 17, 1982.

Smith v. Canada, [1993] 2 C.N.L.R. 190 (Gen. Div.)additional reasons at (1993), 13 O.R. (3d) 215 (Gen. Div.), leave to appeal to Div. Ct. refused (1994), 17 O.R. (3d) 468, 23 Imm. L.R. (2d) 235 (Gen. Div.)

An American Indian cannot rely on the Jay Treaty to enter Canada without a visa.

The Royal Proclamation

October 7, 1763

By the King, A Proclamation George R.

Whereas We have taken into Our Royal Consideration the extensive and valuable Acquisitions in America, secured to our Crown by the late Definitive Treaty of Peace, concluded at Paris, the 10th Day of February last; and being desirous that all Our loving Subjects, as well of our Kingdom as of our Colonies in America, may avail themselves with all convenient Speed, of the great Benefits and Advantages which must accrue therefrom to their Commerce, Manufactures, and Navigation, We have thought fit, with the Advice of our Privy Council, to issue this our Royal Proclamation, hereby to publish and declare to all our loving Subjects, that we have, with the Advice of our Said Privy Council, granted our Letters Patent, under our Great Seal of Great Britain, to erect, within the Countries and Islands ceded and confirmed to Us by the said Treaty, Four distinct and separate Governments, styled and called by the names of Quebec, East Florida, West Florida and Grenada, and limited and bounded as follows, viz.

. . . . .

And whereas it will greatly contribute to the speedy settling of our said new Governments, that our loving Subjects should be informed of our Paternal care, for the security of the Liberties and Properties of those who are and shall become Inhabitants thereof, We have thought fit to publish and declare, by this Our Proclamation, that We have, in the Letters Patent under our Great Seal of Great Britain, by which the said Governments are constituted, given express Power and Direction to our Governors of our Said Colonies respectively, that so soon as the state and circumstances of the said Colonies will admit thereof, they shall, with the Advice and Consent of the Members of our Council, summon and call General Assemblies within the said Governments respectively, in such Manner and Form as is used and directed in those Colonies and Provinces in America which are under our immediate Government; And We have also given Power to the said Governors, with the consent of our Said Councils, and the Representatives of the People so to be summoned as aforesaid, to make, constitute, and ordain Laws, Statutes, and Ordinances for the Public Peace, Welfare, and good Government of our said Colonies, and of the People and Inhabitants thereof, as near as may be agreeable to the Laws of England, and under such Regulations and Restrictions as are used in other Colonies; and in the mean Time, and until such Assemblies can be called as aforesaid, all Persons Inhabiting in or resorting to our Said Colonies may confide in our Royal Protection for the Enjoyment of the Benefit of the Laws of our Realm of England; for which Purpose We have given Power under our Great Seal to the Governors of our said Colonies respectively to erect and constitute, with the Advice of our said Councils respectively, Courts of Judicature and public Justice within our Said Colonies for hearing and determining all Causes, as well Criminal as Civil, according to Law and Equity, and as near as may be agreeable to the Laws of England, with Liberty to all Persons who may think themselves aggrieved by the Sentences of such Courts, in all Civil Cases, to appeal, under the usual Limitations and Restrictions, to Us in our Privy Council.

We have also thought fit, with the advice of our Privy Council as aforesaid, to give unto the Governors and Councils of our said Three new Colonies, upon the Continent full Power and Authority to settle and agree with the Inhabitants of our said new Colonies or with any other Persons who shall resort thereto, for such Lands, Tenements and Hereditaments, as are now or hereafter shall be in our Power to dispose of; and them to grant to any such Person or Persons upon such Terms, and under such moderate Quit-Rents, Services and Acknowledgments, as have been appointed and settled in our other Colonies, and under such other Conditions as shall appear to us to be necessary and expedient for the Advantage of the Grantees, and the Improvement and settlement of our said Colonies.

. . . . .

And whereas it is just and reasonable, and essential to our Interest, and the Security of our Colonies, that the several Nations or Tribes of Indians with whom We are connected, and who live under our Protection, should not be molested or disturbed in the Possession of such Parts of Our Dominions and Territories as, not having been ceded to or purchased by Us, are reserved to them, or any of them, as their Hunting Grounds. — We do therefore, with the Advice of our Privy Council, declare it to be our Royal Will and Pleasure, that no Governor or Commander in Chief in any of our Colonies of Quebec, East Florida, or West Florida, do presume, upon any Pretence whatever, to grant Warrants of Survey, or pass any Patents for Lands beyond the Bounds of their respective Governments, as described in their Commissions; as also that no Governor or Commander in Chief in any of our other Colonies or Plantations in America do presume for the present, and until our further Pleasure be known, to grant Warrants of Survey, or pass Patents for any Lands beyond the Heads or Sources of any of the Rivers which fall into the Atlantic Ocean from the west and North West, or upon any Lands whatever, which, not having been ceded to or purchased by Us as aforesaid, are reserved to the said Indians, or any of them.

And We do further declare it to be Our Royal Will and Pleasure, for the present as aforesaid, to reserve under our Sovereignty, Protection, and Dominion, for the use of the said Indians, all the Lands and Territories not included within the Limits of Our said Three new Governments, or within the Limits of the Territory granted to the Hudson's Bay Company, as also all the Lands and Territories lying to the Westward of the Sources of the Rivers which fall into the Sea from the West and North West as aforesaid.

And We do hereby strictly forbid, on Pain of our Displeasure, all our loving Subjects from making any Purchases or Settlements whatever, or taking Possession of any of the Lands above reserved, without our especial leave and Licence for that Purpose first obtained.

And, We do further strictly enjoin and require all Persons whatever who have either wilfully or inadvertently seated themselves upon any Lands within the Countries above described, or upon any other Lands which, not having been ceded to or purchased by Us, are still reserved to the said Indians as aforesaid, forthwith to remove themselves from such Settlements.

And whereas great Frauds and Abuses have been committed in purchasing Lands of the Indians, to the great Prejudice of our Interests, and to the great Dissatisfaction of the said Indians; In order, therefore, to prevent such Irregularities for the future, and to the end that the Indians may be convinced of our Justice and determined Resolution to remove all reasonable Cause of Discontent, We do, with the Advice of our Privy Council strictly enjoin and require, that no private Person do presume to make any purchase from the said Indians of any Lands reserved to the said Indians, within those parts of our Colonies where, We have thought proper to allow Settlement; but that, if at any Time any of the Said Indians should be inclined to dispose of the said Lands, the same shall be Purchased only for Us, in our Name, at some public Meeting or Assembly of the said Indians, to be held for that Purpose by the Governor or Commander in Chief of our Colony respectively within which they shall lie; and in case they shall lie within the limits of any Proprietary Government, they shall be purchased only for the Use and in the name of such Proprietaries, conformable to such Directions and Instructions as We or they shall think proper to give for that Purpose; And we do, by the Advice of our Privy Council, declare and enjoin, that the Trade with the said Indians shall be free and open to all our Subjects whatever, provided that every Person who may incline to Trade with the said Indians do take out a Licence for carrying on such Trade from the Governor or Commander in Chief of any of our Colonies respectively where such Person shall reside, and also give Security to observe such Regulations as We shall at any Time think fit, by ourselves or by our Commissaries to be appointed for this Purpose, to direct and appoint for the Benefit of the said Trade:

And we do hereby authorize, enjoin, and require the Governors and Commanders in Chief of all our Colonies respectively, as well those under Our immediate Government as those under the Government and Direction of Proprietaries, to grant such Licences without Fee or Reward, taking especial Care to insert therein a Condition, that such Licence shall be void, and the Security forfeited in case the Person to whom the same is granted shall refuse or neglect to observe such Regulations as We shall think proper to prescribe as aforesaid.

And we do further expressly enjoin and require all Officers whatever, as well Military as those Employed in the Management and Direction of Indian Affairs, within the Territories reserved as aforesaid for the use of the said Indians, to seize and apprehend all Persons whatever, who standing charged with Treason, Misprisions of Treason, Murders, or other Felonies or Misdemeanors, shall fly from Justice and take Refuge in the said Territory, and to send them under a proper guard to the Colony where the Crime was committed of which they stand accused, in order to take their Trial for the same.

Given at our Court at St. James's the 7th Day of October 1763, in the Third Year of our Reign.

GOD SAVE THE KING

Case Law:

R. v. Secretary of State (1981), [1981] 4 C.N.L.R. 86, [1982] 2 All E.R. 118 (C.A.)

Obligations under the Royal Proclamation and under the Indian treaties were owed by the Crown in right of Canada and not in right of the United Kingdom. Matters arising out of these obligations are justiciable in the courts of Canada and not those of the United Kingdom. Lord Denning states:

> To my mind the Royal Proclamation of 1763 was equivalent to an entrenched provision in the Constitution of the colonies of North America. It was binding on the Crown "so long as the sun rises and the river flows. [C.N.L.R. p. 91]

Guerin v. R. (1984), [1984] 2 S.C.R. 335, [1984] 6 W.W.R. 481, 59 B.C.L.R. 301, 36 R.P.R. 1, 20 E.T.R. 6, 13 D.L.R. (4th) 321, [1985] 1 C.N.L.R. 120, 55 N.R. 161

The Royal Proclamation confirmed the existence of aboriginal title. It did not create it.

Calder v. British Columbia (Attorney General) (1973), [1973] S.C.R. 313, [1973] 4 W.W.R. 1, 34 D.L.R. (3d) 145, 8 C.N.L.C. 91

The Royal Proclamation

The Supreme Court of Canada split evenly on the point of the application of the Royal Proclamation to the Nishga of British Columbia. Three judges held that the Proclamation did not apply while three others held that it did apply. The seventh judge did not comment on this point.

Mr. Justice Hall described the document as follows:

> This Proclamation was an Executive Order having the force and effect of an Act of Parliament and was described by Gwynne, J., in *St. Catherines Milling* ... as the "Indian Bill of Rights" ... Its force as a statute is analogous to the status of Magna Carta which has always been considered to be the law throughout the Empire. It was a law which followed the flag as England assumed jurisdiction over newly-discovered or acquired lands or territories ...

> In respect of this Proclamation, it can be said that when other exploring nations were showing a ruthless disregard of native rights England adopted a remarkably enlightened attitude towards the Indians of North America. The Proclamation must be regarded as a fundamental document upon which any just determination of original rights rests. [C.N.L.R. p. 150]

Index

All references are to section numbers of statutes and regulations.
The following abbreviations are used in this index:

(blank) = *Indian Act*
p. = *page*
BCTU = *British Columbia Terms of Union*
CA 1867 = *Constitution Act, 1867*
CA 1930 = *Constitution Act, 1930*
CA 1982 = *Constitution Act, 1982*
CIR = *Calculation of Interest Regulations*
DFGCR = *Disposal of Forfeited Goods and Chattel Regulations*
DIANDA = *Department of Indian Affairs and Northern Development Act*
IBCBR = *Indian Band Council Borrowing Regulations*
IBCMER = *Indian Bands Council Method of Election Regulations*
IBCPR = *Indian Band Council Procedure Regulations*
IBER = *Indian Band Election Regulations*
IER = *Indian Estates Regulations*
IMR = *Indian Mining Regulations*
IRR = *Indian Referendum Regulations*
IRTR = *Indian Reserve Traffic Regulations*
IRWDR = *Indian Reserve Waste Disposal Regulations*
ITR = *Indian Timber Regulations*
JT = *Jay Treaty*
MA = *Manitoba Act, 1870*
RP = *Royal Proclamation*

A

ABORIGINAL RIGHTS, CA 1982, 25, 35

ADMINISTRATION, 3

ADMINISTRATION OF ESTATES, *see also* DESCENT OF PROPERTY
- absent/missing heirs, IER, 13
- administrator of estates, IER, 10, 11
- adverse possession, IER, 12
- advertising for creditors/heirs, IER, 8
- affidavits, IER, 7
- application for administration, IER, 6
- definitions, IER, 2
- estate, defined, 2(1)
- executors, IER, 9
- forms, IER, 16
- inventory, IER, 4
- notice of death, IER, 3
- probate of will, IER, 5
- sureties, IER, 10
- wills, IER, 45–47, 49, 50
- women deemed to be widowed, IER, 14

ADVERSE POSSESSION, IER, 12

ALIMONY AND MAINTENANCE, 68, *see also* SUPPORT ORDERS

APPEALS
- decisions of presiding officer of council, IBCPR, 17

APPEALS *(cont'd)*
- elections, IBER, 12–4
- mining claims, IMR, 46
- Minister's decisions in matters testamentary, 47
- protests regarding band list/Indian register, 14.3
- referendums, IRR, 31, 32

APPLICATION, 4, 4.1

APPLICATION OF LAWS, *see also* CONSTITUTIONAL LAW
- provincial laws, 88
- tax laws, 87
- traffic laws/regulations, IRTR

ASSIGNMENTS, 54–56

B

BAND LIST
- band, maintained in decision to leave control with Department, 13.1
- • generally, 10, 13.1(3)
- • return of control to Department, 13.2, 13.3
- copy of, to be provided to band council, 14
- defined, 2(1)
- Department, maintained in entitlement to have name entered on band list, 12
- • generally, 9
- • membership rules, 11
- generally, 8
- inquiries, 14.1
- limitation to one band list, 13
- protests, 14.2, 14.3, 17(3)
- to be posted on reserve, 14(3)
- where band amalgamates/divides, 11(4)

BAND MEMBERS
- ceasing to be, 15, 16
- children of, 18.1
- member of a band, defined, 2(1)

BAND(S)
- amalgamation, 11(4), 17
- defined, 2(1), (2)

- division of, 11(4)
- powers, 2(3)(a)

BORROWING REGULATIONS, IBCBR

BY-LAWS
- certified true copy, 86
- copies to be sent to Minister, 82(1), 85.1(3)
- effective date, 82(2)
- enforcement, 81(2), (3)
- generally, 81
- intoxicants, relating to, 85.1
- money, 83

C

CEASING TO BE BAND MEMBERS, 15, 16

CEASING TO RESIDE ON RESERVE, 25

CERTIFICATE OF ANALYSIS, 101

CERTIFICATE OF OCCUPATION, 20(5),(6), 26, 27

CERTIFICATE OF POSSESSION, 20(2),(3), 26, 27

CHARTER OF RIGHTS AND FREEDOMS, *see also*
- aboriginal rights not affected by Charter, CA 1982, 25
- equality rights, CA 1982, 15

CHIEF, *see also* ELECTIONS
- duty to Band members, 2(1)("Council")

CHILD WELFARE LEGISLATION, 88 (p. 109)

CHILDREN
- child, defined, 2(1)
- education, *see* SCHOOLS
- maintenance of dependants, 68
- money of, 52.1–52.5
- property of, 52
- right to reside on reserve, 18.1

COMMISSIONERS FOR TAKING OATHS, 108

COMMUNITY OF PROPERTY, 48(12)

R

REFERENDUM REGULATIONS

- appeals, IRR, 31, 32
- definition, IRR, 2
- forms, IRR, 33
- holding of referendum, IRR, 3
- subsequent referendums, IRR, 30
- voting by secret ballot, IRR, 4–20
- voting other than by secret ballot, IRR, 21–29

REGISTERED, DEFINED, 2(1)

REGISTRAR, DEFINED, 2(1)

REGULATIONS, POWER TO MAKE

- band/council meetings, 75
- day-to-day operations of reserve, 73
- education, 115
- elected council/chief, 74(3)
- elections, 76
- interest on certain moneys, 64.1(3)
- loans to Indians, 70(2)
- management of revenue moneys by band, 69(2)
- money by-laws, 83(5)
- possession of land by deceased Indian, 42(2)
- surrendered and designated lands, 57

RELIGION, 118, 120, 121

REMOVAL OF MATERIALS FROM RESERVES, 93

RESERVE LAND REGISTER, 21

RESERVE LANDS, *see also* LEASING OF LANDS, SURRENDERS AND DESIGNATIONS

- appropriation of lands, BCTU 13, MA 31
- ceasing to reside on, 25
- compulsory taking/expropriation of reserve lands, 35
- control over lands, 60, BCTU 13, CA 1930, 11
- disposition of grass/timber/non-metallic substances, 58(4)

- exemption from seizure, 29
- generally, 18
- grants/leases void, 28
- not vested in Crown, 36
- possession of, *see* POSSESSION OF LANDS IN RESERVES
- reserve, defined, 2(1)
- surrenders/designations, *see* SURRENDERS AND DESIGNATIONS
- trespass, 30, 31
- uncultivated/unused lands, 58
- use by non-members, 28

ROADS AND BRIDGES, 34

ROYAL PROCLAMATION, RP

S

SALES TAX, 87

SALES/GRANTS OF LAND, 28, 37

SCHOOLS

- agreements with provinces, etc., 114
- attendance, 116
- child, defined, 122
- regulations, power to make, 115
- religious considerations, 118, 120, 121
- school, defined, 122
- truant officers, 119, 122
- when attendance not required, 117

SEARCH AND SEIZURE, 103

SEIZURE

- applicability of provincial legislation, 88
- exemption for reserve lands, 29
- goods, 103, DFGCR
- property on reserve, 89, 90
- timber, of, ITR, 26–29

"SITUATED ON RESERVE", 89, 90

SPECIAL RESERVES, 36

SUPERINTENDENT, DEFINED, 2(1)

SUPPORT ORDERS, 89

SURRENDERED AND DESIGNATED LANDS REGISTER, 55